Walsh-Suzzallo Arithmetics: Business and Industrial Practice

Henry Suzzallo, John Henry Walsh

WALSH-SUZZALLO ARITHMETICS

BOOK THREE
BUSINESS AND INDUSTRIAL PRACTICE

BY

JOHN H. WALSH
ASSOCIATE SUPERINTENDENT OF SCHOOLS
THE CITY OF NEW YORK

AND

HENRY SUZZALLO
PROFESSOR OF THE PHILOSOPHY OF EDUCATION
TEACHERS COLLEGE, COLUMBIA UNIVERSITY

D. C. HEATH & CO., PUBLISHERS
BOSTON   NEW YORK   CHICAGO

THE WALSH-SUZZALLO ARITHMETICS

Three=Book Course

I. **FUNDAMENTAL PROCESSES.** 256 pages.
II. **ESSENTIALS.** 298 pages.
III. **BUSINESS AND INDUSTRIAL PRACTICE.** 376 pages.

Two=Book Course

I. **FUNDAMENTAL PROCESSES.** 256 pages.
II. **PRACTICAL APPLICATIONS.** 511 pages.

D. C. HEATH & CO., PUBLISHERS

COPYRIGHT, 1914,

BY D. C. HEATH & CO.

1H4

PREFACE

THESE texts in arithmetic are devised to train children to meet the ordinary demands of life. Practical efficiency, rather than mental discipline or scholastic thoroughness, has been the chief aim in their organization. Whatever the average man needs to know in mathematical terms, because of its frequency of occurrence in his life or because of its urgency and importance, has been here included. Whatever has small social utility has been omitted. Emphasis has been laid upon practical power and practical thoroughness throughout.

The distribution of topics through the various grades has been greatly influenced by the fact that many children leave school before they have mastered the fundamental processes in arithmetic. It has come to be recognized that essentials should be taught as soon as possible. The most important arithmetical facts and skills should come first and the least significant last. By applying these two principles to the organization of these books, it has been easy to achieve that much-desired end,—the completion of the fundamentals of arithmetic in six school years.

This volume, the third of the three-book series, covers the last two years of the elementary school. While it gives further drill and review of the essentials covered in the preceding books, and adds many special short methods of calculation that increase efficiency, its chief aim is to extend the child's power to make practical applications of arithmetic to life.

In the lower grammar grades he continues to find the more elaborate manipulations of arithmetic troublesome. More than that, the constantly extending applications of arithmetic now lead him into a world foreign to his personal experience, one where right thinking with strange and complicated problems becomes a new and large difficulty.

In the upper grammar grades, the child comes to feel at ease in performing the fundamental processes, only to find their applications more complex than ever. Hence the pressing responsibility of the grammar grades is to teach the children to think. They must be taught to understand the important social institutions with which arithmetical processes are associated, for, without this comprehension, they cannot reason out the successive steps to be taken in solving practical problems. Hence a large part of this text is devoted to the simple social and economic applications of mathematics.

Since the dominant problem in these higher grades is different from that of the lower years, it is necessary that the teacher modify the traditional spirit of mathematical teaching. The work should be formal only in the slightest degree. There ought to be days when teacher and pupils, without once working an example, simply discuss farm production, household management, transportation

and marketing, industrial organization, banking, and
other business practices. In due time, as part of his
general training on a topic, the child will be taught to
compute illustrative problems. This will be done more
to test the correctness of his independent thinking than
to drill him in the manipulation of figures. In many
phases of economic arithmetic the average man needs
merely a critical appreciation of the manner in which
bankers, insurance brokers, lumber dealers, and others
compute their charges from tables. Therefore, much
reading matter is offered and only a necessary amount of
problems and examples.

It would contribute greatly to effective instruction if
the teacher would constantly remember that economic, as
contrasted with formal, arithmetic deals chiefly with applications, and these should be kept vital to the children
taught. While many arithmetical processes are very important to all pupils the whole country over, their applications are not. Each process has many varied uses.
Every child may need to know every fundamental operation, but not every application of the same.

The judicious teacher will omit some of the material
offered in this volume, selecting and amplifying the
portions of most value. Farm problems will interest a
country boy. Girls will see a new worth in arithmetic
intimately associated with household duties. The son of
the skilled carpenter will be eager to master the equations by which his father computes the safe load of a

beam.   The child of a mechanic will be fascinated with industrial construction exercises.   But it would be a serious mistake to make all children study problems that are of no particular concern to them.   The offering is wide; let the teacher select and reject in terms of the community's needs.   With an enriched curriculum that permits flexible choice, there ought never to be a crowded course of study.

Recent investigations show that two urgent demands are being made by practically all school superintendents: (1) that fundamental processes be emphasized in the lower grades in order that early efficiency may result, and (2) that the social and economic applications of arithmetic be taught in the upper grades so that grammar school children will have an insight into the typical business practices of modern life.   These texts are devised to meet both requirements.

CONTENTS

SECTION ONE — GOING INTO BUSINESS

SECTION TWO — REVIEWS AND TESTS

SECTION THREE — BUSINESS ACCOUNTS

SECTION FOUR — AIDING AND PROTECTING BUSINESS

SECTION FIVE — EFFICIENCY IN CALCULATIONS

SECTION SIX — LENDING AND BORROWING MONEY

SECTION SEVEN — BUSINESS PROPORTIONS AND ALIQUOT PARTS

SECTION EIGHT — ECONOMICAL BUSINESS COÖPERATION

SECTION NINE — PRACTICAL USES OF POWERS AND ROOTS

SECTION TEN — GOVERNMENT AND BUSINESS STANDARDS

SECTION ELEVEN — BUSINESS MEASUREMENTS

SECTION TWELVE — EQUATIONS IN BUSINESS

SECTION THIRTEEN — INDUSTRIAL CONSTRUCTION EXERCISES

BUSINESS AND INDUSTRIAL PRACTICE

SECTION I

GOING INTO BUSINESS

Earning and Spending

Everybody that earns and spends may be said to be in business — the boy, the girl, the laborer, the mechanic, the farmer, the physician, the housewife, the clerk, etc.

For the proper management of one's financial affairs the keeping of accounts is essential. An examination of the receipts and expenditures will often suggest ways of increasing the income and of decreasing the outgo.

While yet in school, boys and girls should acquire the habit of keeping a record of money received and spent.

Herewith is shown a simple form of account kept by a boy in an ordinary memorandum book; the first two columns of dollars and cents, containing the sums received, and the last two the sums expended.

			Cash		*Dr.*		*Cr.*
1916							
Jan.	1	*On hand*			*35*		
	2	*Chopping wood*			*25*		
		Skates					*50*
	4	*From Uncle John*	1		—		
	5	*Moving pictures*					*05*
	7	*Balance*				1	*05*
				1	60	1	60
	8	*On hand*		1	05		
	9	*Cleaning snow*			*30*		
	11	*Coffee and cakes*					*10*

1

The first entry shows the cash on hand the day the account is *opened*, the amount being written in the first of the two double columns at the right of the page. Above is written *Dr.*, which indicates that the cash box should contain 35 cents. Each expenditure is written an inch or so to the right of the date column, and the amount is placed in the last double column. Above these items is written *Cr.*, to show that the cash box has paid out the sums specified.

The foregoing account is *balanced* Jan. 7. Space is left for the word *Balance;* then a horizontal line is drawn across both columns. The total of the debits ($1.60) is found and written under the debits and then under the credits. The credits are added and the amount ($1.05) needed to make a total of $1.60 is written in. Since $1.05 belongs in the *Cr.* column, the word *Balance* is written an inch or so from the date column, as in the case of other credits. To indicate that it is not an expenditure, it is sometimes written in red ink.

Double lines are drawn to show that the transactions above them are closed. The red ink credit balance is then entered in black ink as a debit *On hand.*

Written Exercises

1. Copy the foregoing account and insert an additional debit and two additional credits. Balance the account Jan. 14, and reopen it Jan. 15.

2. Make out a girl's cash account showing items as follows: On hand March 1, 1916, $1.25; March 2, spent 30 cents at church fair; March 4, spent for ribbon 25 cents; March 5 received 50 cents from Aunt Mary and spent 10 cents for candy. Balance the account on March 7, and reopen it on March 8.

The accuracy of a balance is determined by counting the money in the cash box, which should contain the sum given by the balance. Any discrepancy will indicate that a mistake has been made.

When the number of items is great, it is better to write the *Dr.* total, and also the balance on a separate piece of paper at first. If the latter does not correspond with the cash on hand, and the omitted debit or credit cannot be recollected, an item is inserted, *U. F.*, which means *Unaccounted for*. If the cash box contained only 84 cents when the foregoing account was balanced, a credit item would be written, " *U. F.* . . . . 21," preceding the *Balance* item, which would then be 84 cents, as is shown in the account below. This also contains a *U. F.* debit item, since the cash box contained 47 cents, and the original balance called for only 44 cents.

			Cash	*Dr.*		*Cr.*	
1916							
Jan.	1	On hand			35		
	2	Chopping wood			25		
		Skates					50
	4	From Uncle John		1	—		
	5	Moving pictures					05
	7	U. F.					21
		Balance					84
				1	60	1	60
	8	On hand			84		
		Cleaning snow			30		
	11	Coffee and cakes					10
	12	Sled					60
	14	U. F.			03		
		Balance					47
				1	17	1	17
	15	On hand			47		

When it is recalled later that the 21 cents " unaccounted for " was a deposit in the school savings bank, and that the *U. F.* item was 3 cents found in the road, a line is drawn through the letters " U. F." in each case, and " Deposit " written alongside the first and " Found " alongside the second.

Written Exercises

1. Make out a girl's account for two weeks. Close it at the end of each week, and reopen it.

2. Make out a boy's account for two weeks, containing at least two debits and three credits each week. Balance the account at the end of each week.

Answering an Advertisement

WANTED. — Boy under 16, grammar-school graduate, good penman, and quick at figures. Steady advancement to the right boy. Address in own handwriting: A. B. S., *Herald Office.*

LETTER

157 MARKET ST.
COVINGTON, KY.
June 23, 1916

A. B. S.
   Herald Office
      Cincinnati, O.
DEAR SIR

I beg leave to offer my services in reply to your advertisement in the *Herald* to-day. I am 15 years of age, and am now completing my first year of high school. I enclose copies of testimonials from my pastor and my teachers.

Respectfully yours

DORSEY KEMP

When the replies to an advertisement of this kind are very numerous, possibly only the best-looking envelopes are opened, and perhaps not more than a half dozen are referred to the person who is to make the selection. It is important, therefore, to pay careful attention to the arrangement of the address, and to write neatly on paper of a business size.

ENVELOPE

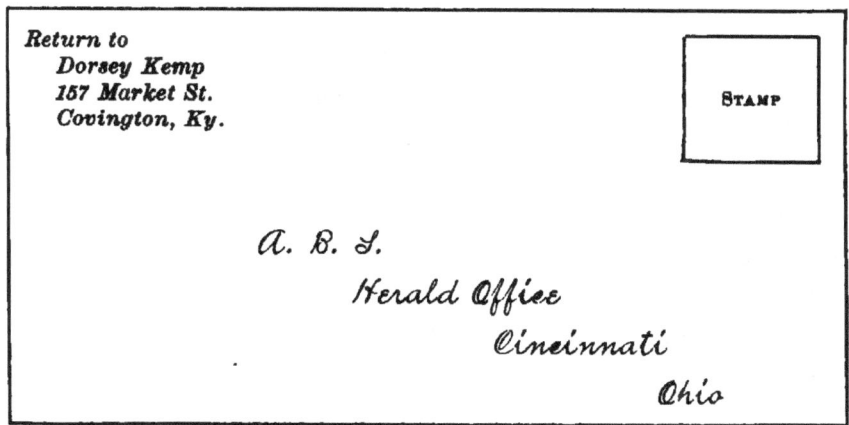

Business men generally omit commas and periods at the end of the lines in the addresses on envelopes and in the heading, the address, and the complimentary close of a letter. The period following an abbreviation is usually retained.

The postal authorities recommend that the name of the state be written in full on the envelope, to prevent mistakes due to the similarity of Penn. and Tenn., La. and Va., etc., when the writing is not distinct. Both the letter and the envelope should always contain the name and the address of the sender as well as those of the person to whom it is written.

Before making his selection of a boy or a girl, the business man writes, in many cases, to the teacher or the pastor, asking more definite information as to the applicant's character and habits.

Written Problems

1. A boy leaves school at 14. He receives $3 per week at first. How much does he earn in 8 years, if his wages are increased $1 per week at the end of each year? (Take 52 weeks to the year.)

Multiply the sum of the weekly rates by 52 instead of multiplying each rate by 52 and adding the separate products.

$$(\$3 + \$4 + \$5 \cdots \text{etc.}) \times 52$$

2. A second boy remains at school 2 years longer and is paid $6 per week at first, receiving an increase of $2 at the beginning of each year. What are his total earnings for 6 years?

3. A boy that was earning $4 per week, with an annual increase of $1, attended a trade night school for three years. His salary for the fourth year was $8, for the fifth $13, and for the sixth $16. What were his total earnings for 6 years?

4. Find the average weekly wages of the following 20 pupils of a trade school:

2 girls receiving $17 per week
3 girls receiving $16 per week
5 girls receiving $15 per week
2 girls receiving $10 per week
4 girls receiving $9 per week
4 girls receiving $8 per week

5. In 1910 the profits of a farm were $1500. By more intelligent management the profits of each year were increased $\frac{1}{10}$ of those of the preceding year. Find the profits (*a*) for 1911; (*b*) for 1912; (*c*) for 1913; (*d*) for 1914; (*e*) the profits from 1910 to 1914, inclusive; (*f*) the average yearly profits for the five years.

Calculating without a Pencil

Boys and girls find it useful all through their lives, either as employers or employees, to be able to perform simple operations without the aid of a pencil.

While still at school, boys and girls should acquire the habit of making mental combinations in the proper way. When a girl shopping for her mother is told that the cost of 15 yards of dress goods at 25 cents per yard is $3.75 and that of 12 yards of calico at 6½ ¢ is 78 cents, she should be able mentally to verify the correctness of these figures, as well as that of the total, $4.53.

This would be difficult if the methods used in written calculations were employed, commencing, in addition, for instance, with the ones' column.

Drills

To remove the tendency to begin with the ones' figures, there should be drills in which numbers to be combined mentally are announced by the teacher.

Combining Mentally

In adding $3.75 and 78¢ mentally, omit dollars and cents, and think four, forty-five (375 + 70); four, fifty-three (adding 8). *Ans.* $4.53.

Use the same method in combining 375 and 78, and omit the word "hundred." Find the sum of 560 + 480, by thinking five, sixty plus four, eighty, making ten, forty, and not one thousand forty.

Find the cost of 15 yards at 25¢ per yard by thinking 15 quarters, 3 and 3 quarters, $3.75; that of 12 yards at 6½¢ by thinking 72 (6×12), 78 (adding ½ of 12).

Oral Drill — Sum of Two Numbers

1. Mrs. Peck buys groceries amounting to $3.47 and dry goods amounting to $2.85. How much does she spend in all?

Think five forty-seven ($3.47 + $2), six twenty-seven (adding $.80), six thirty-two (adding $.05). *Ans.* $6.32.

Omit, however, to think of dollars or of cents until you announce the result.

2. How many pupils are there in a school containing 235 boys and 248 girls?

3. Give sums:

a. $140 + 85$	*b.* $142 + 87$	*c.* $145 + 37$	*d.* $145 + 86$
e. $256 + 91$	*f.* $256 + 28$	*g.* $256 + 78$	*h.* $360 + 73$
i. $369 + 25$	*j.* $369 + 55$	*k.* $482 + 30$	*l.* $482 + 35$

4. What is the cost of a horse at $275 and a buggy at $95?

Since $95 is $5 less than $100, think three seventy-five ($275 + 100$), three seventy (deducting 5). *Ans.* $370.

5. Give sums:

a. $147 + 99$	*b.* $149 + 87$	*c.* $145 + 39$	*d.* $149 + 95$
e. $259 + 91$	*f.* $256 + 28$	*g.* $238 + 85$	*h.* $365 + 79$
i. $365 + 39$	*j.* $367 + 75$	*k.* $482 + 69$	*l.* $489 + 35$

6. How many yards are there in two pieces of cloth, one containing $20\frac{3}{4}$ yards, and the other containing $17\frac{1}{2}$ yards?

Think $37\frac{3}{4}$ ($20\frac{3}{4} + 17$), $38\frac{1}{4}$ (adding $\frac{1}{2}$). *Ans.* $38\frac{1}{4}$ yards.

7. Give sums:

a. $17\frac{1}{2} + 8\frac{1}{2}$	*b.* $15\frac{3}{4} + 6\frac{1}{2}$	*c.* $16\frac{3}{4} + 9\frac{3}{4}$
d. $25\frac{2}{3} + 8\frac{1}{3}$	*e.* $24\frac{3}{8} + 8\frac{3}{8}$	*f.* $34\frac{1}{4} + 5\frac{3}{4}$
g. $35\frac{1}{2} + 7\frac{5}{8}$	*h.* $48\frac{1}{4} + 6\frac{1}{8}$	*i.* $45\frac{1}{6} + 7\frac{1}{6}$

Difference between Two Numbers

1. A girl has $5.60. How much will she have after spending $2.84?

Think three sixty (5.60 − 2), two eighty (deducting 80), two seventy-six (deducting 4). *Ans.* $2.76.

2. Give remainders:

a. 146 − 80	*b.* 229 − 53	*c.* 192 − 38	*d.* 212 − 68
e. 356 − 74	*f.* 256 − 29	*g.* 332 − 77	*h.* 343 − 70
i. 360 − 44	*j.* 417 − 89	*k.* 412 − 32	*l.* 517 − 66
m. 517 − 85	*n.* 623 − 57	*o.* 228 − 69	*p.* 750 − 87

3. A farmer has 275 hens. How many will he have after selling (*a*) 99? (*b*) 48?

(*a*) Think 175 (275 − 100), 176 (adding 1). *Ans.* 176 hens.
(*b*) Think 225 (275 − 50), 227 (adding 2). *Ans.* 217 hens.

Why is 1 *added* in (*a*)? Why is 2 *added* in (*b*)?

4. Give remainders:

a. 140 − 79	*b.* 229 − 99	*c.* 192 − 38	*d.* 225 − 68
e. 356 − 89	*f.* 256 − 28	*g.* 332 − 88	*h.* 340 − 89
i. 360 − 48	*j.* 417 − 98	*k.* 410 − 69	*l.* 514 − 69
m. 576 − 99	*n.* 645 − 58	*o.* 384 − 89	*p.* 447 − 98

5. From a tub of butter containing $49\frac{1}{4}$ pounds, $8\frac{1}{2}$ pounds were sold. How many pounds remained?

Think $41\frac{1}{4}$ ($49\frac{1}{4}$ − 8), $40\frac{3}{4}$ (deducting $\frac{1}{2}$).

6. Give remainders:

a. $56 - 9\frac{1}{3}$	*b.* $57 - 12\frac{1}{4}$	*c.* $60\frac{3}{4} - 9\frac{1}{2}$
d. $34 - 6\frac{1}{8}$	*e.* $34 - 11\frac{1}{8}$	*f.* $35\frac{7}{8} - 8\frac{1}{8}$
g. $46 - 7\frac{1}{4}$	*h.* $60 - 10\frac{1}{2}$	*i.* $34\frac{5}{6} - 6\frac{1}{6}$
j. $87 - 8\frac{3}{5}$	*k.* $45 - 13\frac{2}{3}$	*l.* $48\frac{7}{8} - 5\frac{3}{4}$
m. $23 - 6\frac{1}{2}$	*n.* $72 - 10\frac{4}{5}$	*o.* $76\frac{5}{8} - 9\frac{3}{8}$

Product of Two Numbers

1. How many seats are there in 8 classrooms, each containing 46 seats?

Think three twenty (40×8), three sixty-eight (adding 8×6). *Ans.* 368 seats.

2. Give products:

a. 3×27 *b.* 4×47 *c.* 5×59 *d.* 6×46 *e.* 4×95
f. 5×39 *g.* 6×45 *h.* 7×37 *i.* 5×87 *j.* 5×43
k. 7×34 *l.* 8×28 *m.* 6×78 *n.* 6×52 *o.* 7×16

3. Find the cost (*a*) of 99 cows at $41 each.   (*b*) Of 33 pounds of butter at 29 cents per pound.

(*a*) Think 41 hundred less 41.   *Ans.* $4059.
(*b*) Think nine ninety (30×33) less 33.   *Ans.* $9.57.

4. Give products:

a. 24×19 *b.* 18×99 *c.* 99×99 *d.* 99×34
e. 99×95 *f.* 99×46 *g.* 22×39 *h.* 36×99
i. 12×49 *j.* 47×99 *k.* 99×96 *l.* 78×41

5. Give the cost (*a*) of 39 pounds of coffee at 25 cents per pound.   (*b*) Of 25 pounds of butter at 39 cents per pound.   (*c*) Of 39 suits of clothes at $25 each.   (*d*) Of 25 cows at $39 each.

(*a*) Think 39 quarter dollars, or $9¾.   *Ans.* $9.75.
(*b*) 25 times 39 cents is the same as 39 times 25 cents.
(*c*) 39 suits will cost ¼ of 39 hundred dollars, or 9¾ hundred dollars.
(*d*) 25 times $39 is the same as 39 times $25.

6. Give answers:

a. $48 \times \$\tfrac{1}{8}$ *b.* $49 \times 33\tfrac{1}{3}¢$ *c.* $33¢ \times 33\tfrac{1}{3}$ *d.* $33\tfrac{1}{3} \times 23$
e. $48 \times \$\tfrac{1}{2}$ *f.* $49 \times 50¢$ *g.* $68¢ \times 50$ *h.* 50×79
i. $48 \times \$\tfrac{1}{6}$ *j.* $49 \times 16\tfrac{2}{3}¢$ *k.* $57¢ \times 16\tfrac{2}{3}$ *l.* $16\tfrac{2}{3} \times 67$

7. How many square inches are there in a strip of iron 97 ft. long (*a*) .25 ft. wide?   (*b*) .125 ft. wide?

Omitting Unnecessary Figures

In filling out the extensions in a bill, the beginner frequently sets down on a separate sheet of paper the multiplier and the multiplicand even when this procedure is unnecessary.

Blackboard Exercises

1. Multiply :

Write answers to the following directly from the book:

a. 11 articles @ $1.04   *b.* 845 articles @ $.08
c. 212 articles @ $.24   *d.* 12 articles @ $3.23
e. 254 articles @ $.12   *f.* 113 articles @ $.13
g. 4 articles @ $5.67   *h.* 187 articles @ $.05

In testing the correctness of a bill sent you, cover the extensions with a piece of paper, and write on the latter such products as you can obtain without rewriting the numbers, doing the latter only when it is really necessary.

2. What is the cost (*a*) of $48\frac{1}{2}$ pounds of sugar at 6 cents?   (*b*) Of 12 bushels of wheat at $93\frac{3}{4}$ ¢?

(*a*) Take 6 as the multiplier. Think $3(6 \times \frac{1}{2})$ and $48(6 \times 8)$ are 51; write 1. Think $24(6 \times 4)$, 29 (carrying 5); write 29. *Ans.* $2.91.

3. Write products :

a. $48\frac{1}{2} \times 8$ *b.* $10 \times 62\frac{1}{8}$ *c.* $123\frac{1}{3} \times 9$ *d.* $4 \times 55\frac{1}{4}$
e. $37\frac{3}{4} \times 4$ *f.* $13 \times 31\frac{1}{2}$ *g.* $459\frac{2}{3} \times 3$ *h.* $9 \times 63\frac{1}{3}$
i. $26\frac{3}{4} \times 5$ *j.* $12 \times 46\frac{1}{4}$ *k.* $326\frac{2}{5} \times 5$ *l.* $8 \times 42\frac{5}{8}$

4. Find the cost (*a*) of 2487 pounds of coffee at 25 cents per pound.   (*b*) Of 25 tons of coal at $4.75 per ton.

(*a*) Take the price as $\frac{1}{4}$.   (*b*) Divide $475 by 4. Why?

5. Write extensions :

a. 365 lb. @ 25 ¢   *b.* 25 bu. @ $4.85
c. $12\frac{1}{2}$ pr. @ $1.84   *d.* 678 lb. @ 25 ¢
e. $12\frac{1}{2}$ yd. @ $3.84   *f.* 50 doz. @ $2.75

Business Forms

Everybody is called upon to make out a bill, and he should be able to do so in a businesslike way.

A business house uses "bill heads," giving the name and the address of the concern, with lines for the name and the address of the customer. The two vertical lines at the left enclose a place for dates, and the four at the right provide for two columns of dollars and cents.

The date space is not used when all the articles are bought the same day.

The first of the two double columns at the right is used for the values of the specified quantities. These are called the "extensions." When the bill contains no credits, the sum of the extensions, called the "footing," is generally written in the second double column on the line following the last extension.

The unit price of each item is written to the left of the two double columns, the unnecessary dollar signs or "at" being usually omitted. When a single article is bought, its cost is placed directly in the column of extensions.

The bill is "receipted" by the word "Paid" with the date and the signature of the firm. When the latter is written by a clerk, he follows it with his initials preceded by the word "per."

PHŒNIX, ARIZ., May 12, 1915

MR. GEORGE H. GARTLAND
    475 Manhattan Av.

Bought of MULLALY & WATSON
GROCERS
380–386 Main St.

1 bbl. Flour		6	75
25 lb. Sugar	.06		
3 bu. Potatoes	1.25		
½ lb. Tea	.60		

Paid May 12, 1915
Mullaly & Watson
Per S. M. Y.

Written Exercises

1. Copy and complete the foregoing bill, substituting prevailing prices for those given.

The foregoing bill is for goods bought at one time. In the case of a customer who "runs an account" a memorandum of the purchase is given at the time, and a "statement" is sent at the end of the month.

2. Copy and complete the following :

MONTHLY STATEMENT

GRAND JUNCTION, COL., Nov. 30, 1916

THE A. X. FULLER COMPANY
   Dry Goods
      Clay and Market Sts.

Sold to MRS. D. E. JOHNSON
   345 Washington Square

Nov.	4	4 yd. Cambric	.27					
		2 pcs. Lace	1.15					
	10	1 pr. Gloves		1	25			
	12	27 yd. Silk	.60					
		18 " Lining	.15					
	16	½ doz. Collars	1.50					
	22	6 prs. Socks	.23					
	28	3 yd. Ribbon	.45			$		
		Cr.						
Nov.	15	2 pcs. Lace	1.15	2	30			
	30	3 yd. Ribbon	.45	1	35		3	65
		Balance due				$		

The foregoing monthly statement is merely a bill for goods bought at different times. Insert the dates in the date column. In this bill, write the footing of the purchases in the proper column, but on a line with the last extension. Write the footing of the two credits on the same line as the last credit extension.

3. Copy and complete the following statement sent to a farmer by the grocer from whom he makes purchases, and to whom he sells produce.

STATEMENT OF ACCOUNT

OMAHA, NEB., March 1, 1917

MR. WM. T. FERGUSON
     Haymarket, Iowa

In account with ROSS & SNYDER
Grocers
986 Delafield Av.

1915									
Feb.	6	*To 3 lb. Tea*	.60						
	7	" *1 bbl. Flour*			5	75			
		" *2 lb. Butter*	.35						
	8	" *10 " Coffee*	.25						
		" *20 " Sugar*	.06						
		" *1 sack Salt*			2	35			
	15	" *1 box Soap*			4	80	$		
		Cr.							
Feb.	9	*By 10 bu. Potatoes*	.75						
	14	" *Cash*			5	00			
	28	*Balance due us*					$		

In the foregoing statement the words "In account with" are used instead of "Sold to" or "Bought of." The statement may be rendered by either.

4. Make out the statement that would be rendered by Mr. Ferguson covering the foregoing account.

5. Make out the statement rendered by Mr. Ferguson March 31, during which month he has sold Ross and Snyder 10 bushels of potatoes at three different times at 75 cents per bushel, and bought the same quantity of groceries as in February, and at the same prices.

Bill for Services Rendered and Materials Furnished

The following is a form of bill for services rendered and materials supplied. If the business is too small to warrant the expense of printed bill heads, a pad of ruled blanks can be purchased, which contain a space for the names of the parties. If a blank of this kind is not available, the bill may be made out on ordinary paper. In this case the vertical lines should not be drawn.

CHAMBERLAIN, S.D., *July 8, 1916*

Mr. Wm. F. Foster
  63 Pine St.
      To ARTHUR C. GREENE   *Dr.*
          385 Grove Place

To 3¼ days' work	$ 3.50	12.25
" Hardware		.75
" Lumber		1.80
		$ 14.80

The address of the mechanic is useful in case Mr. Foster desires to mail a check in payment.

Written Exercises

1. Make out a bill for painting the front of a house. Ascertain the quantity of material required for three coats, the number of days of work, with the rate for each.

2. Make out a bill for papering a room. Give the cost of the paper and that of the labor.

3. Write a letter to a plumber asking him to make some repairs, specifying those needed.

4. On the back of the letter draw a rectangle of the proper size to represent an envelope. On it write the plumber's address.

Receipts

The following is a receipt sent by Mr. Greene in acknowledgment of a check received in settlement of the foregoing bill:

RECEIPT IN FULL

CHAMBERLAIN, S.D., *July* 10, 1916

RECEIVED OF *Wm. F. Foster*

Fourteen $\frac{00}{100}$ ——————————————————DOLLARS

in full of account to date

$ 14$\frac{00}{100}$ *Arthur C. Greene*

Blank receipts are generally used, which provide spaces for names, amount, etc. When ordinary paper is used, the same form should be followed, date on first line, name on second, amount in words on third, whether in full settlement or not on fourth, amount in figures on fifth, and also the signature.

RECEIPT ON ACCOUNT

OMAHA, NEB., *Feb.* 15, 1916

RECEIVED OF *Wm. T. Ferguson*

Five $\frac{00}{100}$ ——————————————————DOLLARS

on account

$ 5$\frac{00}{100}$ *Ross & Snyder*
                               Per M. E. K.

The foregoing is the receipt mailed to Wm. T. Ferguson on receipt of his check for five dollars sent in part payment, as shown in the statement of account given on page 14.

A "receipt in full" shows that all indebtedness is settled up to the date of the receipt. A "receipt on account" indicates that there is still a balance due the sender of the receipt.

The receipt given the tenant of a house by the owner specifies on the fourth line the location of the premises and the term covered by the payment, in this form:

"For rent of 93 Madison St., for June, 1915."

The fourth line of a physician's receipt would be as follows:

"For Professional Services to date."

Keeping Bills and Receipts

When making a purchase the buyer should request a memorandum of the articles, prices, etc., whether they are paid for at the time or not. This is frequently made out on a narrow sheet of paper and is called a "sales slip." To the housewife that keeps an account of her expenditures these slips save the writing of numerous items, the totals for a week or a month being the only entry made.

The necessity of retaining receipts and receipted bills is obvious.

Written Exercises

1. Write a letter to a merchant at a distance ordering dry goods at prices given in his advertisement, and stating that a check for the amount is inclosed.

2. Make out his receipt for the sum represented by the check.

3. Make out a rent receipt for one month's rent in advance.

4. Make out a physician's receipt for twenty dollars in part payment of his bill.

Guarding One's Savings

Every boy and every girl should begin as soon as possible to deposit his or her spare money in a savings bank. Most banks receive deposits of a dollar. In some cities there are school banks that receive a deposit of 1 cent and upwards. When the amount to the credit of the pupil reaches one dollar, it is transferred to a regular savings bank, which opens an account with the new depositor.

The following is the form of card used in a

School Bank

Raymond Malarkey
in account with
CENTRAL SCHOOL SAVINGS BANK

Dr.								Cr.
1914					1914			
Jan.	5	Dep.		15	Feb.	2	S. B.	1 00
	12	"		15			Cash	10
	19	"		50				
	26	"		40			Bal.	05
				1 20				1 15
Feb.	2	Bal.		05				

In this school, deposits are received on Monday mornings by the class teacher, who enters the amount on the boy's card. When the total reaches a dollar, an account is opened in a regular savings bank in the boy's name and the withdrawal entered on the card as "S. B." The card shows a further "Cash" withdrawal. The card is generally balanced after each transfer of money to the regular savings bank.

Savings Banks

When a person opens a savings-bank account he receives a book in which is entered on the right-hand page each deposit as it is made, and the interest earned. Each withdrawal is entered on the left-hand page. The two first pages are similar to the foregoing card.

RANCHERS SAVINGS BANK, in account with *John P. Jones*
Dr.   Cr.

1914				1915			
June 28	*Deposit*	*125*	—	*Jan. 4*	*Cash*	*16*	—
Dec. 21	"	*10*	—				
1915							
Jan. 2	(*Int.*)	*2*	*50*				

The account was opened June 28, 1914, with a deposit of $125. On Dec. 21, a further deposit was made of $10. A withdrawal of $16 was made on Jan. 4, 1915. On Jan. 2, 1915, an entry was made of the interest earned, $2.50. This is usually written in red ink.

To withdraw money from a savings bank, a person is generally required to present himself in person at the bank, with his bank book. If the authorities are in doubt as to the identity of the applicant, they ask him certain questions and compare his answers with replies to similar questions made at the time of opening the account.

Savings banks are established for the benefit of depositors. The organizers, other than the officers, receive no pay for their services.

Postal Savings Banks

As a convenience to certain classes of small depositors, and to enable people remote from other banks to protect their money and, at the same time, to increase their accumulations, the government accepts small sums on deposit, on which interest is allowed at the rate of 2 per cent a year.

To accumulate the $1 necessary to open an account, ten cents may be used to buy a *postal savings card*. When nine 10-cent *postal savings stamps* are affixed to the card, the latter is accepted as a deposit of $1. The depositor (who must be at least 10 years of age) then fills out an application and signs it. As evidence of a deposit he receives a certificate bearing his name, the number of his account, the date of issue, the name of the office, and the date on which interest begins (the first of the following month).

Certificates are issued for $1, $2, $5, $10, etc. Interest is paid only on certificates that represent money on deposit for at least one year. When a certificate is lost, a duplicate will be issued.

A depositor may withdraw the whole or any part of his deposits by surrendering properly indorsed certificates for the amount desired.

Postal Savings Bonds

A depositor may exchange certificates amounting to $20, $100, or $500 for registered or coupon bonds dated Jan. 1 or July 1, and bearing interest at the rate of $2\frac{1}{2}\%$, payable semiannually.

The owner of a registered bond receives by mail a check for the interest.

Commercial Banks

While the commercial bank does not, as a rule, pay interest on ordinary deposits, the services it renders are invaluable. It safeguards the money of its depositors and makes it possible for the latter to pay their bills by checks, which pass through the mails without danger of loss to the sender.

A commercial bank is organized for the purpose of earning money for its owners. This it does by loaning the balances of the depositors, and the bank expects that a depositor will generally have some money to his credit in the bank.

Every person who does not use all of his funds should have an account in a commercial bank, paying his bills by check. When the checks are returned to him by the bank, they should be kept as receipts, since they show to whom money has been paid.

Many bank accounts are opened in the joint names of husband and wife, each of whom can draw checks. This is a convenience to the other in the case of the absence, illness, or death of one of them.

Opening an Account

When a person opens an account in a commercial bank, he writes his name in the " signature book " in the form he intends to employ in signing checks. A " pass book " is then given him, which is similar to the one used by a savings bank.

DEPOSITED IN

THE STOCK YARDS BANK

Louisville, Ky.

By *Wm. T. Noonan*

Address *184 Meadow St.*

Sept. 16, 1915

Bills	*250*	*00*
Coin	*40*	*00*
Checks	*18*	*75*
	9	*43*
	106	*77*
	424	*95*

To make a deposit, Mr. Noonan fills out a slip in the accompanying form, inserting his name (as it is signed to his checks), his address, and the date.

The amount in bills is stated, also the amount in coin, then follow the amounts called for by the checks, each of which is "listed" separately.

The receiving teller enters the total in Mr. Noonan's bank book.

In addition to the pass book, each depositor receives a book containing a number of blank checks to be used in withdrawing money from the bank.

The following shows the page of a small book which has a single check to the page. The check book used in a business house has three or more checks to a page.

Page of Check Book

STUB	CHECK
No. _874_ _Sept. 21,_ 19_15_ To _John Whalen_ . _For Horse_ Brought for'd 583.11 Deposited 424.95 Total 1008.06 Amt. this check 300.00 Carried for'd 708.06	No. _874_ LOUISVILLE, KY., _Sept. 21,_ 19_15_ **The Stock Yards Bank** Pay to the order of _John Whalen_ ～～ Three Hundred ～～ $\frac{00}{100}$ Dollars $300 $\frac{00}{100}$ _W. T. Noonan_

Mr. Noonan makes out a check to pay Mr. Whalen for a horse, by writing the date, Mr. Whalen's name, and the amount, signing his name. He places the same details on the stub, which also shows the sum in the bank before the check is drawn and the balance remaining. The check is detached, and the stub remains in the book as a memorandum. In the illustration, "For Horse" indicates the transaction covered by the amount of the check.

"Cashing" a Check

ENDORSEMENT

By *endorsing* the check (which he does by writing "John Whalen" across the back), and presenting it to the paying teller of The Stock Yards Bank, Mr. Whalen will receive $300, if the teller knows that he is Mr. Whalen. If he does not wish to obtain the cash, he can have the check *certified* by the cashier, who writes across the face "certified," with the date and his signature, thereby guaranteeing that the bank will pay this amount.

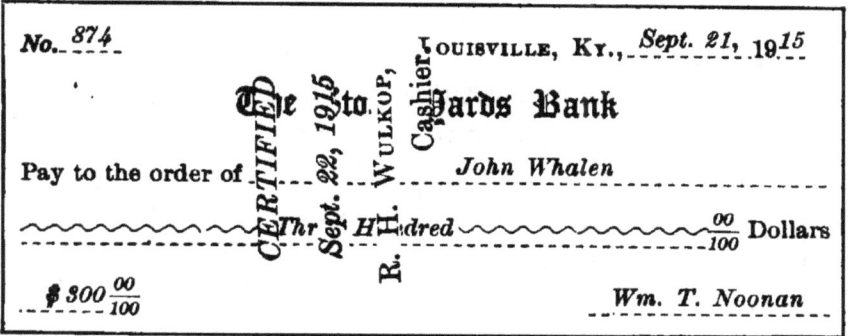

A CERTIFIED CHECK

As its certification binds the bank to pay the check when properly presented, Mr. Whalen can then more readily obtain the cash therefor from a business acquaintance.

Mr. Noonan could have had the check certified if he were a stranger to Mr. Whalen and desired to assure the latter that the check was "good" for $300.

Checks as Receipts

In order to make a check more useful as evidence, some persons use the form shown below, in which they enter the items covered by the check.

The following is in settlement of the account on p. 14.

No. 164   CHAMBERLAIN, S. D., *July 9*, 1915

Brule National Bank

Pay to the order of *Arthur C. Greene* $ 14 80/100

Fourteen 80/100 ~~~~~~~~~~~~~~~Dollars

8¼ days' work .	$8.50	12	25
Hardware			75
Lumber		1	80
		14	80

William F. Foster

This check properly endorsed is considered full receipt for the above bills.

Endorsements

The bare signature of John Whalen on the back of Mr. Noonan's check constitutes an endorsement "in blank," which makes it payable to any holder. This form is used by a business man only when he personally presents it at a bank for deposit or to be cashed, in which case he writes the endorsement at the counter in the bank.

For deposit
John Whalen

If Mr. Whalen sends it to a bank to be placed to his account, he writes "For deposit" on the back above his name, whereby he makes it impossible in case of its loss for the finder to use it.

In Mr. Whalen's absence, the check can be deposited in his bank by a clerk, his wife, etc., the form "for deposit to the credit of John Whalen," being employed, which serves instead of a personal endorsement.

For deposit to the credit of
John Whalen

Mr. Whalen could use the check to pay S. M. Horn $300, by giving it to him endorsed in blank. If it is to be sent by mail, Mr. Whalen writes above his signature "Pay to the order of S. M. Horn," which makes it uncollectible by any other person. If Mr. Horn should receive it with an endorsement in blank, he can secure himself in the event of its loss by writing the same words above Mr. Whalen's signature.

Pay to the order of
S. M. Horn

John Whalen

Liability of an Indorser

By indorsing a check or a note, the indorser guarantees its payment. He can relieve himself of this liability by writing above his name the words "without recourse."

Statement of Account with a Bank

The following is a form of report sent to a depositor:

Statement of

Moore, J. M.,
        2364 Lewis St.

In account with HOME TRUST COMPANY

If no errors are reported in ten days the account will be considered correct.

	Date	Checks			Date	Checks		Date	Credits	Amount	
1	7/1	50		26	8/2	6		July 1, 1915	Bal.	436	50
2	2	10		27	3	5		2		216	50
3		352	85	28		267	50	5		40	
4		10		29		53	50	6		150	
5	3	200		30	4	100		7		250	
6	8	120		31		30		15		50	
7	9	32	64	32	6	30		19		230	
8		5		33	10	18		31		530	
9	10	10		34	11	3		Aug. 2		30	
10	13	78		35	12	15		3		125	
11	14	100		36		4		7		200	
12	19	4		37	13	8		14		50	
13		50		38		C120	60	24		40	
14	21	12		39	14	4		30		750	
15		71	73	40		31	20				
16		5		41		47	50				
17	22	10		42	16	78					
18	24	10		43		5					
19		3		44	17	5					
20	26	14	74	45	18	5					
21	27	5		46	19	7					
22	28	6		47	23	3					
23		6		48	26	3					
24		84	67	49	30	28	15				
25	31	C 93	30			Balance (b)					
						(a')				(a)	
									Balance	(b')	

The number columns show that 49 checks were "honored" by the bank. The *C* prefixed to the checks 25 and 40 indicates that each was certified on the date specified, at which time it was charged against the account, even if it had not been paid by the bank. In this case a slip is sent with the other checks, calling attention to the fact that it has not yet been presented for payment.

Comparison with Check Book

When the depositor finds that the balance agrees with the amount shown on the stub of his check book, he can assume that his figures are correct. If the bank figures show a larger balance than his check book, it may mean that one or more checks are yet outstanding. A difference still existing after all the checks are accounted for, shows a mistake in entering the amount of the check on the stub, a deposit overlooked, an error in adding or subtracting, or the like.

When the depositor makes the necessary corrections on his stub, he files away as further evidence of payments made the checks returned by the bank with the statement.

Written Exercises

1. Find the sum of the credits and write it at (*a*) and and at (*a'*).

2. Insert at (*b*) the balance required to make the total of the checks equal to (*a'*). Write the same sum at (*b'*), to represent the balance to the credit of the depositor at the close of business on Aug. 31. This will appear on the next statement as the balance at the opening of business on Sept. 1.

3. (*a*) Write a letter to the cashier of the Citizens Trust Co., asking him to credit your account with the enclosed deposit. (*b*) Make out a deposit slip for the six checks enclosed.

Special Arithmetic Needed in Business — Percentage

Preparatory Exercises

1. A man bought a lot for $100. What was his profit if he sold it at an advance (*a*) of $\frac{1}{4}$ of the cost? (*b*) Of $\frac{1}{5}$ of the cost? (*c*) Of $\frac{2}{5}$ of the cost? (*d*) Of $\frac{18}{100}$ of the cost? (*e*) Of $\frac{6}{8}$ of the cost? (*f*) Of $\frac{3}{8}$ of the cost?

2. A man sells goods at $40 more than their cost. What does he gain on each $100 of the cost when the latter is (*a*) $100? (*b*) $200? (*c*) $400? (*d*) $500?

A profit of $8 on each $100 is said to be a profit of 8%.

3. When a dealer's profits are $60, what % does he gain if the goods cost:

a. $100?	*b.* $200?	*c.* $300?	*d.* $400?
e. $500?	*f.* $600?	*g.* $150?	*h.* $120?

3% means 3 hundredths, or .03; $12\frac{1}{2}$% means $12\frac{1}{2}$ hundredths, or .125; 100% means 100 hundredths, or .1.

4. A farmer raised 300 bushels of potatoes last year. How many more bushels will he raise this year if the increase should be:

a. 2%?	*b.* 5%?	*c.* 9%?	*d.* 12%?	*e.* 25%?
f. 50%?	*g.* 60%?	*h.* 90%?	*i.* 100%?	*j.* 200%?

5. Change the following per cents to common fractions — lowest terms:

a. 50%	*b.* 25%	*c.* 20%	*d.* $12\frac{1}{2}$%	*e.* $37\frac{1}{2}$%
f. 80%	*g.* 40%	*h.* 10%	*i.* $16\frac{2}{3}$%	*j.* $66\frac{2}{3}$%
k. 90%	*l.* 45%	*m.* 35%	*n.* $33\frac{1}{3}$%	*o.* $87\frac{1}{2}$%

6. Give answers:

a. 3% of $200.	*b.* 25% of 48 lb.	*c.* $12\frac{1}{2}$% of 64 A.
d. 4% of $300.	*e.* 50% of 92 qt.	*f.* $33\frac{1}{3}$% of $96.

Percentage

Drill Exercises

1. Change the following fractions to per cents:

a. $\frac{1}{8}$ *b.* $\frac{3}{8}$ *c.* $\frac{5}{8}$ *d.* $\frac{7}{8}$ *e.* $\frac{2}{3}$

f. $\frac{1}{3}$ *g.* $\frac{1}{6}$ *h.* $\frac{1}{2}$ *i.* $\frac{4}{5}$ *j.* $\frac{2}{5}$

k. $\frac{1}{5}$ *l.* $\frac{1}{4}$ *m.* $\frac{1}{20}$ *n.* $\frac{1}{40}$ *o.* $\frac{1}{80}$

p. $\frac{1}{10}$ *q.* $\frac{9}{10}$ *r.* $\frac{9}{20}$ *s.* $\frac{6}{40}$ *t.* $\frac{1}{12}$

2. What fraction of 24 is (*a*) 12? (*b*) 8? (*c*) 18? (*d*) 4? (*e*) 16? (*f*) 6? (*g*) 9? (*h*) 15? (*i*) 36? (*j*) 30?

3. What decimal of 32 is (*a*) 16? (*b*) 8? (*c*) 4? (*d*) 12? (*e*) 20? (*f*) 28? (*g*) 40? (*h*) 32? (*i*) 48?

4. Give answers:

a. 3% of 200 cows   *b.* 5% of 120 lb.

c. 1% of $237   *d.* $\frac{1}{2}$% of 400 T.

e. 6% of 150 yd.   *f.* 25% of 84 bu.

g. $12\frac{1}{2}$% of 96 A.   *h.* $37\frac{1}{2}$% of $16

i. $33\frac{1}{3}$% of 96 mi.   *j.* $16\frac{2}{3}$% of 48 gal.

5. What per cent

a. Of 80 is 16?   *b.* Of 40 is 32?   *c.* Of 32 is 40?

d. Of 100 is $\frac{1}{2}$?   *e.* Of 90 is 30?   *f.* Of 20 is 12?

g. Of 12 is 20?   *h.* Of 72 is 12?   *i.* Of 35 is 27?

j. Of 28 is 35?   *k.* Of $\frac{1}{2}$ is $\frac{1}{4}$?   *l.* Of $\frac{1}{4}$ is $\frac{1}{2}$?

m. Of $\frac{3}{4}$ is $\frac{1}{4}$?   *n.* Of $\frac{3}{4}$ is $\frac{1}{2}$?   *o.* Of $\frac{3}{4}$ is $\frac{5}{8}$?

6. Find the number of which

a. 20 is 5%   *b.* 30 is 6%   *c.* 42 is 7%

d. 60 is 9%   *e.* 75 is 9%   *f.* 20 is 125%

g. 30 is 150%   *h.* 60 is 75%   *i.* 70 is $87\frac{1}{2}$%

j. 90 is 30%   *k.* 13 is 50%   *l.* 13 is $\frac{1}{2}$%

m. 21 is 25%   *n.* 21 is $\frac{1}{4}$%   *o.* 21 is $\frac{3}{4}$%

Written Problems

1. A man's income is $1080. How much does he save when he saves (a) 12% of his income? (b) 12½% of it?

2. A family uses (a) 17% of its income for rent, (b) 37% of it for food, and (c) 16% for clothing. What sum is used for each when the income is $1200?

3. Last year a village contained 1576 inhabitants. This year the population is 12½% greater. How many more people are there in the village this year?

4. An agent sold a lot for $960. He received from the owner 3% of this sum for selling it. How much did (a) the agent receive? (b) The owner?

5. A man borrowed $1500, on which he paid interest at 5½% per year. What was the yearly interest?

6. How many pounds of butter fat are there in 675 pounds of milk when it contains (a) 4.4% of butter fat? (b) 4.5%?

PROCESS

(a)	675 lb.		(b)	675 lb.
	×.044	In (a) write		.04½
	2700	4.4% as .044.		337½
	2700	In (b) write		2700
	29.7ØØ lb. *Ans.*	4.5% as .04½.		30.375 lb. *Ans.*

---

7. A baseball club won 52.5% of the 80 games it played. How many games did it win?

8. A merchant bought goods for $4500. He sold them at an advance of 45%. What was his profit?

9. If farm machinery loses 15% of its value in a year, what is the loss in value of a machine that cost $960?

10. An agent sold a farm for \$8750. He received 5 % commission on \$1000, 2½ % on \$4000, and 1 % on the remainder. How much was he paid for making the sale?

11. A man's income is \$1095. What per cent of his income does he save when he saves (*a*) \$153.30? (*b*) \$182.50?

PROCESS

(*a*) Since 153.30 is 1095 times the per cent, find the latter by dividing 153.30 by 1095.

Change the quotient, 14 hundredths, to its equivalent, 14 %.

$$.14 = 14\% \ \textit{Ans.}$$

$$1095\overline{)153.30}$$

(*b*) $.16\tfrac{2}{3} = 16\tfrac{2}{3}\%$ *Ans.*

$$1095\overline{)182.50}$$

etc.

$$\begin{array}{r} 1095 \\ \hline 4380 \\ 4380 \end{array}$$

TEST

To prove the correctness of the answer, multiply \$1095 (*a*) by .14, (*b*) by .16⅔ (⅓).

---

12. A family spends annually (*a*) \$240 for rent, (*b*) \$540 for food, and (*c*) \$342 for clothing. When the income is \$1800, what per cent is spent for each of the three items?

13. Last year a village contained 1540 inhabitants. This year the population is 231 greater. What is the per cent of increase?

14. An agent received \$32.50 for selling a lot for \$1300. What per cent of the latter did he receive?

15. A man pays \$63 annual interest on a loan of \$1200. What per cent does he pay?

16. When 825 pounds of milk contain 34.65 pounds of butter fat, what per cent of the milk is the fat?

17. A baseball club played 96 games, of which it won 60. (*a*) What per cent of the games were victories? (*b*) What per cent were defeats?

18. A merchant sold at a profit of $1080 goods that cost $4500. What per cent of the cost was the profit?

19. Farm machinery worth $1080 decreases $160 in value in a year. What is the per cent of decrease?

20. What is a man's income when his annual savings of $192.50 represent (*a*) 14% of his income? (*b*) $12\frac{1}{2}$% of his income?

PROCESS

(*a*) When .14 times the income is 192.50, the income is $192.50 ÷ .14.

Ans. $1375
.14)$192.50

$.12\frac{1}{2}$)$192.50

Get the answer by multiplying the dividend by 8.

---

21. The increase in the population of a village during 1915 was 357, a gain of 17%. What was the population at the beginning of the year?

22. For selling a lot an agent received $26, which was $2\frac{1}{2}$% of the price he obtained for it. What was the selling price?

23. A man pays $3.72 yearly interest on money he borrowed. How much did he borrow if he pays 6% interest?

24. How many pounds of milk will yield 270 pounds of butter fat when 4.5% of the milk is fat?

25. A merchant's profit on goods he sold was $1890. If the profit was 35% of the cost, how much did the goods cost?

26. When the cost of the materials in a five-cent loaf of bread is one half of the selling price, how many loaves must be sold in order to pay from the profits the following monthly expenses:

Rent, $30; expenses of horse and wagon, $30; extra baker, $60; driver, $30?

27. A baker sells on an average 400 five-cent loaves of bread per day. (*a*) What is the cost per loaf when the material costs 2½ cents per loaf and the other expenses amount to $150 per month of 30 days? (*b*) How much remains per month to cover the labor of himself and family and the interest on the money invested?

28. Forty years ago a farmer bought 160 acres of land at $1.25 per acre. He spent $325 in buildings, $150 for machinery, and bought 3 horses at $70 each, 3 cows at $25 each, 4 hogs at $8 each, and 40 chickens at 20 cents each. What was the interest on his investment at 8 %?

29. The same land is worth to-day $100 per acre, including buildings; he has 4 horses worth $250 each, 20 cows worth $60 each, 25 hogs worth $12 each, poultry worth $100, and machinery worth $1400. What is the interest at 8 % on the present value?

30. A girl collected eggs as follows from her 100 hens:

Jan. 662	May 1911	Sept. 648
Feb. 736	Jun. 1635	Oct. 159
Mch. 1410	Jul. 1338	Nov. 225
Apr. 1920	Aug. 912	Dec. 444

She received for them an average of 20¢ per dozen, including those used for cooking. What were the total receipts?

REVIEWS AND TESTS

Quickness at Figures

Accuracy in computation depends largely upon the employment of reasonable rapidity in doing the work. To develop and then to continue the required speed, constant practice is necessary. A minute or two at the beginning of each exercise in arithmetic should be given to rapid oral answers by successive pupils to combinations similar to those contained in the following:

Sight Drills

	A	B	C	D	E	F	G	H	I	J
a.	87	69	25	83	15	34	97	58	49	95
b.	46	34	18	96	78	27	35	17	88	74
c.	54	79	86	37	45	54	89	75	19	66
d.	94	56	48	16	67	99	47	98	85	59
e.	36	29	55	68	26	65	28	39	24	85

1. Add to each of the numbers in the foregoing table:

    a. 70   *b.* 130   *c.* 151   *d.* 189   *e.* 275

2. Subtract each of the numbers in the foregoing table from:

    a. 125   *b.* 259   *c.* 300   *d.* 310   *e.* 420

3. Multiply each of the numbers in the foregoing table by:

    a. $12\frac{1}{2}$ *b.* $16\frac{2}{3}$ *c.* 25   *d.* $33\frac{1}{3}$ *e.* 50   *f.* 99

Testing Progress

Some teachers keep a score in a corner of the blackboard, which gives the date, the exercise, and the number of combinations correctly made within the time limit of, say, two minutes. This score is compared with subsequent drills on the same exercise to note the progress made.

In some schools the same drills are given to classes of different grades and the results compared.

Under ideal conditions, each grade should show a better score than the grade below; and the score of each successive test in the same grade should be better than that obtained in the preceding test.

Oral Answers

Numbers similar to those in the foregoing set, and large enough to be seen from all parts of the room, may be written on a large stout sheet of paper, unless it is preferred to use the text-book. At a signal the class stands, the teacher announces the number to be added (34, for instance), the first pupil says 121 and sits, the next says 103, the next 59, etc. When the last pupil has given his result the class again stands, and the answers continue. When the last combination (69) is made, the next pupil may begin with the first, adding 34 to it, or a new addend may be supplied by the teacher.

Writing the Answers

In order to determine the number of combinations made by each pupil in a given set, a 3-minute test is frequently employed, in which every pupil writes on a strip of paper prepared beforehand the answers to as many examples as possible.

The Scores

When the signal to stop work is given, each pupil lays aside his pen, and takes a lead pencil. At the foot of the strip he writes (1) the number of examples "attempted." The answers are then announced, and the pupil checks his correct ones, drawing his pencil through the wrong ones and those in which he has made any alterations. Under (1) he writes, (2) the number of correct answers and (3) the per cent (2) is of (1).

Sight Reviews — Reducing Fractions

1. Change $\frac{1}{2}$ to
(*a*) 24ths, (*b*) 36ths, (*c*) 48ths, (*d*) 70ths.

2. Change $\frac{1}{4}$ to
(*a*) 16ths, (*b*) 28ths, (*c*) 56ths, (*d*) 72ds.

3. Change $\frac{3}{4}$ to
(*a*) 20ths, (*b*) 32ds, (*c*) 48ths, (*d*) 60ths.

4. Change $\frac{2}{3}$ to
(*a*) 15ths, (*b*) 36ths, (*c*) 60ths, (*d*) 63ds.

5. Change $\frac{4}{5}$ to
(*a*) 25ths, (*b*) 35ths, (*c*) 45ths, (*d*) 55ths.

6. Change $\frac{5}{6}$ to
(*a*) 30ths, (*b*) 36ths, (*c*) 48ths, (*d*) 54ths.

7. Change $\frac{3}{5}$ to
(*a*) 40ths, (*b*) 60ths, (*c*) 70ths, (*d*) 30ths. '

8. Change $\frac{3}{8}$ to
(*a*) 48ths, (*b*) 64ths, (*c*) 72ds, (*d*) 88ths.

9. Change $\frac{5}{8}$ to
(*a*) 24ths, (*b*) 64ths, (*c*) 72ds, (*d*) 88ths.

10. Change $\frac{7}{8}$ to
(*a*) 16ths, (*b*) 24ths, (*c*) 32ds, (*d*) 56ths.

11. Express in lowest terms :

a. $\frac{16}{24}$	*b.* $\frac{18}{40}$	*c.* $\frac{20}{100}$	*d.* $\frac{108}{120}$	*e.* $\frac{63}{81}$
f. $\frac{18}{20}$	*g.* $\frac{19}{95}$	*h.* $\frac{24}{120}$	*i.* $\frac{100}{120}$	*j.* $\frac{48}{60}$
k. $\frac{18}{30}$	*l.* $\frac{17}{51}$	*m.* $\frac{24}{160}$	*n.* $\frac{100}{150}$	*o.* $\frac{37}{74}$
p. $\frac{24}{72}$	*q.* $\frac{34}{51}$	*r.* $\frac{35}{100}$	*s.* $\frac{120}{150}$	*t.* $\frac{23}{92}$
u. $\frac{18}{72}$	*v.* $\frac{39}{65}$	*w.* $\frac{48}{120}$	*x.* $\frac{108}{144}$	*y.* $\frac{69}{92}$

Adding Fractions

1. Give answers in lowest terms. Reduce improper fractions to mixed numbers:

a. $\dfrac{1}{12}$ $+\dfrac{1}{12}$ b. $\dfrac{5}{12}$ $+\dfrac{5}{12}$ c. $\dfrac{1}{12}$ $+\dfrac{7}{12}$ d. $\dfrac{5}{12}$ $+\dfrac{5}{12}$ e. $\dfrac{5}{12}$ $+\dfrac{11}{12}$ f. $\dfrac{7}{12}$ $+\dfrac{7}{12}$

g. $\dfrac{1}{12}$ $+\dfrac{1}{2}$ h. $\dfrac{1}{12}$ $+\dfrac{1}{3}$ i. $\dfrac{1}{12}$ $+\dfrac{1}{4}$ j. $\dfrac{1}{12}$ $+\dfrac{1}{6}$ k. $\dfrac{5}{12}$ $+\dfrac{1}{2}$ l. $\dfrac{5}{12}$ $+\dfrac{1}{6}$

m. $\dfrac{7}{12}$ $+\dfrac{1}{2}$ n. $\dfrac{7}{12}$ $+\dfrac{1}{3}$ o. $\dfrac{7}{12}$ $+\dfrac{1}{4}$ p. $\dfrac{7}{12}$ $+\dfrac{1}{6}$ q. $\dfrac{1}{2}$ $+\dfrac{1}{3}$ r. $\dfrac{1}{3}$ $+\dfrac{1}{4}$

2. Give sums:

a. $1\frac{3}{4}$ $+\frac{3}{4}$ b. $2\frac{2}{3}$ $+\frac{2}{3}$ c. $1\frac{5}{6}$ $+\frac{5}{6}$ d. $2\frac{7}{8}$ $+\frac{3}{8}$ e. $1\frac{7}{8}$ $+\frac{5}{8}$ f. $3\frac{7}{8}$ $+\frac{7}{8}$

g. $1\frac{1}{2}$ $+\frac{1}{3}$ h. $2\frac{1}{3}$ $+\frac{1}{4}$ i. $3\frac{1}{4}$ $+\frac{1}{6}$ j. $2\frac{1}{5}$ $+\frac{1}{6}$ k. $1\frac{1}{3}$ $+\frac{1}{5}$ l. $2\frac{1}{2}$ $+\frac{1}{5}$

m. $2\frac{1}{2}$ $+\frac{2}{3}$ n. $3\frac{1}{3}$ $+\frac{3}{4}$ o. $4\frac{1}{4}$ $+\frac{2}{3}$ p. $5\frac{1}{6}$ $+\frac{2}{3}$ q. $6\frac{5}{6}$ $+\frac{3}{4}$ r. $7\frac{1}{8}$ $+\frac{1}{6}$

Subtracting Fractions

1. Give answers:

a. $\dfrac{1}{2}$ $-\dfrac{3}{8}$ b. $\dfrac{7}{8}$ $-\dfrac{1}{2}$ c. $\dfrac{5}{6}$ $-\dfrac{1}{3}$ d. $\dfrac{1}{2}$ $-\dfrac{5}{12}$ e. $\dfrac{7}{8}$ $-\dfrac{1}{4}$ f. $\dfrac{7}{9}$ $-\dfrac{2}{3}$

g. $\dfrac{7}{12}$ $-\dfrac{1}{2}$ h. $\dfrac{7}{8}$ $-\dfrac{3}{4}$ i. $\dfrac{7}{9}$ $-\dfrac{1}{3}$ j. $\dfrac{2}{3}$ $-\dfrac{1}{9}$ k. $\dfrac{11}{12}$ $-\dfrac{1}{4}$ l. $\dfrac{5}{6}$ $-\dfrac{1}{2}$

2. Give remainders:

a. $1\frac{1}{4}$ $-\frac{3}{4}$ b. $1\frac{1}{3}$ $-\frac{2}{3}$ c. $1\frac{1}{6}$ $-\frac{5}{6}$ d. $1\frac{1}{2}$ $-\frac{1}{3}$ e. $1\frac{1}{2}$ $-\frac{2}{3}$ f. $1\frac{1}{2}$ $-\frac{5}{6}$

g. $2\frac{1}{2}$ $-\frac{5}{6}$ h. $2\frac{1}{2}$ $-\frac{1}{8}$ i. $2\frac{1}{8}$ $-\frac{1}{2}$ j. $2\frac{7}{9}$ $-\frac{1}{3}$ k. $2\frac{1}{8}$ $-\frac{7}{8}$ l. $2\frac{1}{4}$ $-\frac{2}{3}$

Sight Problems

1. Two clocks show the right time at noon Monday. If one gains $7\frac{1}{8}$ minutes per week and the other loses $3\frac{1}{4}$ minutes, what will be the difference in their time at noon the following Monday?

2. Two men start at the same time from points $25\frac{1}{2}$ miles apart and walk towards each other, one at the rate of $3\frac{1}{4}$ miles per hour and the other, at the rate of $3\frac{1}{8}$ miles. How far are they apart at the end of the hour?

3. A tub of butter weighs $49\frac{1}{4}$ pounds with the tub. The latter weighs $8\frac{1}{4}$ pounds. What is the value of the butter at 24 cents per pound?

4. A storekeeper bought $3\frac{3}{4}$ dozen eggs from A and $5\frac{2}{3}$ dozen from B, paying for them 12 cents per dozen. What did the eggs cost him?

5. From a 40-acre field were sold two plots containing $5\frac{3}{4}$ and $6\frac{7}{8}$ acres, respectively. How many acres remained?

6. One man can paint $\frac{1}{8}$ of a fence in a day, another can do $\frac{1}{12}$ of it in a day, and an apprentice can do $\frac{1}{24}$ of it in a day. (*a*) What fraction of the fence can all three together do in a day? (*b*) How many days would it take the three to paint the fence, working together?

7. How many rods of fence will be required to enclose a field $20\frac{3}{4}$ rods long, $16\frac{1}{2}$ rods wide?

8. A boy bought a bicycle for $\$7\frac{1}{4}$ and paid $\$2\frac{3}{4}$ for repairs. What did he gain by selling it for $\$12\frac{1}{2}$?

9. A girl bought for a dress $4\frac{7}{8}$ yards of gingham and $2\frac{3}{8}$ yards of trimming, what did the material cost at 12 ¢ per yard?

Multiplying Fractions

1. Give answers. Change improper fractions to mixed numbers.

a. $\frac{2}{3}$ b. $\frac{3}{4}$ c. $\frac{7}{8}$ d. $\frac{2}{5}$ e. $\frac{4}{5}$
   $\times 8$ $\times 7$ $\times 9$ $\times 6$ $\times 9$

f. 5 g. 4 h. 5 i. 7 j. 6
   $\times \frac{5}{8}$ $\times \frac{2}{3}$ $\times \frac{3}{4}$ $\times \frac{2}{5}$ $\times \frac{6}{7}$

2. Multiply :

a. $1\frac{1}{3}$ b. $1\frac{1}{5}$ c. $1\frac{1}{2}$ d. $1\frac{1}{4}$ e. $1\frac{1}{6}$
   $\times 8$ $\times 6$ $\times 9$ $\times 5$ $\times 7$

f. 3 g. 6 h. 5 i. 4 j. 3
   $\times 1\frac{1}{4}$ $\times 1\frac{2}{5}$ $\times 1\frac{3}{4}$ $\times 1\frac{2}{3}$ $\times 1\frac{5}{8}$

3. Give answers in mixed numbers. Fractions in lowest terms :

a. $\frac{5}{6}$ b. $\frac{5}{6}$ c. $\frac{5}{12}$ d. $\frac{5}{12}$ e. $\frac{5}{12}$
   $\times 3$ $\times 2$ $\times 4$ $\times 2$ $\times 3$

f. 2 g. 4 h. 3 i. 6 j. 4
   $\times \frac{5}{8}$ $\times \frac{7}{8}$ $\times \frac{7}{9}$ $\times \frac{7}{12}$ $\times \frac{11}{12}$

4. Multiply. Express fractions in lowest terms :

a. $2\frac{1}{6}$ b. $4\frac{1}{8}$ c. $3\frac{1}{8}$ d. $5\frac{1}{6}$ e. $5\frac{1}{10}$
   $\times 3$ $\times 4$ $\times 2$ $\times 2$ $\times 5$

f. $3\frac{1}{12}$ g. $6\frac{2}{3}$ h. $7\frac{3}{10}$ i. $8\frac{1}{12}$ j. $6\frac{1}{12}$
   $\times 4$ $\times 3$ $\times 2$ $\times 6$ $\times 4$

5. Give answers :

a. $\frac{1}{2}$ of $\frac{2}{3}$ b. $\frac{1}{3}$ of $\frac{3}{8}$ c. $\frac{1}{2}$ of $\frac{4}{5}$ d. $\frac{1}{4}$ of $\frac{8}{9}$

e. $\frac{2}{3} \times \frac{1}{4}$ f. $\frac{6}{7} \times \frac{1}{6}$ g. $\frac{5}{8} \times \frac{1}{5}$ h. $\frac{2}{3} \times \frac{6}{7}$

i. $\frac{1}{2}$ of $\frac{8}{5}$ j. $\frac{1}{2}$ of $\frac{9}{5}$ k. $\frac{1}{4}$ of $\frac{7}{5}$ l. $\frac{1}{8}$ of $\frac{7}{5}$

Dividing Fractions

1. Give quotients:

a. $2\overline{)1}$　　b. $\tfrac{1}{2}\overline{)1}$　　c. $\tfrac{1}{2}\overline{)15}$　　d. $\tfrac{1}{2}\overline{)32\tfrac{1}{2}}$　　e. $\tfrac{1}{3}\overline{)32\tfrac{1}{3}}$

f. $3\overline{)2}$　　g. $\tfrac{1}{3}\overline{)2}$　　h. $\tfrac{1}{3}\overline{)22}$　　i. $\tfrac{1}{3}\overline{)20\tfrac{2}{3}}$　　j. $\tfrac{1}{3}\overline{)20\tfrac{1}{3}}$

k. $4\overline{)3}$　　l. $\tfrac{1}{4}\overline{)3}$　　m. $\tfrac{1}{4}\overline{)21}$　　n. $\tfrac{1}{4}\overline{)20\tfrac{1}{4}}$　　o. $\tfrac{1}{4}\overline{)20\tfrac{1}{2}}$

2. Divide:

a. $2\overline{)\tfrac{3}{5}}$　　b. $2\overline{)1\tfrac{3}{5}}$　　c. $4\overline{)1\tfrac{3}{5}}$　　d. $3\overline{)1\tfrac{1}{5}}$　　e. $5\overline{)1\tfrac{1}{4}}$

f. $2\overline{)\tfrac{2}{5}}$　　g. $2\overline{)1\tfrac{1}{5}}$　　h. $4\overline{)1\tfrac{1}{5}}$　　i. $3\overline{)1\tfrac{2}{5}}$　　j. $5\overline{)1\tfrac{3}{5}}$

3. Give answers:

a. $2\overline{)64\tfrac{2}{3}}$　　b. $3\overline{)63\tfrac{3}{4}}$　　c. $4\overline{)84\tfrac{4}{5}}$　　d. $5\overline{)50\tfrac{5}{6}}$　　e. $6\overline{)48\tfrac{6}{7}}$

f. $2\overline{)64\tfrac{1}{2}}$　　g. $3\overline{)63\tfrac{1}{3}}$　　h. $4\overline{)84\tfrac{1}{4}}$　　i. $5\overline{)50\tfrac{1}{5}}$　　j. $6\overline{)48\tfrac{1}{2}}$

4. Divide.　Ignore the denominators when they are the same in the divisor and in the dividend.

a. $\tfrac{3}{4}\overline{)\tfrac{9}{4}}$　　b. $\tfrac{3}{4}\overline{)2\tfrac{1}{4}}$　　c. $\tfrac{3}{4}\overline{)4}$　　d. $\tfrac{3}{4}\overline{)1}$　　e. $\tfrac{3}{4}\overline{)2}$

f. $\tfrac{2}{3}\overline{)\tfrac{8}{3}}$　　g. $\tfrac{2}{3}\overline{)2\tfrac{2}{3}}$　　h. $\tfrac{2}{3}\overline{)\tfrac{2}{3}}$　　i. $\tfrac{2}{3}\overline{)1}$　　j. $\tfrac{2}{3}\overline{)2}$

k. $\tfrac{2}{3}\overline{)\tfrac{11}{3}}$　　l. $\tfrac{2}{3}\overline{)3\tfrac{2}{3}}$　　m. $\tfrac{2}{3}\overline{)\tfrac{15}{2}}$　　n. $\tfrac{2}{3}\overline{)5}$　　o. $\tfrac{2}{3}\overline{)6}$

p. $\tfrac{3}{4}\overline{)1\tfrac{1}{4}}$　　q. $\tfrac{3}{4}\overline{)2\tfrac{3}{4}}$　　r. $\tfrac{3}{4}\overline{)\tfrac{20}{4}}$　　s. $\tfrac{3}{4}\overline{)5}$　　t. $\tfrac{3}{4}\overline{)6}$

5. Give quotients:

a. $2\tfrac{1}{4} \div \tfrac{3}{4}$　　b. $3\tfrac{1}{5} \div \tfrac{4}{5}$　　c. $4\tfrac{3}{8} \div \tfrac{3}{8}$　　d. $1\tfrac{1}{9} \div \tfrac{2}{9}$

e. $3\tfrac{3}{8} \div \tfrac{5}{8}$　　f. $4\tfrac{1}{6} \div \tfrac{5}{6}$　　g. $5\tfrac{1}{2} \div \tfrac{2}{2}$　　h. $3\tfrac{1}{9} \div \tfrac{4}{9}$

i. $5\tfrac{1}{3} \div \tfrac{2}{3}$　　j. $4\tfrac{1}{5} \div \tfrac{3}{5}$　　k. $6\tfrac{1}{8} \div \tfrac{7}{8}$　　l. $6\tfrac{1}{6} \div \tfrac{5}{6}$

m. $3\tfrac{1}{4} \div \tfrac{3}{4}$　　n. $2\tfrac{1}{5} \div \tfrac{2}{5}$　　o. $4\tfrac{1}{5} \div \tfrac{4}{5}$　　p. $3\tfrac{1}{9} \div \tfrac{2}{9}$

q. $2\tfrac{1}{8} \div \tfrac{5}{8}$　　r. $3\tfrac{1}{6} \div \tfrac{5}{6}$　　s. $5\tfrac{1}{5} \div \tfrac{5}{5}$　　t. $4\tfrac{1}{8} \div \tfrac{7}{8}$

u. $6\tfrac{1}{3} \div \tfrac{2}{3}$　　v. $4\tfrac{1}{7} \div \tfrac{3}{7}$　　w. $3\tfrac{1}{8} \div \tfrac{3}{8}$　　x. $5\tfrac{1}{7} \div \tfrac{4}{7}$

Sight Problems

1. What is the area of a plot of ground 10½ rods long and 10½ rods wide?

2. When a tablespoonful of coffee weighs ¼ ounce, how many are there in a pound of coffee?

3. At $2½ per dozen, how many dozen handkerchiefs can be bought for $11¼?

4. A field containing 31¼ acres was divided into 5 equal building plots. How many acres were there in each?

5. What is the yield of a 32-acre field at the rate of 20¾ bushels of wheat to the acre?

6. How much more than a dollar will be the cost of 1¾ yards of silk at 60 cents per yard?

7. At $⅝ per yard, how many yards of silk can be bought for $5?

8. What is the cost of a cubic yard of sand at the rate of 75¢ per load of 1¼ cubic yards?

9. There are 1¼ cu. ft. to the bushel. What part of a bushel is a cubic foot?

10. When ¼ of a piece of meat costing 24 cents per pound is fat and bones, what is paid per pound for the lean meat?

11. A boy raised 96½ bushels of corn on ¾ acre. What was the rate per acre?

12. A girl member of a poultry club got 70 eggs from 2 hens in 42 days. What was the average per hen per day?

Reducing Decimals

1. Change the following common fractions to decimals:

a. $\frac{1}{8}$ *b.* $\frac{1}{16}$ *c.* $\frac{1}{20}$ *d.* $\frac{3}{25}$ *e.* $\frac{7}{50}$ *f.* $\frac{1}{40}$

g. $\frac{3}{8}$ *h.* $\frac{3}{16}$ *i.* $\frac{3}{20}$ *j.* $\frac{7}{25}$ *k.* $\frac{11}{50}$ *l.* $\frac{3}{40}$

m. $\frac{5}{8}$ *n.* $\frac{5}{16}$ *o.* $\frac{7}{20}$ *p.* $\frac{9}{25}$ *q.* $\frac{13}{50}$ *r.* $\frac{9}{40}$

s. $\frac{7}{8}$ *t.* $\frac{7}{16}$ *u.* $\frac{9}{20}$ *v.* $\frac{11}{25}$ *w.* $\frac{17}{50}$ *x.* $\frac{11}{40}$

2. Change the following decimals to common fractions — lowest terms:

a. .5 *b.* .6 *c.* .12 *d.* .32 *e.* .125 *f.* .625 *g.* .0625

h. .4 *i.* .8 *j.* .24 *k.* .65 *l.* .375 *m.* .875 *n.* .1875

Decimals of two places are called *per cents.*

3. Change the following per cents to common fractions — lowest terms:

a. 2 % *b.* 1¼ % *c.* 10 % *d.* 12½ % *e.* 18¾ %

f. 4 % *g.* 2½ % *h.* 15 % *i.* 37½ % *j.* 31¼ %

k. 5 % *l.* 6¼ % *m.* 20 % *n.* 33⅓ % *o.* 66⅔ %

p. 6 % *q.* 3⅛ % *r.* 25 % *s.* 62½ % *t.* 93¾ %

u. 8 % *v.* 4½ % *w.* 30 % *x.* 87½ % *y.* 16⅔ %

4. Change the following fractions to per cents:

a. $\frac{1}{8}$ *b.* $\frac{7}{8}$ *c.* $\frac{1}{6}$ *d.* $\frac{1}{20}$ *e.* $\frac{3}{20}$ *f.* $\frac{1}{200}$

g. $\frac{2}{3}$ *h.* $\frac{1}{4}$ *i.* $\frac{5}{6}$ *j.* $\frac{1}{30}$ *k.* $\frac{3}{25}$ *l.* $\frac{3}{200}$

m. $\frac{1}{8}$ *n.* $\frac{3}{4}$ *o.* $\frac{3}{5}$ *p.* $\frac{1}{40}$ *q.* $\frac{3}{50}$ *r.* $\frac{7}{200}$

s. $\frac{3}{8}$ *t.* $\frac{1}{6}$ *u.* $\frac{4}{5}$ *v.* $\frac{1}{50}$ *w.* $\frac{4}{25}$ *x.* $\frac{1}{400}$

Multiplying Decimals

1. Multiply by .15.

a. 6 *b.* 2 *c.* 4 *d.* 10 *e.* 8 *f.* 12 *g.* 20 *h.* 11

2. Multiply by 1.2.

a. 5 *b.* 8 *c.* 9 *d.* 10 *e.* 6 *f.* 20 *g.* 12 *h.* 11

3. Multiply by 24.

a. .3 *b.* .4 *c.* .5 *d.* .01 *e.* .1 *f.* 1.1 *g.* 1.2 *h.* .21

4. Multiply by 2.1.

a. 5 *b.* 6 *c.* 9 *d.* 20 *e.* 3 *f.* 30 *g.* 40 *h.* 11

5. Give products :

a.	1.4	*b.*	100	*c.*	.011	*d.*	300	*e.*	1.1
	× 10		× .12		× 1000		× 1.3		× 110

f.	1.4	*g.*	200	*h.*	.011	*i.*	400	*j.*	1.2
	× 20		× .12		× 2000		× 2.2		× 120

6. Multiply :

a.	48	*b.*	.125	*c.*	624	*d.*	1.25	*e.*	2.5
	× .25		× 64		× .5		× 24		× 8.4

f.	49	*g.*	.125	*h.*	488	*i.*	1.25	*j.*	2.5
	× .25		× 65		× .5		× 32		× 8.5

Dividing Decimals

1. Give quotients :

a. $48 \div 10$ *b.* $48 \div 100$ *c.* $4.8 \div 10$ *d.* $.48 \div 10$

e. $48 \div 20$ *f.* $48 \div 200$ *g.* $4.8 \div 20$ *h.* $.48 \div 20$

2. Divide by .4 :

a. 6 *b.* 8 *c.* 12 *d.* 24 *e.* 3 *f.* 18 *g.* 21 *h.* 5

3. Divide by .3 :

a. .6 *b.* .9 *c.* .12 *d.* 2.4 *e.* 3 *f.* 1.8 *g.* .21 *h.* 9

4. Give quotients :

a. $.25\overline{)21}$ *b.* $.25\overline{)12}$ *c.* $.25\overline{)2.2}$ *d.* $.25\overline{).81}$

e. $25\overline{)12}$ *f.* $25\overline{)20}$ *g.* $25\overline{)1.2}$ *h.* $25\overline{).22}$

5. Give answers :

a. $.125\overline{)31}$ *b.* $.125\overline{)3.1}$ *c.* $.125\overline{).21}$

Sight Problems

1. What decimal of its games is won by a club that wins 40 games out of 64 played?

2. There are 1.25 cu. ft. in a bushel. (*a*) What decimal of a bushel is a cubic foot? (*b*) How many bushels will a bin hold whose capacity is 50 cu. ft. ?

3. What is the quotient (*a*) of .75 divided by .625? (*b*) Of .625 divided by .75?

4. How many square rods are there in a plot 32.4 rods long, 30 rods wide?

5. A mile is 320 rods. What decimal of a mile is (*a*) 128 rods? (*b*) 120 rods?

6. How many rods of fence are required to inclose a field 12.25 rods long, 6.5 rods wide?

7. A player's record of safe hits is .375 of the number of times he goes to the bat. (*a*) How many hits did he make if he batted 80 times? (*b*) How many times at bat with 36 hits would make the same record?

8. What is the width of a plot 3.6 rods long that contains 9 square rods?

9. (*a*) What did I pay per acre for land on which I lost .2 of the cost by selling it at $96 per acre? (*b*) What did I pay per acre for land on which I gained .2 of the cost by selling it at $96 per acre?

10. One clock gains 6.3 minutes, and another loses 4.2 minutes in three weeks. After they are both set right how much will they differ (*a*) in a week? (*b*) In a day? (*c*) How many days would it take to make the difference an hour?

Denominate Numbers

1. Change to the fraction of a day:

a. 6 hr. *b.* 4 hr. *c.* 12 hr. *d.* 16 hr. *e.* 10 hr.
f. 8 hr. *g.* 9 hr. *h.* 18 hr. *i.* 20 hr. *j.* 14 hr.

2. Change to the decimal of a pound:

a. 2 oz. *b.* 6 oz. *c.* 10 oz. *d.* 11 oz. *e.* 5 oz.
f. 4 oz. *g.* 8 oz. *h.* 12 oz. *i.* 13 oz. *j.* 7 oz.

3. Change to the per cent of a ton:

a. 500 lb. *b.* 250 lb. *c.* 1800 lb. *d.* 125 lb.
e. 600 lb. *f.* 375 lb. *g.* 1500 lb. *h.* 625 lb.

4. Change to compound denominate numbers:

a. 67 oz. *b.* 31 in. *c.* 53 mo. *d.* 77 hr.
e. 11 pk. *f.* 97 min. *g.* 10 ft. *h.* 23 da.

5. Change to the fraction of a mile:

a. 20 rd. *b.* 80 rd. *c.* 120 rd. *d.* 160 rd.
e. 40 rd. *f.* 60 rd. *g.* 240 rd. *h.* 180 rd.

6. Change to a lower denomination:

a. .125 T. *b.* $\frac{7}{8}$ da. *c.* 3 lb. 4 oz. *d.* 3 yd. 1 ft.
e. .375 pk. *f.* $\frac{2}{5}$ hr. *g.* 2 qt. 1 pt. *h.* 3 bu. 2 pk.

Compound Numbers

1. Add. Give answers in compound numbers:

a.   10 oz. *b.*   9 in. *c.* 20 hr. *d.* 11 mo.
  + 10 oz.   + 9 in.   + 10 hr.   + 11 mo.

e.   2 ft. *f.* 10 in. *g.* 7 qt. *h.* 12 oz.
  + 2 ft.   + 9 in.   + 7 qt.   + 7 oz.

2. Give sums:

a. 1 lb. 10 oz.
    + 10 oz.

b. 3 yr. 6 mo.
    + 9 mo.

c. 5 bu. 3 pk.
    + 3 pk.

d. 2 yd. 1 ft.
    + 2 ft.

e. 1 lb. 10 oz.
    + 1 lb. 6 oz.

f. 3 yr. 6 mo.
    + 1 yr. 6 mo.

g. 5 bu. 3 pk.
    + 1 bu. 1 pk.

h. 1 yd. 1 ft.
    + 1 yd. 2 ft.

i. 1 lb. 10 oz.
    + 1 lb. 10 oz.

j. 3 yr. 6 mo.
    + 1 yr. 8 mo.

k. 5 bu. 3 pk.
    + 1 bu. 3 pk.

l. 2 yd. 2 ft.
    + 1 yd. 2 ft.

3. Give remainders:

a. 1 lb.
    − 6 oz.

b. 3 yr.
    − 9 mo.

c. 5 bu.
    − 3 pk.

d. 3 yd.
    − 2 ft.

e. 2 lb. 3 oz.
    − 6 oz.

f. 3 yr. 6 mo.
    − 9 mo.

g. 5 bu. 1 pk.
    − 3 pk.

h. 3 yd. 1 ft.
    − 2 ft.

4. Give products in compound numbers:

a. 10 oz.
   × 2

b. 9 in.
   × 3

c. 20 hr.
   × 2

d. 11 mo.
   × 4

e. 2 ft.
   × 5

5. Multiply:

a. 1 lb. 10 oz.
   × 2

b. 3 yr. 6 mo.
   × 3

c. 5 bu. 1 pk.
   × 5

d. 1 ft. 9 in.
   × 2

6. Divide:

a. 6)1 ft.   b. 6)7 ft.   c. 6)6 ft. 6 in.   d. 6)7 ft. 6 in.

e. 2)3 bu.   f. 2)9 bu.   g. 2)8 bu. 2 pk.   h. 2)9 bu. 2 pk.

7. Give quotients:

a. 3 in.)1 ft.   b. 3 in.)2 ft.   c. 1 ft. 3 in.)3 ft. 9 in.

d. 2 pk.)1 bu.   e. 6 in.)5 ft.   f. 1 ft. 8 in.)4 ft. 2 in.

Sight Problems

1. (*a*) How many pounds and ounces of lean meat will supply 20 men with 5 ounces each? (*b*) How many pounds must be bought of meat that contains fat and bone to the extent of $\frac{1}{5}$ of its weight?

2. What decimal of a gallon is 2 qt. 1 pt.?

3. At the rate of 1 second per hour how many minutes and seconds would a watch lose in a week?

4. When the sun rises at 5.10 A.M. and sets at 6.40 P.M., (*a*) how long is the day? (*b*) How long is the night?

5. (*a*) How many 7-inch pieces of wire can be cut from a rod 13 ft. 5 in. long? (*b*) How long a rod is required to make 32 pieces each 5 inches in length?

6. What is the cost of 15 gal. 2 qt. 1 pt. of gasoline at 32 cents per gallon?

7. (*a*) How many furrows 8 inches wide will there be in the width of a field 660 feet wide? (*b*) What is the width of the field in rods of $16\frac{1}{2}$ feet each?

8. How many days are there from June 1 to Sept. 9?

9. (*a*) How many pints of catsup are there to a bottle when a dozen bottles contain $2\frac{1}{4}$ gallons? (*b*) What part of a quart?

10. What pay should a man receive for working 2 hr. 40 min. at the rate of $3 per day of 8 hr.?

11. July 4, 1915, falls upon Sunday. (*a*) On what day does July 4, 1916 fall (leap year)?

12. At $20 per month, what is the rent of a house for 1 yr. 5 mo. 15 da.?

Arithmetical Waste

The combinations used in the preceding drills are such as make it possible for the pupil to give oral answers to all of them, employing, however, different methods from those generally employed in his written work. The next series is composed of large numbers, the answers to which are to be obtained in the regular way, but with the use of fewer figures than the pupil may have previously considered necessary, and without permitting him to rearrange the numbers.

As a preliminary oral exercise, successive pupils may announce the different figures contained in each answer. Thus, in the reduction of $\frac{2022}{15}$ to a mixed number, a boy should say 2, 0, 1, and $\frac{7}{15}$, but without, however, being expected to recall at the end all the figures composing the result.

In changing $321\frac{7}{15}$ to an improper fraction, he thinks 15 (15×1), 22 (adding in 7), and says 2. He then thinks 30 (15×2), 32 (carrying 2), and says 2. He next thinks 45 (15×3), 48 (carrying 3), and says 48. He should not attempt to give the entire answer.

In adding mixed numbers he combines the two fractions, changes the improper fraction in the result to a mixed number, but announces merely the fractional portion, expressed in lowest terms.

Practice in omitting unnecessary figures may be obtained by writing directly from the book answers to all exercises that can be worked in this way.

The employment of this plan will make it possible to work many more examples during the arithmetic period and will be a training in business methods that may prove to be of exceptional value.

Efficiency Sight Drills

Write answers to the following directly from the book on a narrow strip. Use no other paper for side calculations.

1. In 1916 the expenditures of a family of four, living in a large city, were

Rent	$240	Doctor	$24
Food	480	Contributions	20
Clothing	250	Recreations	20
Fuel and light	45	Reading	8
Furniture	15	Repairs	19
Insurance	30	Miscellaneous	85

How much was saved out of a salary of $1500?

PROCESS

Without rewriting the numbers, add the given items and subtract from $1500, writing the balance as follows:

Beginning at the top, think 10, 14, 22, 31, 36, and 4 (writing 4) are 40.

Carrying 4, think 8, 16, 21, 25, 26, 29, 31, 33, 35, 36, 44, and 5 (writing 5) are 50.

Carrying 5, think 7, 11, 13, and 2 (writing 2) are 15.

Savings $254. *Ans.*

---

2. Write the sum required to make the given total:

a.	*b.*	*c.*	*d.*
$146.85	$245.63	$ 38.87	$365.24
23.09	123.45	213.68	9.63
7.76	18.94	5.92	543.21
26.	6.57	27.57	49.18
8.98	92.	8.86	8.57
?	?	?	?
$250.00	$561.23	$300.05	$1056.84

3. Reduce to mixed numbers :

a. $\frac{1815}{8}$ *b.* $\frac{2749}{4}$ *c.* $\frac{8760}{3}$ *d.* $\frac{8741}{12}$ *e.* $\frac{4697}{9}$

f. $\frac{4567}{16}$ *g.* $\frac{8456}{11}$ *h.* $\frac{8236}{8}$ *i.* $\frac{7881}{20}$ *j.* $\frac{6828}{5}$

4. Change to improper fractions :

a. $312\frac{5}{8}$ *b.* $116\frac{8}{9}$ *c.* $511\frac{6}{7}$ *d.* $112\frac{5}{6}$

e. $201\frac{17}{24}$ *f.* $320\frac{8}{15}$ *g.* $356\frac{5}{11}$ *h.* $256\frac{7}{12}$

5. Find sums :

a. $36\frac{1}{2}$ *b.* $39\frac{1}{3}$ *c.* $62\frac{3}{5}$ *d.* $65\frac{3}{4}$ *e.* $68\frac{1}{2}$
$+27\frac{3}{4}$ $+47\frac{5}{6}$ $+59\frac{7}{10}$ $+98\frac{5}{8}$ $+87\frac{7}{8}$

f. $36\frac{1}{4}$ *g.* $30\frac{1}{2}$ *h.* $45\frac{1}{3}$ *i.* $63\frac{1}{4}$ *j.* $50\frac{1}{8}$
$40\frac{1}{6}$ $43\frac{3}{8}$ $72\frac{5}{8}$ $30\frac{3}{8}$ $17\frac{1}{8}$
27 19 35 44 92

6. Find remainders :

a. $77\frac{1}{2}$ *b.* $83\frac{1}{4}$ *c.* $97\frac{1}{6}$ *d.* $56\frac{1}{6}$ *e.* $81\frac{3}{8}$
$-58\frac{3}{4}$ $-46\frac{1}{3}$ $-57\frac{1}{3}$ $-19\frac{7}{10}$ $-62\frac{3}{4}$

f. $90\frac{1}{8}$ *g.* $80\frac{1}{8}$ *h.* $70\frac{1}{4}$ *i.* $60\frac{2}{8}$ *j.* $70\frac{1}{2}$
$-23\frac{5}{6}$ $-34\frac{3}{4}$ $-16\frac{3}{8}$ $-41\frac{5}{6}$ $-30\frac{1}{2}$

7. Find products :

a. $126\frac{1}{2}$ *b.* $243\frac{2}{3}$ *c.* $343\frac{1}{4}$ *d.* $210\frac{3}{4}$
$\times 12$ $\times 9$ $\times 8$ $\times 16$

e. $508\frac{3}{4}$ *f.* $473\frac{2}{3}$ *g.* $622\frac{1}{8}$ *h.* $419\frac{1}{5}$
$\times 5$ $\times 4$ $\times 11$ $\times 6$

8. Divide $7456\frac{2}{3}$ (*a*) by 5.   (*b*) By 6.   (*c*) By 7.

PROCESS	
(*a*) 5)$7456\frac{2}{3}$ *Ans.* $\overline{1491\frac{1}{3}}$	The quotient is 1491, and the remainder is $1\frac{2}{3}$, or $\frac{5}{3}$. Divide $\frac{5}{3}$ by 5.
(*b*) 6)$7456\frac{2}{3}$ $\overline{1242\frac{1}{9}}$	The quotient is 1242, and the remainder is $4\frac{2}{3}$, or $\frac{14}{3}$. Divide $\frac{14}{3}$ by 6.

9. Find quotients:

a. 8)2364$\frac{1}{2}$ *b.* 7)6578$\frac{1}{4}$ *c.* 5)1876$\frac{2}{3}$

d. 9)4375$\frac{2}{3}$ *e.* 6)3857$\frac{1}{2}$ *f.* 4)5835$\frac{2}{3}$

g. 7)3760$\frac{2}{3}$ *h.* 8)7025$\frac{1}{2}$ *i.* 7)8900$\frac{2}{3}$

j. 7)5962$\frac{1}{5}$ *k.* 9)4728$\frac{2}{3}$ *l.* 6)2345$\frac{1}{4}$

10. Find answers:

a. $\frac{1}{4}$ of 764$\frac{4}{5}$ *b.* $\frac{1}{7}$ of 987$\frac{7}{8}$ *c.* $\frac{1}{6}$ of 375$\frac{5}{6}$

d. $\frac{1}{2}$ of 376$\frac{1}{2}$ *e.* $\frac{1}{3}$ of 471$\frac{1}{2}$ *f.* $\frac{1}{4}$ of 564$\frac{1}{2}$

g. $\frac{1}{6}$ of 673$\frac{1}{2}$ *h.* $\frac{1}{3}$ of 676$\frac{1}{2}$ *i.* $\frac{1}{3}$ of 680$\frac{1}{2}$

11. Multiply:

a. 397 by .25   *b.* 489 by .125   *c.* 508 × .3$\frac{1}{3}$

d. 945 by 25   *e.* 315 by 125   *f.* 596 × 16$\frac{2}{3}$

g. 675 by 33$\frac{1}{3}$ *h.* 930 by .66$\frac{2}{3}$ *i.* 832 × .12$\frac{1}{2}$

12. Find products:

a. 84.635 × 20   *b.* 1.487 × 600   *c.* .243 × 9000

d. 28.74 × 30   *e.* 24.63 × 700   *f.* 1.357 × 8000

g. 3.465 × 40   *h.* .248 × 800   *i.* 23.45 × 7000

13. Divide:

a. 84.63 ÷ 20   *b.* 148.7 ÷ 600   *c.* 243 ÷ 3000

d. 2.874 ÷ 30   *e.* 24.64 ÷ 700   *f.* 186 ÷ 2000

g. .846 ÷ 40   *h.* 248.8 ÷ 800   *i.* 952 ÷ 4000

14. Find quotients:

a. 168$\frac{1}{3}$ ÷ $\frac{1}{4}$ *b.* 137$\frac{1}{2}$ ÷ $\frac{1}{5}$ *c.* 243$\frac{1}{4}$ ÷ $\frac{1}{3}$

d. 125$\frac{1}{2}$ ÷ $\frac{1}{6}$ *e.* 315$\frac{1}{3}$ ÷ $\frac{1}{8}$ *f.* 107$\frac{2}{5}$ ÷ $\frac{1}{9}$

g. 212$\frac{1}{4}$ ÷ $\frac{1}{7}$ *h.* 196$\frac{2}{3}$ ÷ $\frac{1}{10}$ *i.* 846$\frac{1}{2}$ ÷ $\frac{1}{12}$

15. Give answers in decimals:

. 157 × .25	*b.* 235 × .125	*c.* 59.3 × .25
. 287 + 25	*e.* 433 + 125	*f.* 48.4 + 25
. 162 × .33⅓	*h.* 188 × .16⅔	*i.* 216 × 8.5
324 + 23⅓	*k.* 142 + 16⅔	. *l.* 183 + 8.5

16. Add:

a. 2 yd. 1 ft. 6 in.
       2 ft. 9 in.
  3 yd. 1 ft.
  4 yd. 2 ft. 10 in.

c. 8 bu. 3 pk. 3 qt.
       2 pk. 6 qt.
  5 bu. 3 pk.
 10 bu.   5 qt.

b. 4 da. 20 hr. 40 min.
  1 da. 14 hr.
       16 hr. 30 min.
  1 da.   40 min.

d. 10 hr. 15 min. 30 sec.
  6 hr. 40 min.
       30 min. 30 sec.
       50 min.

17. Subtract:

a. 10 yd. 1 ft. 6 in.
  2 yd. 2 ft. 9 in.

b. 4 da. 20 hr. 30 min.
  2 da. 30 hr. 40 min.

18. Multiply:

a. 3 yd. — ft. 4 in.
           × 10

c. 2 lb. 4 oz.
      × 9

b. 1 da. 20 hr. 20 min.
            × 4

d. 8 bu. 3 qt.
      × 12

19. Divide:

a. 6)10 yd. 1 ft. 6 in.

c. 7)16 gal. 2 qt. 1 pt.

b. 5)6 da. 5 hr. 10 min.

d. 4)6 bu. 3 pk. 4 qt.

20. Give answers in compound numbers:

a. 33⅓% of 28 yd.
c. 25% of 167 lb.

b. 12½% of 37 bu.
d. 16⅔% of 35 hr.

Be Sure You're Right

While 95% may be considered a high standing in school, a 95% employe is practically worthless in business if this rating means that his figures are wrong once in each twenty calculations. It is assumed that, like every other person, a clerk is liable to make mistakes; but it is expected that he himself will discover them, make the necessary changes, and submit correct results.

Checking Results

In some concerns that employ many clerks, each computation is worked independently by two persons and the figures compared, even when the calculations are made by machine. These precautions are considered necessary owing to the possibility that one person may repeat his original blunder.

When a person must be solely responsible for the correctness of a result, he must be careful to use different combinations in making the test. If the total in an addition is first obtained by adding upwards, he then adds downwards. In multiplication, he reverses the order of factors, when convenient, etc.

In making a test, the original result should always be kept out of sight.

In checking, for instance, the correctness of 246 as the quotient of 159654 ÷ 649, use the latter as the multiplier, since the partial products in the division were obtained by multiplying 649 by the digits of 246, and a mistake made in multiplying 649 by 6 in the division might be repeated in the test.

The pupil should learn by experience the checks that are real tests.

Written Review Exercises

1. Add horizontally and vertically :

a.	\$ 48.33 +	\$ 8.95 +	\$ 24.77 +	\$ 18.63 =	?
b.	165.84 +	28.87 +	184.95 +	68.86 =	?
c.	39.77 +	146.93 +	68.86 +	284.56 =	?
d.	65.80 +	88.75 +	235.79 +	68.77 =	?
e.	209.58 +	94.67 +	65.94 +	357.90 =	?

$$(f) + (g) + (h) + (i) = (j)$$

The work is presumably correct if the value of (j), obtained by adding the vertical column of totals, agrees with the sum of the horizontal row consisting of (f), (g), (h), and (i).

2. Add down. Subtract across :

a.	18.7 − 9.95 = ?	h.	\$23.75 − \$18.98 = ?
b.	103.01 − 63.4 = ?	i.	9. − 3.50 = ?
c.	29. − 8.8 = ?	j.	84.06 − 65.77 = ?
d.	245.7 − 95.47 = ?	k.	50.49 − 9.84 = ?

$$(e) − (f) = (g) \qquad (l) − (m) = (n)$$

3. If a steamer uses 45 tons of coal per hour, how many tons would it use in 1987 hours?

45 T.	PROCESS
× 1987	Use 45 as the multiplier. In checking
9935	the result, cover the last two rows of figures
7948	with a piece of paper, and write on the latter
Ans. 89415 T.	the product of 9935 by 9. Why should this give the original product?

4. Multiply. Test.

a. 2573 × 45   b. 3468 × 48   c. 4597 × 35   d. 5648 × 36

5. What is the cost of 327 acres of land (*a*) at $71 per acre?   (*b*)   At $17 per acre?

PROCESS

In (*a*) take 327 as the multiplicand and write $71 on the same horizontal line. Use 327 as the product by 1, and underneath it write the product by 7 tens, placing the right-hand figure of this product in the tens' column.

(*a*)   327 × $71
        2289
     $23217   *Ans.*

In (*b*) use 327 as the product by 1 ten. Locate properly the right-hand figure of the product by 7 ones.

(*b*)   327 × $17
       2289
    $5559 *Ans.*

Test the correctness of each by taking 327 as the multiplier.

---

6. Find products.   Test.

a. 768 × 18   *b.* 768 × 81   *c.* 634 × 16   *d.* 634 × 61

e. 456 × 71   *f.* 456 × 17   *g.* 375 × 15   *h.* 375 × 51

7. What is the cost of 487 acres of land at $99 per acre?

PROCESS

Under 487, write 100 times 487.   Subtract the former from the latter.

    487 × $99
   48700
  $48213   *Ans.*

---

8. Find products.   Test by multiplying by 99 in the ordinary way.

a. 1345 × 99   *b.* 99 × 5674   *c.* 3579 × 99   *d.* 99 × 4876

9. What is the area of a rectangular plot (*a*) 631 feet long, 378 feet wide?   (*b*) 378 feet long, 136 feet wide?

PROCESS

(*a*)   378 × 631
     1134
    2268
  238518 (sq. ft.)   *Ans.*

(*b*)   378 × 136
    1134
   2268
  51408 (sq. ft.)   *Ans.*

10. Multiply :

a. 148×345 b. 841×234 c. 621×567 d. 136×456

e. 631×345 f. 421×678 g. 189×567 h. 821×456

11. Find the cost (a) of 649 cords of wood at $2.46 per cord. (b) Of 576 barrels of flour at $6.42 per barrel.

PROCESS

(a) 649
   $2.46
   3894
  15576
$1596.54 *Ans.*

(a) To find the product of 24 (tens) multiply by 4 the product by 6 (ones) placing the right-hand figure of the result in the tens' column.

(b) First multiply by 6 (hundreds), placing the right-hand figure of the product in the hundreds' column. To find the product by 42 (ones) multiply the product by 6 (hundreds) by 7. Place the right-hand figure of this product in the ones' column.

(b) 576
   $6.42
   3456
  24192
$3697.92 *Ans.*

---

12. Multiply. Use only two partial products :

a. 357×578 b. 426×635 c. 749×247 d. 273×768

e. 637×457 f. 856×724 g. 436×457 h. 954×683

13. How many ounces are there in $121\frac{7}{8}$ pounds ?

PROCESS

Use 16 as the multiplier. Think $\frac{7}{8}$ of 16 are 14. Think 16, 30 (carrying 14) ; write 0. Think 32 (16×2), 35, (carrying 3) ; write 5. Etc.

     121^{7}
     16 oz·

Note. — Use partial products only when they are necessary.

  Ans. 1950 oz.

---

14. Find products. Write answers from book.

a. $865\frac{2}{3} \times 9$ b. $582\frac{1}{3} \times 10$ c. $245\frac{2}{3} \times 12$ d. $202\frac{1}{3} \times 24$

e. $758\frac{3}{4} \times 8$ f. $473\frac{1}{2} \times 11$ g. $121\frac{1}{4} \times 13$ h. $102\frac{2}{5} \times 25$

15. Multiply (*a*) 876 by $43\frac{2}{5}$. (*b*) $876\frac{2}{5}$ by 43.

PROCESS

(*a*) 876		(*b*) $876\frac{2}{5}$	
$\times\ 43\frac{2}{5}$		43	
5)1752	876×2	5)86	43×2
$350\frac{2}{5}$	$876 \times \frac{2}{5}$	$17\frac{1}{5}$	$43 \times \frac{2}{5}$
2628	876×3	2628	3×876
3504	876×4 tens	3504	40×876
$38018\frac{2}{5}$ *Ans.*	$876 \times 43\frac{2}{5}$	$37685\frac{1}{5}$ *Ans.*	$43 \times 876\frac{2}{5}$

In (*a*) find the product of 876 by $\frac{2}{5}$ by multiplying 876 by 2 and dividing the result by 5; etc.

In (*b*) find the product of $\frac{2}{5}$ of 43; etc.

Test (*a*) by multiplying 43.4 by 876.

Test (*b*) by multiplying 43 by 876.4.

16. Find products:

a. $768 \times 43\frac{4}{5}$ *b.* $768\frac{3}{5} \times 43$ *c.* $168 \times 23\frac{2}{9}$

d. $964 \times 76\frac{2}{3}$ *e.* $964\frac{2}{3} \times 76$ *f.* $246 \times 34\frac{6}{7}$

g. $859 \times 57\frac{3}{4}$ *h.* $859\frac{3}{4} \times 57$ *i.* $359 \times 43\frac{5}{6}$

17. Find the product of $18\frac{3}{4} \times 27\frac{1}{3} \times 8$.

PROCESS

$18\frac{3}{4}$	
$\times\ 8$	Since the product of 8 times $18\frac{3}{4}$ is a whole number,
150	begin with these, and multiply the result by $27\frac{1}{3}$.
$\times\ 27\frac{1}{3}$	

18. Multiply:

a. $27\frac{4}{5} \times 16 \times 31\frac{1}{4}$ *b.* $34\frac{2}{3} \times 2\frac{3}{4} \times 15$

c. $13\frac{2}{7} \times 12 \times 12\frac{5}{6}$ *d.* $43\frac{3}{4} \times 6\frac{2}{7} \times 16$

e. $16\frac{2}{9} \times 24 \times 33\frac{5}{8}$ *f.* $37\frac{1}{2} \times 5\frac{3}{4} \times 12$

g. $14\frac{3}{4} \times 18 \times 16\frac{2}{9}$ *h.* $16\frac{2}{3} \times 4\frac{3}{5} \times 24$

19. Divide (*a*) $23\frac{3}{4}$ by $2\frac{3}{8}$.   (*b*) $86\frac{2}{3}$ by $4\frac{4}{9}$.

PROCESS

(*a*) $23\frac{3}{4} \div 2\frac{3}{8} = \frac{95}{4} + \frac{19}{8} = \frac{\overset{5}{\cancel{95}}}{\cancel{4}} \times \frac{\overset{2}{\cancel{8}}}{\cancel{19}} = 10.$ *Ans.*

(*b*) $86\frac{2}{3} \div 4\frac{4}{9} = \frac{260}{3} + \frac{40}{9} = \frac{\overset{13}{\cancel{260}}}{\cancel{3}} \times \frac{\overset{3}{\cancel{9}}}{\underset{2}{\cancel{40}}} = \frac{39}{2} = 19\frac{1}{2}.$ *Ans.*

---

20. Divide :

a. $\frac{5}{8} + 2\frac{1}{2}$	*b.* $17\frac{7}{9} + 1\frac{2}{3}$	*c.* $24\frac{3}{4} + 2\frac{2}{3}$
d. $1\frac{5}{7} + 3\frac{7}{8}$	*e.* $18\frac{3}{4} + 1\frac{7}{8}$	*f.* $47\frac{1}{2} + 3\frac{3}{4}$
g. $6\frac{1}{4} + 4\frac{2}{3}$	*h.* $25\frac{5}{16} + 2\frac{1}{4}$	*i.* $63\frac{2}{3} + 4\frac{3}{7}$
j. $16\frac{1}{2} + \frac{4}{5}$	*k.* $42\frac{2}{3} + 9\frac{1}{7}$	*l.* $33\frac{2}{5} + 3\frac{1}{8}$
m. $12\frac{5}{7} + \frac{3}{8}$	*n.* $37\frac{1}{2} + 3\frac{1}{3}$	*o.* $40\frac{5}{6} + 5\frac{2}{9}$

21. Simplify the following complex fractions by dividing the numerator by the denominator :

a. $\dfrac{3\frac{1}{2}}{2\frac{2}{3}}$	*b.* $\dfrac{14\frac{1}{4}}{2\frac{2}{5}}$	*c.* $\dfrac{4\frac{7}{8}}{5\frac{2}{5}}$	*d.* $\dfrac{15\frac{2}{5}}{12\frac{1}{4}}$	*e.* $\dfrac{16\frac{1}{3}}{25\frac{1}{6}}$
f. $\dfrac{4\frac{7}{8}}{3\frac{2}{9}}$	*g.* $\dfrac{13\frac{2}{5}}{8\frac{1}{3}}$	*h.* $\dfrac{16\frac{1}{2}}{24\frac{3}{4}}$	*i.* $\dfrac{13\frac{1}{4}}{5\frac{1}{2}}$	*j.* $\dfrac{11\frac{1}{4}}{18\frac{2}{3}}$

22. Divide 1.86 (*a*) by .64.   (*b*) By 6.4.   (*c*) By .064.

PROCESS

(*a*) 2.9 etc. *Ans.*   (*b*) .29 etc. *Ans.*   (*c*) 29.0 etc. *Ans.*

.64)1.86   6.4)1.8.6   .064)1.860.

In (*a*) make the divisor a whole number by moving the decimal point two places to the right and make a corresponding change in the dividend. In (*b*) move the decimal point in the divisor and in the dividend one place to the right. In (*c*) move the decimal point in each three places to the right, annexing the requisite cipher to the dividend.

---

23. Divide:

a. 492.1 ÷ 8.75   *c.* 59.6265 ÷ 22.5

b. 8.512 ÷ 12.8   *d.* 628.224 ÷ .512

24. Find the quotient of 1.96 by 3.7 correct (*a*) to four decimal places. (*b*) To three. (*c*) To two.

```
        .5297
3.7)1,9.6
     1 85
     1 10
       74
      360
      etc.
```

PROCESS

Since the fifth quotient figure is less than 5, the quotient, .5297, is correct to four decimal places. The answer correct to three decimal places is .530, to two decimal places it is .53.

25. Find quotients correct to three decimal places:

a. 101.678 ÷ 2.37   *b.* 187.13 ÷ 123.107   *c.* 199 ÷ 15

26. Divide .87 × 3.4 × 1.2 by .06 × 2.9 × .17.

PROCESS

$$\frac{.87 \times 3.4 \times 1.2}{.06 \times 2.9 \times .17} = \frac{87 \times 34 \times 12 \times 10}{6 \times 29 \times 17}.$$

Change the divisor to whole numbers by canceling its five decimal places. Make a corresponding change in the dividend by canceling four places and inserting 10 as another factor. Why?

27. Divide .87 × 3.4 × 1.2 by 6 × 2.9 × 1.7.

Make the divisor a whole number by canceling its two decimal places. Cancel two in the dividend.

28. Find answers:

a. $\dfrac{.48 \times 2.7 \times 1.6}{.81 \times 3.2 \times .04}$ *b.* $\dfrac{33 \times 6.8 \times .14 \times .5}{9 \times .08 \times 2.2 \times .17}$

c. $\dfrac{1.75 \times 6.4 \times .008}{16 \times 2.6 \times .56}$ *d.* $\dfrac{11.7 \times 2.31 \times .04 \times 75}{4.4 \times .81 \times 1.3 \times .7}$.

Indicating Operations

In the "analysis" of a problem, use the numbers that are given in the problem, in order to show the operation required for its solution.

Thus, in an example asking the price per pound, when 4 pounds of sugar cost 24 ¢, the operation is division, 24 ¢ being divided by 4. When a pupil says the cost per pound is $\frac{1}{4}$ of 24 ¢, he changes 4 to $\frac{1}{4}$ and makes the operation one in multiplication. Although the result is the same, the analysis should contain the given numbers and the sign of division, 24 ¢ ÷ 4.

The "analysis" of an example asking the cost of coffee per pound when $\frac{1}{4}$ costs 8 ¢, frequently states that the result is 4 times 8 ¢, when the numbers given, $\frac{1}{4}$ and 8, require the division of the latter by the former, 8 ¢ ÷ $\frac{1}{4}$.

Sight Exercises

In each of the following examples give the answer, then repeat the numbers and give the sign of operation.

1. At $2 per yard, how much cloth can be bought for $1.75?

2. When $\frac{3}{4}$ yd. cloth costs $1.50, what is the price per yard?

3. Find the cost of $\frac{7}{8}$ yd. silk at 96 ¢ per yard.

4. What is .75 of 84?

5. If 84 is $\frac{3}{4}$ of a number, what is the number?

6. What fraction of 84 is (*a*) 21? (*b*) 42? (*c*) 63?

7. If a man can do $\frac{3}{8}$ of a piece of work in a day, how long will it take him to do the whole work?

8. When silk is 75 ¢ per yard, how much silk can be bought for $1?

Written Exercises

· Before working the first eight examples, indicate the operation required to solve each :

1. At $60 per acre, how much land can be bought for $43.75?

2. When $\frac{2}{3}$ of a man's farm contains 48.74 acres, how many acres are there in the farm?

3. What is the value of $\frac{7}{8}$ of a vessel if the whole vessel is worth $21,000?

4. Find .75 of 3960 yards.

5. If $\frac{3}{4}$ of the length of a road is 3960 rods, how long is the road?

6. What fraction of 50 is (*a*) $43\frac{3}{4}$? (*b*) $56\frac{1}{4}$? (*c*) $33\frac{1}{3}$?

7. If a man can do $\frac{2}{3}$ of a piece of work in $7\frac{1}{2}$ days, how long would it take him to do the whole work?

8. When silk is $56\frac{1}{4}$ cents per yard, how much can be bought for $1?

9. A man working on an average 24 days to the month receives $3.75 per day. What should be his average daily expenses to enable him to save $300 in a year?

$$(\$3.75 \times 24) - (\$300 \div 12).$$

10. If a man loses $\frac{3}{16}$ of the cost of a house when he sells it for $1365, what did the house cost?

$$\$1365 \div (1 - \tfrac{3}{16}).$$

11. A man sold 12 books at $1.50 each, on which his profit was $\frac{1}{4}$ of the cost. What was his profit?

12. A book that is sold at $1.50 has been bought at $\frac{1}{5}$ less than this price. How much does a dealer make on 6 doz. books?

13. After selling $\frac{1}{8}$ of his land a farmer has 286 acres remaining. How many acres did he have at first?

Relation of Numbers

In a question as to the relation of two numbers, either number may precede the other. The same example may be presented in the following form :

32 is what fraction of 24 ?

What fraction of 24 is 32 ?

Some pupils, assuming that only a proper fraction is meant, will make the smaller number the numerator, thus obtaining $\frac{3}{4}$ as the result instead of the correct answer, $\frac{4}{3}$.

This is particularly the case when the rate per cent is required, the larger number being frequently taken as the divisor by pupils that do not carefully read the example.

Sight Exercises

1. What fraction of 24 is 21 ?

2. 24 multiplied by what fraction equals 21 ?

3. 24 multiplied by what decimal equals 21 ?

4. What per cent of 24 is 21 ?

5. 21 is what decimal of 24 ?

6. 24 is how many times 21 ?

7. What fraction of $\frac{5}{8}$ is $\frac{7}{8}$?

8. What decimal of $\frac{4}{5}$ is $\frac{3}{5}$?

9. What fraction of $\frac{6}{8}$ is $\frac{5}{9}$?

10. When butter is 32 cents per pound, what fraction of a pound can be bought for 28 cents ?

11. What per cent of a pound is 14 ounces ?

12. A man buys a cow for $20 and sells it at a profit of $8. What fraction of the cost is the profit ?

13. Muslin costing $6\frac{1}{4}$ cents per yard is sold for 7 cents per yard. What per cent of the cost is the profit ?

Written Problems

When the solution of a written problem involves only multiplication and division, indicate the operations and shorten the work by cancellation.

1. If a factory working only $\frac{3}{4}$ of its capacity burns $292\frac{1}{2}$ tons of coal in a week, what should it burn when working only $\frac{7}{15}$ of its capacity?

PROCESS

At $\frac{3}{4}$ capacity it burns $292\frac{1}{2}$ T.

At 1 capacity it burns $292\frac{1}{2}$ T. $\div \frac{3}{4}$.

At $\frac{7}{15}$ capacity it burns $292\frac{1}{2}$ T. $\div \frac{3}{4} \times \frac{7}{15}$.

$$\frac{585 \times 4 \times 7}{2 \times 3 \times 15}.$$

---

2. A pipe discharges $7\frac{1}{2}$ gal. of water in $\frac{3}{4}$ min. How many gallons will it discharge in $8\frac{1}{4}$ min.?

3. A farmer divided some land among his three sons. To the first he gave $\frac{3}{4}$ of a 600-acre farm. The second received $\frac{7}{8}$ as much land as the first, and the third received $\frac{7}{8}$ as much as the third. (*a*) How many acres did the farmer distribute? (*b*) What fraction of the whole quantity did each receive?

4. If a bicyclist travels 42 miles in 3 hr. 40 min., how long would he require, at the same rate, to travel 60 miles?

5. A girl had 80 hens that laid an average of 120 eggs each. For one half of the eggs she received 15 cents per dozen, for one third of them she received 20 cents per dozen, and 30 cents per dozen for the remainder. (*a*) How much did she receive for all the eggs? (*b*) What was the average price received per dozen?

6. If a 24-acre field yields 452 bushels of grain, how many bushels should an 80-acre field produce, at the same rate?

SECTION III

BUSINESS ACCOUNTS

The Inventory

The first thing to be ascertained upon going into business is the value of one's possessions at that time. This is called making an "inventory," or "taking stock," and is repeated at least once a year.

Every householder should also make an inventory of all of the articles he owns, specifying the quantities, date of purchase, and cost. Such a list is very useful in case of fire, as the owner is otherwise apt to overlook many items in presenting his claim to the insurance company.

The housekeeper's inventory shows the value of the items in each room, with a recapitulation as follows:

INVENTORY OF PERSONAL PROPERTY
Contained in
384 Forest Av., DECATUR, ILL.
Dec. 31, 1914

Halls	$ 80.75
Parlor	875.20
Sitting Room	259.30
Kitchen and Pantry	94.63
Dining Room	225.27
Bedroom 1	84.40
" 2	96.50
" 3	73.00
" 4	37.25
Attic	125.30
Cellar	48.40
Total $	

1. Find the total value of the personal property.

2. Make out an inventory showing the cost of the articles in a sitting room. Insert date of purchase and cost, and add other items.

SITTING ROOM

NUMBER	ARTICLE	DATE OF PURCHASE	COST
1	Table		
6	Books		
1	Carpet		
6	Chairs		
1	Clock		
4	Curtains		
2	Lamps		
1	Mirror		
1	Phonograph		
7	Pictures		

INVENTORY OF FASSIFERN FARM

Dec. 31, 1914

160 acres of Land	$ 150.—		
8 Horses	225.—		
16 Cows	50.—		
28 Sheep	8.—		
40 Hogs	6.50		
Poultry		200	—
Harness		96	—
Vehicles		475	—
Machinery		1500	—
10 T. Hay	9.—		
350 bu. Corn	.75		
125 " Wheat	.96		
75 " Oats	.42		
Other Products		175	—
Household Furniture		987	50
Total		$	

3. Discuss the details of the foregoing inventory. Make one out to suit the values and conditions of your section.

When the individual horses, cows, etc., differ greatly in value, a list is kept stating the value of each. Similar lists are kept of the vehicles, machinery, etc., specifying cost, date of purchase, etc.

The value given in this inventory should be the value of the several items at the time of making the inventory.

Gains and Losses

One's gains or losses during a given period are shown by the difference between the inventory taken at the beginning of the period and the one taken at the close.

Written Problems

1. John Greene's inventory on Dec. 31, 1914, showed the value of his property to be $12,314.75. He had cash on hand and in bank $387.50. He owed $513.25. What was he worth Dec. 31, 1914?

2. On Dec. 31, 1915, his property inventory was $13,986.50. He had cash on hand and in bank $1249.30. He had outstanding debts of $387.50 and there was due him $693.40. (*a*) How much was he worth Dec. 31, 1915? (*b*) How much more was he worth on Dec. 31, 1915, than on Dec. 31, 1914?

3. If farm machinery costing $2000 decreases 12 % in value in a year, (*a*) how much is it worth when it is a year old? (*b*) If it decreases 15 % in value the next year, what is it worth at the end of the second year?

4. If machinery worth $3600 loses 20 % of its value per year when it is not properly painted, oiled, sheltered, etc., how much is saved in a year by care that reduces the depreciation to $12\frac{1}{2}$ % ?

The Day Book

Besides enabling a person to ascertain his resources and his liabilities at a given time, his accounts must show him to whom he owes money and from whom money is due him.   These accounts are kept in a book called the *ledger*.   To keep a list of transactions in the order in which they occur, they may be first entered in a *day book*.

PAGE OF DAY BOOK

AURORA, ILL., Aug. 15, 1915

	23	*M. T. Kennedy*	Cr.			950	00
		By 200 bbl. Flour	$ 4.75				
		"					
	√	*Cash*	Dr.				
		To 25 lb. Sugar	@ .05 1/2	1	38		
		" 6 " Butter	@ .38	2	28	3	66
		"					
	√	*Cash*	Cr.			37,	50
		By 50 bu. Potatoes	.75				
		16					
		Hired J. L. Adams					
		Salary $ 12 per week					
		"					
	47	*William Ziegler*	Dr.				
		To 20 lb. Coffee	.23 1/2	4	70		
		4 " Tea	.44	1	76	6	46
			Cr.				
		By Cash on %				5	00

When a transaction is transferred to the ledger, it is said to be "posted."   The page on which the account appears in the ledger is written in the first column of the day book at the time the transaction is posted.   Thus Mr. Kennedy's account is found on p. 23 of the ledger, and Mr. Ziegler's at p. 47.   As the cash account is generally kept in a separate book, a check mark (√) is sufficient to indicate that a cash item has been posted.

The Cash Account

Accounts are of two general kinds, *cash* accounts and *personal* accounts.

The cash account is frequently kept in a separate book. It is arranged on two pages, or on two halves of the same page, one showing the various sums received and the other giving the sums expended.

The following is a portion of the cash account kept by Mr. Agar, of his personal receipts and expenditures:

Dr							Cash				Cr.	
	1915						1915					
Jan.	1	On hand	46	84	Jan.	6	By Shoes		4	—		
	7	To Salary	15	—		7	" Board		6	—		
	9	To J. F. Tracy	10	—			" Laundry			87		
						8	" Church Dues		1	—		
						9	" Deposit		50	—		
							" Car Tickets		1	—		
						14	" Board		6	—		
							" Laundry			74		
							" Balance		2	23		
			71	84					71	84		
	14	To Balance	2	23								

Two lines are drawn under each total to indicate that the account is closed at that point. It is reopened by writing on the debit side the date, the words "To Balance," and the amount. As this represents the cash on hand, the latter is counted. If it amounts to $2.23, the account is correct.

In a business house the cash book is balanced daily.

Written Exercise

Copy the foregoing account, either in the form given above, or in the form given on page 227.

Personal Accounts

A storekeeper, selling goods for which he is not paid at the time, "charges" them in the *ledger*.

One page of the ledger is given below. The debit side shows items for which Mr. Ferguson is indebted to the proprietors; the credit side shows payments made or goods furnished by Mr. Ferguson, and for which he is credited.

Dr.   *Wm. T. Ferguson*   *Cr.*

	1915						1915			
Feb.	6	To 3 lb. Tea .60		1	80	Feb.	3	By 10 bu. Potatoes .75	7	50
	7	" 1 bbl. Flour		5	75		14	" Cash	5	—
	"	" 2 lb. Butter .35			70					
	8	" 10 " Coffee .25		2	50					
	"	" 20 " Sugar .06		1	20					
	"	" 1 sack Salt		2	35					
	15	" 1 box Soap		4	80		28	By Balance	6	60
				19	10				19	10
Mar.	1	To Balance		6	60					

This account is balanced in the same way as the cash account.

Written Exercises

1. Write out the foregoing account as it would appear on the books of Mr. Ferguson.

Place at the top "Ross & Snyder," the grocers. The debits in the first account will appear as credits in the second, and *vice versa*.

2. Make out a similar account, giving several items of dry goods sold to a farmer, with credits in the form of farm produce, and also a cash credit.

3. Write a letter from the farmer, stating that he encloses a check in part payment of his account.

4. Make out the check.

5. Address the envelope.

Cost of Production

The producer is no longer satisfied with accounts that merely show him that he has made a profit. He knows that continued success depends upon a knowledge of what articles have contributed to make the profit and what ones have been sold at a loss. He keeps an itemized account of the cost of everything that enters into the completion of each article, including material, labor, marketing, and the like, together with its proportionate share of the

"Overhead Charges"

In determining the cost of producing a crop of wheat, for instance, a farmer who charges only for the number of days his horses are actually at work, without taking into consideration the number of days they are idle, overlooks one item. On the other hand, he frequently charges the crop with the entire cost of fertilizer, which may yield some advantage to succeeding crops. He generally omits from consideration the expense connected with the machinery used in making the crop, owing to its deterioration, etc. Such charges as these cannot be overlooked by the producer, whether farmer or manufacturer. Both should take into consideration the interest on the capital invested. A business cannot be considered profitable unless the profits pay its owner a reasonable salary together with a greater rate of interest than his capital would yield if safely invested.

Balance Sheet

The farmer that desires to employ the simplest method of getting at the year's profits or losses is content with the results shown by comparing two inventories. When he desires more detailed information, he keeps an account headed, possibly, "Farm Products." In this he charges for all labor, seeds, fertilizers, etc., and enters as credits the cash received from all sales of grain, milk, vegetables, eggs, etc., together with the value of all articles consumed by his household.

Unit Costs

The one that desires to make real progress must know what it costs to produce each unit of grain, milk, eggs, hay, and the like. When this is ascertained, his efforts are next directed toward a lessening of the unit cost by increasing the yield without a corresponding increase of the expense.

His dairy account, for instance, will be supplemented by one that shows the value of the milk produced by each cow, and its cost. This information will indicate the animals that do not show a profit or one that is insignificant.

Farm Accounts

A farmer with any extended system of accounts keeps one with each field. In the following is included the value of the labor done by the owner, together with one year's interest on the value of the field.

Dr.			Field No. 1 — 40 Acres						Cr.	
	1915						1915			
Mar.	31	Spreading Fertilizer		20	—	Sept.		1020 bu. .96	979	20
Apr.	30	50 bu. Seed	$ 2.50	125	—			Used 30 bu. .95	28	50
May	30	20 da. Plowing	2.00	40	—					
		5 " Harrowing	2.00	10	—					
		5 " Seeding	2.00	10	—					
Aug.	31	40 A. Reaping	.50	20	—					
		40 A. Stacking	.25	10	—					
		Threshing 1050 bu.	.05	52	50					
Sept.	30	Interest on Land		320	—					
		Hauling to R. R.		15	—					
		Net Profit		385	20					
				1007	70				1007	70

Written Problems

1. (*a*) How many bushels of wheat were raised to the acre? (*b*) How much greater is this yield than the average yield of the state, when the latter is 16.7 bushels to the acre? (*c*) How much less is this yield than the average yield to the acre in England when the latter is 31⅛ bushels to the acre?

2. (*a*) What was the total cost of the crop delivered at the railroad station, including interest on the land? (*b*) What was the cost per bushel?

3. (*a*) What would have been the cost per bushel if the farmer had expended $2.50 less per acre and raised seven bushels to the acre less? (*b*) What would have been his profit if the wheat had also brought 1¢ per bushel less because of inferior quality?

4. Find the profit of the foregoing field when the value of the straw is estimated to be $1.93¾ per acre.

5. A cow gives 750 pounds of milk in May. (*a*) How much butter fat does the milk contain when 4½% of its weight is butter fat? (*b*) What is the value of the butter fat at 24 cents per pound?

6. Herd A, 20 cows, averages 20 pounds of milk per cow daily, of which 5¼% is butter fat. Herd B, 20 cows, averages 30 pounds of milk daily, of which 3⅕% is butter fat. Which herd produces the greater amount, (*a*) of milk, (*b*) of butter fat, and how much more than the other?

7. If a pound of porterhouse steak costing 24 cents contains only 10 ounces of lean meat, what is the cost per pound of the latter?

8. When the waste is 11 ounces on a pound of chicken costing 25 cents, what is paid per pound for the meat?

Careful Spending

It has been said that while almost anybody can make money, it takes a wise man to keep it. This does not mean that a man is considered wise because he accumulates money at the expense of proper living; it means that more judgment is required to manage what is earned than it is to earn it.

Household Accounts

A man's earnings do not always grow with his necessities or with the increasing price of articles required in his household. It is then that the intelligent housekeeper puts forth additional efforts to make ends meet and perhaps to overlap a little. She is aided in this work by the keeping of accounts which show the character of her expenditures.

Apportioning One's Income

The accompanying table gives the average per cents spent for rent, for food, and for clothing by certain city families consisting of two adults and two children, and having yearly incomes as specified :

YEARLY INCOME	EXPENDITURES FOR			
	Rent	Food	Clothing	Total
$600	19 %	43 %	13 %	
$800	18 %	42 %	14 %	
$1000	17 %	40 %	15 %	
$1200	17 %	37 %	16 %	

Written Problems

1. Copy the foregoing table, replacing the per cent of expenditure in each case by the amount in dollars. In the total column insert the sum of the three items.

2. Assuming that two children represent one adult, how many meals does a family of 2 adults and 2 children require in a year when three meals are eaten per day and fifteen meals are supplied to visitors during the year?

3. Find the average cost of food used at a meal by an adult, taking 3300 as the number of meals, when the income is (*a*) $600, (*b*) $800, (*c*) $1000, (*d*) $1200, and the sum expended is the per cent given in the preceding table. Give answers in cents and fractions of a cent.

Sight Problems

1. What is the price per pound of the lean meat in a rib roast costing 20 cents per pound, when 50 % of it is waste?

2. What is Mr. A's rent when he spends therefor 15 % of his annual income of $1600?

3. What is the amount spent for clothing during the year by the family spending 16 % of an annual income of $1400?

4. Find the yearly cost of the food for a family spending therefor 40 % of an annual income of $900.

5. What is the cost of a quart of milk at the rate of $\frac{5}{8}$ ¢ per $\frac{1}{8}$ pt.?

6. At 3 ounces for a cent, what is the cost of a 1-pound loaf of bread?

7. When a medium-sized potato weighs 4 ounces, how many will there be in a bushel of 60 pounds?

8. Give the price per pound of each of the following at the given rates. Compare the result with the prices prevailing in the vicinity of the school.

    a. $\frac{1}{2}$ ounce of coffee costs $1\frac{1}{8}$ ¢.

    b. $\frac{1}{2}$ ounce of sugar costs $\frac{3}{16}$ ¢.

    c. $\frac{1}{2}$ ounce of butter costs $1\frac{1}{8}$ ¢.

    d. $\frac{1}{2}$ ounce of flour costs $\frac{1}{8}$ ¢.

    e. $\frac{1}{4}$ ounce of cocoa costs 1 ¢.

    f. $\frac{1}{2}$ ounce of tapioca costs 1 ¢.

    g. 2 ounces of corn meal cost $\frac{3}{8}$ ¢.

    h. 2 ounces of rice cost $1\frac{1}{4}$ ¢.

    i. 2 ounces of canned beans cost 2 ¢.

    j. 2 ounces of canned peas cost $2\frac{1}{4}$ ¢.

    k. 2 ounces of hominy cost $\frac{3}{4}$ ¢.

    l. 2 ounces of prunes cost 1 ¢.

    m. 4 ounces of potatoes cost $\frac{1}{2}$ ¢.

    n. 2 ounces of ham cost $3\frac{1}{2}$ ¢.

    o. 4 ounces of roast beef cost $4\frac{1}{2}$ ¢.

9. When 6 prunes weigh 2 ounces, how many are there to the pound?

10. How many dates to the pound when each weighs $\frac{1}{4}$ oz.?

11. How many pounds do a dozen eggs weigh at 2 ounces each?

12. How many cups of coffee are made from a pound at the rate of $\frac{1}{2}$ oz. to the cup?

13. At the rate of $\frac{1}{8}$ oz. each, how many tablespoons of olive oil are there to the pound?

14. Give the cost of the berries in a dozen quart cans when $1\frac{1}{2}$ quarts of fresh berries at 10¢ per quart are required for one quart of canned berries.

Written Problems

1. Find the cost of a dozen codfish cakes containing 12 ounces of fish at 18 cents per pound, 3 eggs at 24 cents per dozen, and 12 potatoes weighing $\frac{1}{4}$ lb. each at 2 cents per pound.

2. At the rate of $1\frac{1}{2}$ ounces to 6 lettuce leaves, how many are there in a pound?

3. Find the cost of each of the following items in a quart jar of canned peaches, using:

    a. A 16-qt. basket costing $1.50 to make 13 jars.

    b. $\frac{1}{8}$ lb. sugar to the jar @ 6¢ per pound.

    c. A jar costing $7 per gross of 144 jars.

    d. 10 minutes of labor @ 12¢ per hour.

Give the results in cents correct to two decimal places.

4. How many hours are spent in a year in washing dishes (*a*) when 30 minutes are spent 3 times a day? (*b*) 40 minutes? (*c*) How many hours could be saved in a year by the use of conveniences that could save 15 minutes each time the dishes are washed?

5. (*a*) How many hours are spent in washing and ironing for 52 weeks at 12 hours per week? (*b*) What is the cost of the labor at the rate of $7 for 60 hours? (*c*) Of the fuel and soap at 25 cents per week?

6. One hundred farmers contribute $10 each to operate a laundry in connection with their creamery, using heat and power not required by the latter. A room is built at a cost of $325 and machinery is installed at a cost of $575. (*a*) How much is left for the purchase of soap and other supplies? (*b*) What is the cost of the labor for 52 weeks, an engineer being paid $15 per week and two operators at $7 each per week?

Checking Quantities and Extensions

Many persons who are careful in their selection of articles that they purchase, do not always get what they pay for. The seller may make a mistake in the weight, the quantity, or the cost. The careful housekeeper weighs or measures every article when it reaches her home. She verifies the correctness of each extension in a bill rendered, and also the footing. This does not necessarily imply doubt of the honesty of the seller; it means that she wishes a proper return of her money. She is just as prompt to call attention to an undercharge as to an overcharge.

High Cost of Living

When food prices are ascending, incomes increase at a smaller rate, and frequent adjustments between the various items of expenditure become necessary. By careful selection of food and skillful cooking, the good manager can continue to supply palatable and nutritious meals with the decreased amount she is able to allot to this item. She prolongs the life of the clothing without permitting it to become shabby. She sees that recreation is provided to the necessary extent, by directing it into less expensive channels, but without decreasing its amount or its benefit.

The School Kitchen

Following are typical meals cooked in a school kitchen, each containing the proper quantities and the right kinds of food for a man weighing 154 pounds, doing ordinary work.

The weight is that of the raw food ready for cooking. The cost of some materials will be less to the farmer's wife.

MONDAY'S BREAKFAST			TUESDAY'S BREAKFAST		
Kind of Food	Weight	Cost	Kind of Food	Weight	Cost
Stewed Fruit	2 oz.	2.25 ¢	8 Steamed Dates	2 oz.	1.50 ¢
Shredded Wheat	2	1.00	Cornmeal Mush	2	0.40
⅛ pt. Milk	2¼	0.62	⅛ pt. Milk	2¼	0.62
Omelet, 1 egg	2	3.00	2 slices Bacon	1	1.12
2 Rolls	2	2.00	Creamed Potatoes	4⅞	1.52
1 cu. in. Butter	1	2.25	3 slices Bread	3	1.00
2 tb. sp. Coffee	½	1.12	1 cu. in. Butter	1	2.25
1 tb. sp. Sugar	½	0.18	Coffee (2 tb. sp.)	½	1.12
Totals			Sugar (1 tb. sp.)	½	0.18
			Totals		

MONDAY'S DINNER			TUESDAY'S DINNER		
Roast Lamb	4 oz.	4.75 ¢	Cream Soup (spinach)	5½ oz.	1.89 ¢
⅛ pt. Rice	2	1.25	Macaroni and Cheese	5¾	4.39
⅛ pt. Canned Peas	2	2.25	Stewed Corn	2	2.00
4 leaves Lettuce	1¼	2.50	Stewed Tomatoes	2	2.00
1 tb. sp. Oil	¼	0.33	Apple and Celery Salad	2¼	3.00
Tapioca and Apple Pudding	3	2.68	Fruit Gelatine	1⅜	4.62
2 tb. sp. Coffee	½	1.12	3 slices Bread	3	1.00
1 tb. sp. Sugar	½	0.18	½ cu. in. Butter	½	1.12
3 slices Bread	3	1.00	Coffee (2 tb. sp.)	½	1.12
1 cu. in. Butter	1	2.25	Sugar (1 tb. sp.)	½	0.18
Totals			Totals		

MONDAY'S SUPPER			TUESDAY'S SUPPER		
Meat Roll	2 oz.	3.00 ¢	3 Codfish Cakes	5½ oz.	2.12 ¢
Potato Salad	4	0.50	3 slices Bread	3	1.00
Salad Dressing	1	0.75	1 cu. in. Butter	1	2.25
3 slices Bread	3	1.00	Stewed Prunes	2	1.00
1 cu. in. Butter	1	2.25	3 Cookies	1	1.00
3 Canned Peaches	8	3.00	Totals		
2 Sponge Cakes	2	2.00			
Totals					

Written Problems

1. What is (*a*) the daily average weight of the food consumed? (*b*) The daily average cost? (*c*) Find the cost at this rate for the food of a family of 4 adults for a month of 30 days.

2. The following shows the items of one type of a soldier's daily ration, with the cost of each to the government delivered at one of its posts.

(*a–q*) Find the cost of each item, giving the results in cents to four decimal places. (*r*) Find the cost of the entire ration. (*s*) Its total weight, taking the weight of a pint of vinegar as 1 lb., and that of a pint of sirup as 2 lb.

a. 16 oz. bacon at 24 ¢ per pound.

b. 18 oz. flour at $2\frac{3}{4}$ ¢ per pound.

c. .08 oz. baking powder at 9.7 ¢ per ½-lb. can.

d. 2.4 oz. beans at 3.88 ¢ per pound.

e. 20 oz. potatoes at 1.47 ¢ per pound.

f. 1.28 oz. prunes at 5.94 ¢ per pound.

g. 1.12 oz. coffee at 14.75 ¢ per pound.

h. 3.2 oz. sugar at 4.165 ¢ per pound.

i. .5 oz. evaporated milk at 6.67 ¢ per 8-oz. can.

j. .02 pt. vinegar at 14.9 ¢ per gallon.

k. .64 oz. salt at .65 ¢ per pound.

l. .04 oz. pepper at 4.42 ¢ per ¼-lb. tin.

m. .014 oz. cinnamon at 15 ¢ per ¼-lb. tin.

n. .64 oz. lard at 12.98 ¢ per pound.

o. .5 oz. butter at 31.8 ¢ per pound.

p. .04 pt. sirup at 25 ¢ per gallon.

q. .014 oz. lemon extract at 30 ¢ per 8-oz. bottle.

3. Find the cost of rations for 1000 soldiers for 30 days.

4. Find in cents and a fraction the cost of each of the following types of dresses made in the sewing classes of a public school.

(a) Gingham Dress

4 yd. Gingham	@	$\$.11\frac{1}{4}$
$\frac{1}{2}$ yd. Trimming	@	.12
$\frac{1}{2}$ doz. Buttons	@	.10
$\frac{1}{2}$ sp. Cotton	@	.05

(b) Princess Slip

$2\frac{3}{4}$ yd. Cambric	@	$\$.12\frac{1}{2}$
4 yd. Trimming	@	.06
$1\frac{1}{4}$ yd. Ribbon	@	$.02\frac{1}{2}$
$\frac{1}{2}$ doz. Buttons	@	.10
$\frac{1}{2}$ sp. Cotton	@	.05

(c) Dimity Dress

5 yd. Dimity	@	$\$.12\frac{1}{2}$
$2\frac{1}{4}$ yd. Beading	@	.12
$\frac{1}{2}$ doz. Buttons	@	.10
$\frac{3}{4}$ sp. Cotton	@	.05

(d) Graduation Dress

5 yd. Batiste	@	\$.15
4 yd. Lace	@	.12
$\frac{1}{2}$ doz. Buttons	@	.10
$\frac{1}{2}$ sp. Cotton	@	.05

5. How much can be saved (*a*) on clothes that cost \$240 by making them last half again as long through care in cleaning, patching, darning, etc.? (*b*) On farm implements that cost \$720 by making them last $2\frac{1}{2}$ times as long by painting, repairing, oiling, sheltering from rain, etc.

6. Find the expenses shown by the following "Account with 14 Acres of Strawberries":

1 ton Fertilizer	\$34.00
12 M Plants @ \$2	
27 T. Manure @ \$2.20	
$2\frac{3}{5}$ T. Top Dressing @ \$50	
Carting & Spreading Fertilizer	17.82
Labor planting 216 days @ \$1.25	
Labor picking 360 days @ \$1.75	
Labor checking 30 days @ \$2	
Rent at \$10 per acre	

7. Find the returns from the foregoing field as follows:

    3000 qt. Klondikes @ 6 ¢
    6592 qt. Stevens @ 5 ¢
    278 qt. Chesapeakes @ 8 ¢
    32,528 qt. Gaudy Prize @ 7½ ¢

8. (*a*) What was the profit on the foregoing crop? (*b*) What was the average profit per acre?

9. Complete the following pay roll of a builder, in which double pay is given for work done outside of the regular hours. The check mark denotes 4 hours on Saturday and 8 hours on the other working days. The numbers above the check marks denote overtime. The wages specified are those paid for a day of 8 hours.

PAY ROLL FOR WEEK ENDING MAY 26, 1915

No.	WAGES	NAME	MON.	TUE.	WED.	THU.	FRI.	SAT.	TOT.	HRS.	RATE	AMT.
1	$5.00	W. Bauman	✓	✓	✓	✓	✓	✓	44	44	62½ ¢	
2	4.50	J. Bradley	✓	2 ✓	✓	✓	3² ✓	✓	5² 44	55	56¼	
3	4.50	J. Byrnes	6	✓	7	✓	2 ✓	4 ✓	6 41	53	56¼	
4	4.00	E. Whitlock	✓	5	6	1 ✓	1 ✓	1 ✓	3 89		50	
5	4.00	W. S. West	✓	4	4	✓	✓	3			50	
6	4.00	W. McGregor	7	6	✓	7	✓	✓			50	
		Totals	(a)	(b)	(c)	(d)	(e)	(f)	(g)	(h)	—	(i)

Observe that J. Bradley's overtime of 5¼ hours is doubled in combining it with the 44 regular hours.

10. Find the totals (*a*) to (*i*).

11. In the following page from the time book of the Tip-top Manufacturing Company a dash denotes absence, a check mark full time, 1¼ denotes ¼ day overtime.

Pay Roll for Week Ending Oct. 30, 1915

No.	Name	Mon.	Tues.	Wed.	Thur.	Fri.	Sat.	Tot.	Rate	Due
1	A. Cooper	✓	✓	✓	1½	✓	1½	6½	$28.50	$30.88
2	B. Myers	✓	1½	✓	✓	✓	1½	7	16.00	18.67
8	C. Evans	½	✓	✓	✓	✓	✓	5½	15.00	18.75
4	D. Hofman	✓	✓	1½	✓	—	✓	5½	12.50	
5	E. Shaw	½	—	✓	✓	✓	1½		10.00	
6	F. Wenterell	—	1½	✓	✓	✓	✓		10.00	
7	G. Gagnier	✓	✓	½	✓	✓	✓		8.00	
8	H. Laird	1½	—	✓	1½	✓	✓		8.00	
9	I. Seaton	1½	✓	✓	✓	✓	1½		6.00	
10	J. Bradley	✓	✓	✓	✓	✓	—		6.00	
11	K. Ward	1½	✓	1½	✓	1½	✓		5.00	

Fill out the total weekly time of each employee, and the sum due at the given rate for 6 days' work.

12. Before going to the bank for the money, the cashier makes out a memorandum as follows, to ascertain the number of bills and of coins of each denomination needed for the pay envelopes of the several employees.

Complete the memorandum for the pay of the 11 employees and check the correctness of the totals.

No.	Wages	$20	$10	$5	$2	$1	50¢	25¢	10¢	5¢	1¢
1	$30.88	1	1				1	1	1		8
2	18.67		1	1	1	1	1		1	1	2
3	18.75		1		1	1	1	1			
4											
5											
etc.											
Total											

SECTION IV

AIDING AND PROTECTING BUSINESS

Discounts

A person with a small capital would not be able to engage in mercantile business were it not for the time allowed him to pay for the goods in which he deals.

In order, however, to secure prompt payment, and to reduce the risk of carrying his account, the seller frequently deducts a certain per cent for the payment of a bill before it is due.   This is called a *cash discount.*

The bill generally states the time of the credit with the allowance for earlier payment.   In the following bill, the credit is 60 days, with a reduction of 2% if the bill is paid within 10 days.

CEDAR RAPIDS, IA., April 16, 1915

MR. J. R. PAGE
 Columbus, Nebraska

Bought of JOHN J. BARNICLE
COFFEES
485 Highland Av.

TERMS: 60 da. Cash; 10 da. less 2%

12 bags Rio Coffee 1560 lb.	.18¾	292	50		
Less 2%		5	85		
				$286	65
Received Payment					
Apr. 26, 1915					
John J. Barnicle					
per J. H. P.					

82

Written Exercises

1. Find the net amounts required to settle the following bills:

a. $583.75 less 5 %.   *b.* $234.56 less 3 %.   *c.* $635.40 less 2½ %.

PROCESS

(*a*) $583.75
less 5 %   29.19
Ans. $554.56

(*a*) Find 5% of $583.75 by dividing it by 20. Divide by 2, writing the first quotient figure one place to the right; that is, under the 8.

(*b*) $234.56
less 3 %   7.04
Ans. $227.52

(*b*) As the discount should contain only two decimal places, begin by multiplying 4 by 3, but carry 2 since the product of 5 by 3, with 1 carried, is over 5.

(*c*) $635.40
less 2½ %   15.88
Ans. $619.52

(*c*) 2½% = $\frac{1}{40}$. Divide by 4, writing the first quotient figure under 3.

NOTE. — It is important for pupils to acquire the habit of omitting unnecessary figures. In the following examples write the discounts directly under the gross amounts, and subtract.

2. Find the net amounts of the following bills:

a. $483.20 less 5 %   *b.* $298.40 less 2½ %   *c.* $516.50 less 2 %
d. $384.80 less 4 %   *e.* $193.60 less 1¼ %   *f.* $258.50 less 3 %

Sight Exercises

1. Give discounts

a. 1¼ % of $720   *b.* 5 % of $360   *c.* 3 % of $410   *d.* 4 % of $216
e. 2½ % of $840   *f.* 4 % of $250   *g.* 2 % of $320   *h.* 6 % of $621

2. Give net amounts:

a. $800 less 1 %   *b.* $320 less 5 %   *c.* $400 less 2½ %
d. $125 less 2 %   *e.* $450 less 2 %   *f.* $250 less ¼ %

Trade Discount

Catalogues issued by manufacturers frequently give so-called "list prices" of their products, which are, as a rule, much higher than the ones actually charged wholesale purchasers. The latter are informed of the real, or "net," price through a "discount sheet," which states the per cent of deduction from the list price. When a selling price is changed, a new discount sheet is sent to dealers.

Written Exercises

1. When the discount is 40 %, what is the cost of 3 pianos listed at $645 each?

	PROCESS
3 @ $645 $1935	
40 % 774	Under $1935 write at once the product
Ans. $1161	by .4 and deduct.

In the accompanying illustration the work takes the form that would be used in making out a bill.

In the "test" employ different combinations, in order to avoid the possibility of falling into any error that might have been made in the first calculation.

As a discount of 40% is equal to 60% "net," one way would be to find the net cost of a piano by taking 60% of $645, which is $387, and to multiply the latter by 3, which gives $1161, the original answer. Another method would be to divide $1161 by 3 to ascertain the net cost of a piano ($387) and to divide this by 60%.

2. Find answers:

a. List price, $450; rate of discount, 35 %. Discount?
b. List price, $375; rate of discount, 25 %. Net price?
c. List price, $715; rate of discount, 15 %. Discount?
d. List price, $530; rate of discount, 20 %. Net price?

Successive Discounts

The discount sheets of many manufacturers specify two or more successive rates of discount on an article; such as $33\frac{1}{3}$ and 10%; 25, 20, and 5%; etc., the per cent sign being written with only the last. A discount of $33\frac{1}{3}$ and 10% means a deduction of $33\frac{1}{3}\%$ of the list price and a further deduction of 10% of the remainder.

The following bill includes a cash discount of 2% inasmuch as it is settled within 10 days.

MADISON, WIS., Jan. 2, 1915

MR. WILLIAM PRIEDIGKEIT
386 Wabash Av.

Bought of BECK & GODETT

BUILDING MATERIALS

TERMS: 60 days; less 2%, 10 days.   284 Lake St.

1914								
Dec.	29	2400 ft. Pipe		.22½	540	—		
		Less 33⅓%			180	—		
					360	—		
		Less 10%			36	—	324	—
	30	150 bx. Tin		1.48	222	—		
		Less 25%			55	50		
					166	50		
		Less 20%			33	30		
					133	20		
		Less 5%			6	66	126	54
							450	54
		Less 2%					9	01
							$441	53
		Received Payment						
		Jan. 5, 1915						
		Beck & Godett						
		Per J. H. T.						

Written Exercises

1. Find the amount paid in settlement of each of the following bills after the deduction of the specified discounts:

List price $575; trade discount 40 and 10%; cash discount $2\frac{1}{2}$%.

2. Mr. Mullaly sends a check in payment of the following bill:

List prices $3750, with a discount of $33\frac{1}{3}$ and 10%, and $2400, with a discount of 25, 20, and 5%. Cash discount 5% additional.

For what amount should the check be drawn?

3. When the list price is $100, find the net price after the deduction of each of the following discounts:

a. 45%   *b.* 25 and 20%   *c.* 30, 10, and 5%
d. 40 and 5%   *e.* 35 and 10%   *f.* 25, 10, and 10%

Comparing Successive Discounts

Although the sum of the per cents constituting the successive discounts in each of the six items in the last problem is 45%, the net price of each is different.

To compare two or more sets of discounts, change each to its equivalent single discount.

Preparatory Exercise

What fraction of his money has a man spent when he has spent $\frac{8}{10}$ of his money and $\frac{3}{10}$ of the remainder?

PROCESS

Fraction spent $= \frac{8}{10} + \frac{3}{10}$ of $\frac{7}{10} = \frac{80}{100} + \frac{21}{100} = \frac{51}{100}$. *Ans.*

Written Exercises

1. Find the single discount equal to each of the following successive discounts:

a. 25 and 25 %   *b.* 35 and 15 %   *c.* 30, 10, and 10 %

PROCESS

(a)   25 %
(25 % of 75 %) $+18\frac{3}{4}$
            Ans. $\overline{43\frac{3}{4}\%}$

(a) To the first discount (25 %), add $\frac{1}{4}$ of the first net (75 %), which is $18\frac{3}{4}\%$.

(b)   35 %
(15 % of 65 %) $+9\frac{3}{4}$
            Ans. $\overline{44\frac{3}{4}\%}$

(b) The remainder after the deduction of 35 % is 65 %. To 35 % add 15 % of 65 %.

(c)   30 %
(10 % of 70 %)   7
(10 % of 63 %) $6\frac{3}{10}$
            Ans. $\overline{43\frac{3}{10}\%}$

(c) The remainder after the deduction of 30 % is 70 %, $\frac{1}{10}$ of which is 7 %. The remainder after deducting 7 % from 70 % is 63 %, $\frac{1}{10}$ of which is $6\frac{3}{10}\%$.

---

2. Find a single discount equal to each of the following:

a. 40 and 30 %   *b.* 50 and 20 %   *c.* 40, 20, and 10 %
d. 35 and 35 %   *e.* 20 and 50 %   *f.* 80, 30, and 10 %

Sight Exercises

1. What per cent of the list price is deducted when 30 % is deducted and 30 % of the remainder?

PROCESS

Per cent deducted = 30 per cent + 30 % of 70 per cent = 30 per cent + 21 per cent = 51 per cent. *Ans.*

2. What single discount is equal to a discount of 40 and 20 % ?

PROCESS

40 and 20% = 40% + 20 per cent of 60% = 40% + 12% = 52%. *Ans.*

---

3. Find the single discount equal to each of the following :

a. 50 and 50 %   *b.* 60 and 10 %   *c.* 50 and 20 %
d. 10 and 40 %   *e.* 20 and 50 %   *f.* 30 and 30 %

4. What fraction of his money has a man after spending $\frac{1}{4}$ of his money and $\frac{1}{5}$ of the remainder?

PROCESS

After spending $\frac{1}{4}$ of his money, a man still has $\frac{3}{4}$ of it. When he spends $\frac{1}{5}$ of the remainder, he still has $\frac{4}{5}$ of the remainder. The final remainder is $\frac{4}{5}$ of $\frac{3}{4}$, which is $\frac{3}{5}$. *Ans.*

---

5. What fraction of a pound of meat remains when it loses $\frac{1}{8}$ of its weight in trimming and $\frac{1}{5}$ of the remainder in cooking ?

6. What per cent of the list price remains after deducting 30% of it and 40 % of the remainder ?

PROCESS

After the first deduction, the remainder is 70%. When 40% of this is deducted, there remains 60% of it. 60% of 70 per cent is 42 per cent. *Ans.*

---

7. Find the net per cent of the list price remaining after the deduction of the following trade discounts :

a. 50 and 50 %   *b.* 60 and 10 %   *c.* 50 and 20 %
d. 10 and 40 %   *e.* 20 and 50 %   *f.* 30 and 30 %

Commission

A person wishing to sell property finds it advisable, as a rule, to place it in the hands of a real estate *agent*, who charges him a certain per cent of the price obtained for the property.

A salesman sometimes receives, in addition to a fixed salary, a per cent of the amount of his sales.

A mill often purchases cotton through a *factor*, who receives a certain price per 100 bales as a *commission*.

A person desiring to invest money in bonds or stocks sometimes finds it to his advantage to buy them through a *broker*, who receives a commission, or *brokerage*, for his services. This commission is calculated in various ways.

ACCOUNT OF SALES

Thomas McCann, a farmer, ships to Bristol & Son, 200 sacks of potatoes to be sold on commission.

The following is the account of sales rendered by Bristol & Son:

EUREKA, UTAH, Dec. 1, 1915

Sold by BRISTOL & SON
Court House Square

For Account of THOMAS MCCANN

MT. PLEASANT, UTAH

Rec'd Nov. 15

Nov.							
	17	60 sacks Potatoes	2.30	138	—		
	19	50 " "	2.25	112	50		
	24	30 " "	2.45	73	50		
	30	60 " "	2.27½	136	50	460	50
		Charges					
		Freight $6.48 Cartage $4.50		10	98		
		Check on %, Nov. 23		200	—		
		Commission 5%		23	03	234	01
		Net proceeds remitted by check				$226	49

Written Problems

1. Make out an account of sales, substituting local names and prevailing prices. Ascertain, if possible, the rate of freight between the shipping and receiving points, also the cost of cartage.

2. A factor sells for Mr. Saitta 48 bales of cotton, averaging 400 pounds each, at $9\frac{3}{8}$ cents per pound. What is his commission at the rate of $5 per 100 bales, and how much does he remit Mr. Saitta after deducting sundry charges amounting to $19.75, and his commission?

3. An investor purchases, through a broker, 140 shares of stock at $137.50 per share. How much does the stock cost him, including the broker's commission of $12\frac{1}{2}$ cents per share?

4. A salesman receives $100 per month and a commission of $1\frac{1}{8}\%$ on his sales. What does he receive for the year in which his sales amount to $108,000?

5. A broker buys for Mr. H 1250 bags of coffee, weighing 130 pounds each, at 16 cents per pound. What is the cost of the coffee to Mr. H, including the brokerage of $10 per 250 bags?

6. A commission merchant received $23.60 commission on sales amounting to $944. What was the rate of his commission?

7. A real estate agent sold a house for $3500. What was his commission at the rate of 5 % on $1000 and $2\frac{1}{2}\%$ on the remainder?

8. An agent received $25.80 for selling a plot for $860. What per cent of the selling price did he receive?

9. What per cent of the area of a field 120 yd. by 80 yd. is the area of one 20 % longer and 20 % narrower?

Gain and Loss

Preparatory Exercises

1. A newsboy makes 100% profit on the cost of his papers. When his receipts are $1, (*a*) how much do his papers cost? (*b*) How much does he gain?

2. When a newsboy gains 50% of the cost of his papers, how much must be his receipts to give him a profit of $1?

3. A carpet costing $40 is sold for $50. (*a*) What fraction of the cost is gained? (*b*) What per cent?

4. A rug costing $50 is sold for $40. (*a*) What fraction of the buying price is lost? (*b*) What per cent?

5. A village increases from 200 inhabitants to 250. (*a*) What fraction of 200 is the gain? (*b*) What per cent?

6. The population of a village decreases from 250 to 200. (*a*) What fraction of 250 is the loss? (*b*) What per cent?

7. A horse is sold for $300, which is a loss of $100. (*a*) What was the cost? (*b*) What per cent of this was lost?

8. A lot is sold for $500, which is a gain of $100. (*a*) What was the cost? (*b*) What per cent of this was gained?

9. A club won 30 games and lost 20. (*a*) How many games were played? (*b*) What per cent of them were won?

10. By winning 30 games, a club won 75% of the games it played. (*a*) How many games did it play? (*b*) How many games did it lose?

Cost Charges

It is important for a manufacturer to know the actual cost of each product, whether it be a bushel of wheat, a piece of furniture, a machine, or the like. To do this he must ascertain the cost of the material, the cost of the labor, and the " overhead charges." The latter include rent, fuel, light, power, taxes, insurance, repairs, depreciation, etc., and to each unit produced must be assigned its share of these charges.

A planter, for instance, that desires to ascertain the cost of raising a pound of cotton must not limit the charge for the labor of his horses to the comparatively short time they are at field work. If his sole crop is cotton, he should charge it with the keep of the horses for the entire year except for such times as they are engaged in hauling to market, etc.

Buying Price and Selling Price

While the profit on an article is the difference between its cost and the sum obtained for it, diminished by the expenses, it is necessary in determining the percentage of profit to determine what expenses should increase the cost of the article and what ones should diminish the price obtained for it.

The merchant usually considers the price of the article to be its cost when it reaches his store, which may add to the sum paid for it such transportation charges as freight and cartage. The net selling price then is the amount received for it less the cost of delivery and its share of other " overhead charges," which may include, in addition to those previously given, advertising, salaries of salesmen, etc.

Business Efficiency

The better acquaintance with unit expenses of producing, buying, and selling frequently enables a man to change an unprofitable business into one that will yield a satisfactory return for his labor and capital. The cost of material may be diminished by cutting out unnecessary waste, the cost of labor by better arrangement of his machinery, thereby eliminating useless movements, etc.

Before discontinuing the manufacture or sale of such articles as show comparatively no profit, he must consider the effect of such action on the business as a whole. Some articles sold even at a loss draw customers that purchase articles yielding a fair profit.

Some farm crops that give no great revenue may so improve the soil that the yield of succeeding crops is greatly increased.

Sight Problems

1. A farmer had 80 sheep. How many had he after the flock was increased by 25% of that number?

2. A boy had 60 marbles. How many had he after giving 20% of them away?

3. After giving away $33\frac{1}{3}$% of her cherries, a girl has 20 left. (*a*) How many had she at first? (*b*) How many did she give away?

4. A dealer bought a horse for $150 and sold it at an advance of 4%. What did he receive for it?

5. A cow was sold for $60, which was 20% more than it cost. (*a*) What was the cost? (*b*) What was the profit? (*c*) What fraction of the cost is the profit? (*d*) What per cent of the cost is the profit?

6. After a man spends 50% of his money and 30% of the remainder, what per cent of his money is left?

Drill Exercises — Sight and Written

1. Give the gain or the loss.

a. Cost, $20; gain, 25%   b. Cost, 16¢; gain, $6\frac{1}{4}$%

c. Cost, $30; loss, 30%   d. Cost, 24¢; loss, $8\frac{1}{3}$%

e. Cost, $40; gain, 35%   f. Cost, 32¢; gain, $12\frac{1}{2}$%

g. Cost, $50; loss, 40%   h. Cost, 36¢; loss, $16\frac{2}{3}$%

2. Find the selling price (S.P.) of each of the above.

3. Give the gain or the loss in each of the following:

a. S.P., $10; gain, 25%   b. S.P., 60¢; loss, $6\frac{1}{4}$%

c. S.P., $20; loss, 20%   d. S.P., 39¢; gain, $8\frac{1}{3}$%

e. S.P., $30; gain, 20%   f. S.P., 70¢; loss, $12\frac{1}{2}$%

g. S.P., $40; loss, 50%   h. S.P., 42¢; gain, $16\frac{2}{3}$%

4. Find the cost in each of the foregoing examples.

5. Tell what fraction the S.P. is of the cost in each of the following:

a. Cost, $25; S.P., $30.   b. Cost, 30¢; S.P., 48¢.

c. Cost, $30; S.P., $25.   d. Cost, 60¢; S.P., 10¢.

e. Cost, $24; S.P., $36.   f. Cost, 90¢; S.P., 99¢.

g. Cost, $36; S.P., $24.   h. Cost, 80¢; S.P., 70¢.

6. Find the rate per cent of gain or of loss in each of the above.

7. Give answers to the following:

a. Buying price, $30; selling price, $39. Gain %?

b. Loss, 25%; selling price, 60¢. Buying price?

c. Selling price, $50; gain 16%. Buying price?

d. Gain, 30%; buying price, $20. Selling price?

e. Buying price, $90; selling price, $60. Loss %?

f. Gain, 40%; selling price, $70. Buying price?

g. Selling price, $80; loss 50%. Buying price?

h. Loss, 20%; buying price, $70. Selling price?

Written Problems

1. Some years ago a village contained 756 inhabitants. Their number has decreased $8\frac{1}{3}\%$. How many inhabitants are there in the village at present?

2. An agent sold a lot for $840. He received $2\frac{1}{2}\%$ of this amount as commission for selling it. (*a*) What was his commission? (*b*) How much did the seller receive after the deduction of the commission?

3. An importer paid $3620 in Japan for goods. He paid the government a duty of 35% of this sum. How much duty did he pay?

4. A bill of dry goods amounted to $1859.60. A deduction of 5% of this amount was allowed for payment in cash. (*a*) How much was deducted? (*b*) How much was paid?

5. A rectangular field 120 yards long and 80 yards wide was exchanged for a field 10% longer and 10% narrower. (*a*) Find the difference in their respective areas. (*b*) What fraction of the area of the first field is the difference? (*c*) What fraction of the area of the second field is the difference?

6. The owner of farm machinery that costs $2000 considers its value at the end of each year to be 10% less than at the beginning of the year. What does he consider the machinery worth at the end of the fourth year?

7. Goods costing $835.20 are sold at an advance of $17\frac{1}{2}\%$. Find the selling price.

8. An agent sold a house for $6750. He received 5% on $1000, $2\frac{1}{2}\%$ on $4000, and 1% on the balance of the sum obtained for the house. How much did he receive in all?

9. A village that contained 756 inhabitants in 1913 now contains 63 fewer. What per cent did the number decrease?

10. On a bill of dry goods amounting to $2356.40 a deduction of $58.91 was allowed for prompt payment. What per cent of the bill was deducted?

11. A man sold goods that cost him $1560 for $234 less. What per cent did he lose?

12. Goods costing $835.20 are sold for $954.40. What per cent of the cost is the profit?

13. A village that contained 756 inhabitants last year now contains 882. What per cent of 756 is the increase?

14. A village that contained 882 inhabitants last year has now only 756. What per cent of 882 is the decrease?

15. An agent sold a plot for $850 and turned over $816 to his employer. What per cent of $850 did he retain for his services?

16. A bill of $2356.50 was reduced to $2309.37 for prompt payment. What per cent of $2356.50 was deducted?

17. A platform whose dimensions were 24 ft. by 24 ft. is lengthened 25% and made 25% narrower. What per cent is its original area reduced?

18. A dealer lost 20% on his goods by selling them for $234 below cost. (a) What did the goods cost? (b) What was the selling price?

19. A dealer gained 25% on his goods by selling them at $234 above cost. (a) What did the goods cost? (b) What was the selling price?

Safeguarding our Business Interests

Insurance

The chief business of the head of a household is the care of those dependent upon him. This requires the continued setting aside of a portion of the income for the time when it may be interrupted by the producer's illness or terminated by his death. Provision must also be made for increased expenses of various kinds.

Personal Insurance

In many instances, the meager savings of an individual are insufficient to meet his emergency, while the combined small contributions of a number can be so managed as to provide a measure of relief for the comparatively small number that require financial help.

Fraternal Societies

Organizations of various kinds pay a fixed weekly stipend for a stated period to each member unable to work because of illness, and also a definite sum to his family at his death.

Insurance Companies

Insurance companies provide three forms of personal insurance: health insurance, accident insurance, and life insurance. The first gives the insured person a weekly sum for about one half year to each member incapacitated from work by ordinary illness. The second also provides a weekly payment, but only in case the incapacitation is caused by an accidental injury, and also a definite sum when death results therefrom during the period covered by the insurance.

Life Insurance

The most common form of personal insurance is one calling for the payment of a definite amount on the death of the person insured, in consideration of the payment of a stated sum annually, called the *premium*.

The terms of the contract are set forth in a document called the *policy*, which specifies the sum payable by the company upon proof of the death of the *assured*, together with the annual *premium* payable by the latter, and the date on which it is due.

In the *ordinary life policy*, the premium payments continue throughout the life of the assured. This form furnishes the largest insurance for a given premium. A person that fears his ability to keep up payments after his capacity to earn has seriously diminished takes out a 20-payment life policy. In this form premium payments cease after 20 years. A 10-payment life policy is preferred by those whose increase in expenses is likely to be greater than their increase in earnings, and who, therefore, desire to complete their payments within the stated period.

Investment and Insurance

A favorite policy with those who can afford the greater cost is the *endowment policy*. This provides for the payment of the face of the policy by the company at the end of the term, or upon the death of the assured at any time during the term. These policies run, as a rule, for ten or for twenty years.

If, at the end of the term, the assured has no special need of the money, he can purchase therewith a paid-up policy for a stated amount.

The following table shows the premiums payable, at the specified ages, per $1000 of insurance in the ordinary life plan, the 20-payment life, the 10-payment life, and the 20-year endowment. •

ANNUAL PREMIUMS PER $1000

Age	Premiums Payable For			
	Life	20 Years	10 Years	20 Years
20	$18.01	$27.78	$45.51	$47.54
25	20.14	30.07	49.11	48.03
30	22.85	32.83	53.88	48.71
35	26.35	36.17	58.44	49.75
40	30.94	40.34	64.14	51.39
45	37.09	45.69	71.66	54.15
50	45.45	52.83	80.51	58.76
55	56.93	62.66	91.42	66.32
Policy payable at death				In 20 years

Premiums and Dividends

From figures collected for a long period and covering a very large number of people of all ages, it is possible to determine the average number of years persons of a given age will live.

From this is calculated the sum that must be invested annually to yield with interest a given amount, say $1000. To this is added a certain per cent thereof to cover expenses, and an additional per cent to provide for any unusual mortality caused by pestilence, flood, etc. From time to time the portion of the excess premium that can be returned to the assured is determined. This so-called *dividend* is either paid him in cash or used to increase the amount payable at his death.

Insurance on Property

Insurance companies of different kinds afford all classes
of persons the opportunity to avoid a financial loss that
might seriously cripple them. *Fidelity insurance* secures
employers against loss by thefts of employees; *burglary
insurance* reimburses the owner of valuable articles stolen
from his premises; *plate-glass insurance* replaces costly
store windows that have been broken; *casualty insurance*
assures for the owner of buildings any liability for dam-
age because of injuries occurring on his property.

Fire Insurance

Insurance against fire is needed by every householder.
The expense is so insignificant compared with the cost of
replacing the building or the furniture destroyed that no
one is justified in neglecting to insure his property.

The rate of insurance is determined by the risk. It is
greater on a frame building than on one of brick or stone.
It is smaller on a detached building than on one located
in a row. The nature of the business carried on in a
building is a factor in fixing the rate, one in which gasoline, for instance, is sold, being very hazardous. The protection against fire is another factor, a poor water supply
in one section of a city increasing the rate above that
charged in sections in which the water supply is better.

Since an insurance company may be bankrupted by a
local fire that destroys hundreds of houses, a business
man generally distributes his insurance among several
companies, each located in a different city. For convenience, he "places" his insurance through a broker, who is
paid a commission by such company.

The following is the bill of an insurance agent:

CHICAGO, ILL., October 1, 1915

MR. SAMUEL PRATT
   819 Wabash Av.

To HENRY COLLINS & SON, *Dr.*
Insurance Agents and Brokers
LaSalle Building

Oct.		*To premiums on the following policies :*		Amount	Premiums	
	1	*Phœnix of New York*	*Stock*	*1500*	*11*	*25*
	3	*Fireman's of Denver*	*Bldg.*	*9000*	*54*	*00*
		Fidelity of Hartford	*"*	*3500*	*21*	*00*
	5	*Northern of London*	*Stock*	*3000*	*22*	*50*
					$108	*75*

Even the small insurer finds it advantageous to obtain his insurance through a reliable broker, as the latter keeps him informed of the date of the expiration of each policy, the standing of companies, etc., without charge.

The indorsement of a policy of fire insurance shows (*a*) the date of the expiration of the insurance, (*b*) the location of the property, (*c*) the sum for which the company insures it, (*d*) the premium, (*e*) the name of the owner of the property, and (*f*) the name of the insurance company.

The most prominent feature in the indorsement of the policy is the date of its expiration, which should always be kept in mind.

In the case of a building injured by fire, the insurance company has the right to make the repairs needed to restore the building to its condition before the fire, instead of giving the insurance money to the owner. An itemized statement of the value of the goods injured by fire must be supplied by the owner within a definite time and an opportunity given the company to examine their condition, etc. The inventory, from which the details can be supplied, is shown on page 63.

Rates for Short Terms

The owner of a building seldom insures it for less than a year, and generally for three years because of the reduction.

A farmer who intends to sell his hay, grain, etc., can insure it for 2 days, 5 days, 1 month, etc.

The accompanying table gives the per cent of the annual rate charged for each period specified:

2 days 3%	15 days 14%	3 months 40%
5 days 7%	20 days 15%	6 months 70%
10 days 10%	1 month 20%	9 months 85%

A complete table gives the rates for other periods.

Written Exercises

1. What annual premium must Mr. Wilkes pay on a 20-year endowment policy if his age is 30 years?

NOTE. — See table, p. 278.

2. Andrew Jenkins takes out a life policy for $2000 at the age of 30. If he dies after paying 30 annual premiums, (*a*) how much has he paid the company? (*b*) How much less would he have paid if he had taken out a policy on the 20-payment life plan? (*c*) On the 10-payment life plan?

3. Mr. Wade has property worth $6500. He insures it for 80% of its value. (*a*) What is the face of the policy? (*b*) What is the annual premium at 80¢ per $100? (*c*) What must he pay to insure it for three years, the rate being twice that for one year's insurance?

4. A dealer buys 12,000 bushels of wheat at 95 cents per bushel. What must he pay to insure its cost for ` `days at 10% of the annual rate of 50 cents per $100?

Governmental Helps

Among the agencies that help us in the conduct of our business, the most important are the municipal, the county, the state, and the national government. These coöperate by educating the children, by constructing roads and streets, by protecting property against fire and theft, by affording facilities for recreation, by furnishing relief for the poor, by handling our mails, by increasing the commercial advantages of rivers and harbors, by regulating railroads and other public corporations, etc.

Governmental Revenues — Taxes on Persons

Money to pay the expenses of a government is obtained from various sources. A portion of it comes from *license fees* paid by peddlers, storekeepers, owners of vehicles, proprietors of shows, chauffeurs, etc.

In some places a *poll tax* of fifty cents, a dollar, etc., is collected from every male resident that has reached the age of twenty-one.

In many states an *inheritance tax* is levied on the property in the state owned by a person at the time of his death.

An *income tax* is collected by the national government from all persons whose income exceeds a certain sum.

Governmental Debts

When the cost of a much-needed improvement is so great that the taxes for the year in which it is made should not be burdened with the entire expense, money is borrowed, and the cost spread over a number of years. Thus, a portion of the expense of erecting a new school is paid annually for perhaps ten years or longer.

How Tax Money is Spent

The following shows the distribution of the governmental expenditures of Johnson Co., including the city of Blissville:

Interest on Debt, etc.	$ 51,255.17
General administration	3,328.00
Judicial and Correctional	9,870.26
Educational	36,116.31
Health and Sanitation	17,076.18
Protection of Life and Property	30,179.61
Maintenance of Highways, Bridges, etc.	8,053.46
Parks, Public Buildings, etc.	2,373.57
Advertising, Printing, etc.	1,354.00
State Taxes	4,301.65
Charitable Purposes	10,309.38
	$174,217.59
For deficiencies in collections	3,782.41
	$178,000.00

Distributed as follows:

City Charges	$160,873.43
County Charges	9,824.92
State Taxes	4,301.65
	$175,000.00

Assessed value of the property of Johnson County was:

Real Estate	$12,840,500
Personal Property	1,659,500
Total	$14,500,000

Sum to be raised by taxation:

Expenses during 1915	$175,000.00
Less estimated revenues	24,492.90
	$150,507.10

At 12:34 P.M., Sept. 6, 1914, the taxes payable on property become a *lien* thereon, and a buyer after that time deducts from the purchase price the taxes then due, although he is not required to pay them until Oct. 30.

Assessed Value of Property

Officials called *assessors* fix the valuation of property for purposes of taxation. As the owner of real estate is frequently unable to obtain more than 60 or 70 per cent of its actual value, it is customary to assess city property at, perhaps, two thirds of its value, and farm lands still lower. The ratio the *assessed value* bears to the actual value does not affect the taxes on a particular parcel provided the rate is uniform throughout the district in which the taxes are to be levied.

Assuming that the property in a district is worth $8,000,000 and the taxes to be raised are $40,000, A, who owns property worth $8000, should pay $40, or $\frac{1}{2}\%$ of its actual value. If the assessed value is made $4,000,000, the tax rate is 1%, but A's being assessed for $4000, his bill at 1% is still $40.

Real and Personal Estate

Many owners of personal property escape the payment of their share of governmental expenses because of the difficulty of ascertaining their possessions. In the valuation given on the preceding page, that of the personal property is possibly less than one tenth of its real worth.

The Taxpayer

Everybody pays taxes either directly or indirectly. When he is not the owner of the house in which he lives, the rent he pays includes the taxes paid by the owner. His interest in the proper expenditure of every cent raised by taxation is just as great as that of the person who gets a tax bill and pays it.

Assessments

While every property owner in a given district is charged the same rate for the general expenses, the cost of certain local improvements is paid by the persons immediately benefited by them. Thus, when a city constructs a sidewalk, say, 800 feet in length, the owner of 200 feet of property facing the street pays one fourth of the cost. This is generally called an *assessment*, and is not made a part of the regular taxes. The construction of a short road used chiefly by the owners of the adjacent farms is charged against them.

State Taxes

Money required for state expenditures in excess of the revenues is collected through a tax, which is included in the county tax bills. The cost of a long highway may be paid partly by the state, partly by the counties through which it passes, and partly by the owners of abutting property.

Written Exercises

1. (*a*) Find the rate on $1 (correct to seven decimal places) to yield $150,507.10 taxes on property assessed for $14,500,000.

(*b*) What are A's taxes on a house assessed for $3500?

2. Oct. 1, 1914, Frank Phillips agrees to pay Mr. Collins $5000 for his house. How much should he pay after deducting the taxes, the house being assessed at 70 % of its value of $5000, and the tax rate being $10.3798 per $1000 of the assessed value?

3. Find the taxes on the property covered by the following bill.

A Tax Bill

City of Blissville — Department of Finance

Taxes for 1914

Draw check to the order of Receiver of Taxes

Rate 1.03798 per cent   Penalty takes effect Nov. 1

Section	Vol.	Block No.	Lot No.	Location	Valuation	Tax
18	4	6036	30	23d St.	$3000	
					Interest on Tax Rebate on Tax	$

4. In Blissville taxes are received at any time after Sept. 1, a rebate being allowed for payments made during this month at the rate of 6 % per annum for the time between the date of payment and Nov. 1. What rebate is allowed on the foregoing bill if it is paid Sept. 2 ?

5. Taxes paid during October receive no rebate. Those paid after Oct. 31 are subject to a penalty of 7 % per annum from Oct. 1. (*a*) What are Mr. O'Donnell's taxes on property assessed for $10,000 when paid Oct. 30, 1914, the rate being 1.03798 % ? (*b*) What amount is payable Jan. 2, 1915, if interest at 7 % is added from Oct. 1 ? (*c*) How much could he have saved by borrowing the money from a bank at 6 % Oct. 30, and repaying it Jan. 2 ? (360 days to the year.)

6. A town needs to raise $18,950 by taxation. There are 600 persons liable to a poll tax of $1.50 each. The assessed value of the property is $1,900,000. (*a*) How much is raised by the poll tax ? (*b*) How much must be obtained by property taxes ? (*c*) What must be the tax rate on each $1000 of valuation ?

The National Income

The United States government spends nearly 1000 millions of dollars yearly for ordinary expenses. A large part of this is derived from two sources, the *internal revenue* and the revenues from taxes on imported goods.

The greater portion of the internal revenue is paid by manufacturers of liquor and tobacco, the bulk of their payments being represented by stamps affixed to the packages containing their products.

The Tariff

Taxes upon goods brought into the United States from foreign countries are known as *duties*. The existing rates, which were fixed by an Act of Congress adopted in 1913, constitute the *tariff*. These rates are either *specific*, which is a stated price per pound, gallon, etc., or *ad valorem*, which is a per cent of the value.

Payment of Duties

To obtain possession of his goods, the importer pays the *estimated duty*, and gives a bond to pay any additional sum found to be due after the goods are examined.

As a basis for the determination of the estimated duty, the importer files at the custom house the *invoice*, or bill of the foreign seller, which gives the nature and quantity of the goods, with their prices in the currency of the country in which they are bought. He also files an *entry* in which he arranges the items under the rates he thinks are applicable.

The sum actually due, the *liquidated* duty, is determined after the goods are weighed, measured, etc., and their ᵃ *appraised* by the customs authorities.

How Duties are Paid

Arrived 20th day of May, 1915

Entry of Merchandise imported by John Brown & Co.

Date of Invoice, London, May 6, 1915. Seattle, May 20, 1915

Marks	Nos.	Packages and Contents as per Accompanying Invoice	20%	15%	80%	Total
J. B. Co.	44/46	Three (3) cases Mfrs. Metal Steel Wire Scissors	£113 13 2	£3 13 2	£0 14 7	£118 0 11
			$553	$18	$3	$574

Liquidated   553   20   110.60
  May 25, 1915   21   30   6.30
                              116.90

   3   30%   .90
  18   15%   2.70   Amended, 116.90
 553   20% 110.60   Original, 114.20
            114.20   Increase,   2.70

The broker for John Brown & Co. presents the foregoing to an entry clerk at the custom house, who compares the total £118 0 11 with the invoice, checks the reductions to U. S. money, and inserts the estimated duty, which amounts to $114.20. This the importer pays, gives a bond for any additional sum that may be found to be due, and receives an order for the delivery of his employer's goods after the appraiser has inspected them.

Upon the report of the latter that the steel wire is dutiable at 80 % as wire rope, a liquidating clerk inserts the corrected duty in red ink, and notes the increase payable.

The values in U. S. money are found as follows:

$$\begin{array}{rl}
£\ 113.13.2 \ @\ \$4.8665 = & \$553.12, \text{ or } \$553 \\
3.13.2 \ @\ 4.8665 = & 17.81 \qquad 18 \\
14.7 \ @\ 4.8665 = & 3.55 \qquad 3 \\
\hline
£\ 118.0.11 \ @\ \$4.8665 = & \$574.48, \text{ or } \$574
\end{array}$$

As the government omits cents below 50¢ in determining the dutiable value of an invoice, the total is taken as $574, which rejects the cents in two items and makes the third item $18, since it contains the largest number of cents.

Tables of Foreign Money

FRENCH
1 franc (fr.) = 100 centimes

GERMAN
1 mark (*M.*) = 100 pfennige

In French and German money centimes and pfennige are written, respectively, as decimals of the franc and of the mark.

ENGLISH
12 pence (*d.*) = 1 shilling (*s.*)
20 shillings = 1 pound (£)

A farthing is $\frac{1}{4}$ penny, and is generally written as a fraction.

VALUES IN UNITED STATES MONEY

The *intrinsic* value of foreign coin is determined annually by the United States government. In changing foreign money to United States money in calculating duties, the following values are used:

£ 1 = $4.8665
1 mark = 23.8 cents
1 franc = 19.3 cents

Written Problems

1. What is the duty at 35% on goods costing £ 154. 18*s*. 10*d*. ?

$$£ 154 = \$4.8665 \times 154 = \$749.441$$
$$18s. = \ 4.8665 \times \ \ .9 = \ \ \ \ 4.3799$$
$$10d. = \tfrac{1}{24} \text{ of } \$4.8665 = \ \ \ \ \ .2028$$
$$\overline{\$754.0237}$$

Duty = 35% of $754

2. Find the duty at 25% on goods worth 1860 fr. 54.

3. An importer bought 3000 meters of dress goods in Germany at *M*. 0.90 per meter. What is the duty at 35%?

4. Find the cost in Portland, Oregon, of 100 doz. pocketbooks costing in Paris 30 francs per dozen less 5% discount for cash, including the duty at 30%, and freight, etc., amounting to 9½ ¢ per dozen.

5. (*a*) What fraction of a pound sterling is 18*s*. 4*d*.? (*b*) What decimal of a pound sterling is 17*s*. 6*d*.? (*c*) What per cent of a pound sterling is 6*s*. 8*d*.?

6. A London merchant buys tobacco in this country for 61 cents a pound and pays a duty in England of 3*s*. 6*d*. per pound. Find the cost, including duty (*a*) in English money, (*b*) in United States money.

7. At 5 ¢ per lb., find the duty on 100 casks of colors each containing 50 kilograms.

1 kilogram = 2.2046 lb.

8. The owner of a house worth $3750 insures it for 80% of its value. (*a*) What is the face of his policy? (*b*) What is the annual premium at 30 ¢ per $100?

9. A house that is worth $3750 is assessed for 60% of its value. (*a*) What is its assessed value? (*b*) What are the taxes for 1916, if the rate is ¾% of the assessed value?

Written Review Problems

1. A grocer sold sugar that cost him $1000, at a profit of 2%. He sold coffee that cost him $2000, at a profit of 15%. He sold tea that cost him $3000, at a profit of 30%. What per cent did he gain on the total cost of these three articles?

2. A man bought a house for $1250. He paid the agent buying it for him 2%, and spent $125 for repairs. How much must he receive for the house to realize a profit of 10% over his entire outlay?

3. A man buys a house for $1000 and pays the agent 5% commission for buying it. He sells it for $1500 through another agent, who charges him 2% for selling it. (*a*) What is his net profit? (*b*) What per cent of the gross cost of the house is this profit?

NOTE. — The gross cost of an article is the first cost plus the expenses incurred in buying.

4. (*a*) What % is gained on goods bought at $6\frac{1}{4}$¢ per yard, and sold at $8\frac{1}{3}$¢ per yard? (*b*) What per cent is lost on goods bought at $8\frac{1}{3}$¢ per yard, and sold at $6\frac{1}{4}$¢ per yard?

5. A raised 40 bushels of corn to the acre at an expense for labor, etc., of $9.20 per acre; B raised 60 bushels to the acre at an expense of $10.50 per acre; and C raised 75 bushels to the acre at an expense of $12 per acre. Find the cost per bushel in each case for labor, etc.

6. The goods sold each month by a dealer cost him $1000, which he sells at an advance of 25%. (*a*) Find his profit. (*b*) What is his net profit when his monthly selling expenses are $150? (*c*) What are his monthly receipts? (*d*) What per cent of his monthly receipts are his selling expenses?

7. By lowering his prices to 20 % above the cost, he sells goods that cost him $2000. (*a*) Find his profit. (*b*) Find his net profit if his selling expenses have increased 33⅓%. (*c*) What are his monthly receipts? (*d*) What per cent of his monthly receipts are his selling expenses?

8. Find the cost of keeping a cow when she requires 3.5 tons of hay at $7 per ton, 1200 pounds of ground feed at 90 cents per 100 pounds, and pasture worth $8.

9. (*a*) How much is received from a cow that averages daily for 300 days, 13 pounds of milk yielding 4.2 % of butter fat worth 28 cents per pound? (*b*) How much more is received than the cost of the food in the preceding problem?

10. What is received for the milk of a cow that averages 25 pounds daily for 308 days, containing 5.3 % of butter fat worth 28 cents per pound?

11. At the rate of 2400 quarts to the acre, how many quarts can be raised on a plot 8 rods square?

12. (*a*) What is the cost of carrying a bushel of wheat 8 miles to a railroad station at the rate of 20 ¢ per ton per mile? (*b*) What is saved in the transportation of 3000 bushels when the improvement of the road reduces the cost to 12 ¢ per ton per mile?

13. A steam plant consumed an average of 3640 pounds of coal per day. The engineer made certain alterations which saved 260 pounds per day. What per cent was saved?

14. A test showed that an engine developed 190 horse power, 15 % of which was lost by friction, waste, etc. How much power was available for use?

15. Find the cost of the following daily ration of a dairy cow:

40 lb. silage @ $ 2.50 per ton
12 lb. alfalfa @   10.00 per ton
4 lb. bran   @   24.00 per ton
4 lb. meal   @   20.00 per ton

16. By housing implements when not in use, they will last 12 years, while they would become worthless in 5 years if left exposed to the weather. (*a*) What is the yearly saving on tools worth $1800, assuming $\frac{1}{5}$ to be lost in one case and $\frac{1}{12}$ in the other? (*b*) What per cent is realized on the $200 it cost to build the house?

17. A bushel of wheat, 60 pounds, loses 25% of its weight when made into flour. (*a*) Find the weight of the flour. Dough weighs 60% more than the flour used in making it. (*b*) Find the weight of the dough made from a bushel of wheat. Bread weighs $\frac{1}{5}$ less than the dough. (*c*) Find the quantity of bread made from a bushel of wheat. Find the quantity of bread made (*d*) from a pound of wheat. (*e*) From a pound of flour. (*f*) From a barrel of flour containing 196 pounds.

18. To run the machinery of a factory, 190.4 horse-power is required. What horsepower must be developed by the engine if 30% of it is lost by transmission, leakage, etc. ?

19. A cow gives 6000 pounds of milk in a year, from which are produced butter amounting to 5% of this weight, skim milk amounting to 80%, and buttermilk amounting to 15%. Find the value of (*a*) the butter at 32 cents per pound. (*b*) Of the skim milk at 16 ¢ per 100 pounds. (*c*) Of the buttermilk at 12 cents per 100 pounds. (*d*) The total.

20. By making improvements to his engine a man increased its power 14% and reduced the consumption of coal 20% per horsepower. If the engine originally developed 50 horsepower and used $3\frac{1}{2}$ pounds of coal per horsepower per hour, what quantity of coal per horsepower per hour would it use after its improvement, running full capacity?

21. From the farm to the table the following successive losses occur in the weight of a 1000-lb. cow; 5% during transportation to the stockyards, 42% of remainder in killing and dressing, 10% of remainder in cooking, 25% of remainder in bones and fat not eaten. How many pounds of cooked lean meat are furnished by the cow?

22. The following table shows the average weight of a large number of boys and of girls at the ages specified.

Age	Boys			Girls		
	Weight	Yearly Increase	%	Weight	Yearly Increase	%
10	69	——		62	——	
11	73			69		
12	79			78		
13	84			89		
14	92			98		
15	103			106		
	Totals			Totals		

(*a*) Fill in the per cent of increase for each of the five years. (*b*) Find the total increase for the five years and (*c*) the percentage of increase during the five-year period.

Carry out the per cents to two decimal places. Note that (*c*) is not the sum of the yearly per cents.

SECTION IX

EFFICIENCY IN CALCULATIONS

Business Methods

While each calling has its own particular set of " short-cuts " that are inapplicable in other lines, there are some general methods employed by all experienced business men to save unnecessary figures.

Written Exercises

1. Find the cost of 347 pounds of sugar at $5\frac{5}{8}$ cents per pound.

PROCESS		
347		
$5\frac{5}{8}$		Find the product by $\frac{5}{8}$ by dividing
1735	Product by 5	the first product by 8. Do not write
$216\frac{7}{8}$	Product by $\frac{5}{8}$	8 as a divisor.
$1951\frac{7}{8}$	*Ans.* \$19.52	

2. Multiply :

a. $1247 \times 2\frac{2}{5}$ *b.* $2363 \times 5\frac{5}{6}$ *c.* $48 \times 10\frac{10}{11}$

3. Multiply $374\frac{2}{3}$ (*a*) by $\frac{3}{4}$. (*b*) by $\frac{5}{6}$.

PROCESS	
(*a*) $374\frac{2}{3} \times \frac{3}{4}$	(*b*) $374\frac{2}{3} \times \frac{5}{6}$
$93\frac{2}{3}$ Deduct $\frac{1}{4}$	$62\frac{4}{9}$ Deduct $\frac{1}{6}$
281 *Ans.*	$312\frac{2}{9}$ *Ans.*

4. Find products:

a. $753 \times \frac{3}{4}$ b. $645\frac{1}{2} \times \frac{1}{5}$ c. $528\frac{1}{3} \times \frac{2}{3}$

d. $297 \times \frac{7}{8}$ e. $384\frac{1}{2} \times \frac{2}{3}$ f. $613\frac{1}{2} \times \frac{1}{4}$

g. $511 \times \frac{5}{6}$ h. $476\frac{1}{2} \times \frac{5}{7}$ i. $982\frac{2}{3} \times \frac{1}{5}$

5. Multiply 943 (*a*) by 24.   (*b*) by $32\frac{1}{3}$.   (*c*) by $15\frac{2}{3}$.

PROCESS

(*a*) 943×24 (*b*) $943 \times 32\frac{1}{3}$ (*c*) $943 \times 15\frac{2}{3}$

$\quad$ 23575 $\quad$ 31433$\frac{1}{3}$ $\quad$ 15716$\frac{2}{3}$

$\overline{22632}$ *Ans.* $\overline{30490\frac{1}{3}}$ *Ans.* $\overline{14773\frac{2}{3}}$ *Ans.*

Deduct 943 from (*a*) 25 times, (*b*) $33\frac{1}{3}$ times, and (*c*) $16\frac{2}{3}$ times itself.

---

6. Find products:

a. 357×49 b. $456 \times 32\frac{1}{3}$ c. $285 \times 15\frac{2}{3}$ d. $804 \times 49\frac{1}{2}$

e. 972×24 f. $456 \times 34\frac{1}{3}$ g. $285 \times 17\frac{2}{3}$ h. $561 \times 49\frac{3}{4}$

i. 972×26 j. $972 \times 24\frac{1}{2}$ k. $972 \times 24\frac{3}{4}$ l. $972 \times 24\frac{7}{8}$

7. Multiply $146\frac{3}{4}$ (*a*) by $1\frac{1}{8}$.   (*b*) by $1\frac{1}{4}$.   (*c*) by $1\frac{1}{6}$.

PROCESS

(*a*) $146\frac{3}{4} \times 1\frac{1}{8}$ (*b*) $146\frac{3}{4} \times 1\frac{1}{4}$ (*c*) $146\frac{3}{4} \times 1\frac{1}{6}$

$\quad$ 18$\frac{11}{32}$ $\quad$ 36$\frac{11}{16}$ $\quad$ 24$\frac{11}{24}$

$\overline{165\frac{3}{32}}$ *Ans.* $\overline{183\frac{7}{16}}$ *Ans.* $\overline{171\frac{5}{24}}$ *Ans.*

To $146\frac{3}{4}$ add (*a*) $\frac{1}{8}$, (*b*) $\frac{1}{4}$, (*c*) $\frac{1}{6}$ of itself.

Test (*a*) by multiplying $18\frac{11}{32}$ by 9, (*b*) by multiplying $36\frac{11}{16}$ by 5, (*c*) by multiplying $24\frac{11}{24}$ by 7.

---

8. Find products:

a. $144\frac{1}{2} \times 1\frac{1}{3}$ b. $216\frac{1}{2} \times 1\frac{1}{4}$ c. $324\frac{1}{2} \times 1\frac{1}{4}$ d. $486\frac{1}{2} \times 1\frac{1}{6}$

e. $376\frac{8}{9} \times 1\frac{1}{8}$ f. $252\frac{6}{7} \times 1\frac{1}{6}$ g. $108\frac{3}{4} \times 1\frac{1}{3}$ h. $276\frac{2}{5} \times 1\frac{1}{2}$

9. How many square feet are there in a steel plate 12 ft. 3 in. long, 4 ft. 4 in. wide?

PROCESS

$12\frac{1}{4}$ (ft.)   Express each dimension in feet and a fraction.
$4\frac{1}{3}$ (ft.)   Multiply $12\frac{1}{4}$ by 4, then by $\frac{1}{3}$, and combine the
———   partial products. Test by chang-
49   4 times $12\frac{1}{4}$ ing the fractions to improper frac-
$4\frac{1}{12}$ $\frac{1}{3}$ of $12\frac{1}{4}$ tions, etc. $\frac{49}{4} \times \frac{13}{3}$.
$53\frac{1}{12}$ (sq. ft.) *Ans.*

---

10. Find products:

a. $12\frac{2}{3} \times 3\frac{1}{2}$ b. $126\frac{3}{4} \times 4\frac{1}{8}$ c. $245\frac{5}{6} \times 12\frac{1}{6}$

d. $12\frac{1}{4} \times 4\frac{1}{2}$ e. $132\frac{1}{2} \times 6\frac{1}{4}$ f. $376\frac{1}{3} \times 12\frac{1}{3}$

11. How many yards of silk can be bought for $\$374\frac{1}{2}$ when it costs (*a*) $\$\frac{3}{4}$ per yard? (*b*) $\$\frac{7}{8}$ per yard?

PROCESS

In (*a*) divide by $\frac{3}{4}$ by multiplying by $1\frac{1}{3}$; in (*b*) divide by $\frac{7}{8}$ by multiplying by $1\frac{1}{7}$.

(*a*) $\$374\frac{1}{2} \div \$\frac{3}{4}$ (*b*) $\$374\frac{1}{2} \div \$\frac{7}{8}$
      $124\frac{5}{6}$ Add $\frac{1}{3}$ $53\frac{1}{2}$ Add $\frac{1}{7}$
Ans. $499\frac{1}{3}$ (yd.)   *Ans.* 428 (yd.)

Test (*a*) by multiplying $124\frac{5}{6}$ by 4, (*b*) by multiplying $53\frac{1}{2}$ by 8.

---

12. Divide $\$367\frac{1}{2}$ (*a*) by $66\frac{2}{3}$¢. (*b*) By 75¢. (*c*) By $83\frac{1}{3}$¢. (*d*) By $87\frac{1}{2}$¢.

13. Find answers.

a. $846.6 \div .75$ b. $94.64 \div .875$

c. $846.6 \times .75$ d. $94.64 \times .875$

Sight Review Drills

1. Multiply

a. 48×25 b. 25×84 c. 124×25 d. 25×324
e. 49×25 f. 25×86 g. 168×25 h. 25×288
i. 32×25 j. 25×88 k. 165×25 l. 25×368

2. Give products:

a. $18 \times 33\frac{1}{3}$ b. $12\frac{1}{2} \times 88$ c. 16×125 d. 625×16
e. $24 \times 16\frac{2}{3}$ f. $37\frac{1}{2} \times 88$ g. $15 \times 333\frac{1}{3}$ h. 875×16
i. $36 \times 33\frac{1}{3}$ j. $62\frac{1}{2} \times 88$ k. $18 \times 166\frac{2}{3}$ l. 125×48

3. Multiply:

a. 96×99 b. 24×99 c. 96×49 d. 96×24
e. 99×99 f. 86×49 g. 84×24 h. 68×49
i. 88×99 j. 48×24 k. 85×99 l. 36×24

4. Give answers:

a. $99\frac{1}{2} \times 88$ b. $88 \times 49\frac{1}{2}$ c. $88 \times 24\frac{1}{2}$ d. $88 \times 12\frac{1}{2}$
e. $99\frac{3}{4} \times 88$ f. $88 \times 49\frac{3}{4}$ g. $88 \times 24\frac{3}{4}$ h. $88 \times 12\frac{1}{4}$
i. $99\frac{7}{8} \times 88$ j. $88 \times 49\frac{7}{8}$ k. $88 \times 24\frac{7}{8}$ l. $88 \times 12\frac{3}{8}$

5. Multiply:

a. $24 \times 99\frac{2}{3}$ b. $24 \times 49\frac{2}{3}$ c. $24 \times 24\frac{1}{3}$ d. $24 \times 16\frac{1}{3}$
e. $24 \times 99\frac{5}{6}$ f. $24 \times 49\frac{5}{6}$ g. $24 \times 24\frac{5}{6}$ h. $66 \times 16\frac{1}{3}$

6. Give products:

a. $48 \times 25\frac{1}{4}$ b. $48 \times 50\frac{1}{4}$ c. $36 \times 34\frac{1}{3}$ d. $48 \times 12\frac{3}{4}$
e. $48 \times 25\frac{1}{2}$ f. $48 \times 50\frac{1}{2}$ g. $36 \times 17\frac{2}{3}$ h. $48 \times 12\frac{5}{8}$

7. Multiply:

a. $32 \times 19\frac{1}{2}$ b. $16 \times 29\frac{1}{2}$ c. $24 \times 39\frac{1}{2}$ d. $24 \times 19\frac{2}{3}$
e. $32 \times 19\frac{3}{4}$ f. $16 \times 29\frac{3}{4}$ g. $24 \times 39\frac{3}{4}$ h. $24 \times 19\frac{5}{6}$

Special Products

Sight Exercises

To multiply two mixed numbers having the integer the same in each and the sum of the fractions 1, increase one of the integers by 1, multiply it by the other, and to the product annex the product of the fractions.

1. Multiply (*a*) $8\frac{1}{2}$ by $8\frac{1}{2}$.　(*b*) $8\frac{1}{4}$ by $8\frac{3}{4}$.

In (*a*) the product $72\frac{1}{4}$ is 9 times $8 + \frac{1}{2}$ of $\frac{1}{2}$.　In (*b*) the product $72\frac{3}{16}$ is 9 times $8 + \frac{1}{4}$ of $\frac{3}{4}$.

2. Give products :

a. $5\frac{1}{2} \times 5\frac{1}{2}$　*b.* $8\frac{1}{3} \times 8\frac{2}{3}$　*c.* $10\frac{1}{3} \times 10\frac{2}{3}$　*d.* $11\frac{1}{2} \times 11\frac{1}{2}$

e. $6\frac{1}{2} \times 6\frac{1}{2}$　*f.* $9\frac{1}{4} \times 9\frac{3}{4}$　*g.* $10\frac{1}{2} \times 10\frac{1}{2}$　*h.* $11\frac{1}{3} \times 11\frac{2}{3}$

3. Multiply (*a*) 8.5 by 8.5.　(*b*) 7.3 × 7.7.

　　a. $8.5 \times 8.5 = (9 \times 8) + (.5 \times .5) = 72.25$

　　b. $7.3 \times 7.7 = (8 \times 7) + (.3 \times .7) = 56.21$

4. Multiply:

a. 2.5×2.5　*b.* 3.3×3.7　*c.* 4.4×4.6　*d.* 5.5×5.5

e. 2.8×2.2　*f.* 4.2×4.8　*g.* 6.3×6.7　*h.* 8.1×8.9

5. Multiply (*a*) 85 × 85.　(*b*) 73 × 77.

In (*a*) annex to 72 (8 × 9) 25 (5 × 5), making the result 7225.　In (*b*) annex to 56 (7 × 8) 21 (3 × 7), making the result 5621.

6. Give products :

a. 23×27　*b.* 34×36　*c.* 45×45　*d.* 56×54　*e.* 101×109

f. 55×55　*g.* 67×63　*h.* 88×82　*i.* 66×64　*j.* 112×118

Sight Review Problems

1. What is the area of a square having each side 6½ inches long?

2. How many yards are there in 26 rolls of cloth each containing (*a*) 24 yd.? (*b*) 49 yd.?

3. A rectangle is 58 rods long and 52 rods wide; find its area.

4. A solid whose base is a 7-inch square is 41 inches high. What is its volume?

5. What is the cost of 96 bushels of wheat at 99⅞¢ per bushel?

6. At 75¢ per yard, how many more than 123 yards can be bought for $123?

7. How many square inches are there in a rectangle 10⅞ inches long, 10⅛ inches wide?

8. If a man walks for 3 hours 45 minutes at the rate of 3¼ miles per hour, (*a*) how many miles has he walked? (*b*) How many miles and rods? (*c*) How many miles and rods would he walk if he walked for 3 hours and 30 minutes at the rate of 3 miles 160 rods per hour?

9. How many hours are there (*a*) in January? (*b*) In February 1915? (*c*) In February 1916?

10. Give the area of each of the following squares having sides

(*a*) 55 ft. (*b*) 65 yd. · (*c*) 75 rd. (*d*) 8½ mi. (*e*) 10½ in.

11. Under the old tariff Mr. Martin paid 45% duty on an automobile valued at $4500. How much did he pay?

12. At the rate of 56 bushels of corn to the acre what is the yield of 54 acres?

13. (*a*) What fraction of a square foot is there in a pane of glass 8 in. by 6 in.? How many panes of this size are there in a box of glass containing 50 sq. ft.?

14. At $7\frac{1}{2}$ gallons to the cubic foot, how many cubic feet will 3000 gallons of oil occupy?

15. How many shares of stock at $99 per share can be bought for (*a*) 93 hundred dollars, and how many dollars will remain? (*b*) For $9306?

16. How many cubic yards are there (*a*) in 23 cu. ft.? (1 cu. yd. = 27 cu. ft.) (*b*) In 99 cu. ft.? (*c*) In $99\frac{2}{3}$ cu. ft.?

17. At $\frac{7}{8}$ per bushel, how many bushels of wheat can be bought (*a*) for $1? (*b*) For $147?

18. Find the cost of 248 bushels of wheat at $87\frac{1}{2}$ cents per bushel.

19. What per cent is gained on an article (*a*) bought for $60 and sold for $80? (*b*) Bought at 40% below the list price and sold at 20% below the list price? (*c*) Bought at 25% below the list price and sold at the list price?

20. What is the difference on a bill of $100 between a discount of 40% and one of 20 and 20%?

21. In making out a check to pay for 75 shares of stock at $99 per share, Mr. Byrnes found that his balance would be $75 when the check was paid. How much had he in the bank?

22. When a dealer makes a profit of 25% by selling coffee at 30 cents a pound, what per cent would he make by selling it (*a*) for 27 cents per pound? (*b*) For 28 cents? (*c*) For 32 cents?

Written Review Problems

1. What is the cost of plowing an acre of land if one man with three horses plows 2½ acres in 9 hours, at the rate of 20 cents per hour for the man's time and 10 cents per hour for that of each horse?

2. Find the cost when four horses are used and 4 acres are plowed in 9 hours.

3. By the use of a 40-horse-power engine a farmer plows 25 acres per day of 10 hours, at an expense of 15 cents per horse power for gasoline, 40 cents per hour for one man and 20 cents per hour for another, and $4 per day for the rent of the engine. Find the cost per acre.

4. Sheets 20 in. by 28 in. were used for a tin roof. (*a*) How many square inches are covered by each sheet if 1 inch of each side is turned in ("edged") when the sheets are soldered together? (*b*) How many square inches are used in the edging? (*c*) What per cent of each sheet is lost in the edging? (*d*) To cover each 468 square inches of roof, how many square inches of tin must be bought? (*e*) What per cent of 468 square inches must be bought?

5. (*a*) Find the dimensions of the piece of screen wire that will be required to make a screen for a window 36 inches wide 66 inches high when the wood frame is 3 inches wide and the wire overlaps the frame 1 inch on all sides. (*b*) How many square feet of screen wire will be needed?

6. (*a*) Find the dimensions of the piece of screen wire needed for one half a window, the space to be screened measuring 33 in. × 36 in., the wooden frame being 3 inches wide, and the wire overlapping 1 inch on the four sides? (*b*) How many square feet are required?

7. For the frame 2 pieces of wood 33 inches long are needed, and 2 pieces 36 inches long, each 3 inches wide. (*a*) How long a board 3 inches wide must be bought if the boards come only in even feet? (*b*) How many square feet are there in the surface of such a board? (*c*) What is the cost at $3\frac{1}{2}$ ¢ per square foot of surface? (*d*) Find the cost of the wood for 24 windows. (*e*) Of the screen wire for 24 windows at 3 cents per square foot.

8. (*a*) How many superficial square feet of wood are required for the frame of a screen door 7 ft. 6 in. high and 3 ft. 4 in. wide, using two strips for the length and three cross strips, one in the center, the strips being 4 inches wide? (*b*) Find the cost at $1\frac{1}{2}$ times $3\frac{1}{2}$ cents per superficial square foot, the wood being $1\frac{1}{4}$ times as thick as that used for the window frames.

9. (*a*) Find the dimensions of each of the two openings in the door screen which remain after the frame is made. (*b*) Find the dimensions of the screen wire to cover each when it overlaps 1 inch on each side. (*c*) Find the cost of the wire at 3 ¢ per sq. ft. (*d*) Find the cost of the wire for 4 doors. (*e*) Of the wood for 4 doors.

10. The valuation of a school district is $150,000. The school tax is 5 mills on the dollar, which maintains a school of 20 pupils. What is the cost per pupil?

11. Find the cost of a hen's feed for 180 days, consisting of .174 lb. grain per day at 1 ¢ per pound, .07 lb. ground bone at 1 ¢ per pound, and .02 lb. cabbage at $6 per ton.

12. (*a*) How many hens can be accommodated in a house 12 ft. wide by 32 ft. long, if each requires 6 sq. ft. of floor space? (*b*) How many sq. ft. of window are required at the rate of 1 sq. ft. to 16 sq. ft. of floor space?

Adding Mixed Numbers

Written Exercise

1. Find the sum of $18\frac{3}{4}$, $27\frac{5}{8}$, and $9\frac{1}{4}$.

<table>
<tr><td colspan="2" align="center">PROCESS</td></tr>
<tr><td>Since $\frac{3}{4} + \frac{1}{4} = 1$, do not change these fractions to others having a common denominator.
Write the answer.</td><td>$18\frac{3}{4}$
$27\frac{5}{8}$
$9\frac{1}{4}$

$Ans.$</td></tr>
</table>

2. Write the results :

	a.	*b.*	*c.*	*d.*	*e.*
	$16\frac{3}{8}$	$56\frac{3}{7}$	$72\frac{7}{9}$	$123\frac{3}{8}$	$275\frac{5}{6}$
	$48\frac{2}{8}$	$8\frac{4}{7}$	$63\frac{2}{9}$	$84\frac{7}{12}$	$63\frac{3}{4}$
	$9\frac{5}{8}$	$35\frac{5}{8}$	$8\frac{2}{9}$	$17\frac{5}{12}$	$9\frac{1}{6}$

3. Add $4\frac{5}{7}$, $16\frac{3}{8}$, $8\frac{2}{5}$, and $37\frac{1}{8}$.

<table>
<tr><td colspan="3" align="center">PROCESS</td></tr>
<tr><td>Since $\frac{3}{8} + \frac{5}{8} = 1$, omit them in getting the common denominator. Write $+1$ as a reminder that $1\frac{4}{35}$ (the sum of the fractions) must be increased by 1.   Carry 2, therefore, to the whole numbers.</td><td>$4\frac{5}{7}$
$16\frac{3}{8}$
$8\frac{2}{5}$
$37\frac{1}{8}$</td><td>35
25
$\times$
14</td></tr>
<tr><td></td><td align="right">$Ans.$ $67\frac{4}{35}$</td><td>$\times + 1$
$\frac{44}{35} = 1\frac{4}{35}$</td></tr>
</table>

4. Find sums :

a. $63\frac{1}{2} + 8\frac{7}{8} + 35\frac{5}{9} + 5\frac{1}{2} + 23\frac{1}{8} + 16\frac{2}{9}$

b. $28\frac{2}{3} + 9\frac{3}{8} + 61\frac{5}{12} + 4\frac{1}{3} + 37\frac{3}{8} + 22\frac{7}{9}$

c. $15\frac{1}{5} + 7\frac{2}{5} + 84\frac{5}{6} + 1\frac{4}{5} + 56\frac{2}{5} + 18\frac{5}{6}$

d. $30\frac{2}{7} + 4\frac{4}{9} + 23\frac{3}{8} + 3\frac{4}{7} + 13\frac{7}{12} + 25\frac{5}{8}$

e. $50\frac{1}{4} + 6\frac{3}{8} + 75\frac{3}{10} + 7\frac{3}{4} + 42\frac{7}{10} + 14\frac{5}{8}$

5. Add $24\frac{2}{3}$, $47\frac{3}{4}$, $8\frac{1}{6}$, and $15\frac{4}{5}$.

PROCESS

60

Determine the least common denominator by inspection, when possible. Ignoring 3, which is contained in 6, think 12 as the least common multiple of 4 and 6. As 12 and 5 are prime to each other, 60. (their product) is the least common denominator.

$24\frac{2}{3}$
$47\frac{3}{4}$
$8\frac{1}{6}$
$15\frac{4}{5}$

---

6. Find sums :

a. $128\frac{2}{3} + 74\frac{3}{4} + 80\frac{5}{6} + 7\frac{3}{8} + 125\frac{5}{9}$

b. $216\frac{1}{2} + 68\frac{1}{4} + 90\frac{2}{6} + 5\frac{1}{4} + 213\frac{1}{2}$

c. $342\frac{1}{4} + 35\frac{3}{7} + 50\frac{1}{2} + 9\frac{5}{6} + 162\frac{2}{3}$

7. Add $163\frac{7}{10}$, $29\frac{8}{15}$, $7\frac{16}{33}$, and $18\frac{17}{30}$.

PROCESS

330

When the least common denominator cannot be determined by inspection, write each denominator that is not a factor of any other.

$163\frac{7}{10}$ 231

$29\frac{8}{15}$ 22   176

3)30 — 33

10 — 11

3 × 10 × 11 = 330

In this case omit 10 and 15, since they are factors of 30.

$7\frac{16}{33}$

$18\frac{17}{30}$ 187

Ans.

Divide 30 and 33 (the remaining ones) by 3, which is a factor of each. Since 10 and 11, the quotients, are prime to each other, the least common denominator is the continued product of the divisor and the quotients.

In changing the given fractions to 330ths, write the quotient of the latter by a denominator in the first column when necessary, and then write in the second column its product by the numerator.

---

8. Find sums :

a. $26\frac{3}{4} + 9\frac{4}{7} + 8\frac{5}{21} + 10\frac{8}{15}$ *b.* $1\frac{3}{8} + 3\frac{11}{12} + 5\frac{7}{18} + 9\frac{13}{24}$

Subtracting Mixed Numbers

Written Exercises

1. From $135\frac{18}{18}$ take (a) $89\frac{11}{12}$; (b) $77\frac{9}{10}$.

PROCESS

$$
\begin{array}{cc}
 & 36 \\
(a)\quad 135\frac{11}{18} & \boxed{26}\ 62 \\
89\frac{11}{12} & 33 \\
\hline
Ans.\ 45\frac{11}{18} & \frac{11}{18}
\end{array}
$$

(a) Since $\frac{11}{18}$ is greater than $\frac{11}{12}$, the latter is increased by 1, or $\frac{11}{18}$, the sum of 26 and 36 being written alongside.

$$
\begin{array}{cc}
 & 90 \\
(b)\quad 135\frac{11}{18} & \boxed{65}\ 155 \\
77\frac{9}{10} & 81 \\
\hline
Ans.\ 57\frac{11}{18} & \frac{74}{90} = \frac{11}{18}
\end{array}
$$

In (a) an accountant would deduct $\frac{11}{12}$ from $1\frac{11}{18}$ by taking $\frac{11}{12}$ from 1 and adding the remainder, $\frac{1}{18}$, to $\frac{11}{18}$. In (b) he would take 81 from 90 and add 65 to the remainder.

$$36 + 26 - 33 = 36 - 33 + 26$$
$$90 + 65 - 81 = 90 - 81 + 65$$

2. Find remainders:

$a.\quad 236\frac{1}{4}$	$b.\quad 375\frac{2}{3}$	$c.\quad 821\frac{3}{8}$	$d.\quad 672\frac{1}{6}$
$-112\frac{5}{6}$	$-246\frac{5}{8}$	$-179\frac{3}{4}$	$-317\frac{7}{12}$
$e.\quad 300\frac{2}{3}$	$f.\quad 314\frac{5}{6}$	$g.\quad 470\frac{1}{4}$	$h.\quad 239\frac{7}{12}$
$-106\frac{9}{10}$	$-175\frac{7}{9}$	$-206\frac{3}{5}$	$-189\frac{5}{6}$

Decimals — Multiplication

To multiply a decimal by 10, 100, 1000, move the decimal point one, two, three places.

Sight Exercises

Give products:

$a.\ 1.4 \times 10$	$b.\ .12 \times 100$	$c.\ .011 \times 1000$	$d.\ 1.3 \times 300$
$e.\ 1.4 \times 20$	$f.\ .12 \times 200$	$g.\ .011 \times 2000$	$h.\ 2.2 \times 400$
$i.\ 1.4 \times 30$	$j.\ .12 \times 300$	$k.\ .011 \times 3000$	$l.\ 1.1 \times 500$
$m.\ 1.2 \times 40$	$n.\ .12 \times 400$	$o.\ .022 \times 4000$	$p.\ 3.2 \times 200$
$q.\ 1.1 \times 50$	$r.\ .11 \times 500$	$s.\ .011 \times 5000$	$t.\ 4.5 \times 100$

Written Exercises

1. Multiply 84.635 (*a*) by 20.   (*b*) By 400.

PROCESS

(*a*) 846.35
   × 2
———————
1692.7Ø *Ans.*

In (*a*) multiply 84.635 by 10 by moving the decimal point one place to the the right, and in (*b*) multiply it by 100 by moving the decimal point two places to the right. Multiply the changed multiplicands by 2 and by 4, respectively.

(*b*) 8463.5
   × 4
———————
33854.Ø *Ans.*

---

2. Write products from the book:

a. 30 × 28.74   *b.* 600 × 1.487   *c.* 7000 × .2468

d. 40 × 3.465   *e.* 700 × 24.63   *f.* 8000 × 1.357

g. 60 × .1248   *h.* 800 × .1845   *i.* 9000 × 23.45

3. Multiply 87.4 (*a*) by 2.5.   (*b*) By 12.5.

PROCESS

Some accountants prefer to change 2.5 and 12.5 to .25 and .125, respectively.

(*a*) 874
  × .25
————

In (*a*) move the decimal point one place to the right in the multiplicand and one place to the left in the multiplier. In (*b*)

(*b*) 8740
  × .125
————

move it two places to the right in the former and two places to the left in the latter. In (*a*) divide by 4; in (*b*) by 8.

---

4. Find answers :

a. 310.48 × 2.5   *b.* 620.96 × 1.25   *c.* 36 + 1.25

d. 412.96 × .25   *e.* 715.76 × 12.5   *f.* 42 + 12.5

g. 514.32 × 25   *h.* 844.32 × 125   *i.* 84 + 12.5

5. Multiply :

Change multipliers to .75 or .875, then deduct $\frac{1}{4}$ or $\frac{1}{8}$.

a. 10.48 × 7.5   *b.* 12.96 × 8.75   *c.* 14.32 × 87.5

d. 12.96 × 7.5   *e.* 14.32 × 8.75   *f.* 10.48 × 87.5

Adding and Subtracting

Write only the answers:

1. Find the balances in the following cash accounts:

a. $ 374.80	b. $ 1234.56	c. $ 817.74	d. $8.47
97.25	683.59	3256.75	8.47
583.84	88.47	392.48	8.47
1247.56	205.68	176.69	8.47
185.13	1542.80	2216.45	8.47
?	?	?	?
$3247.58	$4000.00	$7123.18	$50.00

Multiplying and Subtracting

2. How much less than $50 will be the cost of 5 coats at $8.47 each?

PROCESS

$50 − 5 times $8.47 = $7.65. Think 35 (5 × 7) and 5 (writing 5) are 40. Think 20 (5 × 4), 24 (carrying 4) and 6 (writing 6) are 30. Think 40 (5 × 8), 43 (carrying 3) and 7 (writing 7) are 50.

NOTE. Use the word "and" only in connection with the remainder that is to be written.

3. Write answers:

a. 896 − (9 × 97)　　b. 650 − (7 × 89)　　c. 737 − (8 × 85)

d. 528 − (6 × 83)　　e. 400 − (5 × 69)　　f. 617 − (6 × 98)

4. Change $\frac{5000}{847}$ to a mixed number.

PROCESS

$\frac{5000}{847} = 5\frac{???}{847}$　　Write 5 as the whole number and 847 as the denominator of the fraction. Think 35(5 × 7) and 5 (writing 5) are 40; etc.

---

5. Write as mixed numbers:

a. $\frac{896}{97}$ b. $\frac{650}{89}$ c. $\frac{787}{85}$ d. $\frac{528}{83}$

e. $\frac{245}{82}$ f. $\frac{298}{37}$ g. $\frac{175}{23}$ h. $\frac{791}{92}$

i. $\frac{202}{35}$ j. $\frac{252}{37}$ k. $\frac{641}{84}$ l. $\frac{145}{19}$

m. $\frac{134}{15}$ n. $\frac{196}{25}$ o. $\frac{147}{22}$ p. $\frac{148}{29}$

6. What is the cost of 5 coats at \$8.47 each and a shawl at \$7.65?

PROCESS

$(\$8.47 \times 5) + \$7.65 = \$50.00$ *Ans.*

Think 35 (5×7), 40 (adding in 5); write 0. Think 20 (5×4), 24 (carrying 4), 30 (adding in 6); write 0. Think 40 (5×8), 43 (carrying 3), 50 (adding in 9); write 50.

---

7. Give answers :

a. $23 + (8 \times 28)$ b. $(9 \times 56) + 27$ c. $53 + (7 \times 84)$

d. $(6 \times 57) + 35$ e. $69 + (5 \times 74)$ f. $(4 \times 84) + 37$

g. $27 + (5 \times 35)$ h. $(6 \times 37) + 30$ i. $19 + (7 \times 12)$

j. $(8 \times 32) + 31$ k. $16 + (9 \times 15)$ l. $(8 \times 15) + 14$

8. Change $5\frac{785}{847}$ to an improper fraction.

PROCESS

$5\frac{785}{847} = \frac{4020}{847}$ Write 847 as the denominator. Find the numerator by thinking 35 (5×7), 40 (adding in 5); write 0; etc.

---

9. Write as improper fractions :

a. $8\frac{23}{28}$ b. $9\frac{27}{56}$ c. $7\frac{18}{84}$ d. $6\frac{85}{57}$ e. $5\frac{69}{74}$

f. $8\frac{27}{41}$ g. $6\frac{18}{37}$ h. $9\frac{15}{23}$ i. $7\frac{18}{39}$ j. $5\frac{18}{47}$

k. $5\frac{27}{35}$ l. $6\frac{30}{37}$ m. $7\frac{12}{19}$ n. $8\frac{31}{32}$ o. $9\frac{15}{16}$

p. $8\frac{14}{15}$ q. $7\frac{21}{25}$ r. $6\frac{15}{22}$ s. $5\frac{24}{25}$ t. $4\frac{27}{29}$

Abbreviated Division

10. A farmer raised 5280 bushels of corn on 83 acres. Find the average yield to the acre.

```
                    PROCESS
Ans. 63¹³⁄₈₃ bu.    Do not write the partial products.
83)5280 bu.         Think 18 (6 × 3) and 0 (writing 0) are 18.
   300              Think 48 (6 × 8) 49 (carrying 1) and 3 (writ-
    51              ing 3) are 52.  To 30 (the first remainder)
                    add 0, making 300 the second partial divi-
dend.  Proceed as before.
```

11. Divide without writing the partial products:

a. 8960 ÷ 97	b. 2931 ÷ 37	c. 4500 ÷ 39
d. 6507 ÷ 89	e. 1756 ÷ 23	f. 4718 ÷ 53

Lowest Terms

12. A tract containing 232 acres was sold for $2871. What was the price per acre?

```
                    PROCESS
$2871⁄232 = $12⁴⁷⁄₂₃₂.  To ascertain the possibility of ex-   87 | 232
pressing the fraction in lower terms, divide 232 by 87.       29 |  58
Omit the quotient figure, 2, but subtract 2 × 87 from 232,
which gives 58 as the remainder.  Divide 87 by 58, which gives 29
as the remainder.  Divide 58 by 29.  Since this leaves no re-
mainder, 29 is the greatest common divisor.  Divide both terms of
the fraction by 29.
```

13. Divide. Find answers in mixed numbers with fractions expressed in lowest terms. Use as few figures as possible.

a. 899 ÷ 203	b. 1231 ÷ 187	c. 2035 ÷ 176
d. 549 ÷ 204	e. 1961 ÷ 444	f. 2329 ÷ 221

Graphs

Numbers, which are usually represented by figures and by words, are sometimes represented by *lines*, especially to enable an interested person to compare at a glance relative quantities, or to determine the nature of numerical changes.

They are used to compare the population of different countries, their exports and imports, temperature, rainfall, etc. A general name for an illustration of this kind is a *graph*.

The accompanying graph shows the quantity of various kinds of grain received by rail during a month, as follows :

Corn 7810 bu.	Rye 6230 bu.	Barley 1475 bu.
Wheat 7250 bu.	Oats 4315 bu.	Buckwheat 420 bu.

each space representing 1000 bushels. Lighter lines are sometimes inserted to show each hundred.

RECEIPTS OF GRAIN DURING MAY, 1914

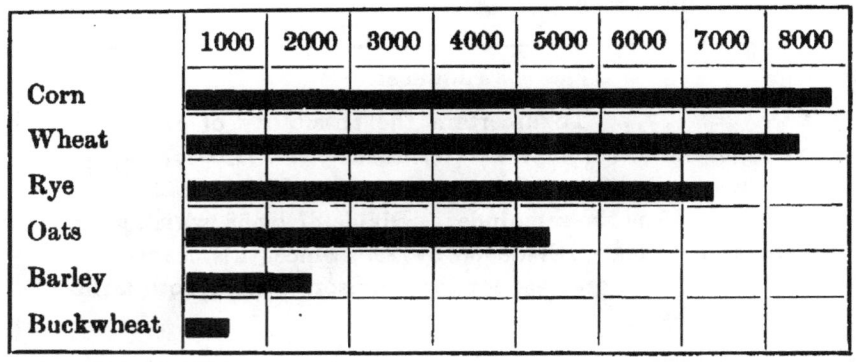

1. Make a similar graph to show the comparative number of pupils in the following grades :

1st	345	4th	200	7th	110
2d	290	5th	170	8th	100
3d	250	6th	150		

Cross-ruled Paper

To save the time required to rule the necessary lines, cross-ruled paper is much used in making diagrams, graphs, etc. The paper is divided into squares of equal size by faint lines $\frac{1}{4}$ in. apart, $\frac{1}{8}$ in., etc. Some forms employ a darker line to denote every tenth one, as an additional help.

The use of this "squared" paper is shown in the following graph, which indicates the changes in the number of passengers carried by a trolley line during each hour of the twenty-four.

PASSENGERS CARRIED, MAY 25, 1916

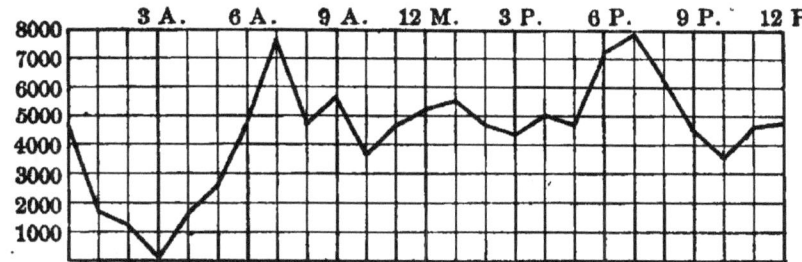

The number of passengers indicated by the foregoing diagram was as follows for each hour:

	12–1, 1550;	4–5, 2750;	8–9, 5600
	1–2, 1230;	5–6, 4800;	9–10, 3790
A.M.	2–3, 475;	6–7, 7925;	10–11, 4900
	3–4, 1880;	7–8, 4710;	11–12, 5300
	12–1, 5600;	4–5, 4900;	8–9, 4550
	1–2, 4810;	5–6, 7200;	9–10, 3800
P.M.	2–3, 4190;	6–7, 7900;	10–11, 4890
	3–4, 5005;	7–8, 6220;	11–12, 4920

Written Exercises

1. Find the number carried (*a*) before noon. (*b*) From noon to midnight. (*c*) All day.

2. On squared paper make a graph to show the changes in temperature indicated by the following record for July 28, 1915.

12 P.M. — 71	6 A.M. — 71	12 M. — 75	6 P.M. — 74
1 A.M. — 70	7 A.M. — 71	1 P.M. — 76	7 P.M. — 73
2 A.M. — 68	8 A.M. — 72	2 P.M. — 78	8 P.M. — 71
3 A.M. — 68	9 A.M. — 74	3 P.M. — 79	9 P.M. — 71
4 A.M. — 68	10 A.M. — 71	4 P.M. — 79	10 P.M. — 72
5 A.M. — 69	11 A.M. — 73	5 P.M. — 77	11 P.M. — 74

TEMPERATURE, JULY 28, 1915

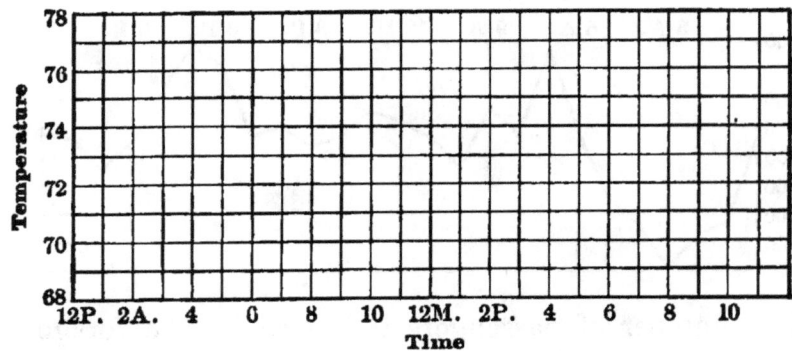

3. Make a graph showing the changes in the average weight of boys at the different ages given in the problem on page 294. On the same paper make a corresponding graph for girls. For the latter use a broken line or ink of a different color.

4. Make a graph showing the changes in the average attendance for the following months:

Sept. 600	Oct. 595	Nov. 605	Dec. 595	Jan. 590
Feb. 595	Mar. 585	Apr. 565	May 570	June 560

Solving Problems by Graphs

A drawing is frequently of great assistance in showing more clearly the conditions involved in a problem; in some types, the graph supplies the answer at sight.

Graphic Solutions

1. A train leaves W at 1 P.M. and travels 30 miles per hour. At 3 P.M. another train leaves W, going at the rate of 40 miles per hour. At what time will the latter train overtake the other?

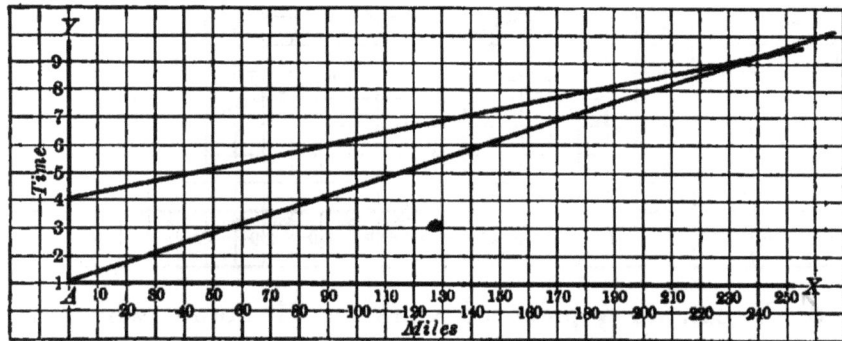

On cross-ruled paper draw AY perpendicular to AX; these lines are called the *axes*. On the axis of X denote the distance of each space from A, taking 10 miles as a convenient unit. On the axis of Y mark the hours beginning at A with 1 o'clock (the starting time of the first train).

Since the first train goes 30 miles per hour, at 2 o'clock it will be 30 miles from A; draw, therefore, a line from A through the point of intersection of the 2 o'clock line with the 30-mile line, and prolong it indefinitely.

For the second train the line begins at 3 on the axis of Y. As it goes 40 miles per hour, at 4 o'clock it will be 40 miles from A. Draw the line, therefore, through the intersection of the 4 o'clock line with the 40-mile line, and prolong it until it intersects the line of the first train. This it does at the intersection of the 9 o'clock line with the 240-mile one. The interpretation is that the trains will be together at 9 o'clock, and at a point 240 miles from A.

TEST. Train 1 travels 8 hours at 30 miles per hour, or 240 miles; train 2 travels 6 hours at 40 miles per hour, or 240 miles.

2. Two trains leave points 315 miles apart, and travel towards each other. One leaves at 3 o'clock and goes at the rate of 30 miles per hour. The other leaves at 6 o'clock and goes at the rate of 45 miles per hour. (*a*) At what time will they meet? (*b*) How far does each travel to the meeting place?

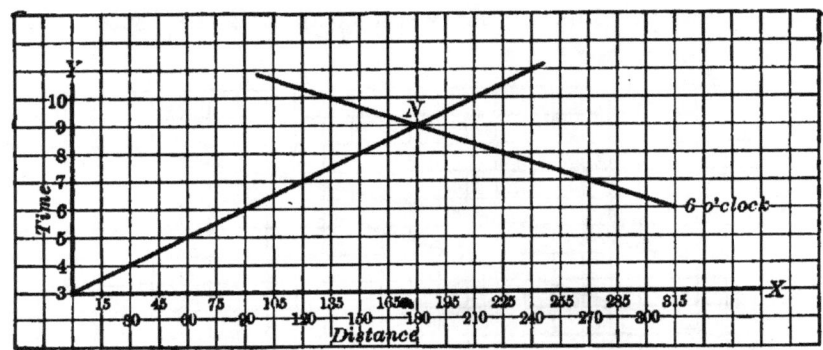

3. V can do a piece of work in 21 hours, which W takes 28 hours to do. In how many hours can both together do it? (See graph below.)

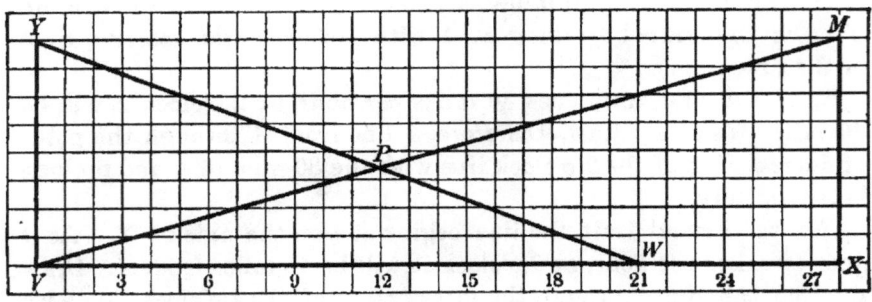

Let *VX* represent 28 hours, and *VY* (of any length) represent the work. Make *XM* of the same length as *VY*. Draw *VM* for *V* working alone and *WY* for *W* working alone. What time is indicated by the intersection at *P*?

4. Draw a horizontal line of any length to indicate the *work*. At one extremity draw a perpendicular 21 divisions long to represent the time required by V; and at the other a perpendicular 28 divisions long to represent the time required by W. From V and W draw lines to the opposite ends of the horizontal line. (*a*) What number of hours corresponds with the point of intersection? (*b*) How many divisions of the horizontal line indicate the portion of the work done by V? (*c*) Done by W?

Use as the length of the horizontal line any multiple of the G. C. D. of 21 and 28 for the number of its divisions : 7 or 21, for instance.

5. Ascertain by a graph how long it would require a boy on a bicycle going 10 miles per hour to overtake a man traveling in a buggy at the rate of 6 miles per hour and who has a start of 12 miles?

6. E and F can paint a house in 12 days which would require 30 days for E to do working alone. How long would F take to paint it by himself?

Using the same letters as in problem 3, make VX 30 spaces long and VY and MX equal to each other and of any convenient length. Draw MV. At 12 spaces from V erect a perpendicular. Through P, its intersection with VM, draw YB. How many spaces from V is the point B?

7. Find the point at which a train leaving 3 hours later and traveling 10 miles faster per hour will overtake one going at an average speed of 30 miles per hour.

SECTION VI

LENDING AND BORROWING MONEY

Investing One's Savings

A person can increase his income by means of the money earned by loaning his savings. While waiting for these to grow to a sum sufficiently large to be invested in a different way, the owner should deposit them in a savings bank. Here they are combined with the savings of many others to make a large total, a portion of which is put out at interest by the officers of the bank, and the remainder retained to be paid over to those wishing to withdraw all or a part of their accounts.

At stated times, generally at the end of the year, the officers of the bank calculate the profits and determine the rate of interest to be paid on sums in the bank at the end of the period, and which have remained on deposit for six months or a year.

The interest is obtainable in cash, or may be entered on the depositor's book and treated as a regular deposit on which interest is payable at the end of the next term.

Net profits not distributed as interest are placed among the funds of the bank to be invested for the benefit of the depositors.

Interest. — Money paid for the use of money is called *interest*. The sum loaned is the *principal*. The per cent of the principal paid for a year's interest is called the *rate*.

The total of the principal and the interest is called the *amount*.

Sight Exercises

1. Give the yearly interest at 4% on

a. $100 *b.* $200 *c.* $300 *d.* $400 *e.* $500 *f.* $150

2. At 4% per year, what per cent of the principal is the interest for ½ year?

3. Give the interest for 6 months at 4% per year on

a. $180 *b.* $270 *c.* $360 *d.* $450 *e.* $540 *f.* $154

4. The interest on $400 for ½ year is equal to the interest on what for 1 year when the rate is the same?

5. Give the interest for ½ year at 3½% on

a. $200 *b.* $400 *c.* $800 *d.* $120 *e.* $240 *f.* $600

Bonds

A person can lend money to a city, a county, a railroad, or any other corporation, by purchasing one or more of its *bonds*. These are issued for different sums; $100, $500, $1000, etc. Each is a kind of mortgage on the property of the corporation for the sum specified on its face, and also for the interest payments.

One who has too little money to put into a mortgage, or who prefers the greater security of a city bond, may buy one representing a loan as small as $10.

The inexperienced investor should not loan his money without disinterested advice. This can usually be obtained without cost from the president of the bank in which he is a depositor.

While the face value of a bond specifies the sum payable by the maker at maturity, the purchaser of a $100 bond may obtain it for $90 or less, or may have to pay $120 or more for it, depending upon the rate of interest payable, the time of its maturity, etc.

Written Problems

1. (*a*) At 5%, how much interest does the owner of a $100 bond receive in 20 years? (*b*) If the bond is paid at the end of 20 years, how much does the owner receive in principal and interest? (*c*) If the bond cost him $110, how much did he gain in 20 years? (*d*) What was his average yearly gain?

2. When $4.50 is the annual interest on $110, what is the rate?

3. (*a*) Find the interest on a 3% twenty-year bond for $100. (*b*) Find the amount, including the face of the bond. (*c*) Find the gain in the 20 years if the bond cost $90. (*d*) Find the average yearly gain.

4. At what rate will $90 yield $3.50 annual interest?

Loans on Real Estate

The prudent lender always requires security for the return of the money loaned and the interest. When he lends to the owner of a house, of a farm, or of other real estate, he first satisfies himself as to the value of the property, limiting the loan to, say, 60% thereof.

Mortgages and Deeds of Trust

When he is satisfied that the loan can safely be made, he obtains a written document, called a mortgage, signed by the owner, in which the latter agrees to a sale of the property in case of failure to pay any interest installment when due, or the face of the loan at the stated time. The owner also guarantees to keep the buildings insured and in repair, to pay taxes as they become due, etc.

A *deed of trust* is a form of mortgage.

Interest

Preparatory Exercises

1. Write from the book the interest for 1 year at 4 % on

a. $1296   *b.* $2345   *c.* $375.50   *d.* $87.25
e. $1475   *f.* $3640   *g.* $493.75   *h.* $47.50

2. Mr. Beck borrows $6540 at 6 %. How much interest does he pay in 3 yr. 6 mo. ?

```
ONE METHOD

$6540   Principal                    The interest for 1
  .06   Rate (in hundredths)       yr. may be found by
392.40  Interest for 1 yr.          multiplying $6540
     3½ Time (in years)             (the principal) by
          etc.                      .06 (the rate in
                                    hundredths), and
this result by 3½(the time in years). A shorter method in this case
is to multiply .06 by 3½ and to multiply $6540 by their product.
```

3. What is the interest on $354.60 at 4 % (*a*) for $1\frac{1}{2}$ yr.? (*b*) For $2\frac{1}{4}$ yr.? (*c*) For 5 yr.? (*d*) For $\frac{3}{4}$ yr.?

```
PROCESS

a.  $354.60 × .04 × 1½ = $354.60 × .06
b.  $354.60 × .04 × 2¼ = $354.60 × .09
c.  $354.60 × .04 × 5  = $354.60 × .2
d.  $354.60 × .04 × ¾  = $354.60 × .03

Write the answers directly from the book.
```

4. Write from the book the interest at 4 % on

a. $350 for 2 yr.   *b.* $34.50 for 180 da.   *c.* $64 for 90 da.
d. $475 for 3 yr.   *e.* $43.75 for 270 da.   *f.* $88 for 45 da.

Written Exercises

1. Mrs. Conklin loans $378 at 6%. How much should she receive in payment of the loan with interest, at the expiration of (*a*) 2 mo. 20 da. ? (*b*) 2 yr. 4 mo. 20 da. ?

$$
\boxed{
\begin{array}{ll}
\text{PROCESS} \\
(a)\quad \dfrac{\$378 \times .06 \times 80}{360} \qquad\qquad (b)\quad \dfrac{\$378 \times .06 \times 680}{360}
\end{array}
}
$$

Time in (*b*), 2 yr. 4 mo. 20 da. = 720 da. + 120 da. + 20 da. = 860 da.

2. Find the amount of $456 at 6% for

a. 1 mo. 20 da.	*b.* 184 da.	*c.* 1 yr. 3 mo. 20 da.
d. 2 mo. 10 da.	*e.* 248 da.	*f.* 2 yr. 1 mo. 18 da.

3. Find the interest on

a. $387.80 at 5% for 80 da.   *b.* $450 at 6% for 1 yr. 20 da.

c. $498.75 at 4% for 72 da.   *d.* $370 at 3% for 2 mo. 18 da.

Sight Exercises

1. Give the interest for 1 year at 4% on

a. $300   *b.* $12   *c.* $312   *d.* $125   *e.* $12.50

2. Give the interest at 4% on

a. $300 for 2 yr.   *b.* $200 for $\frac{1}{2}$ yr.   *c.* $100 for 6 mo.

3. Give the interest for 1 year on

      a. $300 at 6%   *b.* $400 at 4%

      c. $250 at 6%   *d.* $200 at $4\frac{1}{2}$%

4. Give the interest on $100 at 6% for

a. 1 yr. 6 mo.   *b.* 11 mo.   *c.* $4\frac{1}{2}$ yr.   *d.* 2 yr. 9 mo.

5. Give the interest for 1 day on

a. $90 at 4%   *b.* $72 at 5%   *c.* $120 at 3%   *d.* $180 at 4%

Interest-bearing Notes

Money is frequently loaned to a responsible person without further security than his mere promise to pay. The latter is generally given in writing in the form of a note.

A Time Note

A note contains as a rule (*a*) the date on which it is made, (*b*) the length of time it has to run, (*c*) the person to whom it is payable (the *payee*), (*d*) the sum to be paid exclusive of interest, (*e*) the place of payment, (*f*) the rate of interest, and (*g*) the signature of the *maker*.

Some notes do not specify a time for their payment. The following is one form.

A Demand Note

FARGO, N.D., *July 8*, 19*12*

On demand after date I promise to pay to the

order of *Charles Erbrecht*

Seven Hundred $\frac{00}{100}$ ~~~~~~~~~~~~~~~Dollars

at *416 Tenth Av.*

Value received, with interest *at 5* %

$ 700 $\frac{00}{100}$ *James J. Donohue*

Written Exercises

1. Find the amount due on the foregoing note May 3, 1916, in case no interest payments are made after July 8, 1913.

The time from the last interest payment, July 8, 1913, to May 3, 1916, is found by compound subtraction to be 2 yr. 9 mo. 25 da., or 1015 da.

2. Find the interest on :

a. $375 at 4% from Dec. 4, 1913 to May 6, 1915.

b. $480 at 5% from Oct. 7, 1912 to Aug. 10, 1915.

c. $560 at 6% from Aug. 10, 1913 to Oct. 5, 1915.

3. William Johnson buys a house for $3000, paying $600 in cash and giving a mortgage for the remainder, in which he agrees to pay $100 monthly, together with 6% interest on the monthly balances. How much does he pay in six months?

PROCESS

1st month $100 + $\frac{1}{2}$% of $2400 = $112

2d month $100 + $\frac{1}{2}$% of $2300 = ?

3d month $100 + $\frac{1}{2}$% of $2200 = ?

---

4. If he merely agrees to pay $100 per month, how much would Mr. Johnson owe after making six monthly payments of $100 each?

PROCESS

Principal	$2400
Int., 1st month	12
Amount at end of 1st mo.	$2412
1st Payment	100
Balance at end of 1st mo.	$2312
Int., 2d month	11.56
Amount at end of 2d mo.	$2323.56
2d Payment	100
Balance at end of 2d mo.	$2223.56

etc.

Indorsement of Payments

Anything written on the back of a document is an indorsement, whether it be the name of the payee or of a guarantor, or the acknowledgment of the receipt of money paid as interest or as a part of the principal.

To avoid a dispute in the case of the transfer of the note, the maker should see that each interest payment is indorsed on the note. The signature of the payee is not essential, it being assumed that the note remains in his possession.

Written Exercise

1. On June 1, 1914, John C. Maguire gives his note for $1200, payable on demand with interest at 6%. The following payments are indorsed on the note:

> Aug. 1, 1914, $100; Oct. 1, 1914, $100
> Dec. 1, 1914, $100; Feb. 1, 1915, $100

How much is due Apr. 1, 1915?

```
                    PROCESS
Face of note                                  $1200.00
Interest, June 1, 1914 to Aug. 1, 1914           12.00
Amount, Aug. 1, 1914                          $1212.00
Payment, Aug. 1, 1914                            100.00
Balance, Aug. 1, 1914                         $1112.00
Interest, Aug. 1, 1914 to Oct. 1, 1914           11.12
Amount, Oct. 1, 1914                          $1123.12
Payment, Oct. 1, 1914                            100.00
Balance, Oct. 1, 1914                         $1023.12
                      etc.
```

In ascertaining the time between successive payments on a note, each month is taken as $\frac{1}{12}$ yr.

Interest Tables

Clerks obliged to make numerous interest calculations use a book of tables. One style contains 360 pages, each giving the interest at various rates on specified amounts for the number of days stated at the top of the page. The accompanying table shows a portion of the page that gives the interest for 168 days.

168 Days

Principal	5%	6%	7%
1000	23.333	28.00	32.667
1100	25.667	30.80	35.933
1200	28.00	33.60	39.20
1300	30.333	36.40	42.467
1400	32.667	39.20	45.733
1500	35.00	42.00	49.00
1600	37.333	44.80	52.267
1700	39.667	47.60	55.533
1800	42.00	50.40	58.80
1900	44.333	53.20	62.067
2000	46.667	56.00	65.333

In using this portion of the table find the interest of $250 for 168 da. at 5% by taking one fourth the interest of $1000; the interest at 3% by taking one half the interest at 6%; the interest for 56 days by taking one third the interest for 168 days.

Sight Exercises

1. Give the principal that will yield in 168 days the interest yielded by

a. $4000 in 42 da. *b.* $8800 in 21 da. *c.* $7200 in 28 da.
d. $3000 in 84 da. *e.* $4800 in 56 da. *f.* $8400 in 24 da.

2. Using the table write only the answers to the following:

Give the interest on

a. $4000 for 42 da., at 5%   *b.* $4800 for 56 da., at 6%
c. $3000 for 84 da., at 6%   *d.* $7200 for 28 da., at 7%

Interest on Bank Loans

Written Exercises

1. Mr. Rorke borrows $475 from a bank Oct. 22, 1914. How much is required to pay the loan March 15, 1915, with interest at 5 %?

2. Find the interest on

a. $1230, at 4 %, from Jan. 15, 1914 to March 18, 1914
b. $2175, at 5 %, from Dec. 22, 1913 to April 14, 1914
c. $3260, at 6 %, from Aug. 17, 1915 to Jan. 10, 1916

For periods less than a year banks calculate interest for the exact number of days, generally considering the year to consist of 360 days in collecting interest and of 365 days in making interest payments.

A table in some such form as the following is used to ascertain the time between two dates that are not more than a year apart.

DATE TABLE

	JAN.	FEB.	MAR.	APR.	MAY	JUNE	JULY	AUG.	SEPT.	OCT.	NOV.	DEC.
Jan.	365	31	59	90	120	151	181	212	243	273	304	334
Feb.	334	365	28	59	89	120	150	181	212	242	273	303
March	306	337	365	31	61	92	122	153	184	214	245	275
April	275	306	334	365	30	61	91	122	153	183	214	244
May	245	276	304	335	365	31	61	92	123	153	184	214
June	214	245	273	304	335	365	30	61	92	122	153	183
July	184	215	243	274	304	335	365	31	62	92	123	153
Aug.	153	184	212	243	273	304	334	365	31	61	92	122
Sept.	122	153	181	212	243	273	303	334	365	30	61	91
Oct.	92	123	151	182	212	243	273	304	335	365	31	61
Nov.	61	92	120	151	181	212	242	273	304	334	365	30
Dec.	31	62	96	121	151	182	212	243	274	304	335	365

How to use the Table

To find the time from Sept. 3, 1914 to March 5, 1915, take the number at the intersection of the September line and the March column (181) which gives the number of days from Sept. 3 to March 3. To this add 2 days, the time from March 3 to March 5. *Ans.* 183 da.

The time from June 18, 1914 to Dec. 2, 1914 is found by taking the number at the intersection of the June line with the December column, 183 days (which is the time from June 18 to Dec. 18), and deducting 16 days (the time between Dec. 2 and Dec. 18), which gives 167 days as the result.

The time from Nov. 20, 1915 to May 3, 1916 is 181 da. — 17 da. + 1 da., this last being added for the extra day in February of a leap year. *Ans.* 165 da.

Sight Exercises

1. Give the number of days from

    a. Jan. 16, 1914 to March 21, 1914
    b. Dec. 20, 1913 to April 16, 1914
    c. Aug. 10, 1915 to Jan. 15, 1916
    d. April 20, 1914 to Dec. 12, 1914
    e. Feb. 12, 1916 to Dec. 24, 1916
    f. Sept. 15, 1915 to March 18, 1916

2. Give the interest on $900 at 4 % to Jan. 4, 1916 from

    a. Feb. 4, 1915   *b.* Aug. 4, 1915
    c. March 1, 1915   *d.* Nov. 1, 1915

3. Give the amount of $600 borrowed July 1, 1916, and paid with interest at 6 %.

    a. Feb. 1, 1917   *b.* March 2, 1917
    c. April 3, 1917   *d.* May 4, 1917

Written Exercises

1. Mr. Somers borrowed $3700 from the First National Bank Oct. 17, 1914. What sum will be required to repay it Jan. 9, 1915, with interest at 5 %?

PROCESS

The time is 84 days. From the table the interest for 168 days

on $2000 is	$46.667
on $1700 is	39.667

which gives the interest on $3400 for 168 da. as $86.334

Interest for 84 da. is ½ of that for 168 da.

---

2. Find the interest on

  a. $2000 for 168 da., at 3 %
  b. $3500 for 168 da., at 5 %
  c. $1500 for 84 da., at 7 %
  d. $2700 for 84 da., at 6 %
  e. $1800 for 168 da., at 3½ %
  f. $3300 for 42 da., at 6 %
  g. $1200 for 42 da., at 5 %
  h. $2900 for 21 da., at 2½ %
  i. $1500 for 168 da., at 2½ %
  j. $2600 for 91 da., at 7 %

3. Find the amount of

  a. $4000 from Jan. 2, 1915 to June 19, 1915 at 6 %
  b. $4800 from Feb. 1, 1916 to Mch. 14, 1916 at 5 %
  c. $3500 from Nov. 8, 1916 to Oct. 10, 1917 at 3½ %
  d. $2700 from May 7, 1915 to Dec. 3, 1915 at 3 %
  e. $1200 from Apr. 8, 1916 to Mch. 10, 1917 at 6 %

Sight Review Problems

1. If a street is a mile long and 60 feet wide, how many miles must a watering cart travel to sprinkle it, if the cart sprinkles a strip 15 feet wide?

2. How many miles must be traveled by a steam roller 8 feet wide, in order to roll a road 40 feet wide and a mile long, three times?

3. One boat's crew rows 30 strokes per minute and travels 24 feet each stroke, another rows 29 strokes per minute and travels 25 feet at each stroke. How much farther does one go in a minute than the other?

4. If a man obtains 5 sixths of the cost of an article when he sells it for $20, what must he charge for it to obtain 7 sixths of the cost?

5. At 99 cents each, how many baseballs can be bought for $24, and how much money will be left?

6. When 11 tenths of the cost of an article is $66, what is 12 tenths of its cost?

7. A train going 30 miles per hour requires 4 hours to make a trip. How many more miles per hour must it travel to make the trip in 1 hour less?

8. If 5 men dig a ditch 60 feet long in 10 days, how many days would it require 10 men to dig a ditch 30 feet long?

9. At $7\frac{1}{2}$ gallons to the cubic foot, find the capacity in gallons of a tank 5 feet long, 4 feet wide, 2 feet deep.

10. A can copy 15 pages in 3 hours and B can copy 15 pages in 5 hours; (*a*) how many pages can both together copy in 1 hour? (*b*) In what time can both together copy 40 pages?

Written Review Problems

1. A road is 45 feet wide. How many miles of it can be sprinkled in 10 hours by a water wagon traveling at the rate of $2\frac{1}{2}$ miles per hour, if the wagon sprinkles a strip 15 feet wide?

2. If a road is 48 feet wide, how long a strip can be rolled 3 times in 10 hours by a steam roller 8 feet wide moving at the rate of 2 miles per hour?

3. One boat's crew rows 33 strokes per minute and travels 29 feet per stroke; another rows 34 strokes per minute and travels 28 feet per stroke. If they are together at the start of a race, how far apart are they in 6 minutes?

4. If a man loses $16\frac{2}{3}\%$ when he sells an article for $47.50, what price should he receive for it to gain $16\frac{2}{3}\%$?

5. Taking a meter as 39.37 inches, find the number of pieces 1 meter long that can be cut from 20 yards of tape, and the number of inches remaining.

6. If 10% is gained by selling furniture for $171.60, what should be the selling price to make the profit 20%?

7. A steamer traveling 11 miles per hour takes $19\frac{1}{2}$ days to make a voyage. At what rate must it travel to make the voyage in 3 days fewer?

8. If 5 men can dig a ditch 60 feet long in 16 days, how many could dig 45 feet of the same ditch in 10 days?

9. At 231 cu. in. to the gallon, find the number of gallons that will fill a tank 4 ft. 1 in. long, 3 ft. 8 in. wide, and 2 ft. 6 in. deep.

10. A can copy $37\frac{1}{2}$ pages in $7\frac{1}{2}$ hours, and B can copy $13\frac{1}{2}$ pages in $4\frac{1}{2}$ hours; in what time can A and B together copy 280 pages?

To find the Principal, the Rate, or the Time

Sight Exercises

1. Mr. Jones receives $20 a year interest on money lent Mr. Brown at 5 %. How much did he lend?

2. Give the *principal* that will yield in 1 year at 5 %

    a. $20   *b.* $1.20   *c.* $24   *d.* $115   *e.* $.50

3. Give the *principal* that in 1 year will yield

    a. $20 at 4 %   *b.* $1.20 at 3 %   *c.* $4 at 5 %

4. Give the *principal* that at 4 % will yield

    a. $20 in 2 yr.   *b.* $16 in $\frac{1}{2}$ yr.   *c.* $48 in 180 da.

5. Mrs. Lynch receives $24 a year interest on $400 loaned Mrs. Burnet. What is the rate?

6. Give the *rate* at which $300 will yield in 1 year

    a. $18   *b.* $10.50   *c.* $15   *d.* $7.50   *e.* $9

7. Give the *rate* at which $100 will produce

    a. $12 in 2 yr.   *b.* $10 in $2\frac{1}{2}$ yr.   *c.* $2.50 in 6 mo.

8. Give the *rate* at which, in 1 year,

    a. $200 yields $12   *b.* $300 yields $15

9. On a loan of $500 at 6 %, Mr. Melte receives $90 interest. For what time was the money lent?

10. Give the *time* required for $100 at 6 % to produce

    a. $12   *b.* $9   *c.* $1.50   *d.* $12.50   *e.* $27

11. Give the *time* in which, at 6 %,

    a. $200 yields $15   *b.* $100 yields $10

12. Give the *time* in which $300 will yield

    a. $12 at 6 %   *b.* $18 at 4 %   *c.* $27 at $4\frac{1}{2}$ %

Bank Discount

Practically every man having large business interests requires *accommodation* from his bank at certain seasons. The manufacturer needs money to buy raw material. This is supplied by the bank, and it is repaid by the money obtained through the sale of the finished products.

The merchant can obtain money to discount his bills, paying less for the accommodation than the sum saved by the deduction obtained through the cash payment.

The applicant makes out a note for the loan, which frequently takes this form :

```
                          SHOSHONE, IDAHO, May 6, 1915
   Ninety days after date I promise to pay to the order of
                    MYSELF
One Thousand 00/100 ~~~~~~~~~~~~~~~~Dollars
value received, at the Lincoln Co. National Bank.
                              Joseph Huhn
```

As this is payable to himself Mr. Huhn indorses it and has it further indorsed by Frank Philips.

The bank deducts $15, the interest on $1000 for 90 da., and places the remainder, $985, to the credit of Joseph Huhn, entering it in his pass book.

On Aug. 4, the expiration of the 90 days, the bank charges Mr. Huhn's account with $1000, if there are sufficient funds in the bank to his credit, and returns the note, with the other vouchers, when his account is balanced.

In some sections the interest on a bank loan is not deducted in the form of a discount, the borrower paying the note with interest at maturity.

Commercial Paper

Joseph E. Washington owes Barth. S. Cronin $1200, payable in 60 days. As evidence of the debt, he gives Mr. Cronin the following note:

NASHVILLE, TENN., Nov. 1, 1914

Sixty days after date I promise to pay to the order of Barth. S. Cronin Twelve Hundred $\frac{00}{100}$ Dollars, value received, at the First National Bank.

$1200 $\frac{00}{100}$ JOSEPH E. WASHINGTON.

If Mr. Cronin needs cash at once, he may sell the note. He transfers the ownership by indorsing the note, his indorsement also guaranteeing that he will pay the note at the expiration of 60 days if Mr. Washington fails to keep his agreement.

The bank purchases the note at a discount of, say, 6% for a year, which is 1% for the 60 days the note has to run. The discount on the foregoing note is $12, and Mr. Cronin receives $1200 − $12, or $1188, in case it is purchased on Nov 1.

The *bank discount* of a note is the interest on the note for the time it has to run. This interest is paid in advance by the seller of the note.

The sum paid the seller of a note after the deduction of the bank discount is called the *avails* or the *proceeds*.

If Mr. Washington does not pay this note at maturity, the bank *protests* the note. This protest is a statement in writing sent to Mr. Cronin by the bank's attorney. It is mailed after business hours the day the note is due and unpaid. Mr. Cronin pays the $1200 and the protest fee of, say, $2.50.

Maturity of Note .

A note payable *1 month* after Jan. 31, 1915, matures on Feb. 28, the last day of February. A note payable *1 month* after Jan. 31, 1916, matures on Feb. 29. A note payable *30 days* after Jan. 31, 1914, matures 30 days thereafter, or on March 2; one payable *30 days* after Jan. 31, 1916, matures March 1.

In some states a note does not mature until 3 days later than the time specified, these three days being called *days of grace*. In the answers given, no days of grace are considered.

Term of Discount

When a note is discounted on the day it is made, the term of discount corresponds with the time specified in the note.

As the interest, however, is generally taken by days, the discount on a note payable in a month may be taken for 28 days, 29 days, 30 days, or 31 days, according to circumstances.

A 1-month note, for instance, drawn Feb. 15, 1915, is due March 15, 28 days thereafter; one drawn Feb. 15, 1916, is due in 29 days; one drawn April 6, is due in 30 days; one drawn March 9, is due in 31 days.

Sight Exercises

Find the discount at 6 % on a 1-month note for $600 discounted the day it was made, dated as follows:

N.B. The interest on $600 for 1 day at 6% is 10¢.

a. Feb. 4, 1914	*b.* Feb. 7, 1916	*c.* Mar. 8, 1915
d. Jan. 16, 1916	*e.* Apr. 20, 1915	*f.* May 25, 1916
g. June 30, 1915	*h.* May 31, 1916	*i.* July 22, 1915
j. Aug. 14, 1916	*k.* Sept. 14, 1914	*l.* Oct. 3, 1916

Written Exercises

1. Find (*a*) the discount and (*b*) the proceeds of a 3-months' note for $350, dated Jan. 5, 1916, and discounted at 5 % the day it is drawn.

$$\text{PROCESS}$$

$$\text{Discount} = \frac{\$350 \times .05 \times 91}{360}.$$

$$\text{Proceeds} = \text{Face} - \text{Discount}.$$

2. Find the discount on each of the following notes, discounted the day it is drawn, at 6 %:

	TIME	FACE	DRAWN
a.	1 month	$300	Mch. 6, 1915
b.	2 months	$400	Dec. 26, 1916
c.	3 months	$560	Oct. 12, 1915

When the day specified for the maturity of a note is a Sunday or a holiday, the day of payment is fixed by law, which varies in different states. In the examples given, no notice need be taken of holidays.

3. Find (*a*) the discount and (*b*) the proceeds of a 60-days' note for $475, discounted 12 days after its date, at 5½ %.

The interest being taken from the day of discount to the day of maturity, the term of discount in this case is 60 da. — 12 da., or 48 da.

4. Find the discount and the proceeds of each of the following notes :

	FACE	TIME	DISCOUNTED	RATE
a.	$350	60 days	12 days after date	5 %
b.	$420	90 days	10 days after date	6 %
c.	$540	30 days	6 days after date	5 %

5. Find the discount and the proceeds of each of the following notes, discounted at 6 % :

a. Face $3750, discounted 40 days before maturity.

b. Face $2400, discounted 50 days before maturity.

c. Face $1860, discounted 24 days before maturity.

6. Find the discount on a 3-months' note for $1152, drawn Feb. 6, 1915, and discounted April 25, at 6 %.

PROCESS

Day of maturity; 3 mo. from Feb. 6, which is May 6
Term of discount; Apr. 25 to May 6, which is 11 da.

Discount: $$\frac{\$1152 \times .06 \times 11}{360}$$

If the owner of this note had sold it to a bank on the day it was drawn, Feb. 6, the interest for 89 days would have been deducted. By holding it from Feb. 6 to April 25, 78 days, he saved the interest for that period. The term of discount on April 25 is the difference between 89 days and 78 days.

7. Find (I) the date of maturity; (II) the term of discount, *i.e.*, the time between the day of discount and the day of maturity; (III) the discount; and (IV) the proceeds.

	FACE	TIME	DRAWN	DISCOUNTED	RATE
a.	$432	60 da.	July 7	July 10	4 %
b.	$576	3 mo.	Mch. 18	May 3	5 %
c.	$648	90 da.	Sept. 4	Oct. 15	8 %

Sight Exercises

Give the term of discount :

a. Face of note, $475; rate, 6 %; discount, $4.75.

b. Face of note, $387; rate, 5 %; discount, $3.87.

c. Face of note, $295; rate 4½ %; discount, $2.95.

Sight Problems

1. Find the interest on $484 (*a*) for 60 days at 6%. (*b*) For 72 days at 5%. (*c*) For 120 days at 3%. (*d*) For 80 days at $4\frac{1}{2}$%. (*e*) For 90 days at 4%. (*f*) For 5 years at 5%. (*g*) For $6\frac{1}{4}$ years at 4%. (*h*) For 4 years 2 months at 6%.

2. When the discount on a note for $360, discounted for 90 days, is $3.60, what is the rate?

3. (*a*) What per cent is gained on cloth bought at $2 per yard and sold at $2.25? (*b*) What per cent is lost on cloth bought at $2.25 per yard and sold at $2?

4. A carpet covers 45 square yards. If it is made of strips $\frac{3}{4}$ yd. wide, find the total length covered by the strips when they are placed end to end.

5. A man's income in 1909 was $1000. His income in 1910 was 10% greater than in 1909, in 1911 it was 10% greater than in 1910, and in 1912 it was 10% greater than in 1911. What was the increase (*a*) in 1910? (*b*) In 1911? (*c*) In 1912?

6. If a chest of tea contains $\frac{3}{4}$ of a hundred pounds, how many chests will contain 63 hundred pounds?

7. The product of two numbers is 63 hundred. One of the numbers is 84. What fraction of a hundred is the other?

8. If A can do $\frac{1}{10}$ of a piece of work in a day and B can do $\frac{1}{15}$ of it in a day, (*a*) what fraction can both together do in a day? (*b*) How long would A require to do the whole work? (*c*) How long would B require? (*d*) In what time could both do it together?

9. How many tiles $\frac{1}{2}$ ft. square would be required for the floor of a room 20 ft. square?

10. A freight train leaves Holly for Rocky Ford, 90 miles distant, at 9 A.M., traveling 15 miles per hour. At 10 A.M. an express train leaves Rocky Ford for Holly, going 45 miles per hour. (*a*) How far apart are the trains at 10 A.M.? (*b*) How long after 10 A.M. will it be when the latter meets the former?

11. In how many days will $485 produce $4.85 interest (*a*) at 3%? (*b*) At 4%? (*c*) At 5%? (*d*) At 6%?

12. In what time will $485 produce $48.50 (*a*) at 5%? (*b*) At 4%?

13. In what time will $485 produce $485 (*a*) at 5%? (*b*) At 6%? (*c*) At 4%? (*d*) In what time will any sum double itself at 3% simple interest?

14. If 45 pupils are absent in a school of 900, what is the per cent of attendance?

15. A man's purchases amount to $98. If he is allowed 1% for cash, what is the net amount paid?

16. (*a*) Find 99% of $95. (*b*) How many square feet in a rectangle 99 ft. long 98 ft. wide? (*c*) How many times is 99 contained in 8500, and what is the remainder? (*d*) How many times is 99 contained in 8514, and what is the remainder?

17. Find (*a*) the discount and (*b*) the proceeds of a note for $175 discounted at 5% for 72 days.

18. If the proceeds of a note of $200, discounted at $4\frac{1}{2}$%, are $198, what is the term of discount?

19. A freight train leaves Holly for Rocky Ford at 9 A.M., traveling 15 miles per hour. At the same time an express train leaves Rocky Ford for Holly, going 45 miles per hour. What time will they meet, the distance between the cities being 90 miles?

Written Review Problems

1. What is the average age of a class in which there are 7 pupils between 12 and 13 years of age, 9 between 13 and 14, 11 between 14 and 15, 5 between 15 and 16, 7 between 16 and 17, and 1 between 18 and 19?

PROCESS

In finding the average ages, pupils between 12 and 13 are taken as $12\frac{1}{2}$, those between 14 and 15 as $14\frac{1}{2}$, etc.

One Way		*A Shorter Way*	
7 at $12\frac{1}{2}$ yr.	$87\frac{1}{2}$	7 at 0 yr. over $12\frac{1}{2}$	0
9 at $13\frac{1}{2}$ yr.	$121\frac{1}{2}$	9 at 1 yr. over $12\frac{1}{2}$	9
11 at $14\frac{1}{2}$ yr.	$159\frac{1}{2}$	11 at 2 yr. over $12\frac{1}{2}$	22
5 at $15\frac{1}{2}$ yr.	$77\frac{1}{2}$	5 at 3 yr. over $12\frac{1}{2}$	15
7 at $16\frac{1}{2}$ yr.	$115\frac{1}{2}$	7 at 4 yr. over $12\frac{1}{2}$	28
1 at $18\frac{1}{2}$ yr.	$18\frac{1}{2}$	1 at 6 yr. over $12\frac{1}{2}$	6
Total 40 at ? yr.	580	40 at ? yr. over $12\frac{1}{2}$	80
Average age, $14\frac{1}{2}$ yr.		Average age, 2 yr. over $12\frac{1}{2}$ yr.	

By the ordinary method each different age is multiplied by the number of pupils of each age, and the sum of the products divided by the number of pupils.

The other method makes easier multiplications and should be used when possible.

2. Find the average age of the pupils of Washington School from the following data:

19 pupils between 5 and 6
49 pupils between 6 and 7
65 pupils between 7 and 8
71 pupils between 8 and 9
65 pupils between 9 and 10
67 pupils between 10 and 11
67 pupils between 11 and 12
69 pupils between 12 and 13
59 pupils between 13 and 14
43 pupils between 14 and 15
17 pupils between 15 and 16
9 pupils between 16 and 17

3. William's salary is 48 % of John's. If William receives \$576 per year, how much more does John receive?

4. (*a*) A farmer sold his eggs during the year at the following rates :

168 doz. at 20 ¢	75 doz. at 30 ¢
152 doz. at 21 ¢	60 doz. at 32 ¢
136 doz. at 22 ¢	110 doz. at 35 ¢
230 doz. at 25 ¢	37 doz. at 38 ¢
122 doz. at 28 ¢	32 doz. at 40 ¢

What was the average price ?

(*b*) What was his profit per dozen if the cost per dozen was $0.131 for feed, $.026 for labor, and $0.0575 for overhead charges such as interest on capital invested, etc. ?

5. The average number of pupils to a school in 1914, when there were 5 schools, was 158. In 1914, when there were 6 schools, the average was 12 more. What was the increase in the number of pupils ?

6. If a ball rebounds 60 % of the height from which it falls, how high will it rise on the third bound when it is thrown to a height of 50 feet ?

7. From an investment of $15,000 a man's income is $675 per year. How much additional must be invested at the same rate to obtain an income of $75 per month ?

8. A woman has $5835 invested, on which she received 4 % annually. How much additional must she invest at the same rate in order to obtain a total income of $300 per year ?

9. (*a*) What sum must be invested at 4 % to yield an annual income of $900 ? (*b*) What sum must be invested at $4\frac{1}{2}$ % to yield an annual income of $900 ? (*c*) What sum must be invested at 4 % to obtain an annual income of $300 ?

10. A man obtains a loan of $225, and pays for its use 6 % per year. If he repays the loan at the end of 5 years, how much has he paid altogether ?

Accurate Interest

While the convenience attending the use of the year of 360 days has led to its employment in ordinary business calculations of interest on small sums for portions of a year, the 365-day year is the basis in determining the interest payments of the United States and of banks, although the latter generally take the year of 360 days in discounting notes.

Written Exercises

1. The Nassau Trust Company owes Harrison Javins $240, with interest from July 16, 1914. What is the amount of its indebtedness Feb. 20, 1915?

$$\text{Time, 219 days.} \quad Interest = \frac{\$240 \times .03 \times 219}{365}.$$

2. Find the interest on $240 for 219 days, at 3%, taking 360 days to the year.

3. Find the accurate interest on

a. $1460, from Jan. 3, 1915 to Aug. 5, 1915, at 6%.

b. $2000, from March 8, 1914 to May 20, 1914, at 5%.

c. $3650, from May 5, 1916 to Oct. 2, 1916, at 2%.

4. From the accompanying table find the accurate interest on $2760 for 21 days at 5%.

NOTE. — Take from the table the interest on $1600 ($4.603), on $1000 ($2.897), and on $160 ($.460). Combine the three.

5. Find from the table the interest on $1200 for 28 days at 5%.

365 DAYS TO YEAR — 21 DAYS

	5 %	6 %	7 %
$1000	2.887	3.452	4.027
1100	3.164	3.797	4.430
1200	3.452	4.142	4.833
1300	3.74	4.488	5.236
1400	4.027	4.833	5.638
1500	4.315	5.178	6.041
1600	4.603	5.523	6.444

PROCESS

Interest for 21 da. at 5 % on $1200 is $3.452.
Interest for 7 da. is ⅓ of foregoing.   Combine.

---

6. Find the accurate interest on

a. $400 for 21 da. at 5 %   *b.* $350 for 21 da. at 6 %

c. $600 for 7 da. at 3 %   *d.* $800 for 21 da. at 3½ %

e. $700 for 42 da. at 6 %   *f.* $900 for 28 da. at 2½ %

Table of Interest for 1 Day

365 DAYS TO YEAR
INTEREST FOR 1 DAY AT 2 %

PRINCIPAL	INTEREST	PRINCIPAL	INTEREST
$10,000	.55	$210,000	$11.51
11,000	.60	211,000	11.56
12,000	.66	212,000	11.62
13,000	.71	213,000	11.67
14,000	.77	214,000	11.73
15,000	.82	215,000	11.78
16,000	.88	216,000	11.84
17,000	.93	217,000	11.89
18,000	.99	218,000	11.95
19,000	1.04	219,000	12.00

7. Mr. Haupt's bank allows him interest at 2 % on a deposit of $25,000. How much interest is due him per day?

PROCESS

Int. on $10,000   .55
Int. on   15,000   .82
Int. on $25,000 $1.37

---

8. What is the accurate interest on $2500 for 90 days at 2 %?

The interest on $2500 for 90 days is the same as the interest on $225,000 (90 times $2500) for 1 day.

9. Find the accurate interest at 2 % on

a. $3000 for 75 days   *b.* $6000 for 38 days

c. $4000 for 56 days   *d.* $7000 for 33 days

Interest-bearing Deposits

A commercial bank does not, as a rule, pay interest on a depositor's small balances subject to withdrawal at any time by check. It will, however, pay a low rate of interest on a special deposit left with it for a definite period.

James H. Tully has $3000, for which he has no immediate use. This he places in the Citizens Bank, receiving the following certificate:

CERTIFICATE OF DEPOSIT

No. *8376*   BILLINGS, OKLA., *March 1,* 1915

This certifies that *James H. Tully* has deposited in this Bank

Three Thousand and $\frac{00}{100}$ ～～～～～～～～～Dollars

payable *sixty days* after date to *his* order upon return of this certificate, with interest at 2 per cent per annum.

CITIZENS BANK

E. R. Smith,

Cashier.

Written Exercises

1. Find the amount of the foregoing certificate of deposit at the time of its withdrawal, May 24, 1915.

Time between March 1 and May 24 is 84 da.

$3000 × 84 = $252,000.

Take from the table the interest for 1 day on $210,000 and to this add the interest on $42,000 ($\frac{1}{5}$ of $210,000).

2. Find the amount of each of the following certificates of deposit at the expiration of its term:

    a. Face $4000, term 63 days, rate 2%.

    b. Face $3500, term 60 days, rate 3%.

    c. Face $7000, term 30 days, rate $2\frac{1}{2}$%.

Interest on Bank Balances

In the case of depositors whose balances exceed a certain amount (say $500), some commercial banks pay interest at the rate of 2% per year on the balances.

Written Exercises

1. William S. Hurley's account with the Home Trust Company shows the following transactions:

Jan.   1, $1200 balance.   Apr.   5, Deposited $300.
Feb.   2, Deposited $300.   May   6, Withdrew $400.
March 4, Withdrew $600.   June 7, Deposited $800.

If the bank allows 2% on balances, the interest to be credited to his account on July 1 is determined as follows:

		PROCESS	
DATES	TIME	BALANCES	INT. FOR 1 DA. ON
Jan. 1 to Feb. 2	32 da.	$1200	$38,400
Feb. 2 to Mch. 4	30 da.	1500	45,000
Mch. 4 to Apr. 5	32 da.	900	28,800
Apr. 6 to May 6	31 da.	1200	37,200
May 6 to June 7	32 da.	800	25,600
June 7 to July 1	24 da.	1600	38,400

Interest for 1 day on $213,400 = $11.69

The balance of $1200 on Jan. 1 is entitled to interest to Feb. 2, 32 days; the new balance of $1500 is entitled to interest to March 4, 30 days; etc., as shown above.

Instead, however, of finding the interest on each balance, it is changed with its time into the sum entitled to 1 day's interest, and the six sums are combined into one, the interest on which is determined by means of the table.

2. David Roche's account shows balances as follows: July 1, 1914, $1000; Aug. 2, $2000; Sept. 5, $1200; Oct. 12, $1000; Nov. 15, $800; Dec. 3, $1000. How much interest at 2% is credited on these balances Jan. 1, 1915?

Interest Laws

When the rate is not expressed in the paper showing the indebtedness, the *legal rate* of the state is employed.

In some states, a contract to pay a higher rate is not enforceable; in others, the law authorizes the collection of a rate not exceeding a specified one; in a few, any rate agreed upon by the borrower is binding upon him.

The collection of excessive interest is called *usury*.

LEGAL AND CONTRACT RATES

STATES	LEGAL RATE	CONTRACT RATE	STATES	LEGAL RATE	CONTRACT RATE
Alabama	8	8	Nebraska	7	10
Arkansas	6	10	Nevada	7	Any
Arizona	6	Any	New Hampshire	6	6
California	7	Any	New Jersey	6	6
Colorado	8	Any	New Mexico	6	12
Connecticut	6	6	New York	6	6
Delaware	6	6	North Carolina	6	6
Dis. of Col.	6	10	North Dakota	7	12
Florida	8	10	Ohio	6	8
Georgia	7	8	Oklahoma	7	12
Idaho	7	12	Oregon	6	10
Illinois	5	7	Pennsylvania	6	6
Indiana	6	8	Rhode Island	6	Any
Iowa	6	8	South Carolina	7	8
Kansas	6	10	South Dakota	7	12
Kentucky	6	6	Tennessee	6	6
Louisiana	5	8	Texas	6	10
Maine	6	Any	Utah	8	12
Maryland	6	6	Vermont	6	6
Massachusetts	6	Any	Virginia	6	6
Michigan	5	7	Washington	6	12
Minnesota	7	10	West Virginia	6	6
Mississippi	6	10	Wisconsin	6	10
Missouri	6	8	Wyoming	8	12
Montana	8	Any			

Compound Interest

A woman has $100 in a savings bank, drawing interest at 4 % per year. (*a*) How much is there to her credit when a year's interest is added? (*b*) How much interest is due the second year on the first year's principal and interest?

By *compound interest* is meant the interest on the principal and on accrued interest.

Written Exercises

1. (*a*) Find the amount of $400 at 4 % for 4 years, interest compounded annually. (*b*) Find the interest.

	PROCESS	
	Principal	$400.
The interest for each year is calculated on the amount at the end of the previous year.	Int. 1 yr.	16.
	Amount 1 yr.	$416.
	Int. 1 yr.	16.64
	Amount 2 yr.	$432.64
(*b*) The interest for 4 years is $467.94 − $400, or $67.94 *Ans.*	Int. 1 yr.	17.3056
	Amount 3 yr.	$449.9456
	Int. 1 yr.	17.9978
	Amount 4 yr. (*a*)	$467.94 *Ans.*

2. Find the interest on $300 at 5 % for 4 years, compounded annually.

3. Mrs. Peck deposits $600 in a savings bank on Dec. 31, 1913. On June 30, 1914, 2 % of this sum is added as a deposit. (*a*) How much is there to her credit in the bank at this date? (*b*) How much will there be to her credit Dec. 31, 1914, if the amount to her credit on June 30 is increased by an additional 2 % ?

PROCESS

Principal Dec. 31, 1913, $600.
Interest to June 30, 1914,   12. (2 % of $600)
Amount June 30, 1914, $612.
Interest to Dec. 31, 1914,   12.24 (2 % of $612)
Amount Dec. 31, 1914, $624.24

---

4. Find the amount of each of the following at the end of the year, when interest is added half-yearly at the rate of 2 %:

a. $200   b. $250   c. $300   d. $350   e. $550

Compound interest is practically never employed in ordinary business transactions. Even a savings bank that pays interest on the interest left as a deposit, rejects the cents in each new principal, although retaining it in the interest.

5. Mr. Harris deposited $600 in a savings bank on July 1, 1913. To how much interest is he entitled July 1, 1916, if interest at 2 % is placed to his credit semi-annually?

PROCESS

Principal	$600.	
Int. ½ yr.	12.	
Amt. ½ yr.	$612.	(new principal)
Int. ½ yr.	12.24	
Amt. 1 yr.	$624.24	(new principal)
Int. ½ yr.	12.48	2 % of $624
Amt. 1½ yr.	$636.72	(new principal)
Int. ½ yr.	12.72	2 % of $636

In calculating the half-yearly interest, omit the cents, if any, in each new principal.

Compound Interest Tables

Amount of $1 at compound interest, compounded annually.

YEARS	RATE: 2 %	2½ %	3 %	4 %	5 %
1	1.02000	1.02500	1.03000	1.04000	1.05000
2	1.04040	1.05063	1.06090	1.08160	1.10250
3	1.06121	1.07689	1.09273	1.12486	1.15763
4	1.08243	1.10381	1.12551	1.16986	1.21551
5	1.10408	1.13141	1.15969	1.21665	1.27628
6	1.12616	1.15969	1.19405	1.26532	1.34010
7	1.14869	1.18869	1.22987	1.31593	1.40710
8	1.17166	1.21840	1.26677	1.36857	1.47746
9	1.19509	1.24886	1.30477	1.42331	1.55132
10	1.21899	1.28008	1.34392	1.48024	1.62889
11	1.24337	1.32125	1.38423	1.53945	1.71033

Written Exercises

1. What is the interest on $800 compounded annually for 5 years at 5%?

$$\text{Interest} = \$800 \times .27628.$$

2. Find the interest on the following, compounded annually:

a. $800 at 3% for 4 yr.   *b.* $800 at 2% for 6 yr.

c. $800 at 4% for 3 yr.   *d.* $800 at 5% for 7 yr.

3. What is the amount of $800 compounded semi-annually for 5 years at 5%?

$$\text{Amount} = \$800 \times 1.28008.$$

Take from the table the amount of $1 for 10 years at 2½%, since $800 is compounded 10 times at 2½%.

Annual Interest

Written Exercises

1.　　　　DETROIT, MICH., Jan. 15, 1916.

On demand after date I promise to pay to the order of Andrew J. Shipman, Four Hundred Dollars, value received, with interest at six per cent, payable semiannually.

400\frac{00}{100}$　　　　　CLEMENT MANLY.

Find the amount due on the foregoing note on Jan. 15, 1918, if no interest payments have been made.

In most states Mr. Shipman could collect only $72 interest, the laws not permitting the collection of interest on overdue interest. In Michigan, however, and in some other states, the law permits the collection of simple interest on deferred interest payments from the time they are due until they are paid, when the note expressly provides that the interest is to be paid at stated times.

PROCESS

The five semiannual payments of $12 being unpaid for 2½ yr., 2 yr., 1½ yr., 1 yr., and ½ yr., respectively, interest on $12 at 6% is due for 2½ yr. + 2 yr. + 1½ yr. + 1 yr. + ½ yr., or for 7½ yr., together with the interest on $400 for 3 yr.

Principal	$400.00
Interest on $400, for 3 yr. at 6%	72.00
Interest on $12 for 7½ yr. at 6%	5.40
Amount due Jan. 15, 1912	$477.40 *Ans.*

---

2. How much is due Aug. 4, 1916, on a note drawn Aug. 4, 1912, for $600 with 6% interest payable annually, if no payments of interest have been made, and the collection of annual interest is permitted by law?

3. A note for $900 was made Sept. 16, 1913, with interest at 6% payable semiannually. How much was due Sept. 16, 1916, if no interest payments were made except the first?

SECTION VII

BUSINESS APPLICATIONS. PROPORTIONS AND ALIQUOT PARTS

Preparatory Exercises

Four persons engage a vehicle to take them 3 miles 4 miles, 5 miles, and 6 miles, respectively, the total expense of $7.20 to be apportioned among them according to the distance traveled by each.

Taking the sum of the distances, 18 miles, as the basis, the share of each might be determined by ascertaining the cost per mile and multiplying the result by the number of miles.

$a.\ \dfrac{\$7.20}{18} \times 3 \qquad b.\ \dfrac{\$7.20}{18} \times 4 \qquad c.\ \dfrac{\$7.20}{18} \times 5 \qquad d.\ \dfrac{\$7.20}{18} \times 6$

Another method is to multiply the total cost by the fraction of the total distance ridden by each.

$a.\ \$7.20 \times \dfrac{3}{18} \qquad b.\ \$7.20 \times \dfrac{4}{18} \qquad c.\ \$7.20 \times \dfrac{5}{18} \qquad d.\ \$7.20 \times \dfrac{6}{18}$

Each of these fractions, $\frac{3}{18}$, $\frac{4}{18}$, $\frac{5}{18}$, and $\frac{6}{18}$, indicates the *ratio* between the distance traveled by an individual and the total distance.

In expressing each as a ratio, the colon (:) (which is one form of the sign of division) is used instead of the horizontal line employed in the fraction.

Thus, the ratio (*a*) of 3 to 18, (*b*) of 4 to 18, (*c*) of 5 to 18, and (*d*) of 6 to 18, is written

$a.\ $ 3 : 18 $\qquad b.\ $ 4 : 18 $\qquad c.\ $ 5 : 18 $\qquad d.\ $ 6 : 18

Sight Problems

1. If 3 oranges cost 9 cents, what will 8 oranges cost?

2. If 6 men require 11 days to do a piece of work, how many days will 22 men require to do the same work?

Proportion

Preparatory Exercises

Give the missing terms:

1. *a.* $\dfrac{3}{8} = \dfrac{9}{?}$ *b.* $\dfrac{3 \text{ oranges}}{8 \text{ oranges}} = \dfrac{9\cancel{c}}{?\cancel{c}}$ *c.* $\dfrac{3 \text{ lb.}}{9 \text{ oz.}} = \dfrac{48\cancel{c}}{?\cancel{c}}$

    d. $\dfrac{22}{6} = \dfrac{11}{?}$ *e.* $\dfrac{22 \text{ men}}{6 \text{ men}} = \dfrac{\$66}{\$?}$ *f.* $\dfrac{1 \text{ bu.}}{3 \text{ pk.}} = \dfrac{?\cancel{c}}{45\cancel{c}}$

The equality of the ratios (*a*) 3 oranges and 8 oranges and (*b*) 9 cents and 24 cents may be written as a *proportion*, thus:

$$3 \text{ oranges} : 8 \text{ oranges} :: 9 \text{ cents} : 24 \text{ cents,}$$

or, omitting the denominations:

$$3 : 8 :: 9 : 24,$$

which is read "3 is to 8 as 9 is to 24."

It may also be written

$$3 : 8 = 9 : 24,$$

the double colon (::) being replaced by the sign of equality (=), which means the same, each signifying

$$\tfrac{3}{8} = \tfrac{9}{24}.$$

Observe that in the proportion

$$3 : 8 :: 9 : 24$$

the product of 3 and 24 (the *extremes*) is equal to the product of 8 and 9 (the *means*).

Finding a Missing Term

If 18 men can cut 40 acres of grass in a day, how many acres can be cut in a day by 15 men?

Since the ratio of the quantity cut should be equal to the ratio of the men employed, indicate the operations by the following proportion, in which x is used for the missing term:

$$\overset{3}{\cancel{6}} \qquad 5 \qquad 20$$
$$\cancel{18} \text{ (men)} : \cancel{15} \text{ (men)} :: \cancel{40} \text{ (A.)} : x \text{ (A.)}$$

Cancel 18 and 15, also 6 and 40. The product of the extremes, 3 and x, is equal to the product of the means, 5 and 20.

That is: $3x = 100$; which gives $x = 33\frac{1}{3}$ (A.) *Ans.*

Either extreme may be canceled with either mean.

Written Exercises

1. Find the missing term in the following proportion:

MEN MEN DA. DA.
$$13 : 47 :: 26 : x$$

Cancel 13 and 26.

2. Find the missing term:

$$3 \text{ lb. } 6 \text{ oz.} : 5 \text{ lb. } 8 \text{ oz.} :: \$x : \$4.40$$

Change the compound numbers to simple numbers, which gives the following proportion

Oz. Oz. $\$¢$ $¢$
$$54 : 88 :: x : 440$$

Cancel 88 and 440. x equals 5 times 54. Insert the denomination in the result.

In forming a proportion the denominations may be placed above the numbers to indicate that abstract numbers are employed in the preliminary work, the denomination.

3. Find the value of x:

YD. YD. $\$$ $\$$ MI. MI. HR. HR.
a. $18 : 60 :: 27 : x$ *b.* $40\frac{1}{2} : 45 :: x : 40$

Direct Proportion, Inverse Proportion

Preparatory Exercises

1. When 3 men can cut 7 acres of grass in a day, how many acres should 9 men cut at the same rate?

2. When 3 men require 8 days to mow a field, in how many days should 12 men mow it at the same rate?

In Ex. 1, the quantity cut is *directly* proportionate to the number of men. In Ex. 2, the time is *inversely* proportionate to the number of men.

In a builder's handbook it is stated that the load a beam can sustain varies *directly* according to the width of the beam, other things being equal, and *inversely* according to its length between its points of support.

This means that when a beam 2 inches wide will sustain 6 tons, one 4 inches wide will sustain 12 tons; and that when a beam 12 feet long will sustain 16 tons, one 16 feet long will sustain only 12 tons. A beam 6 inches deep will, however, sustain 4 times as much as one 3 inches deep, when both have the same length and width.

The solution of problems by means of proportion should be limited to such industrial and other types as are best treated in this way. Examples of this kind will be found in a later section.

The pupil must not assume, for instance, that the cost of insurance for 3 years is 3 times the cost for 1 year. He must remember that a boy who can walk 3 miles in 1 hour cannot walk 30 miles in 10 hours. He must not jump to the conclusion a pane of glass 9 times the size of a 5-cent one can be bought for 45 cents.

In the solution of the following problems employ any method you prefer.

Sight Problems

1. If 12 men can do a piece of work in 31 days, how long will it take 4 men to do the same work?

2. When a 54-acre field yields 186 tons of hay, (*a*) how many tons should an 18-acre field produce at the same rate? (*b*) If a 27-acre field yields 100 tons, how many tons more or less are obtained than from a corresponding area of the first field?

3. If 18 men can do a piece of work in 4 days working 10 hours a day, how many men will be required to do it in 10 days working 8 hours a day?

4. How many books at 75 ¢ each will be equal in cost to 93 books at $1.50 each?

5. A freight train traveling at the rate of 15 miles per hour requires 69 minutes between two stations. What time does an express train going 45 miles per hour require for the same trip? .

6. If 2 lb. 3 oz. of butter cost 72 cents, what is the cost of 6 lb. 9 oz.?

7. If a train requires 3 hours to go 90 miles, (*a*) how many miles per hour should its speed be increased in order to make the trip in $\frac{2}{3}$ of the time? (*b*) By what fraction of 30 miles is the speed increased?

8. If 30 men can build a wall in 9 days, (*a*) how many fewer men would be required to do the work in 1 day more? (*b*) By what fraction is the time increased? (*c*) By what fraction is the number of men diminished?

9. If it costs $1664 to make a mile of road, what is the share of a man whose land extends 40 rods along the road?

Written Problems

1. When 14 men require 225 days to do a certain piece of work, how long would it take 50 men to do the same work?

SOLUTION BY PROPORTION

The time required to do work is inversely proportional to the number employed: twice as many men requiring one half the time.

50 men : 14 men : : 225 da. : x da.

SOLUTION BY ANALYSIS

If 14 men require 225 da.

1 man requires 225 da. × 14

50 men require $\dfrac{225 \text{ da.} \times 14}{50}$ Cancel

---

2. How long will a train require to go 97.6 miles at the rate of 3.2 miles in 8 minutes?

3. What should be the yield of $3\frac{1}{8}$ A. at the rate of 160 bushels to $8\frac{1}{8}$ A.?

4. If property worth \$15000 pays \$112.50 taxes, what should be the taxes on property worth \$12500?

5. If 9 pieces, each containing $27\frac{1}{2}$ yards, cost \$34.65, how many yards cost \$1.89?

6. By selling goods for \$70 I obtained 80% of their cost. At what price should they be sold to realize 120% of their cost?

7. (*a*) What is the cost of manufacturing an article retailed for \$1 if the retailer pays the manufacturer $\frac{10}{9}$ of the cost and charges the buyer $\frac{10}{9}$ of the price paid the manufacturer? (*b*) What improper fraction of the manufacturing cost does the consumer pay?

Aliquot Parts

A number is an aliquot part of another if it is an exact divisor of the latter. The aliquot parts of 100 are 50, $33\frac{1}{3}$, 25, $16\frac{2}{3}$, $14\frac{2}{7}$, $12\frac{1}{2}$, etc.

Business men frequently employ aliquot parts in working some types of problems generally solved by analysis or by proportion.

8. If 33 acres of land produce 647 bushels of wheat, what should (*a*) 36 acres yield at the same rate? (*b*) 44 A.?

SOLUTION

(*a*) 33 acres yield 647 bushels
(Add) 3 acres yield $58\frac{2}{11}$ bushels ($\frac{1}{11}$ of 647 bushels)
$\overline{36}$ $\overline{705\frac{2}{11}}$ bushels *Ans.*

---

9. How many feet of ditch can 30 men dig in the same time that 33 men dig (*a*) 470 yards? (*b*) 560 yd.?

SOLUTION

(*a*) 33 men dig 470 yards
(Subtract) 3 men dig $42\frac{8}{11}$ yards ($\frac{1}{11}$ of 470 yards)
$\overline{30}$ men dig $\overline{427\frac{3}{11}}$ yards *Ans.*

---

10. If $\frac{3}{4}$ of a farm contains (*a*) 294 acres, how many acres are there in the farm? (*b*) 276 A.?

SOLUTION

(*a*) 3 fourths contain 294 acres
(Add) 1 fourth contains 98 acres ($\frac{1}{3}$ of 294 acres)
The farm contains $\overline{392}$ acres *Ans.*

Interest by Aliquot Parts

Written Exerc...

1. Find the amount of $396.50 ... 5¾% for 3 yr. 10 mo. 23 da.

PROCESS

Principal $396.50		
.05¾		
4)$11.8950	Product by .003	
$ 2.9738	Product by .00¾	
19.8250	Product by .05	
Interest for 1 yr. $22.7988	Product by .05¾	
Interest for 2 yr. 45.5976		
Interest for 8 mo. 15.1992	$\frac{1}{3}$ of interest for 2 yr.	
Interest for 2 mo. 3.7998	$\frac{1}{4}$ of interest for 8 mo.	
Interest for 15 da. .9499	$\frac{1}{4}$ of interest for 2 mo.	
Interest for 8 da. .5066	$\frac{1}{30}$ of interest for 8 mo.	

2. Find the interest :

a. Principal, $1080; rate, 5 % ; time 3 yr. 10 mo. 23 da.

b. Principal, $1440; rate, 6½% ; time 1 yr. 7 mo. 15 da.

c. Principal, $360 ; rate, 6 % ; time 2 yr. 4 mo. 20 da.

d. Principal, $720 ; rate, 7 % ; time 4 yr. 9 mo. 24 da.

e. Principal, $1800 ; rate, 5¾% ; time 5 yr. 3 mo. 10 da.

f. Principal, $1980 ; rate, 4 % ; time 2 yr. 8 mo. 21 da.

g. Principal, $2340 ; rate, 8 % ; time 1 yr. 9 mo. 18 da.

As the interest for 60 days at 6% is 1% of the principal, business men frequently compute interest at 6% for periods expressed in days, by commencing with the interest for 60 days. When the rate is 5%, they begin with the interest for 72 days.

Written Exercises

1. Find the amount of $384.60 for 187 days (*a*) at 6%. (*b*) At 5%.

PROCESS				
(*a*) Rate 6%			(*b*) Rate 5%	
Principal	$384.60			$384.60
Int. 60 da. (1%)	3.846	144 da. (2%)	7.692	
Int. 120 da.	7.692	36 da.	1.923	
Int. 6 da.	.385	6 da.	.321	
Int. 1 da.	.064	1 da.	.053	
	$396.59 *Ans.*		$394.59 *Ans.*	

2. Find the proceeds of a note for $384.60 discounted for 93 days.   (*a*) At 5%.   (*b*) At 6%.   (*c*) At 4½%.

PROCESS					
(*a*) 5%		(*b*) 6%		(*c*) 4½%	
Face $384.60		$384.60		$384.60	
72 da.	3.846	60 da.	3.846	80 da.	3.846
18 da.	.9615	30 da.	1.923	10 da.	.481
3 da.	.1602	3 da.	.192	3 da.	.1443
Procs.	$379.63 *Ans.*		$378.64 *Ans.*		$380.13 *Ans.*

3. Find the amount of

a. $457 for 187 days at 6%.

b. $293 for 187 days at 4½%.

c. $375 for 187 days at 5%.

4. Find the proceeds of a note for

a. $943 discounted for 60 days at 6%.

b. $864 discounted for 63 days at 6%.

c. $588 discounted for 30 days at 5%.

Written Review Problems

1. Furniture catalogued at $60 is bought by a dealer at 40% discount. If he sells it at the catalogue price, what is his per cent of profit?

2. What per cent does A gain on an article that cost him (*a*) 30% below the price he obtains for it? (*b*) 50% below the price he obtains for it? (*c*) 25% below the price he obtains for it?

An article bought at 30 per cent below the selling price is bought at 70 per cent of the selling price.

The cost is, therefore, 70 per cent, and the selling price is 100 per cent. Ignoring the term "per cent," the cost is 70 and the selling price is 100. The profit is 30 on a cost of 70; etc.

3. An article costing $100 is marked 50% above cost. The dealer sells it at 50% below the marked price. (*a*) How many dollars does he lose? (*b*) What per cent does he lose?

4. If goods costing $200 are marked 20% above cost and are sold at 20% below the marked price, (*a*) what is the loss? (*b*) What per cent is lost?

5. If a farmer raised 450 bushels of wheat in 1909, 20% less in 1910, and 20% more in 1911 than he raised in 1910, (*a*) how many bushels did he raise in 1911? (*b*) What was the decrease in 1910 below 1909 in bushels? (*c*) What was the increase in 1911 over 1910 in bushels? (*d*) What was the per cent of increase or decrease of 1911 compared with 1909?

6. The following are the receipts of grain for a week:

Wheat 378 bu., corn 896 bu., barley 64 bu., rye 282 bu., oats 380 bu.

(*a*) Find the total receipts, and (*b*) the per cent of the total represented by each variety.

7. In a year a farmer sold \$4000 worth of produce, which cost him \$2400 in labor, etc. The next year his sales increased \$1000. What should be the increase in the expenses, in order that the rate of profit might be the same?

8. Marching along a good road soldiers take 132 steps per minute, each step being 2 ft. 6 in. (*a*) How many feet do they march in a minute? (*b*) How many minutes would they require to march a mile?

9. At the rate of 99 steps per minute how long would it take a regiment to march 6 miles, if each step measures $2\frac{1}{2}$ ft.?

10. To sell an article costing \$2.40 entails an expense of 5 % of the cost. What is the selling price if the profit is $8\frac{1}{3}$ % on the cost and the expense together?

11. A dealer buys eggs at 15 cents per dozen and sells them at 15 for 25 cents. To make a profit of \$6, (*a*) how many eggs must he sell? (*b*) How many cases of 30 dozen each?

12. A man has $\frac{2}{3}$ of $\frac{4}{5}$ of $\frac{9}{10}$ of his money left. (*a*) What fraction of his money is left? (*b*) If he has \$36 left, how much had he at first?

13. A person sells $\frac{1}{8}$ of his pigs, then $\frac{1}{8}$ of the remainder, then $\frac{1}{10}$ of the remainder. (*a*) What fraction of the original number is left? (*b*) If there are 72 pigs then left, what number had he originally?

14. A buyer is allowed discounts of $33\frac{1}{3}$, 20, and 10 % on an article. Find (*a*) the equivalent single discount. (*b*) The equivalent per cent of the catalogue price. (*c*) The catalogue price, when the net price paid is \$96.

15. Find the cost of making a walk 2 rods long and 6 feet wide at 75 cents a square yard.

Interest by Six Per Cent Method

Preparatory Exercises

Six per cent per year is what per cent for (*a*) 2 yr.? (*b*) 3 yr.? (*c*) 4 yr.?

Six per cent per year is what per cent for (*a*) 1 mo.? (*b*) 2 mo.? (*c*) 4 mo.? (*d*) 6 mo.? (*e*) 8 mo.?

Six per cent per year (*a*) is 1% for how many days? (*b*) Is what per cent for 120 days? (*c*) Is what per cent for 6 days? (*d*) Is what per cent for 24 days?

By the *six per cent method* the interest at 6% is found on $1 for the given time, and this is multiplied by the number of dollars in the given principal.

Written Exercises

1. Find the interest on $396.50 at 6% for 3 yr. 10 mo. 23 da.

PROCESS

Int. on $1 at 6% for 3 yr.	$0.18	
Int. on 1 at 6% for 10 mo.	.05	½ of 10¢
Int. on 1 at 6% for 23 da.	.003⅚	⅙ of 2.3¢
Int. on $1 for 3 yr. 10 mo. 23 da.	$0.233⅚	

$0.233⅚ × 396.5 = $88.85.

At 6¢ per year, the interest for 3 yr. is 18¢.
At ½¢ per month, the interest for 10 mo. is 5¢.
At ⅙ of 1 mill per day, the interest for 23 da. is 3⅚ mills.

---

2. Find the interest at 6%,

a. On $275, for 1 yr. 4 mo. 18 da.

b. On $346, for 2 yr. 6 mo. 24 da.

c. On $409, for 3 yr. 2 mo. 12 da.

d. On $542, for 4 yr. 1 mo. 6 da.

3. When the interest at 6% on a given sum is $294.80, what is the interest on the same sum at (*a*) 5%? (*b*) 4½%? (*c*) 5½%? (*d*) 4%? (*e*) 7%?

NOTE. — (*a*) Deduct ⅙. (*b*) Deduct ¼. (*c*) Deduct 1/12. (*d*) Deduct ⅓. (*e*) Add ⅙.

4. Find the interest at (*a*) 5%, (*b*) 7%, (*c*) 5½%, (*d*) 6½%, (*e*) 4½%, and (*f*) 7½%; when the interest at 6% is $392.40.

5. Find the amount of $396.50 for 3 yr. 10 mo. 23 da. (*a*) At 5½%. (*b*) At 7%.

PROCESS

Int. 6%	$ 92.7149	Int. 6%	$ 92.7149
− ½%	7.7262 (1/12)	+ 1%	15.4525 (⅙)
Int. 5½%	$ 84.99	Int. 7%	$108.17
Principal	396.50	Principal	396.50
Amount	$481.49 *Ans.*	Amount	$504.67 *Ans.*

First find the interest at 6%; from this obtain the interest at 5½% by deducting 1/12 of it, and the interest at 7% by adding ⅙ of it.

---

6. Find the amount of

a. $360, for 1 yr. 2 mo. 24 da., at 4½%.

b. $720, for 3 yr. 3 mo. 19 da., at 5½%.

c. $396, for 2 yr. 4 mo. 6 da., at 6½%.

d. $432, for 5 yr. 8 mo. 15 da., at 7%.

SECTION VIII

ECONOMICAL BUSINESS COÖPERATION

The Market Place

In the early days of a growing community, the house-keeper depended for her supply of fresh vegetables, eggs, etc., upon the passing wagon of a farmer of the vicinity. With an increase of population, the need of a place at which a seller and a buyer could meet developed the "market square" in the center of the village. Here, in the early morning of stated days, were assembled the wagons, from the contents of which were filled the baskets of the customers.

With a larger number of inhabitants comes a market building, in which space is provided to enable the farmer to sell his less bulky products. In the adjacent streets his wagons are permitted to stand during certain hours. Here he sells his load of hay, cordwood, etc.

The Country Store

In sections remote from a village market, the country store serves as a "produce exchange." To it are brought eggs, butter, chickens, and the like, when the quantities are too small to permit of economical consignment by the producer to a city commission merchant; and these are exchanged either for cash or for groceries, dry goods, etc. Every day or two the storekeeper can ship a box or two of eggs, a crate of chickens, to his city agent, to be sold for his account.

Written Problems

1. A farmer brings to a store 8 dozen of eggs, for which he will be allowed 15 cents per dozen in exchange for tea at 60 cents a pound, or 12 cents in exchange for calico at 8 cents a yard. What would the storekeeper gain on the transaction, if he obtained 16 cents per dozen for the eggs and gave in exchange (*a*) tea that cost him 40 cents per pound? (*b*) Calico that cost him 6 cents per yard?

2. A storekeeper paid 12¢ per dozen for 100 dozen eggs, $13\frac{1}{2}$¢ per dozen for 120 dozen, and 13¢ per dozen for 80 dozen. They were sold through a commission merchant for 20 cents per dozen. What is the storekeeper's profit if the expenses for boxes, freight, and other charges amount to $12\frac{1}{2}$% of the sum obtained by the commission merchant?

Coöperation in Selling

While a farmer may produce a large quantity of fruit, berries, vegetables, etc., excellent in quality, he frequently realizes only a fraction of their real value. He packs these berries badly at times, or perhaps sends them to an overstocked market. In California, Florida, Maryland, Texas, Washington, and many other states, associations have been formed to dispose of the foregoing farm products through a competent manager. The latter insists upon attractive packages, uniform quality, and he ships each article to the place at which the best net price can be obtained, as determined by daily dispatches.

A carload of California grapes started for New York is halted by telegraph at Chicago, and its destination is changed to St. Louis, if later information shows an increase of price in this city, making it a better market than New York. The manager may direct the sale at an intermediate point of a carload of Texas peaches intended for Denver, when the quotations received by telegraph show the advisability of this procedure. The weather reports from an intended selling place may indicate the selection of a different city.

The individual farmer is taught by the manager what to raise, how to pack, etc.

Written Problems

1. A farmer shipped 1000 crates of peaches from Texas to Colorado at an expense of 27 ¢ per crate for picking, packing, and hauling; 40 ¢ for freight; 15 ¢ for refrigerating; and $2.60 for handling in Colorado, commission, and other charges. (*a*) What were his net receipts if the peaches sold for $3.75 per crate? (*b*) How much more or less would he receive if he had accepted an offer of 60 ¢ per crate for the peaches on the trees?

2. The manager of a selling association obtained $3.50 per crate for peaches at an expense of 30 ¢ per crate for picking, packing, etc., 25 ¢ for freight, 15 ¢ for ice, and $1.75 for commission and other charges. How much per crate was realized by the producer if his share of the association's expenses was 1 % of the amount remaining after other expenses had been deducted?

Coöperation in Production

When a farmer realizes that butter made by an expert brings a higher price than his product, he is willing to join in the organization of a butter factory ("creamery"), or at least to sell his milk to its owners. In this way he removes from the home the drudgery of churning, and obtains a greater revenue from his milk.

Written Problems

1. Find the cost of the following daily ration of a cow weighing 950 pounds, giving 20 quarts of milk per day:

Bean straw 8 lb. at $4 per ton of 2000 lb.
Mixed hay 12 lb. at $9 per ton of 2000 lb.
Wheat bran 2 lb. at $20 per ton of 2000 lb.
Corn meal 3 lb. at $2.94 per sack of 196 lb.
Cottonseed meal 2 lb. at $27 per ton of 2000 lb.
Oil meal 1 lb. at $28 per ton of 2000 lb.

2. What difference would be made in the cost of a ration in which 30 pounds of ensilage at $3 per ton are substituted for 8 pounds of hay?

3. A cow is pastured for 140 days at the rate of $1.50 per month of 30 days. To feed her for the rest of the year 30 bushels of corn and 30 bushels of oats ground together are required, together with 3 tons of clover hay. Taking the corn at 60 cents per bushel, oats at 40 cents per bushel, and the hay at $8 per ton, find the cost of the food for a year.

Coöperation with Employees

In many lines, work after the regular hours is paid for at double the regular rate.

Some factories fix a standard time for the completion of each article. An operator requiring more time is paid the regular hourly rate; one completing the daily task before the expiration of the working day receives the hourly rate for work done thereafter. The quick man thus increases his pay without diminishing that of his slower mate.

Some corporations set aside a percentage of the net profits for distribution annually among their employees in proportion to their wages.

Written Problems

1. A contractor engages to complete the electric work in a new building in 90 days. When 70 days have elapsed, he finds that it would require 25 days longer for his force of 20 men to finish the task if they continued at the regular rate of 8 hours per day. (*a*) How many hours per day must they work for the remaining time to enable their employer to carry out the terms of the contract? (*b*) What will be the daily pay of each of the employees for the remaining 20 days, at 50 cents per hour for 8 hours and double this rate for the overtime?

2. A factory makes a net profit of $50,000 per year on its capital of $250,000. After distributing 10 % of the capital among the stockholders and deducting 10 % of the profits to cover depreciation of the machinery, it divides the remainder among its employees whose pay roll amounts annually to $500,000. (*a*) What per cent of his salary is given each? (*b*) How much does Mr. Dalton receive, his salary being $1200 per year?

3. If the price of articles needed by the average family has increased 10 % and the expense of placing these articles in a customer's house adds 10 % to their new price because of the cost of telephone messages, packing, delivery, etc., how much more must now be paid for a year's supply of goods previously obtained for $475?

4. A farmer receives 20 % above the market price for butter and eggs delivered to customers who appreciate the superior quality of the articles he produces. How much more does he realize from the sale of goods that will bring $600 at the market rates, with an expense of $80, when the latter is increased 30 % by the delivery of the goods at the houses of his patrons?

Price Fluctuations

The price received by the North Dakota farmer for his wheat is affected by the weather in Argentina and southern Russia. Western Europe produces much less wheat than it needs; the remainder must be procured from the United States, Russia, and Argentina, each of which has a surplus.

The rate to be paid per bushel is determined by the amount of the European shortage and the size of the available surplus. This is first reflected in the quotations from Liverpool, which has finished its transactions for the day before those of Chicago are begun, owing to the time difference of six hours.

The Exchanges

Each city of any size has one or more exchanges; a produce exchange, a cotton exchange, a metal exchange, a tobacco exchange, a stock exchange, etc., either singly, or in combination, as a Board of Trade, for instance.

At each is received a continual stream of telegraphic information concerning the movements of commodities, weather conditions, rates of freight, etc., each of which has some effect on prices. The general effect of the exchange is beneficial, although some persons use it as a means of speculation.

An increase in a local price is reduced by the prompt receipt of a supply from a neighboring section when the cost at the latter is sufficiently less to stand the cost of transportation.

Cabbage and eggs are frequently shipped from Germany to our Atlantic ports, as are potatoes from Scotland and from Ireland. Australia sends meat to California.

Sight Problems

1. Find the brokerage on each of the following:

   a. 4000 bushels of oats at $\frac{1}{8}$ ¢ per bushel.
   b. 320 shares of stock at $12\frac{1}{2}$ ¢ per share.
   c. 240 bags of coffee at 4 ¢ per bag.
   d. 1000 barrels of pork at $2\frac{1}{2}$ ¢ per bbl.
   e. 1500 bales of cotton at 5 ¢ per bale.

2. A broker received a commission of $150 on a sale of wheat. How many bushels did he sell if his commission was $\frac{1}{8}$ ¢ per bushel?

3. At the rate of 4 cents per bag, how many bags of coffee must a broker buy to entitle him to a commission of $100?

4. How much does a broker receive for selling a $10,000 bond at the rate of $\frac{1}{8}$ % ?

Written Problems

1. A broker buys for the Planet Mills 10,000 bushels of wheat at $1.05 per bushel. What is the cost delivered at the mill, including brokerage of $\frac{1}{8}$ ¢ per bushel, and $\frac{1}{8}$ ¢ per bushel for transportation charges?

2. Find the cost of 1000 barrels of pork at $21.75 per barrel and brokerage at $2\frac{1}{2}$ cents per barrel.

3. The Fulton Mills bought 1000 bags of coffee, weighing 130 pounds each, at 12.42 ¢ per pound and paid 4 ¢ per bag brokerage. (*a*) Find the cost of the coffee. (*b*) What will be the cost of the coffee when it is roasted, if the expense of roasting is $\frac{1}{2}$ ¢ per pound? (*c*) If it is then put into bags holding 100 pounds each, how many bags of roasted coffee will there be, if the coffee loses 15 % of its weight by the roasting?

Sharing Expenses

Preparatory Exercises

1. Mr. A needs the use of a traction engine for 120 days in a year. Mr. B needs it for 100 days, and Mr. C for 80 days. (*a*) For how many days do the three need it? (*b*) For what part of this time does Mr. A need it? (*c*) Mr. B? (*d*) Mr. C?

2. If the three unite in the purchase of an engine for $1500, with the understanding that Mr. A should have the use of it for $\frac{2}{5}$ of the year, Mr. B for $\frac{1}{3}$ of the year, and Mr. C for $\frac{4}{15}$ of the year, how much should (*a*) Mr. A contribute to the cost? (*b*) Mr. B? (*c*) Mr. C?

3. Mr. Miller insures his property in Company No. 1 for $2000 and in Company No. 2 for $4000. What share of a loss should be paid (*a*) by No. 1? (*b*) By No. 2?

4. If Mr. Miller's loss by fire is $1200, how much should he receive (*a*) from Company No. 1? (*b*) From Company No 2?

Written Problems

1. A fire loss of $3915 is shared by three companies, company A having insured the property for $4000, B for $6000, and C for $8000. What share of the loss should be paid by each?

PROCESS

$4000 + $6000 + $8000 = $18000.   Total insurance.
18000 : 4000 :: 3915 : A's share
18000 : 6000 :: 3915 : B's share   Test by adding the
18000 : 8000 :: 3915 : C's share   three shares.

---

2. In a storm it was necessary to throw overboard 90 tons of wheat in order to save a vessel. If the cargo consisted of 105 tons belonging to A, 180 belonging to B, and 315 belonging to C, (*a*) what share of the loss should each bear? (*b*) How many tons of the remaining cargo should each receive?

3. A fertilizer contains 10 parts of nitrate of soda, 17 of kainit, and 53 of phosphate. How many pounds of each are contained in a ton?

4. A farmer needs 2700 cu. yd. of concrete. How many cu. yd. (*a*) of cement, (*b*) of broken stone, and (*c*) of cement must he procure if 1 cu. yd. of the first is needed to $1\frac{1}{2}$ cu. yd. of the second and 2 cu. yd. of the third?

Partnership

Wm. Arnold and John Fleming were employed by the same firm at a monthly salary of $100 each. The former had saved $3000 and the latter $2000. They started in business as Arnold and Fleming, each contributing his entire savings to the capital of the new firm. The written agreement provided that the profits should first be devoted to the payment of 6 % interest to each on the sum contributed by him, and that the remainder, if any, should be equally divided between the two partners.

Sight Problems

1. What is the interest at 6 % on the capital of $5000?

2. What remains from profits of $3300 after the deduction of the above interest?

3. What is (*a*) Mr. Arnold's share of the profits, including interest on the capital invested by him? (*b*) Mr. Fleming's share?

Written Problems

1. The year before going into business, Mr. Arnold and Mr. Fleming received 4 % interest on their savings. How much was the income of each increased during the next year ?

2. What would be the share of each in the profits, if he was allowed $ 1200 for his services, and the remainder was divided in proportion to the respective investments?

3. If each left in the business $ 1000 of his profits, how would profits of $ 3920 be divided at the end of the succeeding year on the basis of the original agreement and taking into consideration the new capital ?

Bankruptcy

When a business man (or a firm) finds that he is unable to pay all of his debts, he notifies his creditors, giving them a statement of his *assets* and his *liabilities*, the former including the goods in stock, money due him, etc., and the latter being the money he owes. The creditors may agree to accept a per cent of their respective claims in full settlement, taking a portion of the sum in cash, and the remainder in notes payable at stated intervals. In this way he may continue in business, the profits enabling him to meet the notes as they fall due.

If the creditors are not satisfied with any terms of settlement proposed by him, they may procure an order of a court for the sale of the stock, etc., also other property owned by any of the partners, and the distribution of the proceeds among them in proportion to their respective claims.

Preparatory Exercises

1. M's creditors accept his offer of 70 cents on the dollar. How much does A receive, to whom M owes $500?

2. A's stock, accounts, etc., realized $1200 above the expenses of bankruptcy proceedings, auctioneer's fees, etc. If his debts are $2000, what per cent of them can be paid?

Written Problems

1. Alphin & Co. failed with liabilities of $7240 and assets that were sold for $4525 above expenses. What per cent can be paid each creditor?

2. At the time of the failure of Martin E. Lynch he had four creditors, to whom were due the following:

Mr. A, $500; Mr. B, $600; Mr. C, $700; Mr. D, $800.

His assets realize $2000. What does each creditor receive?

3. Frank Carroll's creditors accept his offer of 20 % in cash, 20 % in 3 months, 20 % in 6 months, and 20 % in 9 months with interest at 5 % on the deferred payments. How much does he pay Gerald Tofte, including interest, to whom he owes $1200, if he makes the foregoing payments according to agreement?

4. Although freed from liability for the remaining 20 %, he pays one half of it one year from the date of failure, and the remainder one year later, with interest at 6 %. What is the amount of these two payments?

5. The books of a concern showed assets of $25,000 and liabilities of $30,000. If the former realized only 66 % of their book value, (*a*) what per cent of his indebtedness can be paid each creditor? (*b*) How much will John Rodman receive, to whom the company owes $375?

Corporations

Believing that a trolley line between Fairfax and Cameron would not only increase the value of their property but would also yield a fair return upon the money invested, a number of the residents agree to organize the Lorton Valley Railway Company. Having ascertained that the line can be built and equipped for $90,000, the *capital stock* is fixed at $100,000, to consist of 1000 *shares* of $100 each.

A dozen men pay up $100 per share to the amount of, say, $5000, and make application to the legislature for a *charter*, giving the name of the company, the names of the incorporators, with the number of shares held by each, and the amount paid therefor in *cash*.

Stockholders. — When the charter is granted, the remaining stock is offered for sale. Each purchaser receives a certificate specifying the number of shares he holds.

Officers. — When sufficient money is obtained from the sales of stock to warrant building operations, the organization of the company is completed by the election of a president, a vice president, a secretary, a treasurer, and a board of, say, twelve directors, each stockholder having one vote for each share of stock owned by him.

Dividends. — At the end of the first year of operation, the profits of the company are found to be $6716.25. To keep the equipment in proper condition, etc., the directors agree to distribute only $4500 among the stockholders as *dividends*, retaining $2216.25 as a *surplus*, to be used as occasion may require. This is added to any portion of the $100,000 not already expended and any other surplus. A dividend of $4\frac{1}{2}$ % is then *declared*, and a check for the sum to which he is entitled is mailed to each stockholder.

Preparatory Exercises

1. A withdraws $1000 from his savings bank and buys 10 shares of the stock. To what fraction of the profits is he entitled?

2. If the profits distributed among the stockholders the first year are $4500, (*a*) how much does A receive? (*b*) What per cent does he receive on his investment?

3. How much more does A receive on the investment than he would have obtained from the bank, which paid 4 % interest?

4. A sells his stock to B at $125 per share. If the latter receives $5 per share from the profits, (*a*) what per cent does he receive on his investment? (*b*) What per cent of the original price paid by A does the latter receive from B?

5. If the profits of the railway company for a year are $7000, (*a*) what surplus will remain after a 5 % dividend is paid? (*b*) What per cent is earned on the capital?

6. When the holder of $100 shares receives dividends of $7 per share, how many dollars per share can a person pay for them to obtain 5 % on the cost?

7. If a woman pays $150 per share and receives dividends of 9 % of the face value ($100) of the share, what per cent of the price paid per share does she receive in dividends?

The Broker. — When the investor, after consultation with a thoroughly reliable and disinterested person, selects the stock he desires to purchase, he may have to employ a broker to obtain it for him, who is paid $⅛ or $¼ per $100 share for his services, which include the transfer of the stock to the buyer.

Sight Problems

1. What does the buyer of 100 shares of stock pay for it at 139\frac{1}{2}$ per share and a brokerage of $$\frac{1}{8}$ per share?

2. What does the seller of 100 shares of stock receive for it at 129\frac{1}{2}$ per share less the brokerage of $$\frac{1}{8}$ per share?

3. What per cent does a man obtain on stock costing $150 per share which gives an annual dividend of $6 per share?

4. What can a man afford to pay per share for stock that gives an annual dividend of $9 per share, if he is satisfied with 4% on the money invested?

Written Exercises

1. Find the cost of 150 shares of stock bought at 143\frac{3}{4}$, brokerage $\frac{1}{8}$.

$$\$(143\tfrac{3}{4} + \tfrac{1}{8}) \times 150.$$

2. How much does Mr. Watson receive for 150 shares of stock sold at 143\frac{3}{4}$, brokerage $\frac{1}{8}$?

$$\$(143\tfrac{3}{4} - \tfrac{1}{8}) \times 150.$$

3. How many shares of stock at 80 can be bought for $9615, brokerage $\frac{1}{8}$?

$$\$9615 \div \$80\tfrac{1}{8}.$$

4. Mr. Romeo realized $17,253 from the sale of stock at 80. If the broker charged $\frac{1}{8}$ for selling, how many shares were sold?

5. When semiannual dividends of 4$\frac{1}{2}$% are received from stock bought at 175, including brokerage, what is the annual rate of income on the investment?

$$9\% \div 1.75.$$

Increasing Capital Stock. — A trolley company that has a capital of $100,000, on which it pays regular dividends of 6%, may consider it advisable to expend $50,000 in the extension of the road, etc. This additional money may be obtained by the issue of five hundred additional shares of stock, each of the existing stockholders being entitled to subscribe at par for one share for each two of the other stock owned by him.

A stockholder not desirous of increasing his holdings, or being without the necessary funds, could dispose of his " rights," obtaining therefor $10 per share from a person willing to invest in the new stock. As the latter gets it at par from the company, it costs him $110 per share, including the price paid for the " right."

Common and Preferred Stock. — Sometimes a corporation decides to make the new issue *preferred stock*, by using the earnings in the first instance to pay a dividend of, say, 5% on it before paying any dividend to the owners of the *common stock*.

This guarantee is an inducement to investors to pay as much as, say, $115 per share for preferred stock.

Assume that the trolley company's net earnings for the first year after the issue of $50,000 preferred stock are $6500. From this must be deducted $2500 dividend on the latter, leaving $4000 for the holders of the common stock, or a dividend of 4%. At this time, the preferred stock may bring $110 per share and the other $90 per share. When the earnings increase to $8500, leaving $6000 for distribution among the holders of the common stock, the latter may go to, possibly, $140.

Some corporations make another issue of preferred stock, which is called *second preferred*, the previous one being the *first preferred*.

Buying and Selling Stocks. — The small investor can seldom afford to risk his savings, and he therefore limits his investments to stocks of corporations that have paid regular dividends for a number of years. Companies are organized every day merely to unload worthless stocks upon foolish buyers, employing for the purpose unscrupulous agents at a large commission. Much of the nominal capital of, say, $100,000 goes into the pockets of the latter; some of it is wasted in the excessive prices paid to the organizers or their friends. The declaration of a dividend of six or seven per cent does not mean that it is warranted by the profits.

Bonds

Instead of increasing the capital to $150,000, the company may conclude to issue bonds for $50,000, bearing interest at, say, 5%. As security, the company mortgages the property in favor of the bondholders.

A person that would not risk his money in stock may be willing to invest in the bonds, owing to the security obtained through the mortgage.

A corporation first pays interest on its bonds, then dividends on preferred stock, then dividends on common stock.

The price of a bond is stated as a per cent of the face value, $109\frac{1}{2}$ meaning that a $100 bond would cost $109.50, exclusive of brokerage; a $10 bond, $10.95; a $500 bond, $547.50, etc. The brokerage of $\frac{1}{8}$ means $\frac{1}{8}$ for each $100 in the face of the bond, regardless of its cost.

A *registered* bond is made out in the name of the buyer and the interest check is mailed to his residence. A *coupon* bond contains a certificate for each interest installment, which is cut off when the interest is due and presented at the company's office for payment.

Sight Problems

1. What is the annual interest on bonds for $10,000 at 6%?

2. What is the cost of $10,000 in bonds at 137¾?

3. What is the brokerage on $10,000 in bonds at ⅛?

4. How many $1000 4% bonds must be purchased to yield $1000 annual interest?

5. What would be the cost of 4% bonds yielding $1000 interest annually when the bonds are selling for 96, including brokerage?

Written Problems

1. An electric-light company pays 5% interest on its bond issue of $100,000, 6% dividends on $50,000 preferred stock, and 7% dividends on $100,000 common stock. What were the net earnings for the year if there remained a surplus of $3745.60 after the foregoing payments were made?

2. A man wishes to invest a sum that will furnish an income of $1500 per year. (a) What will be the face value of 5% bonds that will yield $1500? (b) What is the cost of the bonds at 109⅞, and ⅛ brokerage?

3. How much does the Home Trust Co. pay for 25 one-thousand-dollar bonds at 104¾, brokerage ⅛?

4. What is the annual income from $21,750 invested in 5% bonds bought at 108⅝, brokerage ⅛?

5. A trolley line has a capital of 1000 shares, par value $100. It has issued and sold 5% bonds of the face value of $100,000. If the net earnings for the year are $11,750, what will be the surplus after paying interest on the bonds and a 6% dividend on the stock?

Accrued Interest

Mr. Ziegler is willing on July 2 to pay $120 per share for stock in the Happy Valley Irrigation Company, which pays regular semiannual dividends of $2½ on Jan. 1 and July 1. On October 1 the price might be $121¼ to give the seller the earnings of the three months that elapsed since he received a dividend, the buyer getting the new one in three months.

While the price of the 5% bonds of the same company might remain at 120, Mr. Ziegler would have to pay the seller the interest that *accrued* from the last interest date. If he bought a $100 bond on October 1, at 120, the cost would be $120 plus the interest at 5% on $100 from July 1.

Written Problems

1. (*a*) What does Mr. Ziegler pay for the foregoing bond? (*b*) Find the cost of a bond for $10,000 bought at 120, Dec. 1, brokerage ⅛, and accrued interest.

2. Mr. Bush has a $1000 six per cent bond, interest payable March 1 and Sept. 1. (*a*) How many days are there between these dates? (*b*) What fraction of the half-yearly interest due Sept. 1 has accrued on June 24? (*c*) If Mr. Bush sells the bond at 120 and accrued interest, how much does he receive for it, no brokerage? (*d*) If Mr. Bush cuts off and retains the September coupon, how much should he receive for the bond?

3. The owner of a farm of 242 acres sold it at $160 per acre. He invested one half of the proceeds in 4% bonds at 88, including brokerage, and the remainder in 5% bonds at 110, including brokerage. (*a*) What is the par value of the 4% bonds? (*b*) Of the 5% bonds? (*c*) What annual income is yielded by the bonds?

Maturity of a Bond. Bonds are issued for various terms up to, say, 50 years. At that time interest ceases, and they are redeemable at their face value.

A person purchasing on the day of its issue a 50-year 5% bond of $100 would receive in interest to the time of maturity $250. If he paid $120 for it, he would lose $20 at its redemption for $100, making his net income, at simple interest for 50 years, $230, which is $4.60 per year. As the bond cost $120, the rate received is 4.60 ÷ 120, or 3⅝%, at simple interest.

After the day of issue these bonds must be sold at a lower price to enable a purchaser to realize 3⅝%.

Written Problems

1. A 7% bond for $1000 has 10 years to run. (*a*) How much does it yield in that time at simple interest? (*b*) What is the total sum received in 10 years, including the face of the bond? (*c*) How much more than $1200, the cost of the bond, is received in 10 years? (*d*) What does this average per year? (*e*) What % of $1200 is this average?

2. A 3% bond for $100 maturing in 10 years was bought for $90. (*a*) How much interest is received in 10 years? (*b*) How much is received, including interest and the face of the bond? (*c*) How much more than the cost of the bond? (*d*) What is the average per year? (*e*) What % of $90 is this average?

In determining the rate paid by a bond, bankers take into consideration the interest they can earn upon each dividend (compound interest). A bond paying interest semiannually would show a higher rate than one paying interest annually.

Business Communications

The government takes a letter from a box in which it is deposited and insures its delivery to the addressee in any part of the civilized world. This is done at a nominal cost through the coöperation of the mail wagon, the railroad, the ocean steamer, the letter carrier, etc.

Without leaving his desk, the business man can communicate with a customer in Europe, Asia, etc., telephoning his message to the telegraph office. The reply is telephoned him, if he so desires.

Domestic messages are charged a minimum rate for 10 words, or less, with an additional charge per each word in excess of 10, the name of the sender and the name and address of the person to whom it is sent not being counted.

These rates are usually stated as 25 and 2, 50 and 4, etc., meaning 25¢ (or 50¢) for the first ten words and 2¢ (or 4¢) for each additional word.

Sight Exercises

1. At 50 and 4 what is the cost (*a*) of a 15-word message? (*b*) Of a 30-word message?

2. Give the cost at 25 and 2 of (*a*) a 15-word message. (*b*) A 30-word message.

Day Letters — Night Letters

To secure a fuller use of their lines, telegraph companies accept 50-word messages at reduced rates subject to slight delay in delivery. A *night letter* of 50 words is sent at the regular rate for a 10-word message, and a *day letter* at $1\frac{1}{2}$ times this rate. The latter is delivered the day it is filed, and the former the next morning.

Written Exercises

1. On a telegraph blank write a message to a friend stating that you intend visiting his city. Give the route you will take, state the time you will reach his city, also the address of the place at which you will stop while there. Endeavor to make it as brief as possible by the omission of unnecessary words, but taking care to convey all necessary information.

2. Write on the proper blank a 50-word night letter to a commission merchant stating that you are now digging your potatoes and desire to know the condition of the market in his city. Ask his advice as to the quantity you should send, the time of shipment, etc.

Cable Codes

The high cost of a direct cable message, in which the names and the addresses are counted, makes it necessary for business men to use a *code* in which each word represents a group.

The following are taken from a travelers' cable code distributed gratuitously by a company:

Amble. Arrived here, all well, leaving for home at once.

Askew. Advise you by all means to have a consultation of physicians.

Bayou. Business is quiet; everything all right and everybody well.

Giant. Cannot answer positively at present. Will write.

Punch. Please accept my heartiest congratulations.

State. Please open credit in my favor through . . . for sum of . . . . Wire to me when it is opened, as I wish to draw against it at once.

A code word filed with the company by each business house gives the name and address of the latter.

Cable Letters — Week-end Letters

A 12-word *cable letter* in plain language can be sent to London or to Liverpool at a reduced rate, to be mailed to any part of Europe without an additional fee, or to be delivered by telegraph the next day at a given low rate.

A 24-word *week-end letter* is received Saturday to be delivered by telegraph anywhere on Monday morning or to be sent by mail from London.

Written Exercises

1. Find the cost (*a*) of a 6-word direct message from Tucson, Arizona, to Vienna, Austria, at 44 cents per word. (*b*) Of a 12-word cable letter at the rate of $1.75 to London and 7 cents per word additional to Vienna. (*c*) Of a 24-word week-end letter at $2.15 plus 9 cents per word. (*d*) Of a 24-word dispatch from Boise City to Calcutta at 12 cents per word from Idaho to New York and 74 cents per word from New York to India.

Standard Time

A west-bound traveler passing through a town noticed children issuing from the school and employees from the factory. His watch indicated 12 : 30, while the station clock showed 11 : 30. Upon inquiring, he ascertained that it was just noon in the town, but that the station agent used *central standard time*, while his own watch was set to *eastern standard time*.

He then learned of the coöperation of the railroads in establishing a uniform time throughout each of the four belts into which the United States is divided for this purpose, and making the time difference one hour between any two adjoining belts.

Time Belts. — The belts are approximately 15° in width, each extending about 7½° on both sides of the meridians of Philadelphia (75°), Memphis (90°), Denver (105°), and Virginia City (120°), respectively, which use Eastern (E. T.), Central (C. T.), Mountain (M. T.), and Pacific (P. T.) Time, respectively.

Changing the Time. — The point at which a railroad changes from one time to another is stated on its time-tables. The Santa Fé uses C. T. between Chicago and Dodge City, M. T. between Dodge City and Seligman, and P. T. west of Seligman.

The time used in a city near the dividing line is fixed by the local authorities, being generally that of the railroad passing through it. When a town in longitude 112½° began the use of standard time by putting forward its clocks from 11:30 to 12, the residents changed the time of commencing dinner from 12 to 12:30. When a town in the same longitude a few miles north or south, but on a different railroad, set back its clocks from 12:30 to 12, it fixed the time for the beginning of the midday recess at 11:30.

Sight Problems

1. A baseball match in Chicago (C. T.) is finished at 5 P.M. Allowing 5 minutes for transmission, what time does the score reach a newspaper office (*a*) in New York (E. T.)? (*b*) In San Francisco (P. T.)? In Denver (M. T.)?

2. A train leaves at 9 A.M. C. T., due to arrive at its destination in 24 hours. At what hour should it arrive when the latter is located (*a*) in a section having M. T. ? (*b*) In one having P. T. ? (*c*) In one having C. T. ?

3. A train leaves at 8 A.M. (C. T.) and arrives at 9 P.M. (E. T.). What time is taken for the trip?

Standard Time in Other Countries

Practically all civilized countries have standard time. When the extent of the country east and west is very great, as in the case of the United States, Canada, and Australia, belts are employed, Canada having five, the most easterly using Atlantic Time (A. T.), which is that of Cape Breton (longitude 60°).

As an additional step towards simplification, the time of the meridian of Greenwich (longitude 0°) has been adopted by many other countries as the base, the time of each of these countries being the same as that of England or an exact number of hours earlier or later.

France, Algeria, Tunis, Spain, Belgium, Brazil, etc., use Greenwich time throughout; Germany, Denmark, Norway, Sweden, Italy, etc., use time 1 hour later; Chile uses Eastern Time; etc.

Sight Problems

1. When a message is telegraphed from London at noon, at what time, allowing ten minutes for its transmission, does it reach (*a*) Berlin? (*b*) Chicago? (*c*) Rio de Janeiro? (*d*) Santiago? (*e*) San Francisco?

2. Allowing 15 minutes for transmission, give the time at which messages telegraphed from Denver at noon will reach (*a*) London. (*b*) Paris. (*c*) Chicago. (*d*) San Francisco. (*e*) Cape Breton.

3. A vessel leaves New York Monday noon for Liverpool. Another vessel leaves Liverpool Monday noon for New York. Each makes the trip in 6 days of 24 hours each. At what hour Sunday does (*a*) the first reach Liverpool? (*b*) The other reach New York?

Solar Time

The connection between longitude and time is of importance chiefly to the mariner at sea. A chronometer on the vessel gives the London time. The captain, at noon by the sun, notes the difference between London time and that of the vessel, and calculates therefrom the longitude of the vessel.

Sight Exercises

1. Give the difference in degrees of longitude between a vessel and London when the time difference is

    a. 1 hr.   *b.* 1½ hr.   *c.* 2 hr.   *d.* 6 hr.

2. Give the difference in longitude when it is noon on a vessel and the chronometer gives Greenwich (London) time as follows :

    a. 1 P.M.   *b.* 11 A.M.   *c.* 2 : 30 P.M.
    d. 9 : 30 A.M.   *e.* 4 : 30 A.M.   *f.* 7 : 30 P.M.

3. When a vessel is west of the meridian of Greenwich (*a*) is it noon on a vessel before or after it is noon at Greenwich? (*b*) Does the chronometer show time before or after 12 o'clock noon ?

4. Give the longitude of a vessel at noon, when the chronometer gives London time as follows :

    a. 2 P.M.   *b.* 3 P.M.   *c.* 4 P.M.   *d.* 5 P.M.
    e. 11 A.M.   *f.* 9 A.M.   *g.* 6 A.M.   *h.* 5 A.M.

5. How many minutes of time correspond to a longitude difference (*a*) of 15°? (*b*) Of 1°? (*c*) Of 2°? (*d*) Of ½°? (*e*) Of 6° ?

Railroad Travel

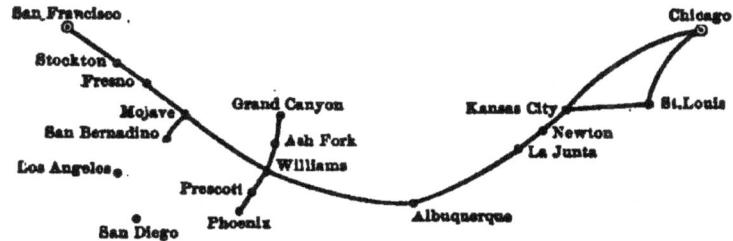

CHICAGO, KANSAS CITY, AND CALIFORNIA

READ DOWN				READ UP	
1	8	Miles	Stations	4	2
10.10 P.M.	8.05 P.M.	0	Lv. (C.T.) Chicago Ar.	11.00 A.M.	10.00 A.M.
11.00 A.M.	8.50 A.M.	454	Ar. Kansas City Lv.	10.30 P.M.	9.00 P.M.
	11.30 P.M.	—	Lv. St. Louis Ar.	7.43 A.M.	
11.30 A.M.	9.10 A.M.	454	Lv. Kansas City Ar.	10.20 P.M.	8.45 P.M.
	2.25 P.M.	654	Lv. Newton (C.T.) Ar.		2.55 A.M.
5.00 A.M.	10.45 P.M.	1024	Lv. (M.T.) La Junta Ar.	6.30 A.M.	4.10 P.M.
8.10 P.M.	11.25 A.M.	1372	Lv. Albuquerque Ar.	6.00 P.M.	4.05 A.M.
11.10 A.M.	10.28 P.M.	1753	Ar. Williams Lv.	5.30 A.M.	4.35 A.M.
	1.30 A.M.	1817	Ar. Grand Cañon Lv.	7.50 P.M.	
12.15 P.M.	11.28 P.M.	1776	Ar. Ash Fork Lv.	4.05 A.M	8.15 A.M.
	3.22 A.M.	1833	Ar. Prescott Lv.	12.23 A.M.	
	9.00 A.M.	1970	Ar. Phœnix (M.T.) Lv.	6.30 P.M.	
2.05 A.M.		2102	Ar. (P.T.) Barstow Lv.		2.20 P.M.
5.35 A.M.	12.10 P.M.	2203	Ar. San Bernardino Lv.	12.05 P.M.	11.00 P.M.
8.30 A.M.	2.35 P.M.	2263	Ar. Los Angeles Lv.	10.00 A.M.	9.00 A.M.
	3.00 P.M.	—	Lv. Los Angeles Ar.	7.15 A.M.	
1.10 P.M.	6.30 P.M.	2389	Ar. San Diego Lv.	2.45 A.M.	2.45 A.M.
2.15 A.M.		2102	Lv. Barstow Ar.		1.55 P.M.
4.25 A.M.	11.00 A.M.	2193	Ar. Mojave Lv.	11.45 A.M.	
10.40 A.M.	4.38 P.M.	2373	Ar. Fresno Lv.	4.15 A.M.	
2.25 P.M.	7.35 P.M.	2496	Ar. Stockton Lv.	12.45 A.M.	
5.30 P.M.	10.30 P.M.	2574	Ar. San Francisco Lv.	9.30 P.M.	8.00 P.M.

Reading the Table

In the time-table on page 369 the names of the stations are placed in the center, the time from Chicago, etc., to San Francisco being given on the left and that from San Francisco to Chicago on the right.

St. Louis is enclosed between lines to indicate that it is not on the main line. A passenger from St. Louis meets train 3 at Kansas City. Returning from the west, he leaves train 4 at the same point.

The stations in the next space are on the main line. A passenger for Grand Cañon leaves the train at Williams.

Ash Fork is on the main line. Passengers leave the train here to take one for Prescott and Phœnix. Barstow is on the main line; from it a train goes to San Bernardino, Los Angeles, and San Diego. Through passengers continue through Mojave, Fresno, etc., to San Francisco.

Sight Problems

1. What is the length of the branch line (*a*) from Williams to Grand Cañon? (*b*) From Ash Fork to Phœnix? (*c*) From Barstow to San Diego?

2. How long does (*a*) train 1 remain in Kansas City? (*b*) Train 2? (*c*) Train 3? (*d*) Train 4?

3. What is the distance (*a*) from Kansas City to Newton? (*b*) From Barstow to San Francisco?

4. How long does it take (*a*) train 1 to go from Chicago to Kansas City? (*b*) Train 3?

How long does it take (*c*) train 2 to go from Kansas City to Chicago? (*d*) Train 4?

5. When it is 10 : 30 P.M. at San Francisco what is the time at Chicago?

Written Problems

1. If a person leaves Chicago by train 1 on Monday, on what day does he reach San Francisco?

2. (*a*) How many hours does it require train 2 to go from San Francisco to Chicago? (*b*) How many miles does the train average per hour, including stops?

3. Find the expense of a trip from San Francisco to Chicago on train 4, allowing $59.75 for fare, $10.40 for sleeping accommodations, and three meals daily at the rate of 60 cents for breakfast, 75 cents for dinner, and 40 cents for supper.

In Italy, Spain, and Belgium the hours are numbered from 1 to 24, the latter being midnight. Some Canadian railroads follow this practice in their time-tables.

Travelers' Checks. — To render it unnecessary for a tourist, commercial traveler, etc., to carry a considerable sum in cash to meet hotel bills and other necessary expenses, associations of bankers issue books containing checks in denominations of $10, $20, $50, etc. Each check is signed by the buyer at the time he obtains it. When he presents one in payment of a hotel bill, etc., he signs it again in the presence of the person to whom he gives it.

Foreign Travel. — Bankers, express companies, etc., issue similar checks for use abroad, the equivalent in the money of various foreign countries being printed on the check. The following is a portion of the equivalents given on one for $20:

In U. S. and Canada	England			France		Germany		Russia	
	£	s.	d.	Fr.	Cent.	Marks	Pf.	Rubles	Kopecks
Twenty Dollars	4	1	8	102	50	83	30	38	46

Written Problems

1. Find the value of each of the following in U.S. money:

a. 102.50 francs at 19.3¢ b. 83.30 marks at 23.8¢
c. 38.46 rubles at 51.5¢ d. £ 410 8d. at $4.8665

2. What per cent of $20 is deducted in each case?

Letters of Credit. — Harold Cox, intending to spend a few months in Europe, obtains from his home bank a check payable in New York. This he presents to a New York banker, obtaining therefor a *letter of credit* for £ 250, travelers' checks for $200, and the remainder in the currency of the country of his steamer's destination. He selects English money for the letter of credit as the one for which he can get the best rates of exchange in the other countries.

With the letter of credit is given a list of bankers in Europe who will pay all or any portion of the sum named, in the money of their respective countries, at the current rate of exchange. Each payment is noted on the letter, to inform other bankers of the amount still remaining to the owner's credit.

When Mr. Cox returns home, he deposits in his own bank any unused travelers' checks and the letter of credit, if any balance remains, to be collected and placed to his account.

Written Exercise

How much does he pay the banker, at the rate of $4.86½ per £ with 1% for commission, $70.59 for the Italian money, and the face value of the travelers' checks plus a commission of ½%?

Transportation of Merchandise

The coöperation of railroads, which enables a passenger to ride for nearly a week without changing cars is extended to the transportation of freight.

An eastern farmer desiring to settle in Oklahoma, Arizona, etc., can load up all his possessions, including live stock, in one or more freight cars, traveling with them to his destination.

Small articles ordered from a distant city are delivered at the door by the parcel post or by the express; larger ones are brought to the nearest railroad station.

Grain is hauled from the farm to the railroad, the loaded cars deliver it to the lake vessel, thence it goes to the canal boat, to be placed upon the ocean steamer for delivery at a European port. In many cases the chief expense is the cost of getting it from the farms to the railroad station.

Parcel Post

Weight	First Zone Local Rate	Weight	Second Zone 150 mi.	Third Zone 150 to 300 mi.	Fourth Zone 300 to 600 mi.	Fifth Zone 600 to 1000 mi.	Sixth Zone 1000 to 1400 mi.	Seventh Zone 1400 to 1800 mi.	Eighth Zone over 1800 mi.
1 lb.	$0.05	1 lb.	$0.05	$0.06	$0.07	$0.08	$0.09	$0.11	$0.12
2 & 3 "	.06	2 "	.06	.08	.11	.14	.17	.21	.24
4 & 5 "	.07	3 "	.07	.10	.15	.20	.25	.31	.36
6 & 7 "	.08	4 "	.08	.12	.19	.26	.33	.41	.48
8 & 9 "	.09	5 "	.09	.14	.23	.32	.41	.51	.60
10 & 11 "	.10	6 "	.10	.16	.27	.38	.49	.61	.72
12 & 13 "	.11	7 "	.11	.18	.31	.44	.57	.71	.84
14 & 15 "	.12	8 "	.12	.20	.35	.50	.65	.81	.96
16 & 17 "	.13	9 "	.13	.22	.39	.56	.73	.91	1.08
18 & 19 " etc.	.14	10 "	.14	.24	.43	.62	.81	1.01	1.20

Sight Problems

1. How many feet long may a package be so that the sum of its length and the perimeter of the end may not exceed 6 feet?

A parcel must not exceed 72 inches in combined length and girth.

2. How long may a package be to keep within the limit of 6 feet when each end is a square measuring ½ foot?

3. Give the volume of a box whose length is 2 feet, the end being 1 foot square.

4. Give the volume of a box whose length is 4 feet, each end being ½ foot square.

Written Problems

1. A dealer in artificial flowers wishes to ascertain the dimensions of the ends of a box 24 inches long that will come under the provisions of the parcel post as to size, and will contain the greatest quantity.

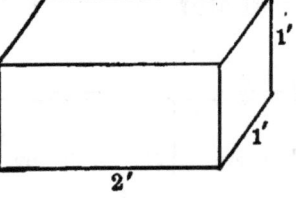

Find the capacity of each of the following boxes in cubic feet and a fraction :

    a. 24 inches long, ends 9 in. by 15 in.
    b. 24 inches long, ends 8 in. by 16 in.
    c. 24 inches long, ends 6 in. by 18 in.
    d. 24 inches long, ends 12 in. by 12 in.

NOTE. — Change each dimension to feet before multiplying.

2. (*a*) What part of a cubic foot will be contained in a box 11 inches long, 9 inches wide, 4 inches deep? (*b*) At ⅘ bushel to the cubic foot, what fraction of a bushel will it hold? (*c*) What is the weight of the wheat it will contain at 60 pounds to the bushel?

Express

Express companies supply transportation of articles too heavy or too bulky to be sent by parcel post, also of goods requiring prompt delivery. A company's wagon collects packages at the residences or stores of the senders and delivers them at the proper railroad station. Another wagon in the distant city takes each package to the designated address.

Freight

Bulky articles and goods in large quantities are transported by freight. The shipper delivers them at the railroad station or steamer dock, and receives from the agent of the company a receipt called a *Bill of Lading*. This is mailed to the person to whom the goods are to be delivered.

Written Problems

1. Change 3*d.*, English money, to cents and a decimal.

2. Find the cost per bushel of sending grain from Chicago to Liverpool at $.0112 for the lake freight, $.043 for the canal freight, 3*d.* for the ocean freight, $\frac{1}{2}$¢ for handling charges at Buffalo and 1¢ in New York.

3. When the all-rail rate from Chicago to New York is 9.6 cents per bushel for wheat weighing 60 pounds to the bushel, what is the freight per ton?

4. What is the cost per bushel per mile for transporting wheat from Chicago to New York, 960 miles?

5. At the rate of 9.6 cents for 960 miles, what would be the rate on a bushel of wheat to New York from a point 1776 miles west of Chicago?

6. Find the canal freight on (*a*) 8500 bushels of corn at .038¢ per bushel. (*b*) 8000 bushels of wheat at .043¢ per bushel.

Transmitting Money

If Thomas Blake in Bismarck desires to send $50 to Daniel Lawler in Chicago, he may do so in any one of the following ways:

He can send his personal check drawn on a Bismarck bank, which Mr. Lawler collects in Chicago, at a small discount.

He can buy from a Bismarck bank a cashier's check payable at a Chicago bank; this may cost him 25 cents in addition to the $50.

He can buy for $50.18 a postal money order payable at the Chicago post office, or an express money order payable at the express company's Chicago office.

He can transmit the money by telegraph by paying $50 at the telegraph office together with the regular fee and the cost of two telegrams. He notifies Mr. Lawler by telegraph, and the latter obtains the money at a telegraph office in Chicago.

Bank Drafts

One form of paying a large sum is by means of a bank draft. The following is a draft purchased from the First National Bank of Seattle by Fred Johnson, to pay Mr. Priedigkeit of Xenia the sum specified.

SEATTLE, WASH., *Aug. 15*, 19*15*

$1248 75/100

At sight pay to the order of *William Priedigkeit*

Twelve Hundred Forty-eight 75/100 ~~~~~~~~~~~ Dollars.

Value received, and charge to the account of the *First National Bank.*

To MERCHANTS' BANK
  XENIA, OHIO

Martin E. Lynch
Cashier

The cost of the foregoing draft depends upon the *rate of exchange*, which varies from time to time. When a draft is purchased for less than its face, exchange is at a *discount*; when it costs more than its face, exchange is at a *premium*. The rates quoted in the daily papers give the premium or the discount on $1000, unless a rate per cent is specified.

The draft shown on page 376 is called a *sight draft*, which is payable upon presentation.

Written Exercises

1. Find the cost of the foregoing draft at a premium of 75¢ per thousand dollars.

$$\$1248.75 + \tfrac{1}{4} \text{ of } \$1.25$$

2. (*a*) What is the cost of a draft for $20,000 purchased at a discount of $\tfrac{1}{8}\%$? (*b*) What rate per thousand corresponds to $\tfrac{1}{8}\%$?

Cashier's Checks

The sight draft is now being displaced by a cashier's check, as follows:

FIRST NATIONAL BANK
SEATTLE, WASH., *Aug. 15*, 1915

MERCHANTS' BANK
XENIA, O.

Pay to the order of *William Priedigkeit*

Twelve Hundred Forty-eight $\tfrac{75}{100}$ ~~~~~~~~Dollars.

1248\tfrac{75}{100}$

Wm. J. Brown
Cashier

Bills of Exchange

A draft payable in a foreign country is called a *bill of exchange*. This is issued in a set of two, the *original* and the *duplicate*. When one is paid, the other has no value.

SAN FRANCISCO, CAL., *Sept. 4, 19//*

£534 3s. 6d.

AT SIGHT of this first of exchange, second unpaid, pay to the order of *Maurice F. Egan*

Five Hundred Thirty-four Pounds Sterling, three shillings, sixpence, ⌇⌇⌇⌇⌇⌇⌇⌇⌇⌇⌇⌇⌇

and charge the same to the account of

To *Pye, Neal, & Co.*
   London, Eng.　　　　　*Jos. F. Lamorelle*

Bills of exchange are generally payable at sight or at a given time after sight. The following is one form of a time bill of exchange :

Exchange for 5000 fr.

ALBUQUERQUE, N. M., *Aug. 4, 19/6*

Sixty days after sight of this second of exchange, first unpaid, pay to the order of *Charles Mette*

Five Thousand Francs, ⌇⌇⌇⌇⌇⌇⌇⌇⌇⌇⌇⌇⌇
and charge to the account of

To *Francolini Frères*　　　　*Barniele & Johnson*
   Marseilles, France

When Mr. Mette receives this bill, he presents it to Francolini Frères for *acceptance*. They agree to pay the bill when due by writing across the face in red ink the word "Accepted," with the date, say, "Aug. 11, 1916." Sixty days after Aug. 11, the bill is payable upon presentation.

The prices of exchange are given in the papers in the following form, the rates varying from time to time :

Rates of Exchange

	SIGHT	60 DAYS
Sterling	4.86	4.84
Francs	$5.17\frac{1}{2}$	5.20
Reichmarks	.95	$.94\frac{1}{2}$

These figures mean that a sight bill on a place in Great Britain costs $4.86 per £, and a 60-day bill $4.84.

The rate for French money means that $1 will purchase a sight bill for $5.17\frac{1}{2}$ francs, or a 60-day bill for 5.20 francs.

The rate for German money means that 95 cents is the cost of 4 marks in a sight bill and $94\frac{1}{2}$ cents in a 60-day bill.

Written Exercises

1. Find the cost of a sight bill for £584 7s. 6d. at $4.86 per £.

2. How much is paid for a 60-day bill on Marseilles for 5000 fr. at the rate of 5 fr. 20 for $1?

$$ \$ (5000 \div 5.2) $$

3. A bill for 1876 marks is bought at the rate of 4 marks for $94\frac{1}{2}$ cents. How much did it cost?

4. How many francs will cost $2500 at the rate of $5.17\frac{1}{2}$ francs to the dollar?

Use of Drafts in Collecting Money

To insure prompt payment, the Wainscott Manufacturing Co. "draws" upon its customers as their bills fall due.

The bill of Henry Jenkins of Hightown, N. D., for $448.75 is due May 6, 1915. The Wainscott Manufacturing Co. makes out the following draft:

MINNEAPOLIS, MINN., *May 1*, 19*15*

At *three days'* sight pay to the order of

THE MANUFACTURERS' BANK

Four Hundred Forty-eight $\frac{75}{100}$ ~~~~~~~~~~ Dollars

and charge to the credit of

To *Henry Jenkins*   WAINSCOTT MANUFACTURING CO.
  Hightown, N.D.   *J. F. Rorke,* Treas.

This draft is deposited "for collection" in the Manufacturers' Bank, in which the Wainscott Manufacturing Company keeps its account. This bank sends it to the First National Bank of Hightown, which it reaches May 3. A messenger from this bank presents it for acceptance to Henry Jenkins, who writes across its face "Accepted, May 3, 1915," and appends his signature. If he keeps an account in the First National Bank, the latter "charges" it with $448.75, and mails the Manufacturers' Bank a cashier's check for the amount.

By this method the Wainscott Manufacturing Company obtains the money by May 8, since Mr. Jenkins would not like to injure his credit with his home bank by refusing to "accept" the draft.

SECTION IX

PRACTICAL USES OF POWERS AND ROOTS

Squares and Square Roots

Preparatory Exercises

1. The front of a shed is 5 feet higher than the back. The shed is 12 feet deep. How long is the roof?

Draw *ABC* on a scale of 4 inches to the foot. Make *CB* 3 inches long. At *C* erect a perpendicular *CA*, 1¼ inches. Measure *AB*.

2. *MNO* is the upper part of the front of a tent. *MO* is 6 feet. *NX* measures 4 feet. How long is *NO*?

Draw a line *XO*, 3 inches long. At *X* erect a perpendicular *XN*, 4 inches long. Draw the line *NO*, and measure its length.

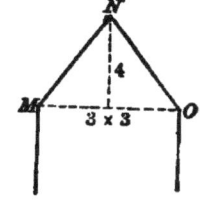

The triangles *ACB* and *NXO* are *right triangles*. The angles at *C* and *X* are *right angles*. The side *AB* or *NO*, opposite the right angle, is the *hypotenuse*. One of the remaining sides of a right triangle is the *base*, and the other the *perpendicular*.

In the right triangle *ABC*, it will be found that $(13 \times 13) = (12 \times 12) + (5 \times 5)$; that is, $169 = 144 + 25$.

13×13 is written 13^2: it is read 13 "*square*." 5×5 is written 5^2; 12×12 is written 12^2.

$$\text{Hypotenuse}^2 = \text{Base}^2 + \text{Perpendicular}^2$$

3

Sight Problems

1. How many square rods are there in a plot of ground 8 rods long 8 rods wide?

2. A piece of ground 12 rods long 12 rods wide is said to be 12 rods square. How many square rods are there in a piece of ground 12 rods square?

3. How many square inches are there in each of the six equal square faces of a cubical box whose edge measures 3 inches?

4. Give answers:

a. $3^2 = ?$ *b.* $6^2 = ?$ *c.* $10^2 = ?$ *d.* $20^2 = ?$ *e.* $90^2 = ?$
f. $4^2 = ?$ *g.* $7^2 = ?$ *h.* $11^2 = ?$ *i.* $30^2 = ?$ *j.* $80^2 = ?$
k. $5^2 = ?$ *l.* $9^2 = ?$ *m.* $12^3 = ?$ *n.* $40^2 = ?$ *o.* $70^2 = ?$

5. How many square rods are there in a 10-acre field?

6. How many rods are there in each side of a square field (*a*) containing 1600 sq. rd.? (*b*) Containing 10 A.?

7. How many inches long is each side of a square piece of paper that contains (*a*) 16 sq. in.? (*b*) 36 sq. in.? (*c*) 100 sq. in.?

8. What are the two equal factors (*a*) of 49? (*b*) Of 25? (*c*) Of 81? (*d*) Of 121?

9. Give answers:

a. $81 = (?)^2$ *b.* $100 = (?)^2$ *c.* $1600 = (?)^2$
d. $49 = (?)^2$ *e.* $121 = (?)^2$ *f.* $8100 = (?)^2$
g. $36 = (?)^2$ *h.* $144 = (?)^2$ *i.* $6400 = (?)^2$

Square Root

To indicate that one of the two equal factors of a number is required, the sign $\sqrt{\ }$ is used.

Thus, $\sqrt{81} = 9$ is read " The *square root* of 81 is 9."

Sight Exercises

1. Give answers:

a. $\sqrt{4} = ?$ *b.* $\sqrt{36} = ?$ *c.* $\sqrt{144} = ?$ *d.* $\sqrt{2500} = ?$

e. $\sqrt{9} = ?$ *f.* $\sqrt{64} = ?$ *g.* $\sqrt{169} = ?$ *h.* $\sqrt{3600} = ?$

i. $\sqrt{1} = ?$ *j.* $\sqrt{49} = ?$ *k.* $\sqrt{121} = ?$ *l.* $\sqrt{8100} = ?$

Architects, surveyors, mechanics, and other business people use tables to ascertain the squares and the square roots of numbers. The following table gives the squares and the square roots of numbers to 60.

Squares and Square Roots

No.	Sq.	Sq. Root	No.	Sq.	Sq. Root	No.	Sq.	Sq. Root
1	1	1.	21	441	4.5826	41	1681	6.4031
2	4	1.4142	22	484	4.6904	42	1764	6.4807
3	9	1.7321	23	529	4.7958	43	1849	6.5574
4	16	2.	24	576	4.8990	44	1936	6.6332
5	25	2.2361	25	625	5.	45	2025	6.7082
6	36	2.4495	26	676	5.0990	46	2116	6.7823
7	49	2.6458	27	729	5.1962	47	2209	6.8557
8	64	2.8284	28	784	5.2915	48	2304	6.9282
9	81	3.	29	841	5.3852	49	2401	7.
10	100	3.1623	30	900	5.4772	50	2500	7.0711
11	121	3.3166	31	961	5.5678	51	2601	7.1414
12	144	3.4641	32	1024	5.6569	52	2704	7.2111
13	169	3.6056	33	1089	5.7446	53	2809	7.2801
14	196	3.7417	34	1156	5.8310	54	2916	7.3485
15	225	3.8730	35	1225	5.9161	55	3025	7.4162
16	256	4.	36	1296	6.	56	3136	7.4833
17	289	4.1231	37	1369	6.0828	57	3249	7.5498
18	324	4.2426	38	1444	6.1644	58	3364	7.6158
19	361	4.3589	39	1521	6.2450	59	3481	7.6811
20	400	4.4721	40	1600	6.3246	60	3600	7.7460

Sight Exercises

1. Give the square roots of the following numbers:

a. 2601 *b.* 1444 *c.* 3136 *d.* 961 *e.* 60 *f.* 38

2. Give the squares (approximately) of

a. 3.3166 *b.* 5.5678 *c.* 7.4162 *d.* 6.9282 *e.* 7.4833

Note. — The product of 4.6904 by 4.6904 is 21.99985216, which is 22 for all practical purposes.

Applications of Square Root

Written Problems

1. How long is the wire rope *SV*, which is employed to keep the pole *MT* perpendicular? One end is fastened to the pole at *S*, 15 ft. from the ground. The other is fastened at *V*, which is 8 ft. from the base of the pole.

PROCESS

$B^2 = 64 \ (8^2)$ Add the squares of *VT* and *TS*. Look in
$P^2 = 225 \ (15^2)$ the column of squares for 289. This is found
$\overline{H^2 = 289}$ to be the square of 17.

Ans. 17 ft.

---

2. Find the length of the hypotenuse of each of the following right triangles, the other sides of which measure, respectively:

a. 12 ft. and 16 ft.   *b.* 7 mi. and 24 mi.
c. 35 rd. and 12 rd.   *d.* 24 in. and 10 in.
e. 9 rd. and 40 yd.   *f.* 20 in. and 21 in.

3. Find the base of a right triangle whose perpendicular measures 11 yards and hypotenuse 61 yards.

PROCESS

$B^2 = ?$

$P^2 = \ \underline{121 \ (11^2)}$

$H^2 = 3721 \ (61^2)$

Ans. 60 yd.

Since 3721 (H^2) represents the sum of 121 (P^2) + B^2, the latter equals 3600, the square root of which is 60.

---

4. Find answers:

a. Hypotenuse, 85; base, 84.   Perpendicular?

b. Perpendicular, 112; hypotenuse, 113.   Base?

Factors and Multiples

Preparatory Exercises

1. What is the square (*a*) of 2? (*b*) Of 5? (*c*) Of 10?

2. Show that $10^2 = 2^2 \times 5^2$.

3. What is the square root (*a*) of 100? (*b*) Of 25? (*c*) Of 4?

4. Show that $\sqrt{100} = \sqrt{4} \times \sqrt{25}$.

Written Problems

1. A piece of tin is 69 inches square. How many square inches does it contain?

PROCESS

$69^2 = 23^2 \times 3^2$

$69^2 = 529 \times 9$, etc.

From the table, $23^2 = 529$

---

2. Find the answers:

   a. 336^2. *b.* 225^2. *c.* 153^2. *d.* 96^2. *e.* 184^2.

3. What is the length of a square field that contains 4761 square rods?

4. Find the square root of

a. 36 × 169.   *b.* 4 × 1369.   *c.* 25 × 2809.   *d.* 16 × 3481.
e. 25 × 289.   *f.* 9 × 1681.   *g.* 81 × 3249.   *h.* 64 × 2209.

5. A number is divisible by 4 or by 25 when its last two figures are ciphers or constitute a multiple of 4 or of 25.   A number is divisible by 9 when the sum of its digits is divisible by 9.

Using 4, 9, or 25 as a factor, find the square root of the following:

    a. 7056.   *b.* 54756.   *c.* 60025.   *d.* 86436.
    e. 4761.   *f.* 34596.   *g.* 38025.   *h.* 60516.

6. What is the length of the diagonal of a rectangular field whose dimensions are 84 rods and 13 rods, respectively?

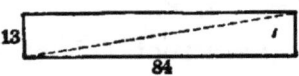

PROCESS

The diagonal is the hypotenuse of a right triangle having sides of 84 rods and 13 rods, respectively.

$B^2 = 7056$
$P^2 = 169$
$H^2 = 7225$

Find the sum of the squares of the sides, 7225. Take 25 as one factor, which gives 289 as the other factor. Indicate the square root $\sqrt{25 \times 289}$, which equals 5 × 17.   *Ans.* 85 rods.

---

7. A 74-foot ladder just reaches a window 70 feet from the ground. How far from the wall is the foot of the ladder?

8. A vessel has sailed 96 miles due north from the starting point, and has then sailed 28 miles due east. How far is the vessel then from the starting point?

Extracting the Square Root

Written Problems

1. How much shorter is a path (XY) along the diagonal of a rectangular field 80 rods long and 39 rods wide than the distance $XW + WY$?

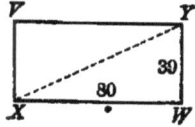

PROCESS

I. To find the square root of 7921 begin at the ones and point off two figures, which leaves 79 as the first period.

$80^2 = 6400$
$39^2 = 1521$
$H^2 = 7921$

Ans. 8 9
$\overline{79'21}$
64
169 $\overline{1521}$
$\underline{1521}$

II. As the largest square contained in 79 is 64, write 64 under 79, and place 8 (the square root of 64) above 79 (the first period).

III. Subtract 64 from 79 and bring down the second period, making 1521 the partial dividend.

IV. Write 16 (twice 8) as a trial divisor. Divide 152 by 16 for the next figure of the root. Place 9 (the quotient) over the second period, and annex it to the trial divisor, making 169 the complete divisor.

V. Multiply 169 by 9. Since the product equals the partial dividend, the required root is 89. $XY = 89$ rods.

2. A bird is at the top of a tree 75 feet high. How far is it from a boy who is 40 feet from the foot of the tree? (Make a diagram.)

3. The foot of a ladder is 13 feet from the bottom of a building 84 feet high and just reaches the roof. (*a*) How long is the ladder? (*b*) How far from the bottom of a building is one end of a 50-foot ladder that just reaches a window 48 feet from the ground?

4. Find the square root of 935089.

```
                9   6   7        PROCESS
               ─────────────     I. Beginning at the ones, point off the
               93  50  89        number in periods of two figures.
               81                   II.  As the largest square contained in
               ──                93, the first period, is 81, write 81 under
       186    1250               93, and place 9, the square root of 81,
              1116               above 93.
              ──────                III.  Subtract 81 from 93, and bring
      1927    13489              down the next period, making 1250 a par-
              13489              tial dividend.
              ─────
```

IV. Write 18 (twice 9) as a trial divisor. Divide 125 by 18 and take 6 (the quotient) as the next figure of the root. Write 6 above the second period and annex 6 to the trial divisor 18, making the complete divisor 186.

V. Multiply 186 by 6 and subtract the product from 1250, leaving 134. To this annex the next period, 89, making the partial dividend 13489.

VI. Write 192 (twice 96) as the next trial divisor. Divide 1348 by 192 and take 7 as the next figure of the root. Write 7 above the last period and also annex 7 to the trial divisor 192, making the complete divisor 1927.

VII. Multiply 1927 by 7. As there is no remainder, the required root is 967.

5. Find the square root of

   a. 56169.   *b.* 37249.

   c. 140625.   *d.* 9.5481.

6. Find the length of the missing side in each of the following right triangles :

a. Hypotenuse, 97 yd. ; base, 72 yd.

b. Perpendicular, 91 ft. ; hypotenuse, 109 ft.

c. Base, 99 rd. ; perpendicular, 20 rd.

7. What is the side of a square steel plate that will contain 150 square inches?

PROCESS

$$\sqrt{150} = \sqrt{25} \times 6 = 5\sqrt{6} = 5 \times 2.4495 = 12.2475 \text{ (in.)} \text{ } \textit{Ans.}$$

Take as the factors of 150, 25 (the largest square) and 6. Write the square root of 25 outside the radical, leaving 6 inside. Take the value of $\sqrt{6}$ from the table.

NOTE. — $5\sqrt{6}$ is read "5 times the square root of 6." Since the square-root sign is also called a *radical*, the foregoing expression is sometimes read as "5 radical 6."

8. Give the values of the following:

    a. $\sqrt{120} = ?$ *b.* $\sqrt{200} = ?$ *c.* $\sqrt{350} = ?$

9. An acre contains 4840 square yards. How many yards long is a square field containing one acre?

10. Find the side of a square the diagonal of which measures 1 inch.

$$\overline{EF}^2 + \overline{FG}^2 = \overline{EG}^2 = 1.$$

Since $EF = FG$, $2\overline{EF}^2 = 1$, and $\overline{EF}^2 = \frac{1}{2}$.

EF is, therefore, equal to $\sqrt{\frac{1}{2}} = \frac{\sqrt{1}}{\sqrt{2}} = \frac{1}{\sqrt{2}}$.

In order to avoid dividing 1 by 1.4142 ($\sqrt{2}$) the radical is transferred to the numerator of the fraction, by multiplying both terms by $\sqrt{2}$.

$$\frac{1}{\sqrt{2}} = \frac{1 \times \sqrt{2}}{\sqrt{2} \times \sqrt{2}} = \frac{\sqrt{2}}{2} = \frac{1.4142}{2} = .7071 \text{ (in.)} \text{. } \textit{Ans.}$$

11. What is the side of a square when its diagonal is 2 feet long?

12. Each side of an aquilateral triangle measures 6 inches. Find its altitude.

Square Root of Decimals

Preparatory Exercises

1. What is the square (*a*) of $\frac{3}{10}$? (*b*) Of .3? (*c*) Of $\frac{7}{10}$? (*d*) Of .7? (*e*) How many decimal places in the result in (*b*) and in (*d*)?

2. How many decimal places are there in the product (*a*) of .03 by .03? (*b*) Of .11 by .11?

3. What is the square root (*a*) of 50? (*b*) Of .50? (*c*) Of .5?

4. Give from the table the square root (*a*) of 6. (*b*) Of 60. (*c*) About how many times the former is the latter?

5. (*a*) Can you give from the table the square root of $\frac{30}{100}$? (*b*) How does this compare with the square root of $\frac{3}{10}$?

Observe that $\sqrt{\frac{30}{100}} = \frac{\sqrt{30}}{10}$ and $\sqrt{\frac{3}{10}} = \frac{\sqrt{3}}{\sqrt{10}}$, which means $\sqrt{3} \div \sqrt{10}$, or $1.7321 \div 3.1623$. By changing .3 to .30, this division is avoided.

The square root of .5 is obtained as follows when a table is not available:

	PROCESS

Ans. .7071 nearly
    .50
    49
1407   10000
      9849
14141 15100
    14141
14142 95900
	I. Begin at the decimal point, and point off two places to the right, annexing a cipher to supply the second place.
	II. Place .7 above .50, and write 49 underneath it. Subtract, and bring down two ciphers (the next period).
	III. Since 14 (the trial divisor) is not contained in 10 (the first two figures of the partial dividend), place a cipher in the root, and

annex one to the trial divisor, making it 140. Bring down another period, making the partial dividend 10000, etc.	

Written Problems

1. A step ladder is 7 ft. 6 in. long. How far apart will be the feet of the ladder when the top is 6 feet above the ground?

2. An octagon having each side 2 inches long is cut from a square piece of paper by cutting off four right triangles. (*a*) What is the length of *Ax* or *xB* when *AB* is 2 inches? (*b*) What is the area of *AxB*?

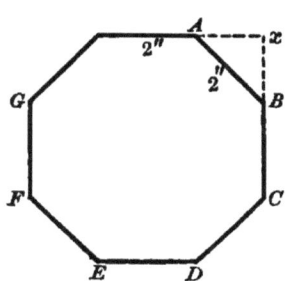

3. Two lead sheets of the same thickness are melted together, one being 10 inches square and the other 10.5 inches square, and made into a single square sheet of the same thickness. What is the size of the latter?

4. A hexagon is cut from a circle 4 inches in diameter. (*a*) How long is each side of the equilateral triangle *MNC*? (*b*) How long is each side of the hexagon? (*c*) Find the length of *xC*, the altitude of one of the triangles. (*d*) How long is *xy*?

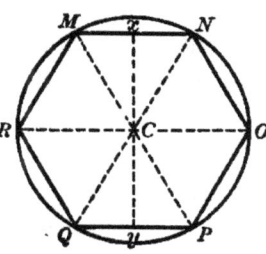

5. The intensity of a light varies inversely as the square of the distance from the light. In testing an electric light it was found that it gave the same illumination at 9 feet as a candle did at $2\frac{1}{4}$ feet. What was the candle power of the former?

Electric : Candle :: $(9)^2$: $(2\frac{1}{4})^2$

6. If a man can just tell the time by his watch when he is 50 feet from a light, how far away from a light 3 times as powerful can he tell it?

Cubes and Cube Roots

$5 \times 5 \times 5$ is written 5^3, the exponent 3 denoting that 5 is taken 3 times as a factor. 5^3 is read "5 *cube*" or "the *third power* of 5."

Sight Exercises

Give answers :

a. $2^3 = ?$ b. $3^3 = ?$ c. $4^3 = ?$ d. $5^3 = ?$

e. $6^3 = ?$ f. $7^3 = ?$ g. $8^3 = ?$ h. $9^3 = ?$

Cube Roots

To denote that the cube root is to be extracted a small 3 is written in the front of the radical sign.

$\sqrt[3]{27} = 3$ is read "the cube root of 27 is 3."

The ordinary method of extracting the cube root is too tedious for business men, who obtain it by using tables, for instance, the following extract from which gives the cubes and the cube roots of numbers to 30 :

Table

No.	Cube	Cube Root	No.	Cube	Cube Root	No.	Cube	Cube Root
1	1	1.	11	1331	2.2240	21	9261	2.7589
2	8	1.2599	12	1728	2.2894	22	10648	2.8020
3	27	1.4422	13	2197	2.3513	23	12167	2.8439
4	64	1.5874	14	2744	2.4101	24	13824	2.8845
5	125	1.7100	15	3375	2.4662	25	15625	2.9240
6	216	1.8171	16	4096	2.5198	26	17576	2.9625
7	343	1.9129	17	4913	2.5713	27	19683	3.
8	512	2.	18	5832	2.6207	28	21952	3.0366
9	729	2.0801	19	6859	2.6684	29	24389	3.0723
10	1000	2.1544	20	8000	2.7144	30	27000	3.1072

SECTION X

GOVERNMENT AND BUSINESS STANDARDS

Weights and Measures

Owing to the variations in the practices of individuals in the United States, the several states, cities, etc., have found it necessary from time to time to fix definite standards both as to quantities and qualities.

In some cities the purchaser of a quart of milk is reasonably certain of obtaining an article containing not less than 3 % of butter fat, that of inferior grade being subject to seizure by the Board of Health. In some localities a loaf of bread must weigh a pound ; in others, a label giving the weight must be affixed.

In many places storekeepers are required to weigh out 15 pounds of potatoes to a customer asking for a peck, the use of a measure not being permitted.

As a protection to honest dealers some states have enacted laws as to the capacity of a barrel, the legal weight to the bushel of grain, etc.

The following table gives a few standard weights prevailing in most of the states :

Wheat	60 lb. to bu.	Potatoes	60 lb. to bu.
Corn	56 lb. to bu.	Rye	56 lb. to bu.
Oats	32 lb. to bu.	Flour	196 lb. to bbl.
Barley	48 lb. to bu.	Pork	200 lb. to bbl.

Whether the bushel will hold only 58 pounds of wheat by actual measurement, or 62 pounds, the seller is paid the bushel price for every 60 pounds delivered.

The basis of all our weights and measures is the yard, an exact copy of the standard yard being kept in Washington and at the various state capitals.

The length of the yard bears a definite ratio to the length of a pendulum beating seconds at the sea level. When the yard is obtained, a cube can be made, each side measuring a foot. The weight of the water of a certain temperature occupying a cubic foot is 1000 ounces. A measure that will hold 231 cubic inches is a gallon; one that will contain 2150.42 cubic inches is a bushel.

Linear Measure

12 inches (in. or ")	= 1 foot (ft. or ')
3 feet	= 1 yard (yd.)
5½ yards	= 1 rod (rd.)
320 rods	= 1 mile (mi.)

A *hand*, used in measuring the height of horses = 4 in. A *fathom*, used in measuring depths at sea = 6 ft. A *knot*, used in measuring distances at sea = 1 geographical mile = 1.15 statute miles. Diameters of buttons are expressed in *lines*, sizes of type in *points*

Liquid Measure

2 pints (pt.)	= 1 quart (qt.)
4 quarts	= 1 gallon (gal.)

A *gill* is ¼ pt. The capacity of cisterns, reservoirs, etc., is sometimes expressed in barrels (bbl.) of 31½ gallons each, or in hogsheads (hhd.) of 63 gallons each. Barrels and hogsheads used in commerce vary in capacity.

A gallon contains 231 cu. in. In making a rough estimate of the capacity of a tank, etc., a cubic foot is taken as the equivalent of 7½ gallons.

Dry Measure

2 pints (pt.)	= 1 quart (qt.)
8 quarts	= 1 peck (pk.)
4 pecks	= 1 bushel (bu.)

A bushel contains, approximately, 2150.4 cu. in. In estimating the capacity of a bin, etc., a bushel is taken as the equivalent of $1\frac{1}{4}$ cu. ft.

Square Measure

144 square inches (sq. in.)	= 1 square foot (sq. ft.)
9 square feet	= 1 square yard (sq. yd.)
$30\frac{1}{4}$ square yards	= 1 square rod (sq. rd.)
160 square rods	= 1 acre (A.)
640 acres	= 1 square mile (sq. mi.)

A square mile of land is called a *section*.

Roofing, slating, and flooring are often estimated by the *square* of 100 sq. ft.

Cubic Measure

| 1728 cubic inches (cu. in.) | = 1 cubic foot (cu. ft.) |
| 27 cubic feet | = 1 cubic yard (cu. yd.) |

A *cord* of wood contains 128 cu. ft. A *perch* of stone or masonry is taken as $24\frac{3}{4}$ cu. ft. in some localities; in others as $16\frac{1}{2}$ cu. ft. In making an agreement to do work at a certain price per perch, its equivalent should be specified.

Avoirdupois Weight

16 ounces (oz.)	= 1 pound (lb.)
2000 pounds	= 1 ton (T.)
2240 pounds	= 1 long ton

The long ton is the only one employed in England. In this country it is used in selling coal and ore at the mines, and in custom house calculations. In some cities dealers are required to sell coal by the long ton.

Troy Weight

24 grains (gr.)   = 1 pennyweight (pwt.)
20 pennyweights = 1 ounce (oz.)

Troy weight is used in weighing gold and silver. Weights of large quantities are expressed in *ounces;* of small quantities in *grains.*   The pennyweight is employed chiefly in denoting the weight of gold jewelry, which is frequently sold by the pennyweight.

Gold and silver are rendered harder by the admixture of other metals. Gold coin consists of 90 parts gold, 9 parts silver, and 1 part copper. Coin silver consists of 9 parts silver and 1 part copper.

The fineness of gold is frequently expressed in carats, 24 carats denoting pure gold. Gold 22 carats fine means that it consists of 22 parts of gold and 2 parts of alloy; gold 18 carats fine contains 18 parts of gold and 6 parts of alloy.

The value of pure gold is practically permanent, being determined by the value of gold coin; that is, a piece of gold of the weight and fineness of a 20-dollar gold coin is worth $20. The price of silver fluctuates.

Written Problems

1. The last government report gives the production of pure gold as 21,380,000 ounces for the year, worth $441,-930,000.   Find the value per ounce.

2. The production of pure silver for the same time was 203 million ounces worth 109 million dollars.   What was its value per ounce?

3. Twenty years ago the production of pure silver was 120 million ounces worth 112 million dollars.   What was its value per ounce twenty years ago?

4. Twenty years ago the production of pure gold was 6 million ounces worth 123 million dollars.   What was the value per ounce?

Comparison of Avoirdupois Weight with Troy Weight

An avoirdupois pound contains 7000 troy grains.

Written Problems

1. How many troy grains are there in an avoirdupois ounce?

2. What is the ratio (*a*) of a troy ounce to an ounce avoirdupois? (*b*) Of an ounce avoirdupois to a troy ounce?

3. How many silver dollars will weigh 33 pounds avoirdupois when the weight of a dollar is 412½ grains?

4. A silver bowl weighs 3 lb. avoirdupois. What did it cost at $1 per troy ounce?

5. Assuming that gold is 19.2 times as heavy as water, (*a*) what is the weight of a cubic foot of pure gold in avoirdupois pounds? (*b*) What is its value at $20 per ounce troy?

Comparison of Dry and Liquid Measures

Dry and liquid measures are compared by means of the cubic inch, a bushel containing 2150.4 cubic inches and a gallon containing 231 cubic inches.

Written Problems

1. Find the number of cubic inches (*a*) in a quart dry measure. (*b*) In a quart liquid measure. (*c*) Find the ratio between the latter and the former.

2. If a man buys 5½ bushels of chestnuts at $2 per bushel, and sells them at the rate of 10 cents per liquid quart, what is his profit?

3. When 1728 cubic inches of water weigh 1000 ounces, find (*a*) the whole number of ounces in a gallon of water. (*b*) The whole number of pounds in a pint of water.

Apothecaries' Weight and Measure

TABLE OF WEIGHT

20 grains (gr.) = 1 scruple (sc. or ℈)
3 scruples   = 1 dram (dr. or ℨ)
8 drams   = 1 ounce (oz. or ℥)

TABLE OF MEASURE

60 minims   = 1 fluid dram (f ℨ)
8 fluid drams = 1 fluid ounce (f ℥)
16 fluid ounces = 1 pint (O.)

The foregoing are used chiefly by physicians in writing prescriptions, and by druggists in compounding them.

Sight Problems

1. How many fluid ounces are there in a gallon?

2. What part of a pint (*a*) does a 4-ounce bottle hold? (*b*) A 2-ounce bottle?

3. If an ordinary tumbler holds $\frac{1}{2}$ pint, how many fluid ounces does it hold?

Written Problems

1. If 30 minims are taken 3 times a day, how long will a 6-ounce bottle of medicine last?

2. How much is received for a gallon of paregoric sold at 5 cents for 2 fluid ounces?

3. A silver dollar weighs $412\frac{1}{2}$ grains and is 90 % pure silver. How many grains of pure silver are there in 100 silver dollars?

4. A $5 gold piece weighs 129 grains and contains 90 % of gold, 9 % of silver, and 1 % of copper. How many grains of each are there in $100?

United States Lands

Principal Meridians. — In laying out government lands a north and south line is run through some point carefully selected. This line is called a *principal meridian*. There are now thirty-two of them, varying in length. The first is the boundary between Ohio and Indiana ; the second runs through Indiana west of the center ; the third runs through the center of Illinois. Some have names ; the Tallahassee, which runs through that city ; Black Hills, Mount Diablo, Bernardino, etc.

North and south rows of townships, called *ranges*, are laid off east and west of a principal meridian.

Base Lines. — Through the starting point of a principal meridian a *base line* is run due east and west. *Tiers* of townships are laid off and numbered north and south of a base line.

Townships. — In locating a township, the word "tier" is usually omitted. The township in which Lansing, Mich., is situated is described as township 4 north, range 2 west of Michigan meridian.

Sections. — A township is six miles square, containing, therefore, 36 square miles. It is divided into 36 sections each 1 mile square and containing 640 acres. The sections of each township are numbered uniformly as shown in the diagram, No. 1 being the northeast section and No. 36 being the southeast. Some of the divisions and subdivisions of a section are shown in the accompanying diagram. A half-section may be either the N. $\frac{1}{2}$, the S. $\frac{1}{2}$, the E. $\frac{1}{2}$, or the W. $\frac{1}{2}$. The four quarters are known, respectively, as the N.E. $\frac{1}{4}$, the N.W. $\frac{1}{4}$, the S.E. $\frac{1}{4}$, or the S.W. $\frac{1}{4}$. Corresponding names are used to designate the subdivision of a quarter-section into halves or fourths.

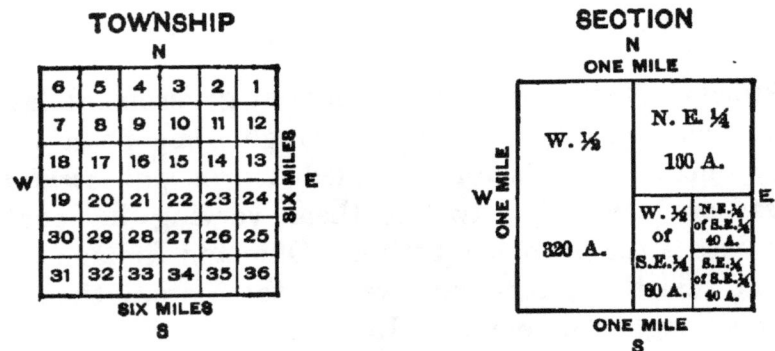

Written Problem

1. (*a*) How many rods of barbed wire are required to enclose the N.E. ¼ of the N.E. ¼ of section 15 with a fence 3 wires high? (*b*) What is the cost at $3\frac{1}{2}$ cents per pound when it weighs 1 pound per rod? (*c*) How many posts 8 feet apart are required?

Variations in Standard

School work would be much simplified if there were throughout the world uniformity in language, in money, and in the system of weights and measures. The American child has more difficulty in learning to read than has the German, owing to the varying sounds of each of our vowels; the latter has more trouble with his grammar and composition. The English currency makes money calculations very complicated in comparison with the decimal ones of most other countries.

Standard Time.— As has already been stated, most civilized nations have as a rule not only standardized the time throughout their respective countries, but each has also established a simple connection between its time and that of other countries.

Uniform Currency. — Even to-day in a few places of the United States small values are expressed in shillings, which mean $12\frac{1}{2}$ cents in some sections and $16\frac{2}{3}$ cents in others. In the latter, the $12\frac{1}{2}$-cent shilling is known as a " York shilling," " levee," "bit," etc.

The first currency improvement consisted in the adoption of the decimal system, which England and a few other countries still resist.

The next was the adoption of a coin of the value of the French franc by Belgium, Finland, Greece, Italy, Spain, Switzerland, Venezuela, etc., although not always taking the same name. The unit in some other countries, Argentine and Haiti, is a coin having the value of five francs.

Weights and Measures. — Many of the countries that decline to bring their currency units into conformity with their neighbors have accepted the advantages of the metric system. The pupil in any of these countries is not burdened with the names of the different units of each table or with their variations in ratio. He has no separate table of dry measure and of liquid measure nor the additional one used by the druggist. To change from cubic measure to dry or to liquid, he moves a decimal point when necessary, requiring no such divisors or multipliers as 231 and 2150.4. Reduction ascending and reduction descending are done in the same way by merely shifting the decimal point.

The Metric System

The metric system is so called from the *meter*, which is the unit of measure.

The length of the meter is 1 ten-millionth of the distance between the equator and one of the poles.

Table of Length

10 millimeters (mm)	= 1 centimeter (cm)
10 centimeters	= 1 decimeter (dm)
10 decimeters	= 1 meter (m)
10 meters	= 1 decameter (dam)
10 decameters	= 1 hectometer (hm)
10 hectometers	= 1 kilometer (km)
10 kilometers	= 1 myriameter (Mm)

The Latin prefixes, *deci*, *centi*, *milli*, denote tenths, hundredths, thousandths, respectively. The Greek prefixes, *deca*, *hecto*, *kilo*, denote 10, 100, 1000, respectively.

The units in common use are the *millimeter*, to measure, for instance, the thickness of wire; the *centimeter*, for such measures as inches and their fractions are employed by us; the *meter* for ordinary lengths; the *kilometer* for long distances.

Compound metric measures are written as mixed decimals, except that final ciphers are sometimes retained.

Thus, 3 meters and 5 decimeters is generally expressed $3^m. 50$, and is read 3 meters 50 centimeters; just as 3 dollars 5 dimes would be called 3 dollars 50 cents.

In writing 25 centimeters it may be expressed 25^{cm}, or as a decimal of a meter, $0^m. 25$, in the same way as 25 cents is indicated by 25 ¢ or $0.25.

Note. — Periods are omitted in writing the abbreviations of metric denominations.

Sight Exercises

1. How many inches are there in 100 meters of 39.37 inches each?

2. Taking the decimeter as 4 inches, (*a*) what fraction of an inch is a centimeter? (*b*) How many centimeters are equal to 16 inches? (*c*) To one foot?

Measures of Capacity

In measuring liquids, grains, etc., the liter (l) is the unit. The divisions and multiples have the same prefixes as are employed with the meter ; deci, centi, hecto, etc.

Small letters are used in writing all the abbreviations except that denoting 10,000 ; the myriameter being written Mm, with a capital to distinguish it from the millimeter, mm. The decaliter is written dal to distinguish it from the deciliter, dl.

The liter is the equivalent of a cube 1 decimeter long, 1 decimeter wide, 1 decimeter deep.

Sight Exercises

1. Taking the decimeter as 4 inches, how many cubic inches are there in the liter ?

2. (*a*) How many cubic inches are there in a quart, when a gallon contains 231 cu. in. ? (*b*) Which is larger, the quart or the liter ?

3. How many cubic inches are there in the difference between the dry quart, of 67.2 cu. in., and the liter?

Larger quantities are measured by the decaliter and the hectoliter.

Measure of Weight

The unit of weight is the *gram*. The weight of a liter of water is 1000 grams, or a kilogram.

The weight of a quart of water is about 2 pounds, that of a liter of water, the kilogram, is 2.2046 lb.

The kilogram is generally called a *kilo*.

1. How many pounds are there (*a*) in 1000 kilos of 2.2046 pounds each ? (*b*) In 500 kilos ?

For large weights the metric ton of 1000 kilos is employed.

Miscellaneous Applications

While the pupil should not burden his memory with the units of tables infrequently used, he has not obtained the greatest possible benefit from his study of arithmetic if he is unable to work an example involving any denominate units whatever, in case he has the table before him.

In the same way, he should be expected to solve a problem involving easily understood conditions, provided they are clearly stated in the problem.

The following examples are given as a test of the pupil's ability to read understandingly.

Written Problems

1. At the rate of 1800 cubic feet per person per hour, how much air will be required in a bedroom by 2 people occupying it for 8 hours?

2. (a) How many cubic feet of air are in a bedroom 10 ft. × 12 ft. × 9 ft.? (b) How many times must the air be changed to supply 2 persons with 1800 cu. ft. each per hour? (c) If the windows are opened sufficiently to change the air 4 times per hour, how many cubic feet are supplied for each?

3. How many persons will receive 1800 cu. ft. of fresh air per hour in a room 24′ × 20′ × 12′, when the open windows change the air four times per hour?

4. (a) How many cubic feet of air per hour are required by 47 pupils and a teacher at the rate of 1800 cubic feet per hour? (b) How many cubic feet are there in a classroom 24′ × 20′ × 12′? (c) How many times per hour must the air in the classroom be changed to supply the necessary quantity of pure air?

5. (*a*) How many cubic feet of air per second are required to furnish 1800 cu. ft. per person per hour to 30 persons? (*b*) If the ventilators admit air at the rate of 5 cubic feet per second for each square foot of opening, how many square feet of the latter are necessary to supply the air? (*c*) How many square feet must the ventilator measure if only three fourths of its surface is unobstructed?

6. Measure the dimensions of your classroom. (*a*) How many square feet of floor space are provided for each pupil and the teacher? (*b*) How many cubic feet of air space are provided for each?

7. (*a*) How much time does a man save in a year for other things, if he requires 30 minutes less per day to do the work in the barn after he has made some changes in its arrangements? (*b*) What is the extra time worth at 20 cents per hour? By improving the house conditions he has made it possible for his wife to save 40 minutes per day. (*c*) How many hours does she save in a year?

8. (*a*) What is the yearly interest on $100 at 6%? (*b*) How much more does a man receive than the interest if an expenditure of $100 for improved machinery will enable him to do 180 hours of extra work worth 20 cents per hour?

9. What interest does a man receive on his yearly payment of $25 for improving the roads, if he saves the equivalent of a man and a team for 34 days, worth $3 per day, in hauling his produce to market, etc.?

10. A foot pound is the work done in lifting 1 foot 1 pound. How many foot pounds of work are done by a man who carries 6000 pounds of bricks and mortar to the top of a 22-foot ladder?

11. A horse power is the power required to do 33,000 foot pounds in 1 minute. What fraction of a horse power is exerted in lifting 6000 pounds 22 feet in 8 hours?

12. The horse power of a gasoline engine may be calculated from the following formula:

$$H.P. = \frac{D^2 \times N}{2.5}$$

in which D represents the diameter of the cylinder in inches and N the number of cylinders.

Find the horse power of a 6-cylinder automobile engine when the diameter of each cylinder is 5 inches.

13. (*a*) Taking the weight of a gallon of water as $8\frac{1}{3}$ lb., find the weight of the water to be pumped per minute for 10 hours to supply 6000 gallons. (*b*) How many foot pounds of labor are required per minute to raise it 40 ft.? (*c*) What decimal of a horse power?

14. (*a*) How many feet per minute does a horse travel when he walks $2\frac{1}{2}$ miles in an hour? (1 mile = 5280 ft.) (*b*) How many foot pounds of power does a horse exert in a minute in carrying a load of 150 pounds 220 feet?

15. The load the average horse can carry on his back for 10 hours per day is about $\frac{1}{10}$ of his weight. This is the power he exerts in drawing a wagon containing a ton on a smooth pavement, or one half ton on an ordinary road. What horse power will a 1500-pound horse develop in overcoming a resistance of 150 pounds, when he travels $2\frac{1}{2}$ miles per hour for 10 hours?

16. The table on the following page shows the results of experiments in raising oats on 5 plots of 1 acre each by 11 different farmers. No fertilizer was used on Plot 1; different ones were tried on each of the others.

TABLE

FARM	No Fertilizer		A Mixture		B Mixture		C Mixture		D Mixture	
	Grain lb.	Straw lb.	Grain lb.	Straw lb.	Grain lb.	Straw lb.	Grain lb.	Straw lb.	Grain lb.	Straw lb.
A	1904	2912	2352	3696	1907	3024	2577	4144	2355	3920
B	2243	5040	2243	5600	1993	4480	2018	5376	2352	6596
C	1680	2128	1907	2464	2352	2464	2577	2912	2465	3136
D	1907	2016	1907	2128	2352	2576	2576	3024	2800	3024
E	1793	2912	1571	3024	1680	3248	2130	4256	2240	4704
F	1458	2912	2128	4256	2801	4480	3248	4704	3363	5040
G	1845	2464	1568	3024	1681	2688	1680	2688	1681	3136
H	2016	2016	2354	2464	2242	2240	2579	2912	2690	2912
I	1569	3472	2016	4256	1792	3920	2241	5040	2688	5600
J	2242	3808	2467	4704	2243	4368	2383	4928	2800	5600
K	2353	3472	2578	4266	2688	4256	2914	4928	3025	5264
Totals	(a)	(b)	(c)	(d)	(e)	(f)	(g)	(h)	(i)	(j)
Increase	——	——	(k)	(l)	(m)	(n)	(o)	(p)	(q)	(r)
Value of inc.	——	——	(s)	(t)	(u)	(v)	(w)	(x)	(y)	(z)
Total value of increase	——		I		II		III		IV	
Cost of fertilizer	——		$ 4.88		$ 4.80		$ 9.86		$ 12.58.	
Profit	——		V		VI		VII		VIII	

Find the total weight of the grain and of the straw raised (a) to (j). Find the increase obtained by the use of the different mixtures (k) to (r). Find the value of the increase at the rate of 40 ¢ per bushel of 32 lb. for the grain (s), (u), (w), (y) and 50 ¢ per 100 lb. for the straw (t), (v), (x), (z). Find the total increase from each mixture, I to IV. Find the net profit following the employment of each by deducting its cost from the value of the increase in the crop, V to VII.

Indicating Operations by Signs

While a person would have no doubt as to the meaning of (a) $20 + 15 + 36$ or of (b) $20 \times 15 \times 36$ he might be uncertain as to the value of (c) $60 - 3 \times 4 + 8$ or of (d) $60 + 30 + 10 - 9$, unless he were familiar with the agreement among mathematicians that two numbers connected by the sign of multiplication or of division constitute a compound quantity that must first be simplified before additions or subtractions are performed. When he learns of this rule, he changes (c) to $60 - 12 + 8$ and (d) to $60 + 3 - 9$. Even then he might have some doubt as to (c) unless he also knew that operations are to be performed from left to right in this case, and that 60 is not to be diminished by $12 + 8$.

Inasmuch as many are unfamiliar with the rule as to multiplication and division signs, it is safer to use a parenthesis in both (c) and (d), writing (c) $60 - (3 \times 4) + 8$ and (d) $60 + (30 + 10) - 9$.

Used in this way, a parenthesis is called a mark of aggregation. A horizontal line is used for the same purpose, $60 - \overline{30 - 10}$ meaning the same as $60 - (30 - 10)$. To indicate that the difference between 30 and 10 is to be divided by 5, the form $(30 - 10) + 5$ is generally replaced by $\dfrac{30 - 10}{5}$, the line between the divisor and the dividend being a mark of aggregation.

When two marks are needed, a bracket may be used as the second.

Thus,

(b) $60 - [(3 \times 4) + 8] = 60 - [12 + 8] = 60 - 20$, etc.

The horizontal line may also be used, thus,

$$60 - (\overline{3 \times 4} + 8).$$

Sight Exercises

Give answers :

a. $60 - 30 - 10 - 5$
b. $60 + 30 - 10 + 5$
c. $(60 + 30 + 10) \div 5$
d. $60 + 30 - 10 \times 5$
e. $60 + 30 \times 10 + 5$
f. $60 - (30 - 10) + 5$
g. $60 - \overline{30 - 10} - 5$
h. $60 \times 30 + 10 \times 5$
i. $60 + [30 - (10 + 5)]$
j. $60 - (\overline{30 - 10} - 5)$
k. $60 \times (30 + 10) \div 5$
l. $(60 + 30) \div 10 + 5$
m. $60 - 30 \div 10 - 5$
n. $60 + 30 \times (10 + 5)$
o. $(60 + 30) \div (10 + 5)$

Written Exercises

1. Simplify the following :

$$2\tfrac{2}{3} \times 3\tfrac{1}{2} + 6\tfrac{1}{4} \times 2\tfrac{1}{5} + \tfrac{8}{10}.$$

When the numbers in an expression are connected by multiplication and division signs exclusively, those immediately preceded by a division sign are made multipliers by using their reciprocals. The foregoing example then becomes,

$$2\tfrac{2}{3} \times 3\tfrac{1}{2} \times \tfrac{4}{25} \times 2\tfrac{1}{5} \times \tfrac{10}{8}.$$

2. Find the quotient of the following :

$$(13\tfrac{1}{2} \times 2\tfrac{2}{3} \times \tfrac{7}{8}) \div (\tfrac{3}{4} \times 1\tfrac{1}{5} \times 16\tfrac{1}{3}).$$

Invert all the fractions in the compound dividend.

3. Find quotients :

a. $(3\tfrac{1}{6} \times \tfrac{3}{7} \times 3\tfrac{1}{8}) \div (1\tfrac{2}{7} \times 3\tfrac{1}{3} \times \tfrac{5}{8}).$
b. $(1\tfrac{1}{25} \times 3\tfrac{1}{2} \times 3\tfrac{1}{4}) \div (\tfrac{1}{8} \times \tfrac{7}{100} \times 4).$

4. Find the value of $\dfrac{1.04 \times 3.5 \times 2.25 \times 7.8}{1.3 \times .125 \times .07 \times 4}.$

Change each divisor into a whole number by making a corresponding change in one or more of the dividends.

Sight Review Problems

1. If the last three figures of a number are 120, what numbers are certainly factors of it?

2. If a number contains all of the following figures in any order whatever, what two numbers will surely divide it: 1, 3, 0, 5?

3. If one pipe can fill a cistern in 2 hours and another in 3 hours, in what time can both fill it running together?

4. If oranges are bought at the rate of 3 for 5 cents and are sold at the rate of 2 for 5 cents, what is the profit (*a*) on 1 orange? (*b*) On 1 dozen?

5. A starts at 9 o'clock and walks at the rate of 3 miles per hour. At 10 o'clock B starts from the same place and follows A at the rate of 4 miles per hour. At what time will he overtake A?

6. A tank is 4 ft. by 2 ft. by 2 ft. (*a*) How many cubic feet of water will it hold? (*b*) How many pounds of water? (*c*) What part of a ton?

7. In working an example a boy multiplied by 2 instead of dividing by 2, and obtained 16 for his answer. If his work was otherwise correct, what is the right answer?

8. Give the smallest number that (*a*) added to 100 will make the sum a multiple of 17. (*b*) Subtracted from 100 will make the remainder a multiple of 14. Give the nearest number to 100 that is a multiple (*c*) of 28. (*d*) Of 29.

9. How many cubic feet of air are there in a room 24 ft. long, 16¾ ft. wide, 9 ft. high?

10. How many strips of carpet ¾ yd. wide will cover a floor 18 ft. wide?

11. A person spent ⅜ of his money and lost ⅜ of the remainder. He then had $31 left. How much had he at first?

12. Four men take 18½ days to do a piece of work. How many men would be required to do it in 1 day?

13. At the rate of 33⅓ bushels of corn to the acre, what would be the yield on 3.9 acres?

14. What is the area of a square each side of which measures 5½ yards?

15. How many times can a vessel containing a pint and a half be filled from one containing a gallon and a quarter, and how much is left over?

16. When 4 men do a piece of work in 12 days, give the time required for the same work by (*a*) 6 men. (*b*) 12 men. (*c*) 3 men. (*d*) 18 men.

17. When a farmer has sufficient food to keep a herd of 30 cows for 40 days, give the time it will last if the herd is increased by:

a. 30 cows   *b.* 10 cows   *c.* 20 cows   *d.* 50 cows

If the herd is diminished by:

a. 15 cows   *b.* 20 cows   *c.* 5 cows   *d.* 25 cows

18. How many cubical boxes, each of which is 3 ft. 6 in. long, can be placed in a bin 14 ft. by 14 ft. by 14 ft.?

19. When the side of a square is 12 inches, (*a*) how many square inches are there in the area of the inscribed square? (*b*) How long is the diagonal of the inscribed square? (*c*) What is the area of a square whose diagonal is 12 inches?

20. The product of three numbers is 121. One of the numbers is 4 and the other two are equal. Find the equal numbers.

21. How long will it take 25 men to do what 10 men can do in 15 days?

22. When the 4th of July falls on Monday, what day will the 4th of August be?

23. If one side of a rectangular field measures 40 rods, what must be the length of an adjacent side so that the field may contain 7¾ acres? (Cancel.)

24. How many square yards more than an acre are there in a field 70 yards square?

25. If a boy walks 2¼ miles in 35 minutes, how many miles will he walk in an hour at the same rate?.

26. How many cubic feet are there in a cubical box 18 inches in depth?

27. A roller is 22 feet in circumference and 9 feet long. How many square feet of ground does it roll in one revolution?

28. Three pipes can fill a tank in 10 minutes. One can fill it alone in an hour, a second can fill it alone in 30 minutes. How long does the third require to fill it alone?

29. The volume of a cube is 27 cubic yards. What is the entire surface?

30. How many square yards are there in a tight fence 6 feet high enclosing a plot 150 ft. square?

31. A 60-day note for $350 is discounted at 6%. Give the proceeds.

32. If the discount of a note for $420 at 5% is $4.20, in how many days is the note due?

Written Review Problems

1. Reduce to their lowest terms

    a. $\frac{888}{720}$ *b.* $\frac{887}{1184}$

2. Divide (*a*) 864 by .024.   (*b*) .0169 by 5.2.

3. How high is a house casting a shadow 24 feet long, when a tree 70 feet high casts a shadow of 42 feet at the same time?

4. Which is the largest and which is the smallest of the fractions: $\frac{17}{150}$, $\frac{28}{200}$, $\frac{14}{125}$?

5. Simplify:

    a. $\frac{1}{3}$ of $(17\frac{1}{2} - 12\frac{1}{4}) + \frac{2}{7}$ of $(3\frac{1}{8} - 1\frac{1}{3})$

    b. $\dfrac{5\frac{1}{2} \times 15\frac{3}{11}}{\frac{1}{2} \times \frac{3}{4} \times 18\frac{3}{4}}$ *c.* $\dfrac{6\frac{3}{4} + (5\frac{1}{2} \times 3\frac{1}{2}) - 7\frac{1}{4}}{6\frac{2}{3} + 5 - 8\frac{1}{3}}$

    d. $(.26 \times .3 \times .02) + (.5 \times .01 \times 1.04)$

6. Find the greatest common divisor (*a*) of 160 and 234.   (*b*) Of 135 and 234.   (*c*) Of 135 and 160.   (*d*) Is there a common factor of 135, 160, and 234?

7. Express as a common fraction the value of

$$.027 \times 2.53 + .099.$$

8. A bathtub is 6 ft. long, 2 ft. 6 in. wide, and 2 ft. deep. There is an overflow pipe 6 inches from the top. (*a*) How long will water entering the tub at 1 cubic foot per minute require to reach the overflow pipe?   (*b*) If the latter is partly stopped and discharges only $\frac{1}{2}$ cu. ft. per minute, how long would it be from the time the water was turned on until it began to flow over the top?

9. Find the per cent of boys and that of girls in a school containing 78 boys and 82 girls.

10. If oranges are bought at the rate of 3 for 5 cents and are sold at the rate of 2 for 5 cents, how many must be sold to make a profit of $3?

11. If a watch that loses .2 min. every hour is set right at noon Jan. 1, what time will it indicate at noon Jan. 11?

12. Express as a decimal the value of each of the following:

a. $\dfrac{3.2-.5}{.04}$ b. $\dfrac{3\ 9-.075}{6}$ c. $\dfrac{3.7\times.15}{.37}$

d. $\dfrac{39.2}{.32}-\dfrac{52.8}{6600}-\dfrac{.00403}{.0124}$

13. Find the exact multiple (*a*) of 4.79 that is nearest to 168.88. (*b*) Of .23 that is nearest to 12.379.

14. How many bricks 8 inches long and 4 inches wide are required to cover a floor 17 ft. 4 in. long and 13 ft. 4 in. wide?

15. A schoolroom is 40 ft. square by 12 ft. high. If it contains 39 pupils and a teacher, (*a*) how many cubic feet of air space are there for each? (*b*) How many square feet of floor space?

16. Find the simple interest on 417.53 francs for $2\frac{1}{2}$ years at $5\frac{1}{2}\%$.

17. A man gives 612.45 francs to 36 persons. He gives 13.60 francs each to 15 of them and divides the balance equally among the others. How much does each of the latter receive?

18. A man divides a farm of 387 acres among his three sons. To the first he gives an 8-acre field, to the second he gives a field 17 acres larger. He then divides the remainder equally among the three. How many acres does each receive, including the two fields?

19. How many packages 10 in. long, $3\frac{3}{4}$ in. wide, and $3\frac{1}{2}$ in. deep can be packed in a case whose inside measurements are 2 ft. 6 in., 3 ft. 4 in., and 3 ft. 6 in., respectively?

20. A man borrows $200, and at the end of each year he gives $50 to pay the interest at 6% and to reduce the principal. How much does he owe at the end of 4 years?

21. How many blocks 2 in. by 3 in. by 5 in. will fill a case measuring on the inside 3 ft. by $2\frac{1}{2}$ ft. by 4 ft.?

22. Three men rent a field for $60. One puts into it 28 sheep for 2 months, another 12 sheep for 8 months, the third 48 sheep for 1 month. How much should each pay?

23. A man borrows $600. At the end of each year he pays $200 to reduce the principal and to pay the interest due at the rate of 6 per cent. How much does he owe at the end of three years, after he has made the regular payment of $200?

24. Find the proceeds of the following note, discounted at 6%, Oct. 14, 1912:

ACCOTINK, VA., Sept. 20, 1912

Ninety days after date I promise to pay to the order of Magnus Schuler, Three Hundred 00/100 Dollars, value received, at the Pohick National Bank.

JOHN McWILLIAMS

25. A owes B $45 and C $30; B owes C $15 and D $50; C owes D $45; D owes A $30 and B $20. What will be the simplest way of settling up?

26. What number multiplied by 4669 gives the same result as 1334 multiplied by 1771?

27. A note for $360 was discounted at 6% on July 7, the proceeds being $357.78. (*a*) In how many days is the note due? (*b*) On what date is it due? (*c*) If it was drawn for 90 days, on what date was it made?

28. When it requires 9 days to finish a certain piece of work, how many days will be required if the work is increased one third and the number of men is decreased one fourth?

29. What is the weight of the water in a tank 13 feet long, 4 yards wide, when the water is 18 inches deep?

30. On each day from Monday to Friday (inclusive) of each week, some workmen repaired 27 yards of a road 7899 yards long; on each Saturday they repaired 12 yards; no work was done on Sunday. If they began work on Monday, the 6th of the month, on what date did they finish?

31. A man increases his fortune each year by $\frac{1}{8}$ of its value at the beginning of the year. At the end of the year he deducts $1800 from his profits for personal expenses. At the end of 1914 he is worth $24,600 after the deduction. What was he worth (*a*) at the beginning of 1914? (*b*) At the beginning of 1913? (*c*) At the beginning of 1912?

32. The capacity of a hall is 300 grown persons or 420 children. If 120 grown persons are present, how many children may be admitted?

33. Find the weight of an iron plate 24 ft. long, 15 ft. wide, and 18 in. thick, when iron is 7.6 times as heavy as water, and a cubic foot of water weighs 1000 oz.

34. Find how much $\frac{18}{25}$ is increased or diminished: (*a*) when 1 is added to each member; (*b*) when 1 is subtracted from each member.

SECTION XI

BUSINESS MEASUREMENTS

Finding Areas

In finding the number of square inches in a rectangle 5 inches by 3 inches the child naturally divides it into 1-inch squares and ascertains their number by counting. In a short time he ascertains that the number of square units into which a rectangle can be divided is equivalent to the number of square units in one row multiplied by the number of rows. At length he formulates the rule:

$$\textit{Area of rectangle} = \textit{Length} \times \textit{Width}$$

with the understanding that the dimensions are expressed in the same linear units, and that their product gives the area in the corresponding square units.

Primitive Method

The early surveyor, whose schooling was limited, developed a method of ascertaining with sufficient accuracy (when land was cheap) the area of an irregular field, such as *ABCD*. On a piece of paper fastened to a horizontal board placed at *A*, for instance, he drew a line in the direction of *AB* and another in the direction of *AD*, thus obtaining the angle at *A*. He then measured *AB*. At *B*, *C*, and *D*, he drew the angles; he also measured the sides *BC*, *CD*, and *DA*.

From these data he made a drawing of the plot to a convenient scale, say, 1 inch to 10 rods. He next divided the drawing into 1-inch squares, counted the whole squares, made due allowance for the fractions, and multiplied 100 square rods by the total number of squares.

Division into Triangles

After he discovered the fact that only one triangle could be made with sides of a given length, the necessity of mapping the corner angles disappeared when the diagonal DB could be measured as well as the other sides.

Later the surveyor found that he could ascertain the area of the given field by measuring DB, the common base of the two triangles, and AX and CY, their respective altitudes, each triangle being one half a rectangle of the same dimensions.

While these three lengths would be sufficient to ascertain the area of the field, they would not determine its shape. For this purpose the points X and Y must be located by measuring, say, DX and DY.

Drawing to Scale

A person is helped in the solution of many problems by the employment of a rough diagram which suggests the required operations. In some cases, however, a drawing must reproduce accurately the proportionate length of each line therein.

To enable a person using a map to determine the distance between any two places, a *scale* is furnished, from which the equivalent in miles can be ascertained.

Map scales vary according to the extent of country represented. A section 300 miles long, 200 miles wide, on a map 6 inches long, 4 inches wide, might be accompanied by a scale 2 inches long to represent 100 miles, with 10-mile subdivisions. The statement that the map was drawn on a scale of 50 miles to 1 inch would, however, be sufficient for most purposes.

Sight Exercises

1. On a scale of 1 inch to 40 rods, how long a line is required to represent:

a. 85 rods?   *b.* 75 rods?   *c.* 125 rods?   *d.* 140 rods?
e. 40 rods?   *f.* 50 rods?   *g.* 150 rods?   *h.* 130 rods?

Written Exercises

1. On a scale of 1 inch to 40 rods draw a line *DB* representing 140 rods. On this line mark a point *X*, 40 rods from *D*, and *Y*, 90 rods from *D*. At *X* erect a perpendicular representing 75 rods and note its upper extremity by the letter *A*. At *Y* let fall a perpendicular representing 120 rods and note its extremity by *C*. Draw *AD*, *AB*, *BC*, and *DC*. (See diagram page 415.)

2. (*a*) How long is *AD*? (*b*) How many rods does it represent? (*c*) How long is *AB*? (*d*) How many rods does it represent? (*e*) How long is *BC*? (*f*) How many rods does it represent? (*g*) How long is *CD*? (*h*) How many rods does it represent?

3. Calculate the length (*a*) of *AB*, when *AX* is 75 rods and *BX* is 100 rods. (*b*) Of *BC*, when *BY* is 50 rods and *YC* is 120 rods. (*c*) Of *CD*, when *CY* is 120 rods and *YD* is 90 rods. (*d*) Of *DA*, when *DX* is 40 rods and *AX* is 75 rods.

Angles

When two intersecting lines make four equal angles, the lines are said to be *perpendicular* to each other and each of the angles is called a *right angle*.

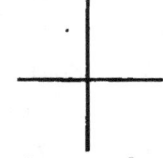

Angles are measured in degrees, the size of the angles depending on the portion of the circumference of a circle embraced between the lines forming the angle when the intersection of the lines is at the center of the circle.

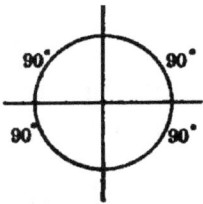

A portion of the circumference of a circle is called an *arc*.

When two lines intersect obliquely, two of the angles are smaller than right angles and two of them are larger. An angle smaller than a right angle is called an *acute* angle; one larger than a right angle is called an *obtuse* angle.

Triangles

Considering the length of their sides, triangles are *equilateral*, having three equal sides; *isosceles*, having two equal sides; *scalene*, having unequal sides.

The three angles of an equilateral triangle are equal, each containing 60°. The angles opposite the equal sides of an isosceles triangle are equal, the side opposite the third angle being called the *base*, regardless of its position.

A triangle containing a right angle is called a *right triangle*; one containing an obtuse angle is called an *obtuse-angled* triangle; one containing three acute angles is called an *acute-angled* triangle.

Quadrilaterals

A *quadrilateral* is any figure of four sides. When the opposite sides are parallel, it becomes a *parallelogram.* The opposite sides of a parallelogram are equal, as are the opposite angles.

When the angles of a parallelogram are equal, the latter becomes a' *rectangle.* A *square* is an equilateral rectangle.

Area of a Rectangle

To find the *area* of a rectangle is to ascertain the number of square units it contains ; square inches, square feet, square miles, etc.

When the rectangle *ABCD* is 9 units long and 4 units wide, the number of square units will consist of 4 rows of 9 square units each, or 9 rows of 4 square units each.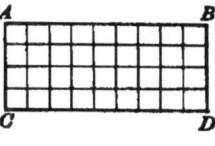

The number of square units in the area of a rectangle is equal to the product of the number of linear units in its length by the corresponding number in its width.

Mathematicians frequently denote one side of a rectangle as its *base* and an adjacent side as its *perpendicular.* In formulating the rule for finding its area, they give it thus:

$$\boxed{\textit{Area of rectangle} = \textit{Base} \times \textit{Perpendicular}}$$

Written Problems

1. How many acres are there in a rectangular field 125 rods long and 84 rods wide ?

2. Find the cost of painting a roof 24 feet wide and 48 feet long at 75 cents per square yard.

Area of a Parallelogram

The parallelogram $ABCD$ may be changed to an equivalent rectangle by cutting along the line Dx, which is perpendicular to AB, and transferring the right triangle AxD to the place marked DyC, thus forming the rectangle $xyCD$.

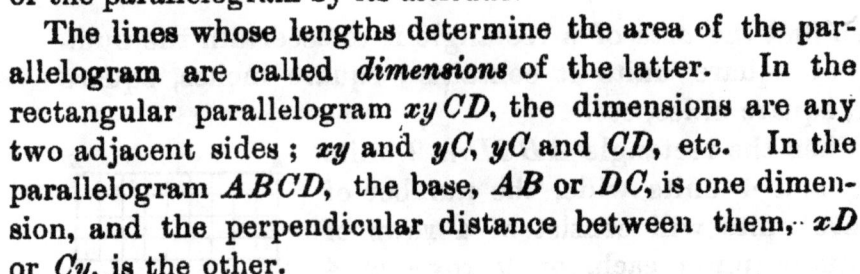

The area of the rectangle $xyCD$ is the product of DC by xD, the base of the parallelogram by its altitude.

The lines whose lengths determine the area of the parallelogram are called *dimensions* of the latter. In the rectangular parallelogram $xyCD$, the dimensions are any two adjacent sides; xy and yC, yC and CD, etc. In the parallelogram $ABCD$, the base, AB or DC, is one dimension, and the perpendicular distance between them, xD or Cy, is the other.

The perpendicular distance between two sides of a parallelogram is called its *altitude*. A side that is perpendicular to the altitude is called the *base*. The dimensions of a parallelogram are the base and the altitude.

$$\boxed{Area\ of\ parallelogram = Base \times Altitude}$$

Written Exercises

1. (*a*) Find the length of AD when Bx measures 8 rods and Ax measures 15 rods. (*b*) What is the area of the parallelogram when CD measures 24 rods?

2. Find the altitude of a 14-acre field in the form of a parallelogram, the length of the base being 56 rods.

3. To a convenient scale draw a parallelogram in which Dx measures 8 rods, CD 24 rods, and Ax 6 rods. (*a*) How long is AB? (*b*) What is the area of the parallelogram?

Area of a Triangle

The area of the triangle ABC is one half the area of the rectangle $xyBC$ formed by erecting perpendiculars at B and C and drawing xy through A.

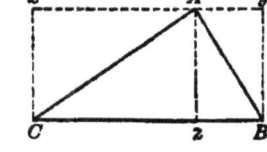

The right triangle AzC is one half the rectangle $AzCx$, and the right triangle AzB is one half the rectangle $AzBy$. The whole triangle ABC is, therefore, one half the whole rectangle $xyBC$. As the area of the rectangle is the product of BC by Az, the area of the triangle is one half the product of its base BC by Az, its altitude.

$$\boxed{Area\ of\ triangle = \tfrac{1}{2}\,(Base \times Altitude)}$$

Sight Exercises

1. Find the area of each of the following parallelograms :

    a. Base, 99 rods ; Altitude, 88 rods.

    b. Base, 125 yards ; Altitude, 24 yards.

    c. Base, 25 feet ; Altitude, $12\frac{1}{2}$ feet.

    d. Base, 48 miles ; Altitude, $83\frac{1}{3}$ miles.

    e. Base, $33\frac{1}{3}$ yards ; Altitude, 63 yards.

    f. Base, 85 inches ; Altitude, 85 inches.

2. Find the area of each of the following triangles :

    a. Base, 88 rods ; Altitude, 99 rods.

    b. Base, 24 yards ; Altitude, 125 yards.

    c. Base, $12\frac{1}{2}$ feet ; Altitude, 25 feet.

    d. Base, $83\frac{1}{3}$ miles ; Altitude, 48 miles.

    e. Base, 63 yards ; Altitude, $33\frac{1}{3}$ yards.

    f. Base, 67 inches ; Altitude, 63 inches.

Dimensions of a Triangle

Preparatory Exercises

1. Take four narrow strips of cardboard (Fig. 1). Make them into a quadrilateral by sticking a pin through each two strips that form a corner. Does the quadrilateral retain its shape under pressure?

Fig. 1.

2. Form three narrow strips of cardboard into a triangle (Fig. 2). Does it retain its shape under pressure?

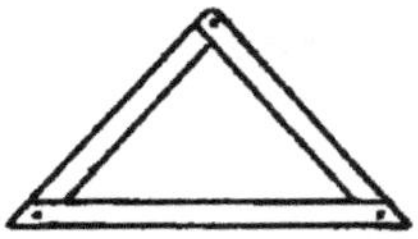

Fig. 2.

There can be only one triangle having sides of given lengths. An indefinite number of quadrilaterals can be formed of sides of given lengths.

As will be seen, the area of a triangle can be calculated when the lengths of the sides are given. The area of a parallelogram or other quadrilateral cannot be ascertained by merely measuring the lengths of the sides. The inclination of the adjacent sides must be known, or the perpendicular distance between two parallel sides, or the length of a diagonal, etc.

Written Exercises

1. The triangle *MNO* (Fig. 3) is right-angled at *M*. The sides *MN* and *MO* measure, respectively, 30 ft. and 40 ft. (*a*) Find its area. (*b*) Find the hypotenuse *NO*. (*c*) Considering *NO* as the base, find the altitude *Mz*, using the area already obtained in (*a*) and the length of *NO* found in (*b*).

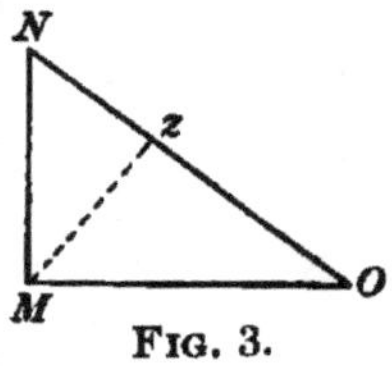

Fig. 3.

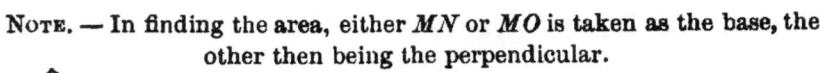

NOTE. — In finding the area, either *MN* or *MO* is taken as the base, the other then being the perpendicular.

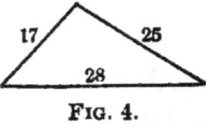

Fig. 4.

2. Find the area of a steel plate (Fig. 4) whose sides measure 17 inches, 25 inches, and 28 inches, respectively.

When the altitude of a triangle cannot be measured, the area may be found from the length of the sides, as follows:

PROCESS

$$17$$
$$25$$
$$28$$
$$2\overline{)70}$$
$$\overline{35} - 17 = 18$$
$$35 - 25 = 10$$
$$35 - 28 = 7$$

The half sum of the sides is 35. From this each side is subtracted separately, giving remainders 18, 10, 7. The square root of the continued product of the half sum and the three remainders is the required area.

Area in square rods $= \sqrt{35 \times 18 \times 10 \times 7} = 210$.

Ans. 210 sq. rd.

In determining the value of $\sqrt{35 \times 18 \times 10 \times 7}$ these numbers may be factored, giving $\sqrt{7 \times 5 \times 9 \times 2 \times 5 \times 2 \times 7}$. This result may be written $\sqrt{7^2 \times 5^2 \times 3^2 \times 2^2}$, which is equal to $7 \times 5 \times 3 \times 2$.

In factoring 18, select 9, which is a square, as one factor.

3. The following is a right triangle. Find its area, however, by the method just given. The sides are 20 yd., 21 yd., 29 yd.

4. Find the area of each of the following triangles: (*a*) 13 in., 14 in., 15 in.   (*b*) 13 ft., 20 ft., 21 ft.

5. Draw two isosceles triangles having sides as follows: (*a*) 5 in., 5 in., 6 in.   (*b*) 5 in., 5 in., 8 in.   (*c*) Find the area of each.

6. (*a*) From the table of square roots find the altitude of an equilateral triangle having 2-inch sides.   (*b*) Find the area by multiplying the altitude by one half the base. (*c*) Find the area by the method given in example 2.

7. Compare the area of a 4-inch equilateral triangle with that of a 2-inch equilateral triangle.

The Trapezoid

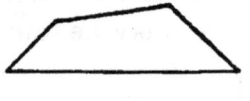

A quadrilateral that has no parallel sides is called a *trapezium*.

The quadrilateral *ABCD*, which has two sides parallel, is called a *trapezoid*.

The trapezoid is divisible into two triangles *ABC* and

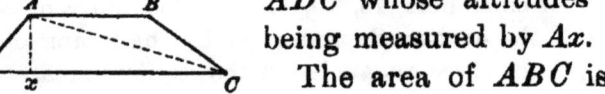

ADC whose altitudes are the same, being measured by *Ax*.

The area of *ABC* is $\frac{1}{2}(AB \times Ax)$; the area of *ADC* is $\frac{1}{2}(CD \times Ax)$; the area of the trapezoid is $\frac{1}{2}(AB + DC) \times Ax$; that is:

Area of trapezoid = $\frac{1}{2}$ *Sum of parallel sides* × *Perpendicular.*

The length of a line drawn midway between the parallel sides and parallel to them is one half the sum of the lengths of the parallel sides. The line *ab* is $\frac{1}{2}(MN + OP)$.

8. Cut out a trapezoid *MNOP*, making *MN* 4 inches long and *OP* 6 inches, and the perpendicular distance between them 5 inches. Mark the middle points *a* and *b*. Draw a perpendicular from *a* to *PO* and one from *b* to *PO*. Cut along these perpendiculars and rearrange the pieces to make a rectangle. (*a*) What are the dimensions of the latter? (*b*) Find its area. (*c*) What is the length of *ab*?

9. *ABCD* is one end of a shed 12 feet deep, 18 feet high in the back, and 23 feet high in the front. (*a*) How many square feet are there in the surface of this end? (*b*) Find the length of *BC*, one side of the roof.

The Trapezium

The area of a trapezium is obtained by dividing it into two triangles by a diagonal, which constitutes their common base. The altitude of each triangle is the perpendicular let fall on the diagonal from one of the opposite corners.

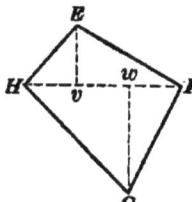

The area of the two triangles constituting $EFGH$ is $\frac{1}{2}(FH \times Ev) + \frac{1}{2}(FH \times Gw)$, which is equal to $\frac{1}{2}[HF \times (Ev + Gw)]$.

10. One diagonal of the field $EFGH$ measures 48 rods. The perpendiculars Ev and Gw let fall on the diagonal from the corners opposite measure, respectively, 24 rods and 30 rods. (*a*) How many square rods are there in the field? (*b*) How many acres?

> *Area of trapezium = Diagonal × one half sum of the two perpendiculars let fall on the diagonal from the opposite corners.*

11. A five-sided field is divided into three triangles by the two diagonals MJ and MK, their respective lengths being 18 rods and 22 rods. The altitude Ia is 6 rods, the altitude Jb is 12 rods, and the altitude Lc is 6 rods. (*a*) How many square rods does the field contain? (*b*) How many acres?

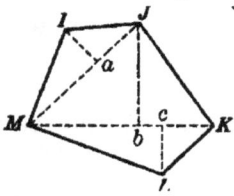

12. The adjacent sides of a parallelogram are 7 ft. and 9 ft. and a diagonal measures 8 ft. (*a*) Find its area. (*b*) Find the area of a parallelogram having a diagonal of 14 ft. and adjacent sides measuring 7 ft. and 9 ft.

Note. — In each parallelogram find the area of the two equal triangles into which it is divided by the diagonal.

Area of Polygons

A surface bounded by straight lines is called a *polygon*. A triangle is a polygon of three sides and a quadrilateral is one of four sides. Polygons of five, six, seven, eight, etc., sides are called *pentagons, hexagons, heptagons, octagons*, etc., respectively.

A polygon is said to be *regular* when it is both equilateral and equiangular. An equilateral triangle and a square are regular polygons. The rhombus is not a regular polygon since it is not equiangular.

The area of an irregular polygon may be obtained by dividing it into triangles, as in No. 11. In the next example an irregular pentagon is divided into triangles and a trapezoid by perpendiculars *Bx*, *Cz*, and *Ey* let fall on *AD*.

13. From the following measurements: *Ax* 10 yd., *Bz* 10 yd., *yD* 15 yd., *EC* 18 yd., find (*a*) the area of *ABCE*. (*b*) Of *CED*. (*c*) Of *ABCDE*.

Regular Hexagons

A regular hexagon is divisible into six equal equilateral triangles.

14. When each side of the regular hexagon *ABCDEF* is 1 inch, find the length (*a*) of *xy*, the altitude of one of the triangles. (*b*) The area of one triangle. (*c*) The area of the hexagon.

15. A summer house has the form of a regular hexagon, each side of which is 6 feet. Find the cost of making a cement floor at $9 per square yard.

Circumference of Circle

A *circle* is a surface bounded by a curved line called the *circumference*, each point of the latter being at the same distance from the *center*.

The *diameter* of a circle is any straight line extending from one point in the circumference to another and passing through the center; a straight line between two points in the circumference but which does not pass through the center is called a *chord*. XY and ZW are diameters, XZ and XV are chords. The radius of a circle is a line extending from the center to the circumference, and is one half the diameter. CX, CW, CY, and CZ are radii.

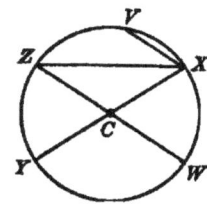

The ratio between the diameter and the circumference of a circle may be experimentally determined as follows:

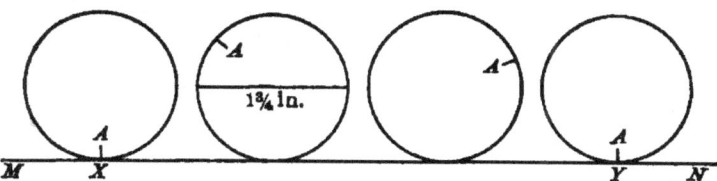

Make a cardboard circle having a diameter of $1\frac{3}{4}$ inches and mark a point A on its circumference. Roll it along a line beginning at X. When A again reaches the line, mark the point Y. The length of XY will be found to be $5\frac{1}{2}$ inches.

The ratio of $1\frac{3}{4}$ inches to $5\frac{1}{2}$ inches is 7 to 22, which is approximately the ratio of the diameter to the circumference.

$$Circumference\ of\ circle = 3\tfrac{1}{7} \times Diameter$$

Sight Exercises

1. Give the circumference of a circle having a diameter of (*a*) 3½ yd.   (*b*) 7 ft.   (*c*) 14 rods.   (*d*) 21 meters.

2. Give the circumference of a circle having a radius of (*a*) 3½ mi.   (*b*) 6 meters.   (*c*) 7 rods.   (*d*) 3 in.

3. Give the diameter of a circle having a circumference of (*a*) 22,000 mi.   (*b*) 44 ft.   (*c*) 220 yd.   (*d*) 11 in.

Written Problems

1. The inner circumference of a circular track is 1 mile (1760 yards).   What is the diameter in yards?

2. When the inner circumference of a circular track is ½ mile, (*a*) what is its diameter in yards?   (*b*) What is the outer diameter, if the track is 7 yards wide?   (*c*) How much greater is the outer circumference than the inner one?   (*d*) What is the length of one side of a square that will exactly contain the track?

3. What is the diameter of the earth at the equator, assuming the circumference to be 25,000 miles?

4. Find the length of a degree of longitude at the equator, there being 360 degrees in the circumference.

5. A bicycle wheel has a diameter of 2 ft. 4 in. (*a*) How many feet will the bicycle travel in each revolution of the wheel?   (*b*) How many revolutions must the wheel make in going a mile?

6. A cog wheel 14 inches in diameter has 66 cogs.   What is the distance between the cogs at the top, assuming the distance to be equal to the width of a cog?

Area of Circle

Cut a paper circle into as many equal parts as possible. Arrange the pieces as shown below to form a parallelogram as nearly as possible.

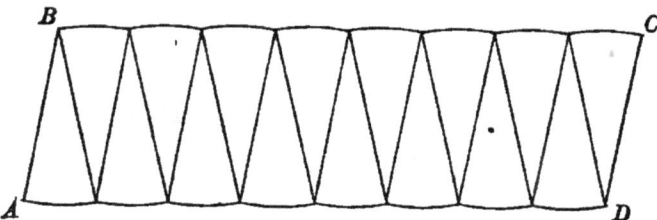

As the number of pieces increases, the nearer to a rectangle does the parallelogram become, so that when the number of pieces is indefinitely large, the figure is a rectangle.

The height of this rectangle is the radius of the circle; the length of the rectangle is one half the circumference of the circle, or $3\frac{1}{7}$ times the radius; the area is, therefore, $3\frac{1}{7}$ times the square of the radius.

Area of circle = $3\frac{1}{7}$ × Square of radius

This may be expressed: $A = \pi R^2$, the Greek letter π (*pi*) representing $3\frac{1}{7}$, the ratio between the diameter and the circumference.

Written Exercises

1. (*a*) Find the area of a circle whose radius is 42 feet. (*b*) Find the area of a circle whose diameter is 42 feet. (*c*) How do the areas compare?

2. The circumference of a circle is 220 yards. (*a*) Find the diameter. (*b*) The radius. (*c*) The area.

3. (*a*) What is the diameter of a circle whose area is 616 square rods? (*b*) The circumference?

PROCESS

First obtain the radius by using the formula

$$3\tfrac{1}{7} R^2 = 616$$

$$R^2 = 616 \div 3\tfrac{1}{7} = 616 \times \tfrac{7}{22} = 196$$

$$R^2 = 196; \quad R = \sqrt{196} = 14$$

When the radius is 14 rods, the diameter is twice 14 rods, or 28 rods.

---

4. The area of a circle is 12,474 sq. ft. Find (*a*) the radius. (*b*) The diameter. (*c*) The circumference.

5. What will be the area of the top of the stump made by sawing down a tree at a point where its circumference is 44 feet?

When the circumference is given, the area can be obtained by multiplying ½ the circumference by ½ the diameter.

6. Find the area of a window the lower part of which is a rectangle 4 ft. wide 6 ft. high, and the upper part a semicircle.

7. A circular window is 7 feet in diameter. Find its area.

8. Find the area of a circular walk 7 feet wide surrounding a plot 28 feet in diameter.

Find the difference between the area of the outer circle and that of the inner one.

9. Find the cost of resilvering a circular mirror 1 ft. 9 in. in diameter at 32 cents per square foot.

Sectors and Segments

A portion of a circle bounded by two radii and an arc is called a *sector*.

ABC is a sector of 60°; *BCD* is a sector of 90°, *C* being the center of the circle.

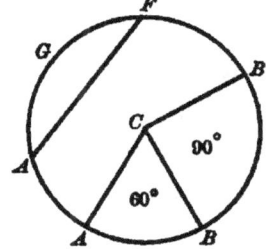

A sector of 90° is called a *quadrant;* one of 60° is called a *sextant.* What is the name of a sector of 180°?

A *segment* is a portion of a circle bounded by an arc and its chord. *EFG* is a segment.

Sight Exercises

1. In a circle whose diameter is 7 in., give (*a*) the length of the circumference. (*b*) The length of a semicircumference. (*c*) The length of an arc of 90°. (*d*) The length of an arc of 60°. (*e*) The length of an arc of 120°.

2. In a circle whose diameter is 14 inches, give the area (*a*) of the circle. (*b*) Of a semicircle. (*c*) Of a quadrant. (*d*) Of a sextant. (*e*) Of a sector of 120°.

Written Exercises

1. Find the area of a sextant, when the radius of the circle is 14 inches.

2. Find the area of a quadrant of a circle whose radius is 21 feet.

3. In the sector *XYZ*, the length of the arc is 33 yards, and the sides *XY* and *XZ* measure 14 yards each. Find the area.

Since *Area of circle* $= \frac{1}{2}(R \times circumference)$
Area of sector $= \frac{1}{2}(R \times arc)$.

4. In a circle having a diameter of 70 inches, find the length of an arc (*a*) of 180°. (*b*) Of 90°. (*c*) Of 72°. (*d*) Of 60°.

5. What is (*a*) the area of a sector of 72°, the sides being 35 inches long? (*b*) The length of the arc?

6. The hexagon *ABCDEF* is inscribed in a circle having a radius of 7 ft. (*a*) What is the length of *AB*, the chord of an arc of 60°? (*b*) Find the length of *xz*, the altitude of one of the six equilateral triangles composing the hexagon. (*c*) Find the area of each of the six triangles.

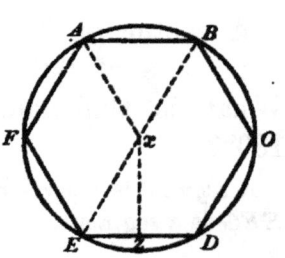

7. The square *ABCD* has sides 14 inches long. (*a*) Find the area. (*b*) Find the area of the square *mnop*. (*c*) Find the area of the circle inscribed in *ABCD*.

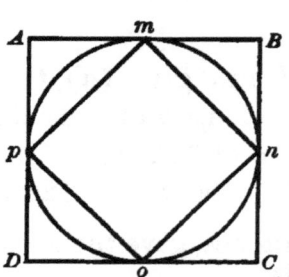

8. (*a*) How many times will a wagon wheel 3½ feet in diameter revolve in going a mile? (*b*) How many times will a bicycle wheel 28 inches in diameter revolve in going a mile?

9. If a steam roller is 7 feet high and 8 feet long, how many square feet of ground will it roll at each revolution?

10. Four circles each 3 inches in radius are cut from a square piece of cardboard. (*a*) Find the area of the smallest piece of cardboard that will answer, and (*b*) the area of the four circles.

11. The lower part of a window 7 feet wide, is 10 feet long. The upper part is a semicircle. What is the area of the window?

Capacity and Volume

Preparatory Exercises

1. How many 1-inch cubes would cover the bottom of a rectangular box 8 inches long and 6 inches wide, inside measurement?

2. How many layers would be required to fill a box 4 inches high?

3. What is the capacity in cubic inches of a box 8″ × 6″ × 4″?

The sign ″ denotes inches, ′ denotes feet, × denotes "by."
8″ × 6″ × 4″ is read 8 inches by 6 inches by 4 inches.

4. What is the volume of a rectangular block 8″ × 6″ × 4″?

5. The bottom of an octagonal candy box has an area of 24 square inches. When it is 4 inches high, what is its capacity?

6. What is the volume of a marble block 4 inches high whose bottom and top are equal hexagons, each having an area of 21 square inches?

7. How many cubic inches of water will a tumbler hold when the inside area of its circular bottom is 10 square inches and it is 4 inches high, the opening at the top having the same area as at the bottom?

8. How many cubic feet of marble are there in a block whose bases are circles containing 20 square feet each, the distance between the bases being 10 feet?

9. (*a*) At 7½ gallons to the cubic foot, what is the capacity of a cylindrical tank 10 feet deep and having a base containing 20 square feet? (*b*) Give the capacity in bushels of a bin of this size, taking ⅘ bu. to the cu. ft.

Prisms and Cylinders

In mensuration, a box, a tumbler, a block, etc., is called a *solid*. The term *volume* means its capacity, its cubical contents, etc.

Each of the boxes and blocks in the first six of the foregoing examples is a *prism*. One of them is called an *octagonal* prism, another a *hexagonal* prism, and the others *rectangular* prisms.

A rectangular prism has six *plane faces* and twelve *edges*. Two of its opposite faces are called its *bases*, which are parallel to each other and equal in area. Each edge is perpendicular to an adjacent one.

In the hexagonal prism, the two equal parallel faces are hexagons, and the remaining six, called the *lateral* faces, are rectangles; in the octagonal prism two are octagons and the eight lateral faces are rectangles. The hexagons in the former are called the bases, and the octagons in the latter.

The tumbler and the block in Examples 7 and 8 are called *cylinders*, the bases in each of which are equal circles. A cylinder has two plane faces and one curved face.

The foregoing are called *right* prisms or cylinders, each lateral edge in the former being perpendicular to the adjacent edge of the base.

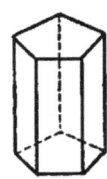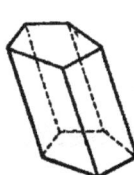

The accompanying figures show a right pentagonal prism and an oblique one. Each of the ten lateral faces is a parallelogram, the five in the former being rectangles and the five in the latter being rhomboids.

Unless the term *oblique* is used, a right prism or cylinder is intended.

Volume of Prism or of Cylinder

> *Volume of right prism (or cylinder) = Area of base × altitude.*

Written Problems

1. Find (*a*) the area of the base and (*b*) the volume of a square prism 8 feet high, the sides of the base measuring 5 ft. 6 in. each.

2. A cylindrical vessel is 7 inches in diameter and 6 inches high. (*a*) What is the area of its base? (*b*) What is its capacity? (*c*) How many gallons of water would it hold? (Take 231 cu. in. to the gallon.)

3. A cubical block of granite 7 feet each way was made into the largest cylinder possible. (*a*) How many cubic feet of granite were there in the original block? (*b*) How many cubic feet of granite are there in the cylinder? (*c*) What fraction of the area of the base of the cube is the area of the base of the cylinder? (*d*) What fraction of the block was cut away?

4. A piece of iron 6 inches square and 6 inches thick has a cylindrical hole bored through it $3\frac{1}{2}$ inches in diameter. (*a*) How many cubic inches of iron were there in the original piece? (*b*) How many cubic inches of iron are removed in making the hole? (*c*) How many cubic inches of iron remain?

5. A piece of timber 15 ft. long is 6 inches square at the ends. (*a*) Find its volume. (*b*) If its weight is one half that of an equal volume of water, how heavy is it? (A cubic foot of water weighs 1000 oz.) (*c*) Find the weight of a piece 32 ft. long and with ends 1 foot square.

6. The outer diameter of an iron pipe 7 feet long is 14 inches, and the iron is 2 inches thick. (*a*) How many cubic inches of iron are there in the pipe? (*b*) How many cubic feet?

The volume of the pipe is the difference between the volume of two cylinders, both 84 inches high, and having diameters of 14 inches and 10 inches respectively.

Volume in cubic inches = $(7^2\pi - 5^2\pi) \times 84$; or $(7^2 - 5^2) \times 3\frac{1}{7} \times 84$.

Number of cubic feet = $\dfrac{(7^2 - 5^2) \times 3\frac{1}{7} \times 84}{1728}$ Cancel.

7. The water in a swimming tank 60 ft. long and 25 ft. wide is 3 ft. deep at one end and 7 ft. at the other. How many gallons does it contain at $7\frac{1}{2}$ gallons to the cubic foot?

Consider as the base of the prism one side of the tank, which is a trapezoid having two parallel sides of 7 ft. and 3 ft., respectively, with a perpendicular distance between them of 60 ft. The altitude is 25 ft.

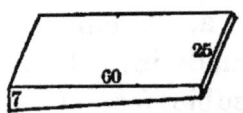

8. A two-story and attic house without a cellar is 24 feet wide, 30 feet long, 16 feet high to the eaves and 25 to the ridge pole. (*a*) Find the number of cubic feet in the attic. (*b*) The number of cubic feet in the rest of the house. (*c*) The outside surface.

The house is a prism, the ends being the bases. The attic may be considered a triangular prism 30 ft. in altitude, the base being a triangle with a base of 24 ft. and an altitude of 9 ft.

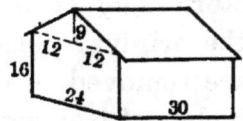

9. A builder agrees to erect it at the rate (*a*) of 60 cents per square foot of outside surface, or at the rate (*b*) of 6 cents per cubic foot for the cubic contents of the attic, and 13 cents per cubic foot for the cubic contents of the rest of the house. Find the cost of the house at each rate.

10. The roof of this house extends one foot beyond the walls on all sides. (*a*) What are the dimensions of each half of the roof? (*b*) What is the total area of the roof? (*c*) At 9 shingles to the square foot, how many shingles will be required?

11. How many cubic feet of ensilage will a rectangular silo contain, the interior dimensions of the base being 14 ft. by 14 ft., and its height 30 ft. ?

12. (*a*) Find the cubical contents of a cylindrical silo 14 feet in diameter (interior) when filled to the height of 30 feet. (*b*) Find the weight of the contents at 40 pounds to the cubic foot. (*c*) When a cow is fed 35 pounds per day, how many cows will it supply for 176 days? (*d*) At the rate of 14 tons to the acre how many acres of ground will furnish the necessary fodder to fill the silo to the height of 30 ft.?

13. Each half of the roof of a house is 40 ft. by 25 ft. The top of the roof is 20 ft. above the bottom. How many cubic feet of snow are there on the roof after a 6-inch fall?

Note that the snow on a sloping roof is the same in volume as it would be on the space covered by the roof if the latter were removed.

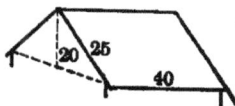

In the determination of the quantity of iron, etc., in rods, beams, etc., business men use the following formula :

$$Volume = Length \times Area\ of\ cross\ section.$$

in which "cross section" is substituted for the word "base," and "length" for "height."

14. Find the number of cubic feet in 4 rods each 18 ft. long with a cross section 2 inches square.

15. How many cubic inches are there in a circular rod 5 ft. 4 in. long and 1¾ inches in diameter?

16. A ring is made of an iron bar having a rectangular cross section 2 inches square. (*a*) When the interior diameter of the ring is 6 inches, what is the exterior diameter? (*b*) What is the radius (R) of the outer circle? (*c*) What is the radius of the inner circle ($R_{//}$)? (*d*) How many times π is $R^2\pi - R_{/}^2\pi$? (*e*) How many square inches are there in the surface of the top of the ring? (*f*) What is the depth of the ring? (*g*) Find the number of cubic inches in the ring.

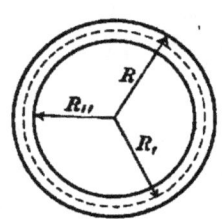

17. This ring is made from a bar of iron having a cross section of 2 inches square and equal in length to the circumference of a circle whose radius is $R_{/}$ in the diagram, the distance from the center of the enclosed circle to the middle of the ring. (*a*) How long is the bar? (*b*) How many cubic inches does it contain?

18. (*a*) How long a circular rod 2 inches in diameter will be required to make an "anchor" ring having an interior diameter of 6 inches, the length being equal to the circumference of a circle having a diameter halfway between that of the outer and the inner diameter of the ring? (*b*) What is the area of a cross section of the rod?

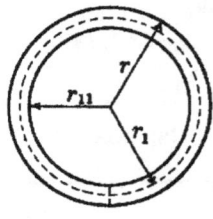

(*c*) How many cubic inches of iron are there in the ring? (*d*) Find the ratio between the area of a cross section of this ring and that of the ring made from the bar. (*e*) Find the ratio between the quantity of iron in this ring and the quantity in the other.

Reading a Working Drawing

The lines on the paper on which the following diagrams are drawn, are $\frac{1}{8}''$ apart.

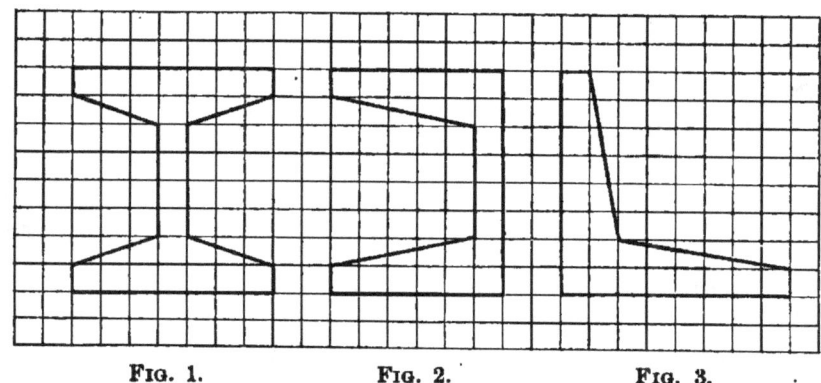

FIG. 1.　　　FIG. 2.　　　FIG. 3.

Sight Exercises

When the scale is $16''$ to $1''$, (*a*) how high is each of the beams whose cross sections are shown above? (*b*) If the cross section in Fig. 1 is divided into four trapezoids and a rectangle, what are the dimensions of the latter?

Written Exercises

1. (*a*) Find the area in square inches of the cross section represented in Fig. 1. (*b*) Find the number of cubic feet in a beam 18 ft. long. (*c*) Find its weight at 480 pounds to the cubic foot.

2. (*a*) Find the area of the cross section of a channel beam (Fig. 2). (*b*) Find the number of cubic feet in a beam 16 ft. long. (*c*) Find its weight.

3. (*a*) Find the area of the cross section of an angle beam (Fig. 3). (*b*) Find the number of cubic feet in a beam 12 feet long. (*c*) Find its weight.

Development (Pattern) of Prism

The illustration shows the *development* of a right prism. This may be cut from cardboard, the edges folded and fastened with gummed paper.

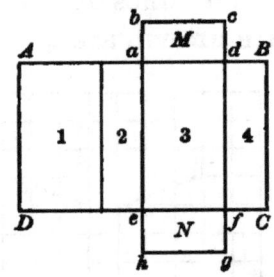

The four lateral faces together form a rectangle *ABCD*, the base of which, *DefC*, is the perimeter of the base of the prism and the altitude of which, *AD*, is the altitude of the prism.

By the *convex surface* of a solid is meant the sum of the lateral surfaces. The *entire surface* includes also the surface of the two bases.

Preliminary Exercises

1. When *BC* is 6 inches and *Cf* is 2 inches, what is the area of *dBCf*?

2. What is the area of rectangle No. 2?

3. What is the area of *adfe* when *ad* is 4 inches?

4. What is the area of rectangle No. 1?

5. What is the combined area of rectangles Nos. 1, 2, 3, and 4?

6. What is 6 times $(4 + 2 + 4 + 2)$?

7. What is the value of $(6 \times 4) + (6 \times 2) + (6 \times 4) + (6 \times 2)$?

8. What is the area of *ABCD*?

Convex surface of prism = Perimeter of base × Altitude.

Convex Surface

Sight Exercises

1. Give the perimeter of one base of each of the following prisms, when the bases are, respectively,

  a. Equilateral triangles, each side 6 ft.
  b. Regular hexagons, each side 4 ft.
  c. Rectangles, 2 ft. by 7 ft.
  d. Right triangles; hypotenuse 5 ft., perpendicular 3 ft.
  e. Rhombuses (parallelograms), each side 5 ft.

2. Give the convex surface of each prism, when its altitude is 10 ft.

Entire Surface

The entire surface of a prism is the convex surface increased by the area of the bases.

Written Exercises

1. Find the entire surface of a square prism 7 in. high, the area of each base being 9 sq. in.

PROCESS	
Area of base,	9 sq. in.
Each side of base,	? in.
Perimeter of base,	? in.
Convex surface,	? sq. in. ⎫ Add.
Area of two bases,	? sq. in. ⎭

2. How many square yards are there in the floor, the walls, and the ceiling of a room 16 ft. 6 in. long, 13 ft. 4 in. wide, and 9 ft. high?

Cylinder

The development of a right cylinder is a rectangle and two circles. The height of the former is the altitude of the cylinder, and its length is equal to the circumference of either base. The rectangle constitutes the convex surface.

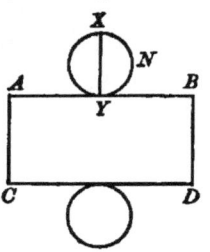

Sight Exercises

Give the convex surface of each of the following cylinders :

    a. Altitude, 7 in.; circumference of base, 21 in.

    b. Altitude, 10 ft.; diameter of base, 7 ft.

    c. Altitude, 5 ft.; radius of base, $3\frac{1}{2}$ ft.

    d. Altitude, 9 in.; circumference of base, 9 in.

    e. Altitude, $1\frac{1}{2}$ in.; diameter of base, 14 in.

Written Problems

1. A cylinder is 22 inches in circumference and 7 inches high. What is the entire surface ?

PROCESS	
Circumference of base,	22 in.
Radius of base,	? in.
Area of each base,	? sq. in.
Of both bases,	? sq. in. ⎫ Add
Convex surface,	? sq. in. ⎭

2. At 50 ¢ a square yard find the cost of polishing a granite shaft 10 ft. high, $3\frac{1}{2}$ ft. in diameter, omitting both ends. (The convex surface.)

3. A rectangular granite block is 6 ft. high and has a base 8 ft. by 2 ft. Find the cost of polishing the sides and the top at 5¢ per square foot.

4. The entire surface of a square prism is 90 sq. ft. If a side of the base measures 3 ft., (*a*) what is the convex surface? (*b*) What is the height of the prism?

5. The convex surface of a cylinder 9 in. high is 198 sq. in. Find (*a*) the circumference of the base. (*b*) The area of each base. (*c*) The entire surface.

6. The entire surface of a cube is 1536 sq. in. (*a*) How many square inches are there in each face? (*b*) What is the length of each edge?

7. Find the convex surface of a regular hexagonal prism 6 inches high, each side of the base measuring 2 inches.

8. How wide a strip of iron will be required to make a stovepipe 7 inches in diameter if $\frac{1}{2}$ inch is used in making the seam?

9. How many square feet of sheet iron will it take to make a stovepipe 6 feet long and 7 inches in diameter, allowing $\frac{1}{2}$ inch for the lap in making the seam?

10. A farmer has a concrete roller $2\frac{1}{8}$ feet in diameter and $5\frac{1}{2}$ feet wide. (*a*) How many square yards does it roll in going 1 mile; that is, how many square yards are there in a strip 1760 yd. long and $5\frac{1}{2}$ ft. wide? (*b*) What fraction of an acre? (*c*) How far must the team travel to roll an acre? (*d*) How many acres are rolled when the team travels 24 miles? (*e*) How many cubic feet of concrete are there in the roller?

11. How many feet of sheet iron will it take to make a pipe 7 inches square and 6 feet long allowing $\frac{1}{2}$ inch for the lap?

Measurements

Sight Review Problems

1. A roll of oilcloth contains 30 square yards; give its length (*a*) when the oilcloth is 2 yards wide. (*b*) When it is $1\frac{1}{2}$ yards wide.

2. Give the length (*a*) of a strip of carpet $\frac{3}{4}$ yd. wide, containing 30 square yards. (*b*) Of one 27 in. wide containing 27 square yards. (*c*) Of one 27 in. wide containing 30 square yards.

3. How many running feet of boards will contain 1200 sq. ft., (*a*) when the boards are 6 in. wide? (*b*) 4 in.? (*c*) 8 in.? (*d*) 9 in.?

4. Find, as a fraction of a square foot, the top surface of a brick (*a*) 8 in. long, 4 in. wide. (*b*) How many square feet will 900 bricks cover when each covers $\frac{2}{9}$ sq. ft.? (*c*) How many bricks, each covering $\frac{2}{9}$ sq. ft., are required to cover a surface of 1000 sq. ft.?

5. A strip of land $\frac{1}{2}$ yard wide contains an acre (4840 sq. yd.); (*a*) how long is it? (*b*) Give the length of a strip 18 inches wide, which contains an acre.

6. (*a*) What fraction of a square foot is covered by a shingle when it covers a space 4 in. by 4 in.? (*b*) How many shingles are required to cover 100 sq. ft. when each covers $\frac{1}{9}$ sq. ft.? (*c*) When each covers a space $\frac{5}{12}$ ft. by $\frac{1}{3}$ ft.?

7. (*a*) What is the volume of a brick whose dimensions are $\frac{2}{3}$ ft. by $\frac{1}{3}$ ft. by $\frac{1}{8}$ ft.? (*b*) How many bricks are there to the cubic foot if each brick contains $\frac{1}{27}$ cu. ft.? (*c*) How many cubic inches are there in a paving brick whose dimensions are 8 in. by 4 in. by $2\frac{1}{2}$ in.?

Written Review Problems

1. A strip of ground is 5 miles long and 9 inches wide. Find its area (*a*) in square yards. (*b*) In acres.

As there are 1760 yards in a mile, the area in square yards will be 1760 × 5 × ¼. As there are 4840 square yards to an acre, the area in acres will be 1760 × 5 × ¼ ÷ 4840.

2. How many miles does a team travel in plowing 1 acre when the plow makes a furrow 9 inches wide?

Omitting from consideration the distance traveled in making turns, the plowed ground may be considered as a rectangle 9 inches wide, having an area of 1 acre. Changing the area to 4840 sq. yd., and the width to ¼ yd., the length in yards is 4840 ÷ ¼, and the length in miles is 4840 ÷ ¼ ÷ 1760; that is, $\dfrac{4840 \times 4}{1760}$.

3. Find the distance in miles traveled by a team (*a*) in cutting an acre of grass when the machine cuts a strip 4 ft. 6 in. wide; (*b*) in cutting an acre of wheat when the machine cuts a strip 6 ft. wide.

4. If a team travels 15 miles in a day, (*a*) find the number of acres it can plow when the furrow is 9 inches wide; (*b*) the number of acres of grass it can cut when the mowing machine cuts a strip 4½ ft. wide; (*c*) the number of acres of grain it can cut when the reaper cuts a strip 6 ft. wide.

5. An hexagonal mirror *abcdef* is made from a rectangular plate, *ABCD*. (*a*) Find the dimensions of the plate required for a mirror having sides 6 inches long. (*b*) Find the area of the four triangles cut from the plate in making the mirror. (*c*) Find the number of square inches in the mirror.

6. In a picture frame 2 inches wide, (*a*) how many square inches are used, including waste, when the outside 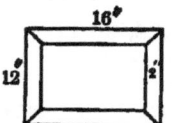 dimensions are 16 in. by 12 in.? (*b*) How many square inches are cut off in making the four corners? (*c*) How many square inches are there in the frame?

7. (*a*) What is the area of the largest circular piece of tin that can be cut from a sheet $3\frac{1}{2}$ feet square? (*b*) How many square feet of tin remain? (*c*) What fraction of the original sheet is left?

8. Two wheels are connected by a continuous belt. Find the length of the belt when the radii of the wheels are 11 inches and 24 inches respectively and the centers are 84 inches apart, assuming that the belt touches each wheel for one half of its circumference.

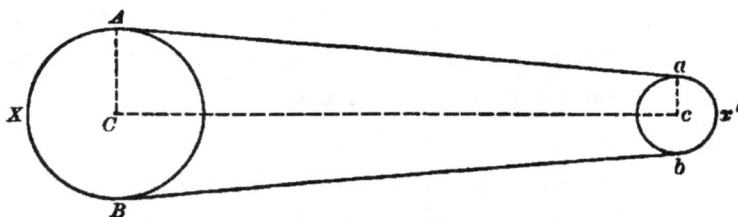

Note that Aa is the hypotenuse of a right triangle whose base is Cc and whose perpendicular is $AC - ac$.

9. To make the top of a vegetable can a piece of tin 7 inches in diameter is required. (*a*) How many square inches are used for the top and the bottom? (*b*) What is the length of the strip used in making the side when $\frac{1}{2}$ inch is required by the seam? (*c*) What is the breadth of the strip required for a can 6 inches high when $\frac{1}{2}$ inch is used for the seam at each base? (*d*) How many square inches of tin are required for a can? (*e*) Find the capacity of the can.

The Cone

A cone is a solid which slopes regularly from a point called the *apex* to its circular base.

In the pattern of a cone shown herewith, the sector *AB'DC'* forms the convex surface. The circumference of the base is equal in length to *BDC*, the arc of the sector *ABDC*. The sector is folded by bringing together the radii *AB* and *AC*, *DCB* then becoming the circumference of the base. The cone is completed by attaching a circular base.

The slant height of the cone is the distance between the apex and the circumference of the base, *AB*, or *AC*, or *AD*.

In a right cone the apex is directly above the center of the base.

Convex Surface of Cone

As the area of the sector *ABDC* is one half of the product of the arc by one of the equal sides,

> *Convex surface of cone = Circumference of base × one half slant height*

Sight Exercises

Find the convex surface of the following cones:

a. Circumference of base, 99 ft.; slant height, 168 ft.
b. Radius of base, $3\frac{1}{2}$ in.; slant height, 10 in.

Written Exercises

1. How many square feet of sheet lead will cover a conical roof 7 feet in diameter and having a slant height of 9 feet?

2. How many square yards of canvas are there in a conical tent 14 ft. in diameter, slant height 10 ft.?

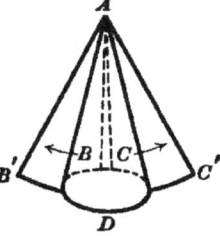

Entire Surface of Cone

The entire surface of a cone is the area of the convex surface increased by the area of the base.

Written Exercises

1. Find the entire surface of a cone when the circumference of the base measures 99 ft. and the slant height is 168 ft.

PROCESS

I. Convex surface in sq. ft. $= \frac{1}{2}(168 \times 99)$.

II. (*a*) Diameter of base in ft. $= 99 \div 3\frac{1}{7}$.

    (*b*) Area of base in sq. ft. $= (\frac{1}{2} \text{ of } 99) \times (\frac{1}{2} \text{ of } 99 \div 3\frac{1}{7})$

$$= \frac{99 \times 99 \times 7}{2 \times 2 \times 22}.$$

III. Entire surface = convex surface + surface of base.

    I. In multiplying 84 by 99, use the short method, and write the product at once.

    II. (*a*) *Indicate* the length of the diameter $(99 \div 3\frac{1}{7})$ ft.

        (*b*) Next *indicate* the area of the circle by indicating the product of the half diameter by the half circumference.

        (*c*) Then shorten the work by cancellation.

    III. Combine the two areas.

2. Find the entire surface of cones as follows:

a. Circumference of base, 98 ft.; slant height, 84 ft.

b. Radius of base, 28 yd.; slant height, 49 yd.

c. Diameter of base, 35 ft.; slant height, 125 ft.

d. Circumference of base, 9 in.; slant height, 24 in.

e. Radius of base, 3 ft.; slant height, 7 ft.

f. Diameter of base, 5 yd.; slant height, $11\frac{1}{2}$ yd.

3. Find the cost of slating a conical steeple 25 feet in diameter, slant height 42 feet, at $18 per 100 square feet.

The Pyramid

A pyramid is a solid having a polygon for the base, and a triangle for each lateral face. The triangles have a common vertex, which constitutes the apex of the pyramid.

Surface of Pyramid

In a right pyramid, the apex is directly over the center of the base; and when the pyramid is also regular, the lateral triangles have equal bases and equal altitudes, any one of the latter constituting the slant height of the pyramid.

As the area of the triangle ABC is $\frac{1}{2}$ ($BC \times AY$), that of ACD is $\frac{1}{2}$ ($CD \times AY$), that of ADE is $\frac{1}{2}$ ($DE \times AY$), and that of EF is $\frac{1}{2}$ ($EF \times AY$), the area of all the triangles is $\frac{1}{2}$ the product of the sum of the lines constituting the edges of the base of the pyramid by the slant height.

Convex surface of pyramid = Perimeter of base × one half slant height.

Sight Exercises

1. Find the convex surface of the following pyramids, the slant height being 10 ft., and the base being :

a. An equilateral triangle, each side 6 ft.

b. A regular hexagon, each side 4 ft.

c. A square, each side 7 ft.

Written Exercise

Find the entire surface of a pyramid, the slant height being 20 ft. and the base (*a*) a 10-foot square, (*b*) a 6-foot equilateral triangle.

Volume of Cone or of Pyramid

If a wooden cylinder be placed on one scale-pan and three cones, each having its base and altitude respectively equal to those of the cylinder, be placed on the other, the weight of the cylinder will exactly balance that of the three cones when all four are made of the same kind of wood.

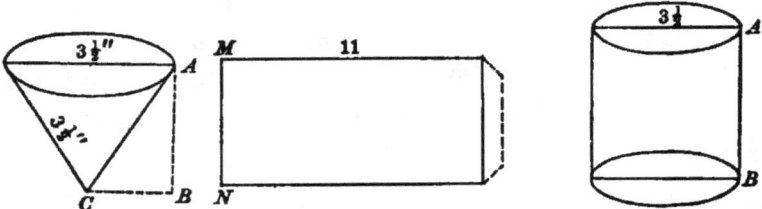

A hollow paper cone can be filled three times with sand from a hollow cylinder having its base and its altitude respectively equal to those of the cone.

Similar experiments with prisms and pyramids will show that the volume of a pyramid is one-third that of a prism having base and altitude equal, respectively, to those of the pyramid.

> *Volume of pyramid (or cone) = Area of base × one third altitude.*

Written Exercises

1. Find the volumes of pyramids, as follows :
a. Altitude, 12 inches ; base a 7-inch square.
b. Altitude, 9 feet ; base a 4-inch equilateral triangle.

2. Find the volumes of cones as follows :
a. Altitude, 12 inches ; diameter of base, 7 inches.
b. Altitude, 9 feet ; radius of base, 2 inches.
c. Altitude, 3 yards ; circumference of base, 6 yards.

Board Measure

Board measure is used in selling sawed lumber, including boards, beams, joists, rafters, planks, etc.

> *Number of board feet = Length in feet × Width in feet × Thickness in inches.*

Thus, the number of board feet in a board 12 feet long, 4 inches wide, and 1 inch thick or less, is $12 \times \frac{1}{3} \times 1$.

The unit of board measure is the *board foot*, which is 1 foot long, 1 foot wide, and 1 inch thick. Boards less than 1 inch thick are considered as having a thickness of an inch.

Table

Lumber dealers use a table in determining the board in a given piece of timber. The following is a portion of such a table.

Size in Inches	Length in Feet							
	10	12	14	16	18	22	26	30
2 × 4	$6\frac{2}{3}$	8	$9\frac{1}{3}$	$10\frac{2}{3}$	12	$14\frac{2}{3}$	$17\frac{1}{3}$	20
2 × 6	10	12	14	16	18	22	26	30
2 × 8	$13\frac{1}{3}$	16	$18\frac{2}{3}$	$21\frac{1}{3}$	24	$29\frac{1}{3}$	$34\frac{2}{3}$	40
2 × 10	$16\frac{2}{3}$	20	$23\frac{1}{3}$	$26\frac{2}{3}$	30	$36\frac{2}{3}$	$43\frac{1}{3}$	50
2 × 14	$23\frac{1}{3}$	24	$32\frac{2}{3}$	$37\frac{1}{3}$	42	$51\frac{1}{3}$	$60\frac{2}{3}$	70
$2\frac{1}{2}$ × 12	25	30	35	40	45	55	65	75
$2\frac{1}{2}$ × 14	$29\frac{1}{6}$	35	$40\frac{5}{6}$	$46\frac{2}{3}$	$52\frac{1}{2}$	$64\frac{1}{6}$	$75\frac{5}{6}$	$87\frac{1}{2}$
$2\frac{1}{2}$ × 16	$33\frac{1}{3}$	40	$46\frac{2}{3}$	$53\frac{1}{3}$	60	$73\frac{1}{3}$	$86\frac{2}{3}$	100
3 × 6	15	18	21	24	27	33	39	45
3 × 8	20	24	28	32	36	44	52	60
3 × 10	25	30	35	40	45	55	65	75
4 × 6	20	24	28	32	36	44	52	60
6 × 10	50	60	70	80	90	110	130	150

Sight Exercises

1. Give the number of board feet in the following boards, each 1 inch thick :

a. 14 ft. long, 1 ft. wide.
b. 10 ft. long, 6 in. wide.
c. 12 ft. long, 3 in. wide.
d. 18 ft. long, 4 in. wide.
e. 16 ft. long, 9 in. wide.

f. 12 ft. long, 8 in. wide.
g. 16 ft. long, 4 in. wide.
h. 10 ft. long, 6 in. wide.
i. 18 ft. long, 9 in. wide.
j. 14 ft. long, 3 in. wide.

2. Give the number of board feet in the following planks, rafters, etc., each 2 in. thick :

a. 14 ft. long, 9 in. wide.
b. 10 ft. long, 6 in. wide.
c. 12 ft. long, 4 in. wide.
d. 18 ft. long, 6 in. wide.

e. 12 ft. long, 6 in. wide.
f. 16 ft. long, 8 in. wide.
g. 10 ft. long, 9 in. wide.
h. 18 ft. long, 4 in. wide.

3. Give the number of board feet in the following, each being 12 ft. long :

a. 2 in. by 4 in.
b. 2 in. by 6 in.
c. 3 in. by 4 in.
d. 4 in. by 4 in.

e. 2 in. by 10 in.
f. 3 in. by 8 in.
g. 5½ in. by 6 in.
h. 8 in. by 10 in.

i. 3 in. by 6 in.
j. 4 in. by 5 in.
k. 2 in. by 10 in.
l. 3 in. by 12 in.

Written Problems

1. At $30 per M (thousand) find the cost of 120 planks 16 ft. long, 8 in. wide, 2 in. thick.

$$\text{Cost} = \frac{\$30 \times 120 \times 16 \times \frac{2}{3} \times 2}{1000}$$

2. What is the weight of a piece of timber 16 ft. long, 8 in. wide, 2 in. thick at 36 pounds to the cubic foot?

3. How many board feet are there in 100 rafters 2 in. by 7 in., 12 ft. long?

Matched Boards

Boards used for floors and ceilings are " tongued and grooved," the tongue of one board being fitted into the groove of the next one. These boards are generally 3 inches or 6 inches wide, including the tongue.   When laid, each board covers a strip $\frac{1}{2}$ inch less in width.

4. (*a*) How many matched boards 16 ft. long, 3 in. wide will be required for a floor 16 ft. long, $12\frac{1}{4}$ ft. wide when the tongue is $\frac{1}{2}$ inch wide ?

$$\text{Number} = 12\frac{1}{4} \text{ ft.} \div 2\frac{1}{2} \text{ in.}$$

(*b*) Find the cost of the boards at $36 per M, considering them as 3-inch boards.

$$\text{Cost} = \frac{\$36 \times \text{number of boards} \times 16 \times \frac{1}{4}}{1000}$$

5. (*a*) How many square feet are there in the ceiling of a porch 27 ft. 6 in. long, 8 ft. wide?   (*b*) How many feet of boards 3 inches wide are required when $\frac{1}{2}$ inch is lost in matching?   (*c*) How many feet of boards 6 inches wide are required when $\frac{1}{2}$ inch is lost in matching?

Siding

Boards used for the outside covering of a house are generally beveled.   Siding is $\frac{1}{4}$ in. thick at the top and $\frac{5}{8}$ in. at the bottom.   It is generally 6 inches wide and 12 or 16 ft. long.   It is laid horizontally, each row overlapping one fourth of the one below it.   A 6-inch board, therefore, covers only $4\frac{1}{2}$ inches of surface.

6. (*a*) How many rows of siding will be required for one side of a building 18 feet high?

$$18 \text{ ft.} \div 4\tfrac{1}{2} \text{ in.}$$

(*b*) When the boards are 12 feet long how many boards will be needed for each row in the side of a building measuring 36 feet? (*c*) How many boards will be needed for a side of a building 36 feet long 18 feet high, deducting for 6 windows, each 6 ft. by 3 ft.?

Shingles

Shingles are usually 16 and 18 inches long, but each row overlaps the one below, leaving only 4 or 5 inches exposed. They range in width from $2\tfrac{1}{2}$ to 14 or more inches, but the unit of measure is 4 inches. They are put up in bundles of a quarter of a thousand, a "thousand" meaning the equivalent of 1000 shingles 4 inches wide.

7. (*a*) When shingles are laid 4″ "to the weather," how many 4-in. shingles cover a square foot? (*b*) How many are required when laid 5″ "to the weather"?

In (*a*) each covers 4″ × 4″; in (*b*) 4″ × 5″.

8. How many square feet will 1000 shingles cover when they are laid (*a*) 4 inches "to the weather"? (*b*) 5 inches "to the weather"?

9. (*a*) How many bundles of shingles (250) will be required for a roof 40 ft. by 25 ft. when they are laid 4 inches to the weather? (*b*) How many slates 16 inches wide laid 10 inches to the weather would be needed?

10. How many thousand shingles will be required for the side of a house 36 ft. long, 18 ft. high, deducting for 6 windows each 6 ft. by 3 ft., if they are laid 5 inches to the weather and 112 shingles are allowed for waste?

Laths

Ordinary laths are 4 ft. long, $1\frac{1}{2}$ in. wide, $\frac{1}{4}$ in. thick. They are sold in bunches of 100. Being laid $\frac{1}{4}$ in. apart, 1 lath is required for a space 4 ft. by 2 in.

11. How many laths are required for 100 sq. yd. when 1 lath is needed for a space 4 ft. by 2 in., and no allowance is made for waste?

12. (*a*) How many square yards of plastering are there in the walls and the ceiling of a room 15 ft. long, 12 ft. wide, 9 ft. high deducting for 2 doors, each 3 ft. by $7\frac{1}{2}$ ft., and 2 windows each 3 ft. by 6 ft.? (*b*) Adding $2\frac{1}{2}\%$ for waste, how many laths are required?

13. Find the total cost of the materials required to lath and plaster 100 square yards, at the following quantities and prices:

> 10 bushels of lime at 40 ¢ per bushel.
> $1\frac{1}{2}$ cubic yards of sand at 75 ¢ for $1\frac{1}{4}$ cu. yd.
> 2 bushels of hair at 40 ¢ per bushel.
> 100 pounds of plaster of Paris for 50 cents.
> 1400 laths at $2.75 per M.
> 10 pounds of nails at 14 ¢ per pound.

Painting

14. How many gallons of paint will be required for 3 coats on two sides of a house 36 ft. deep and 18 ft. high, if the first coat takes 1 gal. for 60 sq. yd., the second 1 gal. for 72 sq. yd., and the third coat 1 gal. for 90 sq. yd.?

15. The front of a house is 24' wide, 18' high to the eaves, and 27' to the ridgepole. (*a*) Find the number of sq. yd. in the surface, deducting for a door $7\frac{1}{2}' \times 3'$, 3 windows, each $6' \times 3'$, and 1 window $4' \times 3'$.

Wall Paper

Wall paper is generally 18 inches wide. It is sold by
the single roll of 8 yards, or the double roll of 16 yards.
Borders are either 9 inches wide or 18 inches wide. A
wide border at the top of a wall is called a *frieze*.

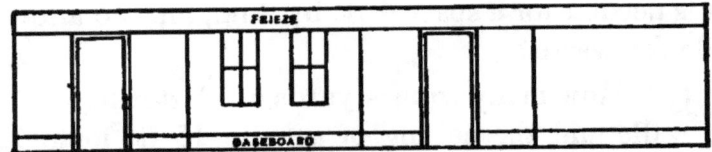

16. A room is 15' long, 12' wide, and 10½' high.

(*a*) How many sq. ft. of baseboard 1' wide does it
contain, deducting for 2 doors 3' wide? (*b*) How many
rolls of border 8 yd. long and 18 in. wide are required for
the frieze? (*c*) How many single rolls of paper are required to cover the walls above the baseboard and below
the frieze, deducting for 2 doors, each 9' × 3', and 2 windows, each 6' × 8', and allowing 12 sq. ft. for waste?

17. How many square yards of plastering are required
for the walls and the ceiling of the same room, the plaster
extending to the bottom of the baseboard?

18. How many board feet of 3-inch matched flooring
are required, allowing ½ inch for waste on each board?

Carpeting

19. (*a*) How many square yards of carpet are required
to cover a floor 5⅓ yards wide, 6¾ yards long? (*b*) Find
the number of running yards of carpet employed to cover
the floor when the carpet is ¾ yard wide.

20. At $1.25 per yard laid upon the floor, what will be
the cost of carpeting a floor 15 ft. long, 12 ft. wide, when
the carpet is 27 inches wide?

21. How many yards of carpet 1 yd. wide must be purchased for a floor 20 ft. 3 in. long, 16 ft. wide, when the strips run lengthwise?

When the strips run lengthwise, 5¼ strips are required, but 6 strips must be purchased. The length of the room being 6¾ yd., the number of yards is 6¾ × 6, etc.

22. How many yards of carpet 27 in. wide will be needed for the floor of a room 20 ft. 6 in. long, 16 ft. wide, when the strips run crosswise?

Number of strips: 20½ ft. ÷ 27 in. = 246 in. ÷ 27 in. = 9⅓; 10 strips must be used. Length of each strip, 16 ft., or 5⅓ yd. Quantity of carpet to be bought: 5⅓ yd. × 10, etc.

23. A floor is 20 ft. 3 in. long, 16 ft. wide. How many yards of carpet are needed (*a*) when the carpet is 1 yard wide and the strips run crosswise? (*b*) Find the number of yards of carpet 27 inches wide that must be bought when the strips run lengthwise. (*c*) When they run crosswise.

Matching Patterns. — In "making" a carpet for a given floor, the strips are sewed together in such a way as to "match the patterns." This frequently requires that a portion of each strip except the first be cut off, the amount varying according to the pattern.

24. How many yards of carpet, 27 inches wide, are required for the floor of a room 20 ft. 3 in. long, 16 ft. wide, when 4 inches are wasted on each strip except the first, and the strips run lengthwise?

25. How many inches must be cut off every strip except the first to match the pattern when the first strip is 20 ft. 3 in. long, and the pattern is repeated (*a*) every 9 inches? (*b*) Every 12 inches? (*c*) Every 8 inches?

Deductions for Openings

In building walls by the cubic yard; in painting, plastering, etc., by the square yard, contractors do not make a full allowance for openings. In some cases no deduction is made for openings below a certain size; in other cases one half of the area of the openings is deducted.

In ascertaining the quantity of material required, the actual surface or volume is used, due consideration, however, being given to material necessarily wasted.

26. (*a*) At 30¢ per square yard, find the cost of plastering the walls and the ceiling of a room 15 ft. long, 12 ft. wide, and 10½ ft. high, making one half allowance for 2 doors, each 9 ft. by 3 ft., and 2 windows, each 6 ft. by 8 ft. (*b*) Find the cost of tinting the walls and the ceiling at 8¢ per square yard, making the same allowance. (*c*) At 35 cents per square yard, find the cost of painting the baseboard, which is 1 ft. wide, the doors and the windows, making no allowance in the last for the space occupied by the glass.

27. The outside dimensions of the walls of a cellar are 36 ft. by 24 ft. (*a*) How many square feet remain for the floor of the cellar, if the walls are 2 ft. thick? (*b*) How many square feet are occupied by the walls? (*c*) If the walls are 9 ft. high, how many cubic yards of material do they contain, if there is one opening 9 ft. by 4 ft. and three openings each 3 ft. square? (*d*) How many tons of stone are required, if one ton is sufficient for a perch of 16½ cu. ft.? (*e*) Find the cost of building the walls at $3 per perch of 22 cu. ft., if the walls are measured on the outside and one half allowance is made for the openings.

The walls are considered by the contractor as equivalent to a wall (36 ft. + 24 ft. + 36 ft. + 24 ft.) long, 8 ft. high, 2 ft. thick.

28. A finished road consists of 3 inches of fine broken stone laid on 12 inches of coarser material. (*a*) How many cubic yards of each must be spread before rolling for a mile of road 27 feet wide, assuming that the steam roller will compress it into three fourths of the space it occupied when loose? (*b*) How many cart loads will be required at ⅝ cu. yd. to the load?

29. A printer has an order for 1500 cards 3″ by 2¼″. He has 25 sheets of pasteboard measuring 24″ by 18″. What is the largest number of cards he can get out of this material?

30. Two rectangular cisterns, with lids, are to be made of sheet iron. One measures 12′ × 8′ × 6′, the other 16′ × 9′ × 4′. (*a*) Find the number of square feet of material required for each, making no allowance for seams. (*b*) What is the capacity of each in cubic feet?

31. Find the difference in the number of cubic inches between a solid 12″ × 8″ × 6″ and one 14″ × 10″ × 8″.

32. How many board feet of inch boards will be required for a covered box having inside dimensions 12″ × 8″ × 6″?

33. A window sash whose outside dimensions are 5′ × 3′ 6″ contains 4 panes of glass of the same size. The frame is 2″ wide and the panes are separated from each other by strips 1″ wide. Make a drawing showing the dimensions of each pane.

34. A stair carpet covers 18 steps, 10″ tread and 7″ rise, with 18″ extra at both the bottom and the top of the staircase. How many yards of carpet are required?

SECTION XII

EQUATIONS IN BUSINESS

Formulas

A builder is asked what load a certain beam will bear. Turning to his handbook he finds the following formula for the safe load of a rectangular beam supported at both ends and uniformly loaded over the entire span.

$$\text{Safe load} = 2 \times \frac{w \times d^2 \times C}{l}$$

An explanatory note states that w represents the width of the beam in inches, d its depth in inches, and l its length in feet between the points of support. The value of C is given in a table which shows the equivalent in pounds for different woods; yellow pine, oak, spruce, white pine, hemlock, etc.

If the beams are of spruce 3 inches wide, 6 inches deep, and 12 feet long, and the table gives 70 pounds as the safe unit for spruce, these figures are substituted in the foregoing formula, thus:

$$\text{Safe load (in pounds)} = 2 \times \frac{3 \times 36 \times 70}{12}$$

Preparatory Exercises

1. Find the result.

2. What is the safe load when yellow pine is used in a similar case, its unit being 100 pounds?

302

Equations

The foregoing formula constitutes an equation which consists of two *members* connected by a sign of equality, one of the members containing an *unknown number* whose value is to be determined.

NOTE. — The expression $6 + 5 = 11$ is not an equation; it is called an *identity*.

In these two examples the result is determined by substituting the given numbers and performing the indicated operations. In the following, intermediate steps are required to obtain the result.

3. A builder wishes to ascertain the depth of a yellow pine beam 12 feet long between supports and 3 inches wide that will sustain a load of 1800 pounds uniformly distributed.

He substitutes in formula (*a*) the given numbers, producing the following equation:

$$1800 = \frac{2 \times 3 \times d^2 \times 100}{12}.$$

He first *simplifies* the second member by cancellation, making it $50\,d^2$, which gives the following:

$$1800 = 50\,d^2,$$

or, as it is customary to make the first member the one containing the unknown number:

$$50\,d^2 = 1800.$$

Dividing both members by 50, the equation becomes

$$d^2 = 36.$$

Extracting the square root of both members,

$$d = 6. \quad Ans. \quad 6 \text{ inches deep.}$$

Test by substituting 36 for d^2 in the formula, which should give 1800 lb. for the safe load.

Written Exercises

1. How wide should be a yellow pine 12-foot beam, 6 inches deep, to sustain a load of 2400 pounds?

2. What should be the distance between the points of support of a yellow pine beam 3 inches wide and 6 inches deep to enable it to sustain a load of 2400 pounds?

$$2400 = \frac{2 \times 3 \times 36 \times 100}{l}.$$

Simplify the second member, producing the following:

$$2400 = \frac{21600}{l}.$$

Remove the fraction from the second member by multiplying both members by l.

$$2400 \, l = 21600.$$

3. Find the equivalent required for C to enable a 12-foot beam, 3 inches wide and 6 inches deep, to sustain a load of 1350 pounds; that is, solve the equation:

$$\frac{2 \times 3 \times 36 \times C}{12} = 1350.$$

4. Find the area of a field in the form of a trapezoid whose parallel sides measure 30 and 50 rods, respectively, and having a perpendicular distance between them of 35 rods.

$$A = \frac{(30 + 50) \times 35}{2}.$$

First combine the numbers in the parenthesis. Then cancel.

5. The area of a trapezoid is 1200 square rods. The parallel sides are, respectively, 25 rods and 35 rods long. Find the perpendicular distance between them.

$$\frac{(25 + 35) \times p}{2} = 1200.$$

Percentage

The general formula for finding a per cent of a number is

$$P = \frac{B \times R}{100},$$

in which B represents the number, R the *rate*, and P the result. The letter B is called the *base* and P the *percentage*.

When the cost of an article is given and the rate of gain or of loss, the gain or the loss is obtained by multiplying the cost by the rate expressed as hundredths.

The difference in the live weight of a cow and the weight of its meat in the butcher shop is about 48%. If the live weight is 950 lb., the loss is 48% of 950 lb.

In applying the formula care must be used to select the proper number for the base. As a rule this is expressed in the problem, but such is not the case in the following:

6. The population of a city was 18,000 in 1915, an increase over 1914 of $12\frac{1}{2}$%. What was the increase?

7. A dealer sold goods for $18,000, which represented a profit of $12\frac{1}{2}$%. What was his profit?

In example 6, the base is the population of 1914; in 7, it is the *cost*, unless it be specified that in this case the profit is $12\frac{1}{2}$% of the receipts.

A person called upon to calculate the interest on $300 for 67 days at 6% could refer to the formula:

$$I = \frac{P \times R \times T}{100}.$$

Replacing the letters in the formula by the given numbers, he obtains the following:

$$I = \frac{\$300 \times 6 \times 67}{100 \times 360}.$$

To find Principal, Rate, Time, etc.

Written Exercises

1. What principal at $3\frac{1}{2}\%$ will yield $34.23 interest in 2 yr. 8 mo. 18 da. ?

PROCESS

Represent the principal by P, the rate in hundredths as $\frac{7}{200}$, and the time (978 days) in years as $\frac{978}{360}$. The combined product of the foregoing represents the interest, $34.23.

$$\frac{P \times 7 \times 978}{200 \times 360} = 34.23$$

Clear this of fractions by multiplying both members by 200 × 360, which gives

$$P \times 7 \times 978 = 34.23 \times 200 \times 360$$

Cancel the decimal point in 34.23 and the two ciphers in 200, which gives

$$P \times 7 \times 978 = 3423 \times 2 \times 360$$

Indicate the division of both members by 7 × 978, which gives

$$P = \frac{3423 \times 2 \times 360}{7 \times 978}$$

Cancel and find the result.

Test by calculating the interest on the principal thus found.

---

2. Find the interest on $360 for 2 yr. 8 mo. 18 da. at $3\frac{1}{2}\%$.

3. At what rate will $540 produce $88.83 interest in 4 yr. 8 mo. 12 da. ?

PROCESS

Represent the rate by R, change 4 yr. 8 mo. 12 da. to $\frac{1692}{360}$ yr., which gives

$$\frac{540 \times R \times 1692}{100 \times 360} = 88.83$$

from which

$$R = \frac{88.83 \times 100 \times 360}{540 \times 1692}$$

Reject the decimal and cancel 100.

---

4. Find the amount of $540 for 4 yr. 8 mo. 12 da. at $3\frac{1}{2}\%$.

5. At what rate will $360 amount to $419.22 in 4 yr. 8 mo. 12 da. ?

PROCESS

First find the interest, which is $419.22 — $360. Substitute the result in the formula, as in the preceding example.

---

6. In what time will $240 at $3\frac{1}{2}\%$ yield $38.99 interest?

PROCESS

Represent the time (in years) by T.

$$\frac{240 \times 7 \times T}{200} = 38.99$$

Indicate the value of T.

$$T = \frac{38.99 \times 200}{240 \times 7}$$

Cancel the decimal point, etc. Change the fraction of a year in the result to months and a fraction, and the latter to days.

---

7. In what time will $240 at $3\frac{1}{2}$ % amount to $278.99·? First, find the interest ($278.99 — $240).

8. What principal will amount to $563.82 in 3 yr. 10 mo. 17 da. at $4\frac{1}{2}$ %?

PROCESS

Indicate the interest on P at $4\frac{1}{2}$ % for 3 yr. 10 mo. 17 da. (1397 da.).

$$\frac{P \times 9 \times 1397}{200 \times 360} = \text{Interest}$$

Simplify the first member by cancellation, etc., making the equation

$$\frac{1397 \times P}{8000} = I$$

Find the amount by adding the principal

$$P + \frac{1397\,P}{8000} = A = 563.82$$

That is, $\quad \dfrac{8000\,P}{8000} + \dfrac{1397\,P}{8000} = 563.82$

Combine the two terms in the first member

$$\frac{9397\,P}{8000} = 563.82$$

$$P = \frac{563.82 \times 8000}{9397}$$

---

9. Find principal, rate, time, etc., as required.

a. Principal, $420; rate, 5%; time, 4 yr.   Interest?

b. Principal, $350; rate, 4%; time, 3 yr.   Amount?

c. Principal, $480; rate, 6%; interest, $86.40. ·Time?

d. Principal, $270; time, $2\frac{1}{2}$ yr.; interest, $37.50.   Rate?

Written Review Problems

1. What interest is yielded by $4500 at 3% in 3 years 7 months 12 days?

2. A man sells his farm for $12,000. He pays the agent for selling it 5% on $1000, $2\frac{1}{2}$% on $4000, and 1% on the remainder. He loans the net proceeds on a mortgage bearing 5% interest. What is his annual income from the mortgage?

NOTE. — Do not use the equation unnecessarily.

3. A person borrows $5000 on July 1, at $4\frac{1}{2}$%. What sum will pay the loan with interest on December 1? (Find time in days.)

4. When the amount of $360 for 1 year is $378, (*a*) what is the interest for 2 years? (*b*) What is the amount for 2 years?

Use the equation to find the rate. Use it in the next to find the principal.

5. If the amount of a certain sum at 5% is $504 for 1 year, what is the amount of the same sum for 2 years?

6. When a number increased by $\frac{1}{3}$ of itself is 84, what is the number when it is increased by $\frac{2}{3}$ of itself?

7. If a dealer gains 20% when he sells an article for $252, what must be the selling price to make the profit twice as large?

8. A selling price of $9.60 represents a profit of 60%. What per cent of profit would be represented by a selling price of twice $9.60 for the same article?

9. (*a*) What per cent of the list price is 40% of 75% of 90% of the list price? (*b*) What per cent of the list price remains after the deduction of successive discounts of 60, 25, and 10%?

Equations in General

Preparatory Exercises

a. What number added to 54 gives 72?
b. What number subtracted from 54 leaves 18?
c. What number multiplied by 72 gives 54?
d. What number divided by 4 gives 18?

One method of solving such problems is to write them as follows:

$$a. \quad \begin{array}{r} 54 \\ +? \\ \hline 72 \end{array} \qquad b. \quad \begin{array}{r} ? \\ -54 \\ \hline 18 \end{array} \qquad c. \quad \begin{array}{r} 72 \\ \times? \\ \hline 54 \end{array} \qquad d. \quad \frac{?}{4} = 18 \text{ or } 4\overline{)\underset{18}{?}}$$

and then to determine the number that will produce the result.

A general method for the solution of problems of this kind is to write each as an equation, thus:

$$a. \; 54 + x = 72 \quad b. \; x - 54 = 18 \quad c. \; 72\,x = 54 \quad d. \; \frac{x}{4} = 18$$

and then to solve the equation.

Only + and − signs should be used in equations, the product of an ordinary number by an unknown number being indicated by writing them together ($72\,x$), and division being indicated by writing the divisor as the denominator of a fraction of which the dividend is the numerator. The product of two ordinary numbers is generally obtained before the equation is written.

A number written before a letter without a sign connecting them, is called a *coefficient* of the letter. Thus, 72 in (*c*) is the coefficient of *x*. When no coefficient is expressed, the coefficient is 1.

The solution of an equation consists in finding the value of the unknown number.

Sight Exercises

1. Supply the missing number:

a. $? + 3 = 19$ e. $3 \times ? = 24$ i. $? + 2 = 15$

b. $? - 9 = 18$ f. $? \times 5 = 40$ j. $6 + ? = 12$

c. $? - 7 = 25$ g. $9 \times ? = 81$ k. $? + 4 = 10$

d. $8 + ? = 90$ h. $? \times 4 = 68$ l. $5 + ? = 15$

Collecting Terms

To solve the equation

$$6x + x - 2x - 4x + 3x = 68 - 80 + 60$$

it is necessary to combine the five terms of the first member into a single term, and also the three terms of the second member.

The five terms of the first member consist of three *positive* terms $+6x$, $+x$, and $+3x$, whose sum is $+10x$. The sum of the two *negative* terms, $-2x$ and $-4x$, is $-6x$. The first member is, therefore, equivalent to $10x - 6x$, which is combined into $4x$.

The two positive terms of the second member, $+68$ and $+60$, are combined into 128, the second member becoming $128 - 80$, which is combined into 48.

The simplified equation, $4x = 48$, is solved by dividing both members by 4, the coefficient of x, which gives $x = 12$.

To test the result, replace x in the *original* equation by 12, which gives: $72 + 12 - 24 - 48 + 36 = 68 - 80 + 60$.

Collect the terms in each member.

Sight Exercises

Give value of x:

a. $x + 2x = 60 - 30$ b. $x + 2x + 3x = 30 + 18$

c. $2x + 3x = 20 + 10$ d. $x - 2x + 3x = 30 - 10$

e. $3x - x = 40 - 10$ f. $2x - 3x + 5x = 20 + 28$

Written Problems

1. A boy paid $220 for a horse, a buggy, and a set of harness. The buggy cost 4 times as much as the harness and the horse cost $1\frac{1}{2}$ times as much as the buggy. Find the cost of each.

· PROCESS

Let $x =$ cost of the harness

Then $4\,x =$ cost of buggy

And $6\,x =$ cost of horse

$$x + 4\,x + 6\,x = 220$$

Collect terms $11\,x = 220$

Divide by 11 $x = 20$, cost of harness in dollars

$4\,x = 80$, cost of buggy in dollars

$6\,x = 120$, cost of horse in dollars

Test : $\overline{\text{Sum} = 220}$ *Ans.* $20, $80, $120

In equations, only abstract numbers are employed, x in this problem denoting the *number* of dollars. In writing the answers, the dollar sign is prefixed.

2. In four flocks there are 360 sheep. The first numbers twice as many as the second, and the second as many as the third and the fourth together. If these two contain the same number, how many are there in each flock?

Let $x =$ number in the fourth flock

Then $x =$ number in the third flock

     $2\,x =$ number in the second flock

And $4\,x =$ number in the first flock

     $x + x + 2\,x + 4\,x = 360$

Collect terms.

3. Divide 78 marbles between two boys so that one will have 5 times as many as the other.

4. A man spends $3.04 for coffee at 16 cents per pound and tea at 60 cents per pound, buying the same number of pounds of each. How many pounds of each does he buy?

Let x = number of pounds of each
$$16 x + 60 x = 304$$

As the cost of the articles is given in cents, the sum spent, $3.04, is written as cents.

5. A drover bought sheep, cows, and horses, an equal number of each, for $4440, paying 6 times as much for a cow as for a sheep, and 5 times as much for a horse as for a cow. How many of each did he buy?

6. A farmer obtained from 60 acres in wheat and 40 acres in corn, a total yield of 3600 bushels of grain. The corn field produced three times as much grain per acre as the wheat field. How many bushels were obtained from each?

7. Mr. Adams has 3 farms containing together 360 acres. The first contains $1\frac{1}{8}$ times as many acres as the second, and the second contains $1\frac{1}{2}$ times as many as the third. How many acres are there in each?

Let $2 x$ = number of acres in the third

8. A boy buys three times as many 1¢ stamps as he buys of 2's, and twice as many 2's as he buys of 5's. How many of each does he buy if he pays 90 cents for the lot?

Let x = number of 5-cent stamps
Then $2 x$ = number of 2-cent stamps
And $6 x$ = number of 1-cent stamps
$5 x$ = cost of 5-cent stamps
$4 x$ = cost of 2-cent stamps
$6 x$ = cost of 1-cent stamps
$$5 x + 4 x + 6 x = 90$$

Transposing Terms

Sight Exercises

1. Give value of x:

a. $x + 20 = 40$ b. $x + 30 = 70$ c. $x + 40 = 90$

d. $x - 20 = 40$ e. $x - 30 = 70$ f. $x - 40 = 90$

2. Give value of $2x$:

a. $2x + 2 = 10$ b. $2x + 2 = 16$ c. $2x + 4 = 20$

d. $2x - 2 = 10$ e. $2x - 2 = 16$ f. $2x - 4 = 20$

3. Give value of x:

a. $2x + 2 = 10$ b. $2x + 2 = 16$ c. $2x + 4 = 20$

d. $2x - 2 = 10$ e. $2x - 2 = 16$ f. $2x - 4 = 20$

g. $3x + 2 = 17$ h. $3x - 2 = 19$ i. $4x - 4 = 20$

To find the value of x in the equation $x + 20 = 40$, the first member must be diminished by 20; and to preserve the equality, 20 must also be subtracted from the second member.

$$x + 20 - 20 = 40 - 20$$

Combining terms in each member

$$x = 20$$

To find the value of x in the equation $x - 20 = 40$, the first member must be increased by 20, and to preserve the equality, 20 must be added to the second member.

$$x - 20 + 20 = 40 + 20$$

Combining terms in each member

$$x = 60$$

In practice, however, it is not customary to take the unnecessary steps of increasing or decreasing both members of an equation by writing the members on both sides.

The equations, $x + 20 = 40$ $x - 20 = 40$

are changed to $x = 40 - 20$ $x = 40 + 20$

by transposing 20 to the second member with a change of sign.

Written Exercises

1. Find the value of x in the following equations:

(a) $160 - 3x = 250 - 12x$

PROCESS

Given,	$160 - 3x = 250 - 12x$
Transpose,	$-3x + 12x = 250 - 160$
Collect terms,	$9x = 90$
Divide by the coefficient of x,	$x = 10$ *Ans.*

TEST

Substitute -30 in the first member for $-3x$, and -120 in the second member for $-12x$. This gives $160 - 130 = 250 - 120$, which becomes $130 = 130$.

(b) $3x + 240 - 5x = 460 + 4x - 310$

PROCESS

Given,	$3x + 240 - 5x = 460 + 4x - 310$
Transpose,	$3x - 5x - 4x = 460 - 310 - 240$
Collect terms,	$-6x = -90$
Change signs,	$6x = 90$
Divide by coefficient of x,	$x = 15$ *Ans.*

TEST

$$(3 \times 15) + 240 - (5 \times 15) = 460 + (4 \times 15) - 310$$
$$45 + 240 - 75 = 460 + 60 - 310$$
$$285 - 75 = 520 - 310$$
$$210 = 210$$

NOTE. — In the equation $-6x = -90$, the negative signs can be made positive by transposing $-6x$ to the second member and -90 to the first member, thus: $90 = 6x$, which becomes $15 = x$, by dividing both members by 6; but it is customary to change the negative sign of each member.

2. Solve the following equations. Test each result:

a. $19x - 22 = 90 + 3x$

b. $17x + 18 = 94 - 2x$

c. $96 + 4x = 16x - 48$

d. $14x + 63 = 198 - x$

e. $9x - 15 = 24 - 6x + 18 - 4x$

f. $6x - 42 + 5x = 34 - 3x - 5x$

g. $57 - 6x + 9 = 3x + 8 - x + 2$

h. $24 - 3x - 6x = 33 - 4x - 64$

Sight Problems

1. When 7 is subtracted from 5 times a number the remainder is 28. What is the number?

2. What number increased by twice itself and by 13 will be 43?

3. Henry has 40 marbles, which is 12 fewer than twice as many as William has. How many has William?

4. Mr. Smith has 45 head of stock. He has 10 more cows and 20 more sheep then he has horses. How many has he of each?

5. When 10 is added to 3 times a number the sum is 100. Find the number.

6. In a class of 40 pupils the girls outnumber the boys by 2. How many boys are in the class?

7. A team of horses and a wagon cost together $750. What is the cost of each horse if it is $150 more than that of the wagon?

8. The length of a field exceeds its width by 10 rods. Its perimeter is 140 rods. Give the dimensions.

Sight Exercises

1. Solve the following equations:

a. $4x + 9 = 53$

b. $5x = 16 - 3x$

c. $5x - 17 = 3x + 11$

d. $3x - 4 = 23$

e. $4x = 28 + 2x$

f. $7x + 20 = 50 - 3x$

g. $6x + 2 = 38$

h. $7x = 36 - 2x$

i. $2x - 15 = 18 - 9x$

Written Problems

1. The difference of two numbers is 24 and their sum is 86. Find the numbers.

PROCESS

Let $\quad\quad\quad x =$ the smaller number

Then $\quad\quad x + 24 =$ the larger

$$x + x + 24 = 86$$

Transpose $\quad x + x = 86 - 24$

Combine $\quad\quad 2\,x = 62$

Divide $\quad\quad\quad x = 31$, the smaller number

$\quad\quad\quad x + 24 = 55$, the larger number

Test. $\quad\quad \overline{31 + 55 = 86}$

In testing the accuracy of a result, be careful to select the proper condition. Since 55, the larger number, is obtained by increasing the smaller number, 31, by 24, their difference, which is the first condition in the problem, the correctness of the answer 31 is not determined by subtracting it from 55. Test by the other condition, which gives 86 as the sum. Since $31 + 55$ gives this result, the answers are correct.

2. A girl planted tulips, hyacinths, and crocuses; 20 more hyacinths than tulips, and 25 more crocuses than hyacinths. How many of each were there, if she planted 95 in all?

PROCESS

Let $\quad\quad\quad x =$ number of tulips

Then $\quad\quad x + 20 =$ number of hyacinths

And $\quad\quad x + 45 =$ number of crocuses

$$3\,x + 65 = 95 \quad\quad\quad\quad \text{etc.}$$

After the pupil has had some practice, he can write the equation

$$x + x + 20 + x + 20 + 25 = 95$$

without the preliminary statement.

In writing the latter, he should employ only as many words as he finds necessary, regardless of the number given in the sample statements.

3. Find two numbers whose sum is 115 and whose difference is 43.

4. A man has two fields, containing together 73 acres, one of which contains 19 acres more than the other. How many acres are there in each?

5. The length of a rectangle is 44 yards greater than its width, and the perimeter is 240 yards. (*a*) Find the dimensions. (*b*) Find the area.

$$x + x + 44 + x + x + 44 = 240.$$

6. When 3 times a number is subtracted from 142, the result is the same as the subtraction of 18 from 5 times the number. Find the number.

Clearing of Fractions

Preparatory Exercises

Give the value of x, when

a. $\frac{1}{4}$ of x is 12   *d.* $\frac{3}{4}$ of x is 12   *g.* $1\frac{1}{2}$ times x is 12

b. $\frac{1}{5}$ of x is 10   *e.* $\frac{2}{5}$ of x is 10   *h.* $3\frac{1}{3}$ times x is 10

c. $\frac{1}{7}$ of x is 21   *f.* $\frac{3}{7}$ of x is 21   *i.* $1\frac{2}{5}$ times x is 21

The expression $\frac{1}{4}$ of x is written $\frac{x}{4}$; $\frac{2}{5}$ of x is written $\frac{2x}{5}$; $3\frac{1}{3}$ times x is written $\frac{10x}{3}$, a mixed number being generally written as an improper fraction.

Written Exercises

1. Find the value of x in the following equation :

$$3x - 60 + \frac{2x}{3} = 58 - \frac{5x}{4}.$$

In order to obtain an equation without fractions multiply both members by the L. C. M. of the denominators of the fractions.

PROCESS

Given $\qquad 3x - 60 + \dfrac{2x}{3} = 58 - \dfrac{5x}{4}$

Multiply each term by 12

$\qquad\qquad 36x - 720 + 8x = 696 - 15x$

Transpose $\quad 36x + 8x + 15x = 696 + 720$

Combine $\qquad\qquad\qquad 59x = 1416$

Divide $\qquad\qquad\qquad\qquad x = 24$ *Ans.*

Test. $\quad 72 - 60 + 16 = 58 - 30$; or $28 = 28$

---

2. Solve the following equations. Test each result.

a. $\dfrac{x}{2} + \dfrac{x}{3} + \dfrac{x}{4} = 91$

f. $\dfrac{x}{3} + 19 = \dfrac{x}{4} + 20$

b. $x + \dfrac{x}{3} + \dfrac{x}{5} = 92$

g. $\dfrac{2x}{5} + \dfrac{2x}{3} = x + 25$

c. $2x + \dfrac{x}{2} - \dfrac{x}{3} = 26$

h. $\dfrac{x}{3} + \dfrac{x}{4} = \dfrac{5x}{8} - \dfrac{11}{12}$

d. $\dfrac{2x}{3} + \dfrac{x}{4} - \dfrac{x}{5} = 43$

i. $3x - 7 = \dfrac{5x}{3} + \dfrac{7}{3}$

e. $\dfrac{x}{3} - \dfrac{x}{4} + \dfrac{x}{5} = 34$

j. $\dfrac{x}{3} + \dfrac{x}{4} = \dfrac{2x}{5} + 11$

Written Problems

1. What number increased by 50 % and $33\frac{1}{3}$ % of itself will equal 66 ?

$$x + \frac{x}{2} + \frac{x}{3} = 66.$$

2. The difference between 75 % and $66\frac{2}{3}$ % of the same number is 13. Find the number.

3. A certain number is increased by 56 and the sum divided by 12, giving 10 for the quotient. What is the number ?

$$\frac{x + 56}{10} = 12.$$

4. After selling $\frac{1}{2}$ and $\frac{1}{3}$ of his land, Mr. Yates has still 100 acres. How many acres had he originally ?

$$x - \frac{x}{2} - \frac{x}{3} = 100.$$

5. After a discount of 50 % of the list price and $33\frac{1}{3}$ % of the remainder, an article cost $100. What is the list price ?

$$x - \frac{x}{2} - \frac{x}{3} = 100.$$

6. My crop of wheat this year is 561 bushels, which is $37\frac{1}{2}$ % larger than last year's crop. How many bushels did I raise last year ?

7. A man leaves $7500 to his widow, two sons, and three daughters, each son to have twice as much as a daughter, and the widow $500 more than all the children together. What is the share of each ?

Let x = the share of each daughter
Then $2x$ = the share of each son
$3x$ = share of three daughters
$4x$ = share of two sons
$7x + 500$ = widow's share

8. Divide 57 stamps among 3 girls in such a manner that the second will receive $1\frac{1}{2}$ times as many as the first, and the third will receive $1\frac{1}{4}$ times as many as the second.

9. The sum of two numbers is 75, one being $1\frac{1}{2}$ times the other. Find the numbers.

10. The perpendicular distance between the parallel sides of a trapezoid is 60 rods. One of the parallel sides is 50 rods. Find the other, when the area is 3300 square rods.

$$\frac{(50 + x) \times 60}{2} = 3300.$$

Removing Parentheses

A parenthesis is used to combine two or more terms into a single compound term. The expression $60 - (30 + 10)$ is considered as composed of two terms, the first of which, 60, is to be diminished by the second, the latter being a compound expression indicating the difference between 30 and 10. The two numbers written within the parenthesis are considered positive, the — sign preceding the parenthesis indicating the operation to be performed.

When a parenthesis preceded by a — sign is removed, the signs of the contained numbers are changed. Thus, the foregoing expression is written $60 - 30 - 10$. The expression $60 - (30 - 10)$ is written $60 - 30 + 10$ when the parenthesis is removed.

A number immediately preceding, or following, a parenthesis, and not connected with it by any sign, indicates that it is a multiplier of the enclosed expression. Thus, $60 - 2 (30 - 10)$ means that 60 is to be diminished by twice the difference between 30 and 10. The multiplier, 2, may be placed within the parenthesis by performing the indicated multiplication, which gives $60 - (60 - 20)$, and the parenthesis may then be removed, which gives $60 - 60 + 20$.

Written Exercises

1. Find the value of x in the equation :

$$x - 3(x - 10) = 4x - 42.$$

PROCESS

Given	$x - 3(x - 10) = 4x - 42$
Remove the parenthesis	$x - 3x + 30 = 4x - 42$
Transpose	$x - 3x - 4x = 42 - 30$
Combine	$-6x = -72$
Change signs and divide	$x = 12$, *Ans.*

Another method is to transpose the negative compound term, making it positive

$$x = 4x - 42 + 3(x - 10).$$

In making such transposition change only the sign *prefixed* to the compound term.

---

2. Solve the following equations.   Test results.

a. $4(x - 3) + 7(x - 1) = 5x - 1.$

b. $4(x + 3) - 7(x - 3) = 2(x + 4).$

c. $8(x + 2) - 9(x - 2) = 3x + 2.$

d. $6(10 - x) - 9(8 - x) = x + 1.$

e. $48 - 3(4x - 5) = 27 - 3(2x - 4).$

Fractional Terms

1. Find the value of x in the following equation :

$$\frac{2x - 4}{9} - 1 = \frac{x + 1}{12}.$$

Multiply by 36	$\dfrac{36(2x - 4)}{9} - 36 = \dfrac{36(x + 1)}{12}$	*(a)*
Simplify	$4(2x - 4) - 36 = 3(x + 1)$	*(b)*
Remove parentheses	$8x - 16 - 36 = 3x + 3$	*(c)* etc.

The illustration shows the successive steps in the process.   The pupil should omit steps *(a)* and *(b)* unless he finds them necessary.

2. Solve the following equation:

$$6 - \frac{2x - 1}{9} = 14 - \frac{5x - 4}{6}.$$

PROCESS

Given
$$6 - \frac{2x - 1}{9} = 14 - \frac{5x - 4}{6}$$

Transpose the fractions
$$6 + \frac{5x - 4}{5} = 14 + \frac{2x - 1}{9}$$

Transpose 6 and combine
$$\frac{5x - 4}{6} = 8 + \frac{2x - 1}{9}$$

Multiply by 18
$$3(5x - 4) = 144 + 2(2x - 1)$$
etc.

By transposing a negative fractional term, thus changing it to a positive one, the beginner sometimes avoids mistakes. The transposition of 6 and its combination with 14 reduces the number of terms.

3. Solve the following equations:

a. $\dfrac{x - 9}{12} - \dfrac{x - 6}{8} + 1 = \dfrac{x - 10}{4}.$

b. $\dfrac{x + 1}{5} - \dfrac{2 - x}{7} = \dfrac{x - 3}{2}.$

c. $\dfrac{2x + 3}{9} - \dfrac{x - 3}{3} = 9 - \dfrac{5x - 6}{6}.$

d. $\dfrac{x + 1}{6} = \dfrac{x - 1}{4} - \dfrac{20 - x}{3}.$

e. $\dfrac{3x + 2}{7} - \dfrac{x + 3}{2} + 5 = \dfrac{3x - 21}{4}.$

f. $\dfrac{3x + 1}{4} - \dfrac{4x + 1}{3} = \dfrac{x - 28}{6}.$

Written Problems

1. In a factory 36 men and 66 boys are employed, each man receiving $2 per day more than a boy. What is the pay of each if the daily pay of all is $225?

$$36(x + 2) + 66\,x = 225.$$

2. A fraction is equal to $\frac{3}{4}$, and the difference between its numerator and its denominator is 5. What is the fraction?

$$\frac{x}{x + 5} = \frac{3}{4}.$$

When each member consists of a single fraction, the equation is cleared of fractions by multiplying the numerator of the fraction in the first number by the denominator of the fraction in the second, and the numerator of the fraction in the second by the denominator of the fraction in the first.

$$4\,x = 3(x + 5).$$

3. If 3 be added to both terms of a fraction whose value is $\frac{3}{4}$, the value will become $\frac{4}{5}$. What is the fraction?

Representing the fraction by $\frac{3\,x}{4\,x}$,

$$\frac{3\,x + 3}{4\,x + 3} = \frac{4}{5}.$$

4. A train going 15 miles per hour faster than a second train travels 180 miles while the other travels 120 miles. At what rate does each travel?

$$\frac{180}{x + 15} = \frac{120}{x}.$$

5. What fraction equal to $\frac{5}{7}$ will become equal to $\frac{2}{3}$ when 10 is subtracted from both terms?

6. What per cent of $18\frac{3}{4}$ is $16\frac{2}{3}$?

$$\frac{x}{100} \text{ of } 18\frac{1}{4} = 16\frac{2}{3}.$$

7. A man bought a number of bicycles at $14 each. He sold $\frac{2}{3}$ of them at $19 each, 2 of them at $18 each, and the remainder at $16 each, realizing a profit of $100. How many did he buy?

Representing by x the number bought, $\frac{2x}{3}$ is the number sold at $19 each. There are then $\frac{x}{3}$ left, of which 2 are sold at $18 each, leaving $\frac{x}{3} - 2$, which are sold at $16 each.

The profit in dollars on the first lot is 5 times $\frac{2x}{3}$, or $\frac{10x}{3}$; on the second lot, 8; on the third lot, 2 times $\left(\frac{x}{3} - 2\right)$, or $\frac{2x}{3} - 4$.

The whole profit, in dollars, is $\frac{10x}{3} + 8 + \frac{2x}{3} - 4$, which is equal to 100.

8. A dealer buys a certain number of bicycles at $13 each. He sells $\frac{2}{3}$ of them at $18 each, 3 at $17 each, and the remainder at $15 each, making a total profit of $78. How many did he buy?

9. What per cent of $16\frac{2}{3}$ is $18\frac{3}{4}$?

10. By what fraction of itself must $16\frac{2}{3}$ be increased to become $18\frac{3}{4}$?

$$16\frac{2}{3} + 16\frac{2}{3}\, x = 18\frac{3}{4}.$$

11. By what fraction of itself must $18\frac{3}{4}$ be diminished to become $16\frac{2}{3}$?

12. The perimeter of a rectangle is 48 rods. Find the area when one side is 4 rods longer than the adjacent side.

Let x = length of short side.
Find the area after dimensions are determined.

13. A and B purchase together 350 tons of hay at $12 per ton. If A takes 60 tons more than B, what should each pay?

14. A man wishing to divide a number of stamps among some boys finds, if he gives 5 to each, he will have 10 over, and that he requires 5 more in order to give 6 to each. How many stamps has he?

Let x = number of boys.

$$6x - 5 = 5x + 10.$$

After ascertaining the number of boys, the number of stamps can be found.

15. I had $4 in my pocket. I spent 60 cents for a book and I bought two pairs of gloves, one pair costing 40 cents more than the other. I then had $1.80 left. What was the price of each pair of gloves?

16. By purchasing cloth at $2.40 per yard, I have 40 cents left. If I had bought cloth at $2.80 per yard, I should have been 70 cents short. How many yards did I buy?

17. How many pounds of coffee costing 24¢ per pound can be mixed with coffee costing 18¢ per pound to make 150 pounds costing 22¢ per pound? Solve and test.

	PROCESS
Let	x = quantity of 24¢ coffee
Then	$150 - x$ = quantity of 18¢ coffee
	$24x$ = cost of first (in cents)
	$18(150 - x)$ = cost of second (in cents)
and	150×22 = cost of mixture (in cents)
	$24x + 18(150 - x) = 3300$
	$24x + 2700 - 18x = 3300$
	etc.

The richness of milk depends upon the percentage of butter fat it contains. Below 3% its sale in cities is generally forbidden as not being sufficiently nutritious for young children. Above 18% it is considered cream.

18. A creamery has an order for 150 gallons of 4 % milk. (*a*) There is on hand a lot of milk testing 5 % and another lot testing $3\frac{1}{2}$ %. How many gallons of each can be used in a mixture that will fill the order?

Taking x as the quantity of 5 % milk and $150 - x$ as the quantity of $3\frac{1}{2}$ % milk, the equation becomes,

$$\frac{5\,x}{100} + \frac{3\frac{1}{2}(150 - x)}{100} = \frac{4(150)}{100}.$$

Clear the equation of the denominator 100 by rejecting it from each term. Solve the equation. Test.

(*b*) How could the same order be filled with skim milk and 6 % milk?

$$\frac{5\,x}{100} + \frac{0(150 - x)}{100} = \frac{4(150)}{100}.$$

Since skim milk has no butter fat, its per cent is 0; hence the second term of the first member of the foregoing equation disappears.

19. If there is a call for 75 pounds of milk containing 8.5 % of fat, and milk containing 6 % is to be used, how much skim milk can be added?

20. A boy weighing 100 pounds is sitting on one end of a 5-ft. crowbar, the other end of which is under a stone. (*a*) How far from the stone must a support be placed in order that his weight will exert a lifting force of 300 pounds upon the stone?

In a lever, the energy (E) multiplied by its distance from the fulcrum (F) is equal to the work (W) multiplied by its distance from the fulcrum.

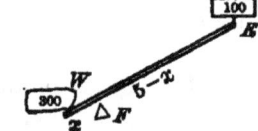

Representing the distance FW by x, EF will be $5 - x$. Multiplying the former by 300 and the latter by 100, the following equation results:

$$300\,x = 100(5 - x).$$

(*b*) Assuming that the crowbar extends 6 inches under the stone, how far from the edge of the stone must the fulcrum be placed?

$$300 \, x = 100(4\tfrac{1}{2} - x).$$

21. A dairyman wishes to deliver 100 pounds of cream testing 18%. How many pounds of 5% milk and of 25% cream can he use?

22. A portion of a field in the form of a right triangle was cut off by a line parallel to the base, making a trape-

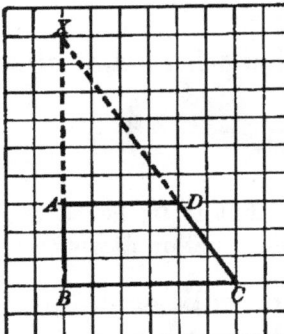

zoidal field with parallel sides measuring, respectively, 48 rods and 72 rods, the perpendicular distance between them being 36 rods. What was the length of the perpendicular of the original triangle?

This may be worked experimentally on cross-ruled paper by drawing *ABCD* to scale, making *BC* 6 spaces, *AD* 4 spaces, and *AB* 3 spaces. Extend *CD* and *BA* until they meet?

PROCESS

The line *AD*, parallel to *BC*, makes two *similar* triangles, *AXD* and *BXC*. In triangles of this kind the homologous (corresponding) sides are proportional; that is,

$$XA : XB :: AD : BC$$

Representing *XB* by x, *XA* will be $x - 36$;

therefore $x - 36 : x :: 48 : 72$

or, $:: 2 : 3$ (Canceling)

Making the product of the extremes equal to the product of the means, the following equation results:

$$3 \, x - 108 = 2 \, x$$

or, $x = 108$ *Ans.* 108 rods

Test. Compare this result with the one obtained by the drawing.

23. The upper portion of a cone was cut off, leaving a frustum with bases 8″ and 12″ in diameter, respectively, and a slant height of 9″. What was the slant height of the original cone?

Find the value of x in the following proportion:

$$x : 12 :: x - 9 : 8.$$

24. An 18-foot plank weighing 24 pounds rests on a fulcrum placed 12 feet from one end. (*a*) What weight must be placed on the other to balance the plank?

The weight of each portion is assumed to be concentrated at its center, that of the larger part (16 lb.) being located 6 ft. from the fulcrum, and that of the smaller part (8 lb.) 3 ft. from the fulcrum.

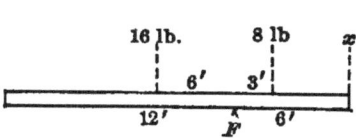

The balancing weight (x) is 6 ft. from the fulcrum.

Using a dot to denote multiplication,

$$x \cdot 6 + 8 \cdot 3 = 16 \cdot 6,$$

that is, $6x + 24 = 96.$

25. A boy weighing 80 pounds is sitting at one end of an 18-ft. plank that weighs 24 pounds. If he is 12 feet from the fulcrum, how heavy a man can he balance at the other end of the plank?

80 (lb.) × 12 (ft.) + 16 (lb.) × 6 (ft.) must balance x (lb.) × 6 (ft.) + 8 (lb.) × 3 (ft.).

Two Unknown Numbers

Preliminary Exercises

1. If 1 lb. tea and 2 lb. coffee cost 100 cents, and 1 lb. tea and 3 lb. coffee cost 125 cents, (*a*) What is the price of a lb. of coffee? (*b*) What is the price of a lb. of tea?

Express by the following equations, x representing the price of tea per lb. and y the price per lb. of coffee:

(i) $\quad x + 2\,y = 100$
(ii) $\quad x + 3\,y = 125$

Subtract (i) from (ii) $\qquad\qquad y = 25$

Substitute in (i) for $2\,y$ its value.

$$x\ 50 = 100$$

Transpose $\qquad\qquad x = 50$

Ans. Tea, 50¢ per lb., coffee, 25¢ per lb.

2. If twice A's money added to three times B's money amounts to $700, and twice A's money added to five times B's money amounts to $900, (*a*) What is twice B's money? (*b*) How much money has B? (*c*) How much money has A?

This problem may be expressed by the two following equations, x representing A's number of dollars, and y representing B's:

(i) $\quad 2\,x + 3\,y = 700$
(ii) $\quad 2\,x + 5\,y = 900$

Subtract (i) from (ii) $\qquad\qquad 2\,y = 200$

$$\text{or, } y = 100$$

Substitute in (i) 300 for $3\,y$,

$$2\,x + 300 = 700$$

Transpose $\qquad\qquad 2\,x = 700 - 300$
Collect terms, $\qquad\qquad 2\,x = 400$
Divide $\qquad\qquad\qquad x = 200$

Ans. A has $200, B has $100.

When two unknown numbers have the same value in each of two different equations, the latter are said to be *simultaneous*.

The equations $x + 2\,y = 100$ and $2\,x + 4\,y = 200$ are called *identical equations*, since the second is a multiple of the first, and is, therefore, reducible to it.

The foregoing method of reducing two simultaneous equations each containing two unknown numbers to an equation containing only one unknown number is called the method of *elimination*.

Elimination by Combination

Written Exercises

1. Given $2x + 3y = 25$ and $2x - 3y = 7$; to find the value of x and of y.

PROCESS

Given	$2x + 3y = 25$ (i)	Since the sum
	$2x - 3y = 7$ (ii)	of $+3y$ and $-3y$
Adding (i) and (ii)	$\overline{4x = 32}$	is 0, add the two
or,	$x = 8$ *Ans.*	equations.

To find the value of y, substitute this value of x in (1), which then becomes $16 + 3y = 25$. By transposition, $3y = 25 - 16 = 9$, and $y = 3$. As a test substitute these values in the first member of (ii), which then becomes $16 - 9$. As this gives 7, which is the second member of (ii), the values are correct.

Since the value of y was found by substituting the value of x in equation (i), test the results by substituting both values in in equation (ii).

---

2. Given $4x - 7y = 10$ and $2x + 3y = 18$; to find the value of x and of y.

PROCESS

Given	$4x - 7y = 10$	(i)
	$2x + 3y = 18$	(ii)
	$- + -$	
(i)	$4x - 7y = 10$	
Multiply (ii) by 2,	$\underline{4x + 6y = 36}$	(iii)
	$13y = 26$	
	$y = 2$ *Ans.*	

Find the value of x by substituting 2 for y in either (i) or (ii) and test the two values by substituting both in the other equation.

To eliminate x, it must have the same coefficient in both equations; therefore multiply by 2 both members of equation (ii), and mark the new equation (iii). Since $4x$ is positive in (i) and (iii), change the signs of all the terms in (i) and combine the two equations, thereby eliminating $4x$. The signs of (i) are changed rather than those of (iii) in order that the coefficients of y may be positive when the two equations are combined.

Write the changed signs above (or below) the numbers.

3. Given (i) $2x + 3y = 31$ and (ii) $5x - 4y = 3$; to find the value of x and of y:

PROCESS	
Multiply (i) by 5,	$10x + 15y = 155$ (iii)
Multiply (ii) by 2,	$10x - 8y = -6$ (iv)
Change signs of (iv) and	$-\quad+\quad+$
combine with (iii),	$23y = 161$
	$y = \quad 7$ *Ans.*

4. Find the value of x and of y:

a. $3x + 14y = 81$ *c.* $7x - 2y = 41$ *e.* $4x + y = 65$
$\quad 5x + 9y = 92$ $3x + 5y = 41$ $3x - 4y = 44$

b. $4x + 11y = 6$ *d.* $3x - 9y = 5$ *f.* $x - 8y = 7$
$\quad 3x - 7y = 1$ $5x + 6y = 98$ $5x + 7y = 129$

Written Problems

1. A boy buys 1-cent and 2-cent stamps, 25 in all, at a cost of 30 cents. How many of each does he buy?

Represent the number of 1-cent stamps by x and the number of 2¢ stamps by y, obtaining the following equations

$$x + y = 25 \text{ and } x + 2y = 30$$

Solve also by one unknown number, representing the number of 2-cent stamps by x and the number of 1-cent stamps by $25 - x$, which produces the following equation:

$$2x + 25 - x = 30.$$

2. A and B together have $50. If A were to spend $\frac{1}{4}$ of his money, he would still have $6 more than B. How much money has each?

$$\frac{3\,x}{4} - y = 6. \quad \text{Clear of fractions.}$$
$$x + y = 50.$$

3. When the numerator of a fraction is increased by 5, its value becomes $\frac{1}{3}$; when its denominator is increased by 7, its value becomes $\frac{1}{4}$. Find the fraction.

Represent the fraction by $\frac{x}{y}$. Then $\dfrac{x+5}{y} = \dfrac{1}{3}$ and $\dfrac{x}{y-7} = \dfrac{1}{4}$.

4. The sum of two numbers is 43 and their difference is 25. What are the numbers?

5. Find two numbers whose sum is 73 and twice whose difference is 70.

6. One half the difference of two numbers is 18, and one third of their sum is 24. What are the numbers?

7. Four colts and three cows cost together $435. Three colts and five cows cost together $450. What is the cost (*a*) of a colt? (*b*) Of a cow?

8. A number of geese at $1.50 each and of turkeys at $2.50 each cost $58. If the geese had cost 25¢ apiece less and the turkeys 25¢ apiece more, the total cost would have been $1 more. How many of each were bought?

9. A's annual income is 4 times B's, and his annual expenditures are 5 times B's. If each saves $1000 per year, what is the annual income of each?

Let x = B's income   Let y = B's expenditures
Then $4\,x$ = A's income   Then $5\,y$ = A's expenditures

$$x - y \text{ (B's savings)} = 1000$$
$$4\,x - 5\,y \text{ (A's savings)} = 1000$$

10. The perimeter of an isosceles triangle is 51 inches, and 6 times the length of the base is equal to 5 times the length of each of the equal sides. Find the length of the base.

11. A driver bought 3 horses and some sheep for $900. He sold the horses at a profit of $10 each and the sheep for $6 each, gaining altogether $75. How many horses did he buy, if the sheep cost him $5 each?

Let x = cost of horses, y = number of sheep.
$3x + 5y = 900$; $3(x + 10) + 6y = \$975$.
Solve also without using x and y.

12. If 35 cu. in. of brass and 16 of iron weigh 239 ounces, and 11 cu. in. of brass and 25 of iron weigh 155 ounces, find the weight of a cubic inch of each.

13. If both terms of a fraction are increased by 1, its value becomes $\frac{4}{7}$; when both terms are increased by 2, its value becomes $\frac{8}{10}$. What is the fraction?

14. The sum of two digits of a number is 9. Find the number when it is 45 greater than the number formed by interchanging the digits.

Represent the tens' digit by x and the units' digit by y, which makes the number $10x + y$, and the number formed by interchanging the digits $x + 10y$, then $x + y = 9$; $10x + y = x + 10y + 45$.

15. The sum of a number and the number formed by interchanging the digits is 110; the difference between them is 54. What is the number?

16. If a number of two digits is divided by the sum of its digits, the quotient is 8 and the remainder is 2; if the number formed by reversing the digits is divided by the sum of its digits, the quotient is 2 and the remainder is 8.

$$\frac{10x + y - 2}{x + y} = 8. \qquad \frac{x + 10y - 8}{x + y} = 2.$$

17. A boy has 15 coins, quarters, and half dollars. If he exchanges the quarters for dimes and the half dollars for nickels, he will have 8 times as many coins. How much money has he?

$$x + y = 15, \quad 5x + 2\tfrac{1}{2}y = 15 \text{ times } 8.$$

When the number of coins of each denomination is ascertained, the sum of money is computed.

18. One day the receipts for 160 straight tickets and 80 round trip tickets between two cities were $680; the next day the receipts for 84 straight tickets and 156 round trip tickets were $756. What is the price of a ticket of each kind?

19. Find a fraction whose value is increased $\tfrac{1}{30}$ when both terms are increased by 2.

Product of two Binomials

The product (a) of $(x + 6)$ by $(x + 9)$, (b) of $(x - 6)$ by $(x - 9)$, (c) of $(x + 6)$ by $(x - 9)$, obtained as follows:

(a)	(b)	(c)
$x + 6$	$x - 6$	$x - 6$
$x + 9$	$x - 9$	$x - 9$
$x^2 + 6x$	$x^2 - 6x$	$x^2 + 6x$
$9x + 54$	$-9x + 54$	$-9x + 54$
$x^2 + 15x + 54$ *Ans.*	$x^2 - 15x + 54$ *Ans.*	$x^2 - 3x - 54$ *Ans.*

First write the partial product by x, then the partial product by $+9$ or -9, and combine the two. Observe that in multiplying -6 by -9, the product is $+54$, and that when one factor is preceded by $+$ and the other by $-$ the sign preceding the product is $-$. The rule is stated as follows:

Like signs give $+$; unlike signs give $-$.

Written Exercises

1. Find the value of x in the following equation :

$$(x + 20)(x - 30) = x^2 - 1200$$

PROCESS

Given $(x + 20)(x - 30) = x^2 - 1200$

Perform indicated multiplication $x^2 - 10x - 600 = x^2 - 1200$

Transpose and combine $-10x = 600$

Test $x = 60$ *Ans.*

---

2. Find the value of x in the equation :

$$(30 - x)(20 + x) = 1200 - x^2.$$

3. Solve the equation $\dfrac{x + 1}{x + 5} = \dfrac{x + 4}{x + 9}$.

PROCESS

Given $\dfrac{x + 1}{x + 5} = \dfrac{x + 4}{x + 9}$

Clear of fractions by cross multiplication :

$$(x + 1)(x + 9) = (x + 4)(x + 5)$$

Solve

---

4. Find the value of x :

     a. $\dfrac{7 - x}{8 - x} = \dfrac{9 - x}{11 - x}$ *b.* $\dfrac{x + 1}{x + 9} = \dfrac{x + 5}{x + 15}$

5. Find the value of x in the following proportion :

$$x + 1 : x + 4 :: x + 5 : x + 9.$$

Form an equation making the product of the extremes equal to the product of the means. $(x + 1)(x + 9) = (x + 4)(x + 5)$

6. Find the value of x :

     a. $x - 7 : x - 6 :: x = 1 : x + 2$

     b. $5 - x : 6 - x :: 11 - x : 14 - x$

     c. $(x + 1)^2 - x^2 = 35$

Written Problems

1. When one side of a square field is increased by 30 yards and the other is decreased by 40 yards, the area is decreased by 2400 square yards. Find the length of the field.

2. What number subtracted from both terms of $\frac{4}{5}$ and of $\frac{7}{9}$ will make the resulting fractions equal?

$$\frac{4-x}{5-x} = \frac{7-x}{9-x}.$$

3. What number must be added to 9, to 11, to 22, and to 26, in order that the new numbers may form a proportion?

$$x+9 :: x+11 : x+22 : x+26.$$

4. The difference between the squares of two successive numbers is 49; find the numbers.

Representing the numbers by $x+1$ and x, $(x+1)^2 - x^2 = 49$.

5. The difference between the squares of two successive even numbers is 64. What are the numbers?

6. The hypotenuse of a right triangle is 1 inch longer than the base, and the perpendicular is 5 inches. How long is the base?

7. The side of one square is 4 yards longer than that of a second, and the area of the first is 96 square yards greater than the area of the other. Find the length of the side of each.

8. By what number must 3, 5, 9, and 13 be increased in order that they may form a proportion?

9. A 5-foot path surrounding a square plot contains 625 sq. ft. What is the area of the plot?

Area of plot and path $= (x+5)^2$. Area of plot $\equiv x^2$. Area of path $\equiv (x+5)^2 - x^2$.

Quadratic Equations

An equation containing the second power of the unknown number (x^2), is called a *quadratic* equation.

Sight Exercises

Give the value of x:

a. $x^2 = 36$	b. $2x^2 = 32$	c. $3x^2 = 48$
d. $2x^2 = 50$	e. $2x^2 = 12\frac{1}{2}$	f. $3x^2 = 5\frac{1}{3}$
g. $\dfrac{x^2}{3} = 12$	h. $\dfrac{3x^2}{4} = 36$	i. $x^2 = \dfrac{16}{25}$

Written Exercises

Find the value of x:

a. $(x+2)^2 + (x-2)^2 = 40$ b. $x(x+7) = 7(x+28)$

c. $(2x+3)(2x-4) = 2(26-x)$ d. $(x-3)(x+2) = 19 - x$

e. $(3x+1)(3x-1) = 35$ f. $x(x+5) = 5(x+1) + 20$

Written Problems

1. The side of one square is 3 times as large as that of another square, and both together have an area of 117 square feet. Find (*a*) the area of each. (*b*) The length of a side of each.

2. The difference between two numbers is 4 and the sum of their squares is 136. What are the numbers?

Represent the numbers by $x + 2$ and $x - 2$.

3. The sum of the squares of three consecutive numbers is 149. What are the numbers?

Represent the numbers by $x + 1$, x, and $x - 1$.

4. The area of a circle is 616 square inches. Find the radius.

Area $= 3\frac{1}{7} R^2$, $3\frac{1}{7} R^2 = 616$.

Sight Exercises

1. Give answers :

a. $(x+1)^2$ b. $(x-4)^2$ c. $(x+7)^2$ d. $(x-10)^2$

e. $(x-2)^2$ f. $(x+5)^2$ g. $(x-8)^2$ h. $(x+11)^2$

i. $(x+3)^2$ j. $(x-6)^2$ k. $(x+9)^2$ l. $(x-12)^2$

2. Give the number required to make each of the following a complete square :

a. $x^2 + 4x + ?$ b. $x^2 - 6x + ?$ c. $x^2 + 8x + ?$

d. $x^2 - 10x + ?$ e. $x^2 + 12x + ?$ f. $x^2 - 14x + ?$

g. $x^2 + 16x + ?$ h. $x^2 - 18x + ?$ i. $x^2 + 20x + ?$

j. $x^2 - 22x + ?$ k. $x^2 + 24x + ?$ l. $x^2 - 26x + ?$

3. Extract the square root of each member of the following equations :

a. $x^2 + 2x + 1 = 24 + 1$ b. $x^2 + 24x + 144 = -44 + 144$

c. $x^2 + 8x + 16 = 9 + 16$ d. $x^2 + 16x + 64 = -60 + 64$

e. $x^2 + 20x + 100 = 44 + 100$ f. $x^2 + 12x + 36 = -11 + 36$

Written Exercises

1. One side of a rectangle is 20 yards longer than the other, and the area is 384 square yards. What are the dimensions ?

PROCESS

Given $\qquad x^2 + 20x = 384$

Complete the square

$$x^2 + 20x + \left(\frac{20}{2}\right)^2 = 384 + 100 = 484$$

Extract the square root, $x + 10 = \pm 22$

Transpose, $x = (a)\ 22 - 10$ and $(b) - 22 - 10$

or $\qquad x = 12$, or -32

Ignoring the negative result, *Ans.* 12 yd., 32 yd.

Test. 12 (yd.) × 32 (yd.) = 384 (sq. yd.)

---

2. Find the value of x in the following equation:
$$x^2 + 24\,x = 81$$

PROCESS

Given $\qquad\qquad\qquad x^2 + 24\,x = 81$

Complete the square,
$$x^2 + 24\,x + 144 = 81 + 144 = 225$$

Extract square root, $\qquad x + 12 = \pm\,15$

Transpose, $\qquad\qquad\qquad x = 15 - 12,\ \text{or} - 15 - 12$
$$x = 3,\ \text{or} - 27\ \textit{Ans.}$$

Test. When $x = 3$, $\quad x^2 = 9$, $\quad 24\,x = 72$; $\qquad 9 + 72 = 81$

When $x = -27$, $\ x^2 = 729$, $24\,x = -648$; $\ 729 - 648 = 81$

---

3. Find the values of x in the equation:
$$x^2 + 300 = 36\,x + 25$$

PROCESS

Given $\qquad\qquad\qquad x^2 + 300 = 36\,x + 25$

Transpose, and combine like terms,
$$x^2 - 36\,x = -275$$

Complete the square,
$$x^2 - 36\,x + 324 = -275 + 324 \equiv 49$$

Extract the square root, $\ x - 18 = \pm\,7$

Transpose and combine, $\qquad x = 7 + 18,\ \text{and} - 7 + 18$
$$x = 25,\ \text{or } 11\ \textit{Ans.}$$

Test. When $x = 25$, $\qquad\qquad x^2 = 625$ and $36\,x = 900$
$$625 + 300 \equiv 900 + 25$$
$$925 \equiv 925$$

When $x = 11$, $\qquad\qquad\qquad x^2 = 121$ and $36\,x = 396$
$$121 + 300 \equiv 396 + 25$$
$$421 \equiv 421$$

Note that there are two positive values of x.

---

4. Find the value of x in the equation:
$$x^2 - 100 = 44$$

Two Values of the Unknown Number

Since $-7 \times -7 = 49$, the square root of 49 is $+7$ or -7. This is written ± 7, which is read "plus or minus 7."

This gives rise to *two* values of x in a quadratic equation. When one of the values is negative it is generally omitted in giving the answer to a problem.

Written Exercises

Solve the following equations by adding to both members of each the square of one half the coefficient of x:

a. $x^2 + 2x = 15$ b. $x^2 - 2x = 15$ c. $x^2 + 8x = -15$

d. $x^2 - 8x = -15$ e. $x^2 - 2x = 48$ f. $x^2 + 2x = 48$

g. $x^2 - 14x = -48$ h. $x^2 + 14x = -48$ i. $x^2 + 2x = 63$

j. $x^2 - 2x = 63$ k. $x^2 + 16x = -63$ l. $x^2 - 16x = -63$

Written Problems

1. One side of a rectangle is 6 inches longer than another and the area is 135 square inches. Find the length of two adjacent sides.

$x(x + 6) = 135$. Solve also by employing $x + 3$ and $x - 3$ to represent the sides.

2. The product of two numbers is 96. One of the numbers is 4 less than the other. What are the numbers?

3. The walls and the ceiling of a square room 9 feet high require 108 square yards of plaster. What are the dimensions of the ceiling?

Let $x =$ the length and the width in *yards*.

The area of each of the four walls in *square yards* will be $3x$.

4. A girl bought two pieces of muslin, paying 40 cents for each, one costing 2¢ per yard more than the other. She received 1 yard less of the dearer kind. What was the price of each?

PROCESS

Let $\qquad x = $ cost per yard of one

Then $\qquad x + 2 = $ cost per yard of other

Then $\qquad \dfrac{40}{x} = $ number of yards of cheaper kind

And $\qquad \dfrac{40}{x + 2} = $ number of yards of dearer kind

which gives the equation $\dfrac{40}{x} - \dfrac{40}{x + 2} = 1$

Clear of fractions by multiplying all terms by $x(x + 2)$, which gives $\qquad 40(x + 2) - 40\,x = x(x + 2)$

or $\qquad 40\,x + 80 - 40\,x = x^2 + 2\,x$

Combine terms of first member. $\quad 80 = x^2 + 2\,x$

or $\qquad\qquad\qquad\qquad x^2 + 2\,x = 80$

Test, using only the positive value.

5. A certain number is subtracted from 25 and the remainder is multiplied by the number, giving a product of 114.   What is the number?

$$(25 - x)x = 114, \quad 25\,x - x^2 = 114.$$

Test both answers. Changing signs,

$$x^2 - 25\,x = -114. \quad x^2 \text{ should be made positive.}$$

6. In a trip of 100 miles one train travels 5 miles more per· hour than a second, and finishes the trip in 1 hour less.   Find the speed of each.

7. A flower bed 18 feet by 12 feet is surrounded by a walk the area of which is equal to that of the bed.   Find the width of the walk.

$$(18 + x)(12 + x) = (18 \times 12) + (18 \times 12).$$

8. The perpendicular of a right triangle is 7 yards longer than the base and 2 yards shorter than the hypotenuse.   What are the respective lengths of the three sides?

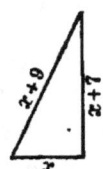

9. Find the radius of a circle when the diameter is 4 inches longer than a chord that is 6 inches from the center.

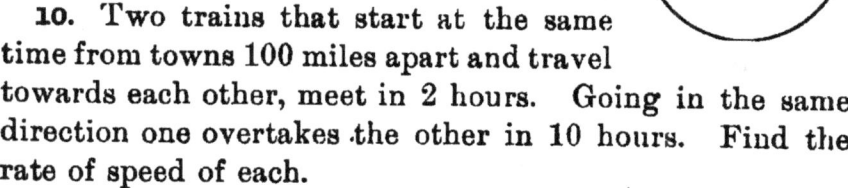

$$x^2 + 6^2 = (x - 2)^2.$$

10. Two trains that start at the same time from towns 100 miles apart and travel towards each other, meet in 2 hours. Going in the same direction one overtakes the other in 10 hours. Find the rate of speed of each.

11. A boat goes 75 miles with the current in 3 hours, and against the current in 5 hours. (*a*) How many miles per hour does the boat travel? (*b*) What is the rate of the current?

12. What is the volume of a cube when the entire surface contains 96 sq. in.?

Representing an edge by x, $6 x^2 = 96$, when the length of an edge is found, find the volume.

13. The sum of the adjacent sides of one rectangular field is 62 rods. The dimensions of a second field are, respectively, 16 rods greater and 8 rods less. Find the dimensions of the first if both have diagonals of the same length.

Let $\qquad x =$ one side of first.
Then $\qquad 62 - x =$ adjacent side.

(*a*) $x^2 + (62 - x)^2 =$ length of diagonal.

Then $\qquad x + 16 =$ one side of second.
And $\qquad 54 - x =$ adjacent side.

(*b*) $(x + 16)^2 + (54 - x)^2 =$ length of diagonal. (*a*) = (*b*).

Make the equation, solve, and test.

SECTION XVII

INDUSTRIAL CONSTRUCTION EXERCISES

Angular Measure

60 seconds (″)	1 minute (′)
60 minutes	1 degree (°)
360 degrees	1 circle

Angles

At 12 o'clock the two hands of a clock coincide; at any other hour they form an angle. The angle formed at 6 o'clock, when both hands are in a line, is called a *straight angle*. At 9 o'clock the hands form a *right angle*. At 2 o'clock the angle formed by the hands is called an *acute angle*, which is smaller than a right angle. At 4 o'clock the hands form an *obtuse angle*, which is larger than a right angle.

Acute and obtuse angles are also known as *oblique* angles.

Draw a straight angle, a right angle, an acute angle, and an obtuse angle, and write the correct name under each.

In the following exercises, straight angles will not be considered. Although the hour hand has traveled through 270° in going from XII to IX, the angle between its hands at 9 o'clock is a right angle, being measured by the smaller of the two arcs intercepted by the hands.

344

Sight Exercises

1. How many degrees are passed over in an hour (*a*) by the minute hand? (*b*) By the hour hand?

2. What angle is formed by the hands (*a*) at 10 o'clock? (*b*) At 2 o'clock? (*c*) At 4 o'clock? (*d*) At 5 o'clock? (*e*) At 7 o'clock? (*f*) At 8 o'clock? (*g*) At 1 o'clock? (*h*) At 11 o'clock?

3. How many degrees does the hour hand pass over (*a*) in one half hour? (*b*) In 20 minutes? (*c*) In 40 minutes?

4. How many degrees are there in the angle formed by the hour and the minute hand (*a*) at 6:30? (*b*) At 4:20? (*c*) At 5:40? (*d*) At 7:30?

Designating Angles

When two lines, *OP* and *ON* for instance, form an angle, the lines are called the *sides* of the angle, and the common point *O* is called the *vertex*.

The angle is called the angle *NOP* or *PON*, the letter at the vertex being placed between the other two. It may also be designated as the angle *O*. A letter placed between the lines, near the vertex, is sometimes used to designate an angle; as, for instance, the angle *x*.

One of the two angles having the common vertex shown in the illustration is called *ABC* and the other *CBD*. Each may also be designated by a letter or a figure placed between the lines; as, for instance, angle 1 and angle 2, respectively.

Angles having a common vertex and a common side are called *adjacent angles*. Angles 1 and 2 are adjacent angles.

Supplementary angles are made by two lines that form only two angles, the common vertex being on one of the sides. *wvu* and *uvx* are supplementary angles.

When two lines intersect to form four angles, the opposite pairs are called *vertical angles;* thus, *a* and *b* are vertical angles, as are *x* and *y*.

The lengths of the sides of an angle do not affect the size of the angle. The angle formed by *AB* and *CB* may be called *ABC,* or *uBC,* or *uBv,* etc.

The angle *ABD* is the sum of the angles *ABC* and *CBD.* It may also be called *uBD, ABy,* etc.

Oral Exercises

1. How many straight lines can be drawn (*a*) through one point? (*b*) Through two points?

2. How many straight lines are required to form (*a*) one angle? (*b*) Two angles? (*c*) Four angles?

Mechanical Drawing

In the construction exercises, use a hard pencil, a ruler, a pair of compasses, a right triangle, and a protractor.

Draw circles and arcs by means of the compasses. One use of the compasses is shown in the following exercise, which requires that a line be drawn equal in length to a given line *AB.* A————————B

Draw lightly a line, *XY,* of indefinite length. Place one foot of the compasses on *A,* and make the other (containing a pencil) fall on *B.* Keeping the feet of the compasses this distance apart, place the first foot on *X,* and

draw a short arc by the pencil across *XY* at *Z*. Rule
XZ, the required line, in ink or darken it by a soft pencil.

Do not erase the arc and the remainder of the line. In the following exercises leave such construction lines and arcs to show the method
pursued. Finish the required figure with a darker line.

Use a right triangle, made of wood or of stiff cardboard,
to determine the direction of a line perpendicular to a given
line, also of one parallel to a
given line.

To draw from *P* a line
parallel to *AB*, place the perpendicular of the triangle on
AB and place the ruler *XY*
against the base. Holding
the ruler firmly, slide the
triangle along it until the
point *P* touches the perpen-

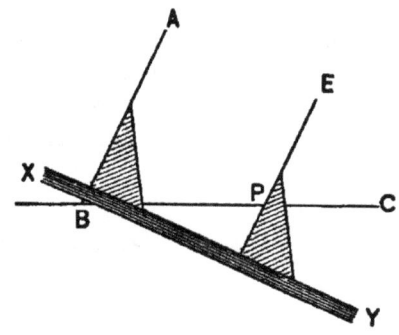

dicular. Draw a line from *P* along the perpendicular.

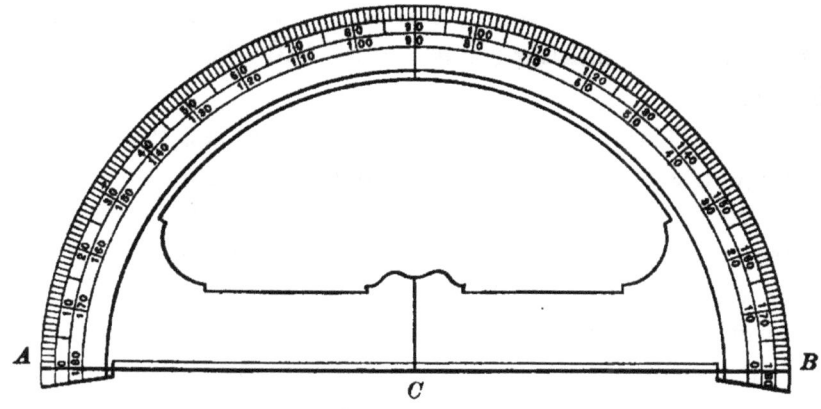

Measuring Angles

To measure an angle is to determine the number of
degrees in the arc intercepted by its sides, the vertex being
the center of the measuring circle.

For this purpose a *protractor* is used. The simplest form is the semicircular protractor shown in the illustration.

To measure the angle *GDE* place the point *C* of the protractor on *D*, the vertex of the angle, and the point *B* on the line *DE*. The number of degrees on the protractor at *F*, the point cut by the line *DG*, gives the measure of the angle.

The protractor has two sets of figures each extending to 180°. In measuring the angle *GDE*, the point *B* of the protractor being on *DE*, use the lower row of figures, which extends from 0° at *B'* to 180° at *A'*.

Angles

Construction Exercises

1. Draw two lines in such a way as to make (*a*) four angles. (*b*) Two angles. (*c*) One angle.

2. Using the protractor, draw two lines making (*a*) an angle of 40°. (*b*) An angle of 75°, one line being vertical. (*c*) Two lines making an angle of 120°, both lines being oblique.

3. (*a*) Draw two lines forming two angles, one of which contains 50°, and write in each angle the number of degrees it contains. (*b*) Draw two lines forming two angles, one of which measures 110°, and write in each angle the number of degrees it contains. (*c*) What is the sum of the two supplementary angles in each case?

4. Draw (*a*) two lines making two equal supplementary angles. (*b*) Two lines forming four equal angles. (*c*) Mark in each of the six angles the number of degrees it contains.

NOTE. — A line is perpendicular to another when the supplementary angles are equal.

5. Using the protractor, draw a perpendicular (*a*) to a horizontal line. (*b*) To a vertical line. (*c*) To an oblique line.

6. (*a*) Draw two lines cutting each other at an angle of 60°, and write in each of the four angles the number of degrees it contains. (*b*) Draw two lines cutting each other at an angle of 140°, and write in each of the four angles the number of degrees it contains.

7. (*a*) To a horizontal line draw two lines an inch apart, each making an angle of 90° with the first line. (*b*) Where will the last two lines intersect each other? (*c*) Using the protractor, draw two·lines perpendicular to a vertical line. (*d*) Two perpendicular to an oblique line.

8. By means of the ruler and the triangle draw (*a*) several perpendiculars to a given line. (*b*) Several oblique lines parallel to each other.

9. To a given line draw a second line making an angle of 40° with the first. By means of the ruler and the triangle draw a third line parallel to the second. (*a*) How many degrees are contained in the angle made by the third line with the first line on the same side? (*b*) How many degrees are there in each of the two supplementary angles?

10. By means of the protractor draw several lines running in the same direction and each making an angle of 60° with a vertical line. Where will the oblique lines intersect?

11. Draw two parallel lines, using the ruler and the triangle. Draw a line intersecting one of the parallel lines at an angle of 50°. Write in each of the eight angles the number of degrees it contains.

Triangles

12. On a line 3 inches long construct a triangle having two base angles of 60 degrees each. (*a*) Measure the third angle. (*b*) Measure each of the other two sides. (*c*) Write in each angle the number of degrees it contains and the length of each side. (*d*) How many degrees are there in the three angles?

Draw the base line the given length. Make the next line sufficiently long to intercept the third line. Do not prolong this last line unnecessarily.

13. (*a*) Construct a triangle having base angles of 65° each. (*b*) Mark in each angle the number of degrees it contains. (*c*) How many degrees are there in the three angles? (*d*) How do the other sides compare in length with the base? (*e*) With each other?

14. Construct an isosceles triangle having its base (*a*) vertical. (*b*) Oblique. (*c*) Having its vertex below the base.

15. Construct a triangle having one base angle of 50° and one of 60°. (*a*) Measure the third angle and write in it the number of degrees it contains. Measure the three sides. (*b*) The longest side is opposite which angle? (*c*) The shortest side is opposite which angle? (*d*) How many degrees do the three angles contain?

16. (*a*) Construct a triangle containing one right angle. (*b*) Find the number of degrees contained in the two oblique angles. (*c*) Try to construct a triangle containing two right angles. (*d*) Construct a triangle containing an obtuse angle. (*e*) Find the number of degrees contained in the three angles. (*f*) Try to construct a triangle containing two obtuse angles.

Oral Exercises

1. How many degrees are there in the sum of the three angles (*a*) of a right triangle? (*b*) Of an isosceles triangle? (*c*) Of an obtuse-angled triangle? (*d*) Of a scalene triangle? (*e*) Of an equilateral triangle?

2. How many degrees are there in each angle of an equilateral triangle?

3. How many degrees are there in an angle supplementary to one of (*a*) 60°? (*b*) 90°? (*c*) 140°? (*d*) 30°?

4. (*a*) If one angle of a right triangle contains 30°, how many degrees are there in the other oblique angle? (*b*) If one of the angles of an isosceles triangle is 120°, how many degrees are there in each of the other two angles? (*c*) How many degrees are there in each angle of an isosceles right triangle? (*d*) When one of the base angles of an isosceles triangle contains 40°, how many degrees are there in each of the other two angles?

5. Give the number of degrees in the third angle of a triangle when two of the angles contain, respectively, (*a*) 30° and 40°. (*b*) 50° and 60°. (*c*) 70° and 80°. (*d*) 30° and 50°.

Quadrilaterals

Construction Exercises

1. Using the protractor, draw (*a*) a square. (*b*) A rectangle. Using the triangle, draw (*c*) a square on a 3-inch oblique line. (*d*) A rectangle 3 inches by 2 inches having an oblique line for the base.

2. (*a*) Draw a line 3 inches long making an angle of 60° with a 4-inch line. (*b*) Using the ruler and the triangle, complete the parallelogram. (*c*) Write in each of the four angles its contents in degrees.   (*d*) Write on each of the four sides its length.

3. On a base 3 inches long, construct a parallelogram having a side $2\frac{1}{2}$ inches long and containing (*a*) an angle of 30°.   (*b*) Draw a line constituting its altitude. (*c*) Mark the length of the altitude and of each of the two remaining sides.   (*d*) Mark in each angle of the parallelogram the number of degrees it contains.   (*e*) Construct a parallelogram having sides of the same length as the foregoing but containing an angle of 53°.   (*f*) What is its altitude?   (*g*) Draw a parallelogram having sides of $2\frac{1}{2}$ and 3 inches, respectively, and an angle of 37°. (*h*) What is its altitude?   (*i*) Write in each of the three foregoing rhomboids its area.

4. Construct a rhombus having each side 3 inches and (*a*) an angle of 60°.   (*b*) An angle of 150°.   (*c*) Altitude 2 inches.

5. Construct three trapezoids of different shapes each having an altitude of $2\frac{1}{2}$ inches and parallel sides 3 inches and 4 inches, respectively.

6. Construct three trapeziums of different shapes each having a diagonal of 4 inches and perpendiculars of 2 inches and 3 inches, respectively, from this diagonal to the angles opposite.

7. (*a*) From each extremity of a 2-inch line draw two lines, each $2\frac{1}{2}$ inches long and making with the first line angles of 70° and 110°, respectively.   (*b*) Complete the quadrilateral.   (*c*) What kind of quadrilateral is it?

8. (*a*) From each extremity of a 2-inch line draw two lines making angles of 80° and 100°, respectively, and measuring $2\frac{1}{2}$ and 3 inches, respectively.   (*b*) Complete the quadrilateral.   (*c*) What kind of quadrilateral is it?

Oral Exercises

1. How many degrees are there in the sum of the four angles (*a*) of a square? (*b*) Of a rectangle? (*c*) Of a rhomboid? (*d*) Of a trapezium? (*e*) Of a rhombus?

2. Give the number of degrees in each of the remaining angles of a parallelogram when it contains one angle of (*a*) 90°. (*b*) 60°. (*c*) 120°. (*d*) 40°. (*e*) 80°.

3. A quadrilateral contains two angles of 90° each and one angle of 40°. (*a*) How many degrees are there in the fourth angle? (*b*) What kind of a quadrilateral is it?

4. A quadrilateral contains three angles of 80° each. (*a*) How many degrees are there in the fourth angle? (*b*) What kind of a quadrilateral is it?

5. How many degrees are there in the second base angle of a parallelogram when the first contains (*a*) 75°? (*b*) 110°? (*c*) 65°? (*d*) 135°?

Polygons

A polygon is said to be *inscribed* in a circle when each vertex lies on the circumference of the circle; it is said to be *circumscribed* about a circle when each side touches the circumference at a single point.

Construction Exercises

1. (*a*) Draw a circle having a radius of 2 inches. (*b*) Using the protractor draw two diameters intersecting at an angle of 90°. (*c*) Draw the chords of the four arcs of 90°, forming an inscribed square. (*d*) Draw perpendiculars touching the extremities of the diameters, forming a circumscribed square. (*e*) How do the two squares compare in area?

2. (*a*) Draw a circle having a radius of 2 inches. (*b*) Draw two radii meeting at an angle of 60°. (*c*) How many degrees are there in the intercepted arc? (*d*) Draw the chord and on it write its length. (*e*) Using the compasses mark off on the circumference as many successive arcs as possible equal in length to the first. (*f*) Draw the chord of each arc. (*g*) How many inches in length is each arc?

Note. — The space between the points of the compasses represents the length of the chord of each of the successive arcs.

3. (*a*) Inscribe an equilateral triangle in a circle by dividing the circumference into six equal arcs, and drawing the chords of arcs of 120°. (*b*) Circumscribe a similar triangle by making each side of the circumscribed triangle pass through a vertex of the inscribed triangle. (*c*) Compare the areas of the two triangles.

A *regular polygon* is one having equal sides and equal angles. To inscribe a regular polygon in a circle the protractor may be used to determine one arc of the proper size, the others may then be laid off with the compasses.

4. Inscribe in a circle (*a*) a regular hexagon. (*b*) A regular octagon. (*c*) A regular pentagon.

5. Divide a circumference into five equal arcs, and number the divisions 1, 2, 3, 4, and 5. Draw chords from 1 to 4, 1 to 3, 2 to 4, 2 to 5, and 3 to 5, forming a five-pointed star.

6. Inscribe in a circle a six-pointed star.

7. Divide a regular hexagon into six equal triangles. (*a*) What kind of triangle is each? (*b*) In each angle of two adjacent triangles mark the number of degrees it contains. (*c*) How many degrees are there in the angle formed by two adjacent sides of a regular hexagon?

8. Without drawing a circle, construct a regular hexagon having 2-inch sides.

NOTE. — At each end of a line 2 inches long draw a line 2 inches long making the required angle, using the protractor. From the other end of each of these two lines draw a line making the required angle. Connect these last lines. Test the accuracy of the drawing by measuring the last two angles.

9. Divide a regular octagon into eight equal triangles (a) What kind of triangle is each? (b) How many degrees are there in each of the eight equal angles m at the center of the octagon? (c) How many degrees are there 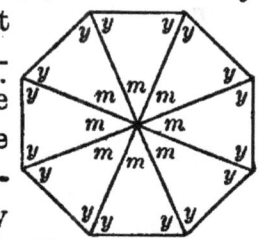 in each of the other two angles y of one of the triangles? (d) How many degrees are there in the angle formed by two adjacent sides of the octagon? (e) How many degrees are there in the supplementary angle formed by extending one side of the octagon? (f) How does the latter angle compare with one of the angles at the center?

10. Find the number of degrees in each angle of (a) a regular pentagon. (b) A regular nonagon.

11. On a 3-inch line construct (a) an equilateral triangle. On the same line construct (b) a square. (c) A regular pentagon, etc.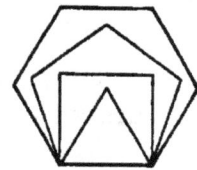

Sight Exercises

1. (a) How many degrees are there in the sum of the angles of a triangle? (b) To how many right angles is this sum equal?

2. (a) How many degrees are there in the sum of the angles of a quadrilateral? (b) To how many right angles is this sum equal?

3. (*a*) Is each angle of a regular pentagon acute or obtuse? (*b*) How many degrees does it contain? (*c*) How many degrees are there in the five angles? (*d*) To how many right angles is the sum equal? (*e*) How many degrees are there in the supplementary angle *s* formed by producing one of the sides? (*f*) What fraction of 360° does the supplementary angle contain?

4. How many sides has a regular polygon when each of its angles measures (*a*) 60°? (*b*) 120°? (*c*) 90°? (*d*) 135°? (*e*) 108°? (*f*) 140°?

Construction Problems

In the following exercises do not use the triangle and the protractor; use only ruler and compasses.

Concentric circles have the same center but unequal radii. Eccentric circles have different centers.

1. Draw (*a*) two concentric circles. (*b*) Two eccentric circles, one entirely within the other. (*c*) Two circles tangent (touching) internally. (*d*) Two circles tangent externally, having equal radii. (*e*) Two having radii unequal. (*f*) Two intersecting circles having equal radii. (*g*) Two having radii unequal.

2. Using each extremity of a 2-inch line as a center, (*a*) draw two circles of 3-inch radius. (*b*) Draw radii to the points at which the circumferences intersect. (*c*) Give the lengths of the sides of each of the two triangles thus formed. (*d*) Connect the two intersecting points. (*e*) How does this line divide the common base of the two triangles?

3. On a 2-inch base construct two isosceles triangles, having the equal sides of each triangle 3 inches long. Use short arcs to determine the vertex of each triangle.

Draw the arcs lightly and do not erase them. Complete the triangle in dark lines.

4. Draw a short line and bisect it, without measuring the line.

Use arcs intersecting above and below the line as in No. 3. Placing the ruler on the points of intersection cut the given line by a short line. Test the accuracy of the work by using the compasses to measure the length of each half.

5. Erect a perpendicular (*a*) at the center of a line. (*b*) At a point in a line not the center.

To erect a perpendicular at *A* in the line *MN*, mark off with the compasses *B* and *B'* equidistant from *A*. The problem now is to erect a perpendicular at *A*, the middle point of *BB'*.

The whole of the arc shown in the illustration need not be drawn; two very short portions will locate *B* and *B'*.

With *B'* and *B* as centers, and with a radius greater than *B'A*, draw arcs intersecting at *Y*.

Why must these radii be longer than *B'A* ?

Why is it unnecessary to have an additional set of arcs intersecting below *A* ?

6. To a given line draw a perpendicular passing through a given point outside the line.

To draw to *OP* a perpendicular which will pass through *Q*, an arc is drawn with *Q* as a center and cutting the line *OP* in two points, *r* and *s*. With these as centers, the intersection at *t* is obtained.

Why is it better to have this intersection below the given line rather than above it ?

7. Draw two intersecting circles having radii of 3 inches and 2 inches, respectively, with centers $2\frac{1}{2}$ inches apart. (*a*) Connect each center with but one of the two points of intersection. (*b*) Give the lengths of the sides of the triangle thus formed.

8. Construct (*a*) a triangle having a base of $2\frac{1}{2}$ inches and sides of 2 inches and 3 inches, respectively. (*b*) An isosceles triangle having a base of 2 inches and equal sides of 3 inches each. (c) An equilateral triangle having 2½-inch sides.

9. Draw two lines each 2½ inches long, forming one angle of 60°.

10. Construct, if possible, a triangle whose sides measure, respectively, (a) 1, 1½, and 2 inches. (b) 1, 2, and 3 inches. (c) 2, 3, and 4 inches. (d) 1, 3, and 5 inches.

11. Construct a triangle whose sides measure, respectively, 2, 2½, and 3 inches, and on the 3-inch side construct a second triangle, completing a parallelogram.

12. Construct three different parallelograms having sides of 2 and 2½ inches, respectively.

NOTE. — Draw the given lines meeting at different angles.

13. Inscribe a square in a circle (a) by drawing two diameters intersecting at right angles, cx. (b) By employing short intersecting arcs.

Locate two corners, x and x', by the ruler placed on the center c.

Using x and x' as centers, and with the same radius make an intersection at y. Place the ruler on y and c to locate z and z'.

NOTE. — In all of these exercises endeavor to show variety. Do not always employ a horizontal base line. Draw intersecting arcs below a line, as well as above, or to one side, etc.; have them as few as is consistent with accurate results.

14. Construct an arc (a) of 180°. (b) Of 90°. (c) Of 60°. (d) Draw the chord of each. (e) Draw a line bisecting each chord and its arc. First draw an arc somewhat larger than is needed, then darken the required part.

NOTE. — DC is an arc of 60°, DF is an arc of 120°. Bisect DC to get an arc of 30°. Bisect CF, which gives an arc of 90° from D to point of bisection.

15. Draw two lines forming an angle (*a*) of 30°. (*b*) Of 120°. (*c*) Of 90°. (*d*) Of 45°. (*e*) Of 22½°.

16. Inscribe an octagon in a circle.

Bisect one of the arcs of 90°, Exercise 13, and set off the remaining arcs by means of the compasses.

17. (*a*) Construct a 2-inch hexagon.

Draw a circle having a radius of 2 inches, and divide the circumference into 6 equal parts, keeping the compass points 2 inches apart.

(*b*) How long is the chord of each of the six arcs?

18. Construct a 2-inch square using arcs of 3-inch radius exclusively.

The construction points are shown in the following diagram, in which *A B* is the 3-inch base.

With *A* as a center and a 3-inch radius (which is kept throughout this exercise) draw an arc greater than 90° to *m*. Lay off an arc of 60° at *n*. Bisect *Bn* at *X* by means of arcs intersecting at *o*, centers being at *B* and *n*, respectively. With *X* as a center, locate *C*. Draw *A C* to make the second side of the square. With *B* and *C* as centers, locate *D*.

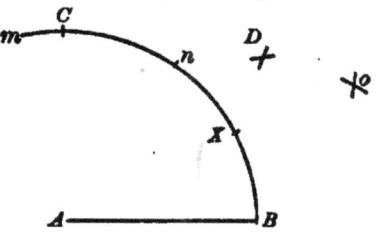

19. Without producing the line, erect a perpendicular at one end (*a*) of a horizontal line. (*b*) Of a vertical line. (*c*) Of an oblique line.

NOTE. — See Exercise 14.

20. Draw two 2-inch lines meeting (*a*) at an angle of 120°. (*b*) At an angle of 135°.

NOTE. — An angle of 135° is equal to an angle of 90° + one of 45°.

21. On a 2-inch line construct (*a*) a regular hexagon. (*b*) A regular octagon.

22. Draw two lines forming any angle. To a second line draw a line making an equal angle.

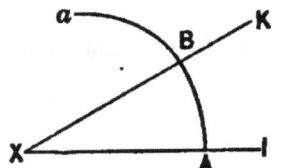 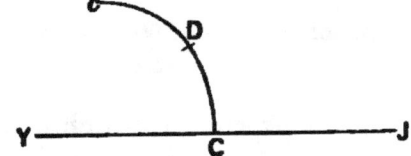

Draw *XI* and *XK* at random. It is required to draw from *Y* a line *YD*, making at *Y* an angle equal to *KXI*.

With *X* as a center, draw an arc, and with *Y* as a center, and keeping the same radius, draw another arc. Measure the chord of *AB* with the compasses, and lay off *CD* equal to it. A line *YD* will make an angle at *Y* equal to that at *X*.

23. To a horizontal line draw two oblique parallel lines.

This requires that two lines be drawn, making equal angles with the horizontal line on the same side of the latter.

24. From a point without the line draw two equal lines (*a*) to a horizontal line. (*b*) To a vertical line. (*c*) To an oblique line.

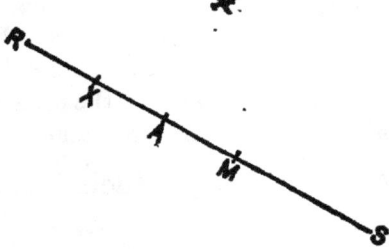

With the given point *J* as a center, draw arcs intersecting the given line, *RS*, at *M* and *X*. Draw *JX* and *JM*.

25. From a point without the line draw a perpendicular (*a*) to a horizontal line. (*b*) To a vertical line. (*c*) To an oblique line.

NOTE. — See Problem 6.

26. Construct four triangles, each having a base of 4 inches and base angles of 45° and 60°, respectively. (*a*) In one, let fall a perpendicular from each vertex on he side opposite. (*b*) In the second, draw a line from each vertex to the middle of the opposite side. (*c*) At the center of each side of the third, erect a perpendicular, extending it until it meets one from a second side. (*d*) Bisect each angle of the fourth by a line extending to the opposite side.

27. Draw two rhombuses having sides of $3\frac{1}{4}$ inches each and one diagonal of $2\frac{1}{2}$ inches. (*a*) Divide one rhombus into two acute-angled triangles. (*b*) Divide the other into two obtuse-angled triangles.

28. Compare the areas of two triangles, one having sides of $3\frac{1}{4}$ inches, $3\frac{1}{4}$ inches, and $2\frac{1}{2}$ inches, respectively, and the other having sides of $3\frac{1}{4}$ inches, $3\frac{1}{4}$ inches, and 6 inches, respectively.

29. Construct an equilateral triangle. From each vertex draw a perpendicular to the opposite side. (*a*) Inscribe a circle. (*b*) Circumscribe a circle. (*c*) Compare the radii of the respective circles.

30. Draw a circle. (*a*) In it draw two chords not parallel to each other. (*b*) Bisect each chord by a perpendicular. (*c*) Where do the perpendiculars meet?

31. Bisect the chords of two adjacent arcs of a circle by perpendiculars. Where do these meet?

32. Using a cup, or other suitable object, draw an arc of a circle. Without completing the circle, find its center.

(Draw two chords, etc.)

33. (*a*) Draw several circles through a given point. (*b*) Several through two given points. (*c*) Draw a circle through three given points. (*d*) How many different circles can be drawn through three given points? (*e*) Circumscribe a circle about a triangle having sides of 2, 2½, and 3 inches, respectively.

34. Draw three right triangles of different dimensions. Circumscribe a circle about each. (*a*) Upon what line does the center of the circle fall? (*b*) At what part of the line? (*c*) If the hypotenuse of a right triangle is 5 inches, what is the radius of the circumscribing circle?

35. (*a*) Construct a right triangle having a hypotenuse of 3⅛ inches and one side of 3 inches. (*b*) Measure the remaining side. (*c*) Construct a right triangle having a hypotenuse of 3⅛ inches and a side of 2½ inches. (*d*) Measure the other side.

36. Erect a perpendicular at the end of a line.

To erect a perpendicular at the end of a line AB, a point C is taken, and with the radius CA an arc is drawn cutting AB at x. A line is drawn through xC cutting the arc at y. Why is AM (or Ay) perpendicular to AB?

(See also Problems 15 and 18.)

As a triangle whose sides are in the ratio of 3, 4, and 5 contains a right angle, a perpendicular may be erected at F by laying off on the line FG five equal divisions; at 1, 2, 3, 4, and 5. With 3 as a center, and a radius equal to five of the divisions, an arc is drawn. With F as a center, and a radius equal to *four* of the divisions, a second arc is drawn, intersecting the first at L. A line from F through L is perpendicular to FG.

This method is frequently employed by mechanics in laying out a " square corner."

Oral Review Problems

Make a rough diagram, if necessary, before answering.

1. How many circles can be drawn (*a*) through one point? (*b*) Through two points? (*c*) Through three points?

2. In a circle of 7 inches in diameter, how long is an arc (*a*) of 180°? (*b*) Of 60°? (*c*) Give the ratio of an arc of 180° to an arc of 60° in the same circle.

3. In a circle of 7 inches in diameter, how long is a chord (*a*) of 180°? (*b*) Of 60°? (*c*) Give the ratio of a chord of 180° to one of 60° in the same circle.

4. (*a*) How does the length of an arc of 120° compare with that of an arc of 240° in the same circle? (*b*) How does the length of a chord of 120° compare with that of a chord of 240° in the same circle?

5. What other arc in the same circle has a chord equal in length to that of a chord (*a*) of 60°? (*b*) Of 100°? (*c*) Of 160°?

6. (*a*) How many triangles different in area can be constructed having sides of 4, 5, and 6 inches, respectively? (*b*) How many rhomboids different in area can be constructed having two opposite sides measuring 4 inches each and the other two opposite sides measuring 5 inches each? (*c*) How many rectangles different in area can be constructed having two opposite sides measuring 4 inches each and two opposite sides measuring 5 inches each?

7. (*a*) How many degrees are there in each angle of an inscribed equilateral triangle? (*b*) How many degrees are there in the arc of which one side of the triangle is the chord? (*c*) What is the ratio between the number of degrees in the angle and the number in the arc?

Similar Triangles

Construction Exercises

1. (*a*) Construct a 2-inch equilateral triangle. (*b*) Divide it into 1-inch triangles. (*c*) How many of the latter are there? (*d*) Divide a 3-inch equilateral triangle into 1-inch triangles. (*e*) How many are there? (*f*) How many degrees are there in each angle of the large triangle? (*g*) In each angle of the small triangle?

2. Construct an isosceles right triangle. (*a*) Mark in each angle the number of degrees it contains. (*b*) Bisect each side of the large triangle and divide it into small ones by connecting the points of bisection. (*c*) Mark in each angle of each of the small triangles the number of degrees it contains. (*d*) How do the angles of one of the small triangles compare with the corresponding angles of the large one? (*e*) How do the sides of a small triangle compare with the corresponding sides of the large one? (*f*) How does the area of a small triangle compare with the area of the large one?

Two triangles are similar when the angles of one are equal each to each with the corresponding angles of the other. Corresponding sides of two similar triangles are proportional to each other.

3. Construct a right triangle having a hypotenuse of $2\frac{1}{2}$ inches and one side of 2 inches. (*a*) Measure the third side. Two of the angles are 37° and 90°, respectively. (*b*) Write these in their proper places, and write in the third angle the number of degrees it contains. (*c*) Give the sides and the angles of a similar triangle having an area four times as great.

4. Divide a line into 5 equal parts.   To divide the line *KL* into 5 equal parts, a line *Km* is drawn, and from *L*, the other extremity, *Ln* is drawn, making the angle *KLn* equal to the angle *mKL*. With the dividers mark off five equal divisions on *Km*, beginning at *K*; and beginning at *L*, mark off five of the same size on *Ln*.   Place the ruler successively on 1 *d*, 2 *c*, 3 *b*, etc., and mark off the intersections on *KL*.

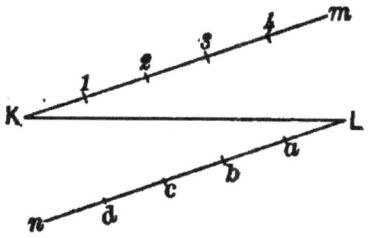

Calculating Heights and Distances

The height of a building, a tree, etc., is frequently obtained by comparing the length of the shadow cast by the building, tree, etc., with the length of the shadow cast by a perpendicular object the height of which is known.

Written Problems

1. If a man 6 ft. tall casts a shadow of 7 ft. 3 in., how high is a tree that casts a shadow of 58 ft. at the same time ?

Owing to the very great distance of the sun, its rays strike all objects with the same angle.   The triangles *abc* and *ABC* are, therefore similar, and the corresponding sides are proportional.

That is,

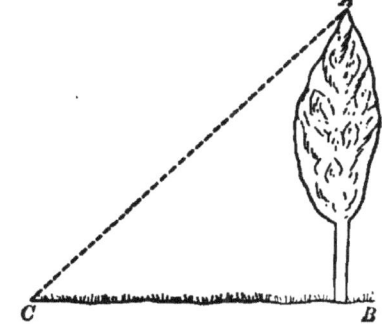

$$bc : BC :: ab : AB$$
$$7\tfrac{1}{4} : 58 :: 6 : x \text{ (ft.)}$$

2. When the eye of a man lying on the ground is 10 feet from the foot of a fence 6 feet high, he can just see the top of a house whose foot is 50 feet from his eye.

How high is the house?

$MN = 10$ ft., $NP = 6$ ft., $MO = 50$ ft. Find OQ.

3. Wishing to determine the length (RS) of a pond, two boys placed a stake at X. They then measured the distance SX, which was 135 rods, and on a line with SX, placed a stake at M, 45 rods from X. Finding RX to measure 120 rods, they placed a stake at N, 40 rods from X. The distance from M to N was measured and found to be 48 rods. How long is the pond?

4. By means of a convenient form of protractor a line from the top of a tree was found to make an angle of 45° with the level ground at a distance of 120 feet from the foot of the tree. How high is the tree?

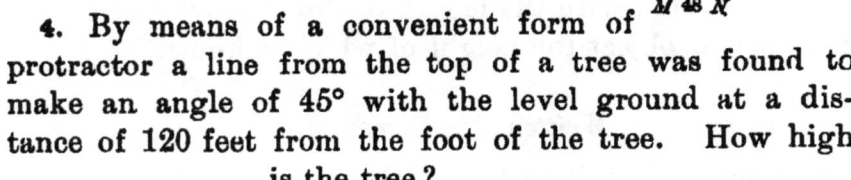

5. A line from the top of a flagstaff VW makes an angle of 60° with the ground at X, 30 feet from its base. (*a*) How far is a gunner at X from a bird on the top of the staff? (*b*) What is the height of the staff?

Note. — Draw a triangle having angles of 30°, 60°, and 90°, respectively, and determine the ratio between the longest and the shortest side. The side opposite 90° is not 3 times as long as the side opposite 30°.

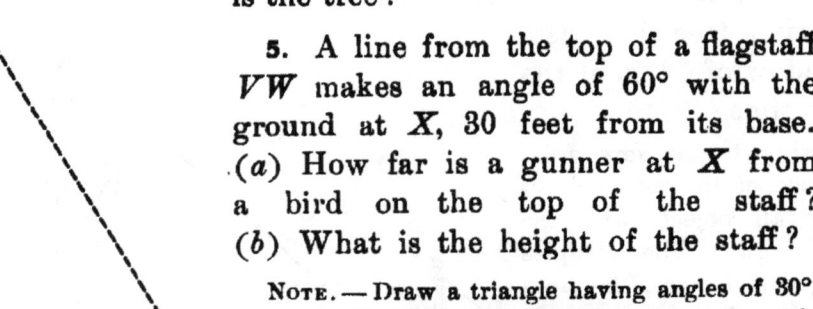

Elementary English

Allen and Hawkins's School Course in English. Book I, 35 cts.; Book II, 50 cts.

Allen's School Grammar of the English Language. A clear, concise, adequate book for upper grades. 60 cents.

Badlam's Suggestive Lessons in Language and Reading. A manual for primary teachers. Plain and practical. $1.50.

Badlam's Suggestive Lessons in Language. Being Part I and Appendix of Suggestive Lessons in Language and Reading. 50 cents.

Benson's Practical Speller. Contains nearly 13,000 words. Part I, 261 Lessons, 18 cents; Part II, 270 Lessons, 18 cents. Parts I and II bound together, 25 cents.

Benson and Glenn's Speller and Definer. 700 spelling and defining lists. 30 cts.

Branson's Methods in Reading. With a chapter on spelling. 15 cents.

Buckbee's Primary Word Book. Drills in articulation and in phonics. 25 cents.

Clapp and Huston's Composition Work in Grammar Grades. 15 cents.

Fuller's Phonetic Drill Charts. Exercises in elementary sounds. Per set (3) 10 cts.

Haaren's Word and Sentence Book. A language speller. Book I, 20 cents; Book II, 25 cents.

Hall's How to Teach Reading. Also discusses what children should read. 25 cts.

Harrington's Course for Non-English Speaking People. Book I, 25 cents; Book II, 30 cents. Language Lessons to accompany Book I, 25 cents.

Harris's Spiral Course in English. Book I, 35 cents; Book II, 60 cents.

Heath's Graded Spelling Book. 20 cents.

Hyde's Two-Book Course in English, Book I. Practical lessons in the correct use of English, with the rudiments of grammar. 35 cents.

Hyde's Two-Book Course in English, Book II. A carefully graded course of lessons in language, composition and technical grammar. 60 cents.

Hyde's Practical Lessons in English. Book I, 35 cents; Book II, 50 cents. Book II, with Supplement, 60 cents. Supplement bound alone, 30 cents.

Hyde's Practical English Grammar. 50 cents.

Hyde's Derivation of Words. With exercises on prefixes, suffixes, and stems. 10 cts.

MacEwan's The Essentials of the English Sentence. A compendious manual for review in technical grammar preparatory to more advanced studies in language. 75 cents.

Mathew's Outline of English Grammar. With Selections for Practice. 70 cents.

Penniman's New Practical Speller. Contains 6500 words. 20 cents.

Penniman's Common Words Difficult to Spell. Contains 3500 words. 20 cents.

Penniman's Prose Dictation Exercises. 25 cents.

Phillip's History and Literature in Grammar Grades. 15 cents.

Sever's Progressive Speller. Gives spelling, pronunciation, definition and use of words. 25 cents.

Smith's Studies in Nature, and Language Lessons. A combination of object lessons with language work. 50 cents. Part I bound separately, 25 cents.

Spalding's Problem of Elementary Composition. Practical suggestions for work in grammar grades. 40 cents.

See also our lists of books in Higher English, English Classics,
Supplementary Reading, and English Literature.

D. C. HEATH & CO., Publishers, Boston, New York. Chicago

Elementary Mathematics

Atwood's Complete Graded Arithmetic. New edition. Work for each grade from third to eighth inclusive, bound in a separate book. Six books. Each, 25 cts. *Old edition:* Part I, 30 cts.; Part II, 65 cts.

Badlam's Aids to Number. Teacher's edition—First series, Nos. 1 to 10, 40 cts.; Second series, Nos. 10 to 20, 40 cts.; Pupil's edition — First series, 25 cts.; Second series, 25 cts.

Bigelow and Boyden's Primary Number Manual. For teachers. 25 cts.

Branson's Methods of Teaching Arithmetic. 15 cts.

Hanus's Geometry in the Grammar Schools. An essay, with outline of work for the last three years of the grammar school. 25 cts.

Heath's Beginner's Arithmetic. For first and second years. 30 cts.

Heath's Primary Arithmetic. Illustrated in color. 35 cts.

Heath's Complete Practical Arithmetic. 65 cts.

Howland's Drill Cards. For middle grades. Each, 3 cts.; per hundred, $2.40.

Hunt's Geometry for Grammar Schools. The definitions and elementary concepts taught concretely. 30 cts.

Joy's Arithmetic Without a Pencil. Mental Arithmetic. 35 cts.

Pierce's Review Number Cards. Two cards, for second and third year pupils. Each, 3 cts.; per hundred, $2.40.

Safford's Mathematical Teaching. A monograph, with applications. 25 cts.

Siefert's Principles of Arithmetic. A teacher's guide. 75 cts.

Sloane's Practical Lessons in Fractions. 25 cts. Set of six fraction cards, for pupils to cut. 10 cts.

Sutton and Bruce's Arithmetics. Lower, 35 cts.; Higher, 60 cts.

The New Arithmetic. By 300 teachers. Little theory and much practice. An excellent review book. 65 cts.

Walsh's New Arithmetics. New Primary, 30 cts. New Grammar School, 65 cts. New Grammar School, Part I, 40 cts.; Part II, 45 cts. Alternate Arithmetic, for upper grades, oo cts.

Walsh's Arithmetics. *Two Book Series*—Primary, 30 cts.; Grammar School, 65 cts. *Three Book Series*—Elementary, 30 cts.; Intermediate, 35 cts,; Higher, 65 cts.

Walsh's Algebra and Geometry for Grammar Grades. 15 cts.

Watson and White's Arithmetics. Primary, 35 cts. Intermediate, 45 cts. Complete, in preparation.

Wells and Gerrish's Beginner's Algebra. For grammar grades. 50 cts.

White's Arithmetics. Two Years with Number, 35 cts. Junior Arithmetic, 45 cts. Senior Arithmetic, 65 cts.

For advanced works see our list of books in Mathematics.

D. C. HEATH & CO., Publishers, Boston, New York, Chicago

Elementary Science

Austin's Observation Blanks in Mineralogy. Detailed studies of 35 minerals. 35 cents.

Bailey's Grammar School Physics. Practical lessons with simple experiments that may be performed in the ordinary schoolroom. 50 cents.

Ballard's The World of Matter. Simple studies in chemistry and mineralogy; for use as a textbook or as a guide to the teacher in giving object lessons. $1.00.

Brown's Good Health for Girls and Boys. Physiology and hygiene for intermediate grades. Illustrated. 45 cents.

Brown's Health in the Home. Illustrated. 50 cents.

Clark's Practical Methods in Microscopy. Gives in detail descriptions of methods that will lead the careful worker to successful results. Illus. $1.60.

Clarke's Astronomical Lantern. Intended to familiarize students with the constellations by comparing them with facsimiles on the lantern face. With seventeen slides, giving twenty-two constellations. $4.50.

Clarke's How to Find the Stars. Accompanies the above and helps to an acquaintance with the constellations. Paper. 15 cents.

Colton's Elementary Physiology and Hygiene. For grammar grades. 317 pages. Illustrated. 60 cents.

Eckstorm's The Bird Book. The natural history of birds, with directions for observation and suggestions for study. 301 pages. Illustrated. 60 cents.

Guides for Science Teaching. Teachers' aids for instruction in Natural History.
    I. Hyatt's About Pebbles. 26 pages. Paper. 10 cts.
    II. Goodale's A Few Common Plants. 61 pages. Paper. 20 cts.
    III. Hyatt's Commercial and other Sponges. Illustrated. 43 pages. Paper. 20 cts.
    IV. Agassiz's First Lesson in Natural History. Illus. 64 pages. Paper. 25 cts.
    V. Hyatt's Corals and Echinoderms. Illustrated. 32 pages. Paper. 30 cts.
    VI. Hyatt's Mollusca. Illustrated. 65 pages. Paper. 30 cts.
    VII. Hyatt's Worms and Crustacea. Illustrated. 68 pages. Paper. 30 cts.
    XII. Crosby's Common Minerals and Rocks. Illustrated. 200 pages. Paper, 40 cts. Cloth, 60 cts.
    XIII. Richards's First Lessons in Minerals. 50 pages. Paper. 10 cts.
    XIV. Bowditch's Physiology. 58 pages. Paper. 20 cts.
    XV. Clapp's 36 Observation Lessons in Minerals. 80 pages. Paper, 30 cts.
    XVI. Phenix's Lessons in Chemistry. 20 cts.
    Pupils' Note-book to accompany No. 15. 10 cts.

Hoag's Health Studies. Practical hygiene for grammar grades. Cloth. Illustrated. 75 cents.

Rice's Science Teaching in the School. With a course of instruction in science for the lower grades. 46 pages. Paper. 25 cents.

Ricks's Natural History Object Lessons. Information on plants and their products, on animals and their uses, and gives specimen lessons. $1.50.

Ricks's Object Lessons and How to Give Them. — Vol. II. Lessons on elementary science for grammar and intermediate grades. 90 cents.

Scott's Nature Study and the Child. A manual for teachers, with outlines of lessons and courses, detailed studies of animal and plant life, and chapters on methods and the relation of nature study to expression. $1.50.

Sever's Elements of Agriculture. For grammar grades. Illustrated. 50 cents.

Shaler's First Book in Geology. A helpful introduction to the study of modern textbooks in geography. Illustrated. Cloth, 60 cents. Boards, 45 cents.

Spear's Leaves and Flowers. An elementary botany for pupils under twelve. Illustrated. 25 cents.

Weed's Farm Friends and Farm Foes. An elementary textbook on weeds and insects. Cloth. Illustrated. 90 cents.

Wright's Seaside and Wayside Nature Reader, No. 4. Elementary lessons in geology, astronomy, world life, etc. Illustrated. 50 cents.

See also our list of books in Science.

D. C. HEATH & CO., Publishers, Boston, New York, Chicago

Heath's Home and School Classics.

FOR GRADES I AND II.

Mother Goose : A Book of Nursery Rhymes, arranged by C. Welsh. In two parts. Illustrated. Paper, each part, 10 cents; cloth, two parts bound in one, 30 cents.

Perrault's Tales of Mother Goose. Introduction by M. V. O'Shea. Illustrated after Doré. Paper, 10 cents; cloth, 20 cents.

Old World Wonder Stories: Whittington and his Cat; Jack the Giant Killer; Jack and the Bean-Stalk; Tom Thumb. Edited by M. V. O'Shea. Illustrated. Paper, 10 cents; cloth, 20 cents.

Craik's So-Fat and Mew-Mew. Introduction by Lucy Wheelock. Illustrated by C. M. Howard. Paper, 10 cents; cloth, 20 cents.

Six Nursery Classics : The House That Jack Built; Mother Hubbard; Cock Robin; The Old Woman and Her Pig; Dame Wiggins of Lee, and the Three Bears. Edited by M. V. O'Shea. Illustrated by Ernest Fosbery. Paper, 10 cents; cloth, 20 cents.

FOR GRADES II AND III.

Sophie : From the French of Madame de Segur by C. Welsh. Edited by Ada Van Stone Harris. Paper, 10 cents; cloth, 20 cents.

Crib and Fly : A Tale of Two Terriers. Edited by Charles F. Dole. Illustrated by Gwendoline Sandham. Paper, 10 cents; cloth, 20 cents.

Goody Two Shoes. Attributed to Oliver Goldsmith. Edited by Charles Welsh. With twenty-eight illustrations after the wood-cuts in the original edition of 1765. Paper, 10 cents; cloth, 20 cents.

Segur's The Story of a Donkey. Translated by C. Welsh. Edited by Charles F. Dole. Illustrated by E. H. Saunders. Paper, 10 cents; cloth, 20 cents.

FOR GRADES III AND IV.

Trimmer's The History of the Robins. Edited by Edward Everett Hale. Illustrated by C. M. Howard. Paper, 10 cents; cloth, 20 cents.

Aiken and Barbauld's Eyes and No Eyes, and Other Stories. Edited by M. V. O'Shea. Illustrated by H. P. Barnes and C. M. Howard. Paper, 10 cents; cloth, 20 cents.

Edgeworth's Waste Not, Want Not, and Other Stories. Edited by M. V. O'Shea. Illustrated by W. P. Bodwell. Paper, 10 cents; cloth, 20 cents.

Ruskin's The King of the Golden River. Edited by M. V. O'Shea. Illustrated by Sears Gallagher. Paper, 10 cents; cloth, 20 cents.

Browne's The Wonderful Chair and The Tales It Told. Edited by M. V. O'Shea. Illustrated by Clara E. Atwood after Mrs. Seymour Lucas. In two parts. Paper, each part, 10 cents; cloth, two parts bound in one, 30 cents.

FOR GRADES IV AND V.

Thackeray's The Rose and the Ring. A Fairy Tale. Edited by Edward Everett Hale. Illustrations by Thackeray. Paper, 15 cents; cloth, 25 cents.

Ingelow's Three Fairy Stories. Edited by Charles F. Dole. Illustrated by E. Ripley. Paper, 10 cents; cloth, 20 cents.

Ayrton's Child Life in Japan and Japanese Child Stories. Edited by William Elliot Griffis. Illustrated by Japanese Artists. Paper, 10 cents; cloth, 20 cents.

Ewing's Jackanapes. Edited by W. P. Trent. Illustrated. Paper, 10 cents; cloth, 20 cents.

Carové's Story Without an End. Fourteen illustrations. Cloth, 25 cents.

Heath's Home and School Classics—*Continued.*

FOR GRADES V AND VI.

Lamb's The Adventures of Ulysses. Edited by W. P. Trent. Illustrations after Flaxman. Paper, 15 cents ; cloth, 25 cents.

Gulliver's Travels. I. A Voyage to Lilliput. II. A Voyage to Brobdingnag. Edited by T. M. Balliet. Fully illustrated. In two parts. Paper, each part, 15 cents ; cloth, two parts bound in one, 30 cents.

Ewing's The Story of a Short Life. Edited by T. M. Balliet. Illustrated by A. F. Schmitt. Paper, 10 cents ; cloth, 20 cents.

Tales From the Travels of Baron Munchausen. Edited by Edward Everett Hale. Illustrated by H. P. Barnes after Doré. Paper, 10 cents ; cloth, 20 cents.

Muloch's The Little Lame Prince. Preface by Elizabeth Stuart Phelps Ward. Illustrated by Miss E. B. Barry. In two parts. Paper, each part, 10 cents ; cloth, two parts bound in one, 30 cents.

FOR GRADES VI AND VII.

Lamb's Tales From Shakespeare. Introduction by Elizabeth Stuart Phelps Ward. Illustrated by Homer W. Colby after Pillé. In three parts. Paper, each part, 15 cents ; cloth, three parts bound in one, 40 cents.

Martineau's The Crofton Boys. Edited by William Elliot Griffis. Illustrated by A. F. Schmitt. Cloth, 30 cents.

Motley's The Siege of Leyden. Edited by William Elliot Griffis. With nineteen illustrations from old prints and photographs, and a map. Paper, 10 cents ; cloth, 20 cents.

Brown's Rab and His Friends and Other Stories of Dogs. Edited by T. M. Balliet. Illustrated by David L. Munroe after Sir Noel Paton, Mrs. Blackburn, George Hardy, and Lumb Stocks. Paper, 10 cents ; cloth, 20 cents.

FOR GRADES VII, VIII AND IX.

Hamerton's Chapters on Animals : Dogs, Cats and Horses. Edited by W. P. Trent. Illustrated after Sir E. Landseer, Sir John Millais, Rosa Bonheur, E. Van Muyden, Veyrassat, J. L. Gerome, K. Bodmer, etc. Paper, 15 cents ; cloth, 25 cents.

Irving's Dolph Heyliger. Edited by G. H. Browne. Illustrated by H. P. Barnes. Paper, 15 cents ; cloth, 25 cents.

Shakespeare's The Tempest. Edited by Sarah W. Hiestand. Illustrations after Retzch and the Chandos portrait. Paper, 15 cents ; cloth, 25 cents.

Shakespeare's A Midsummer Night's Dream. Edited by Sarah W. Hiestand. Illustrations after Smirke and the Droeshout portrait. Paper, 15 cents ; cloth, 25 cents.

Shakespeare's The Comedy of Errors. Edited by Sarah W. Hiestand. Illustrations after Smirke, Creswick and Leslie. Paper, 15 cents ; cloth, 25 cents.

Shakespeare's The Winter's Tale. Edited by Sarah W. Hiestand. Illustrations after Leslie, Wheatley, and Wright. Paper, 15 cents ; cloth, 25 cents.

Defoe's Robinson Crusoe. Edited by Edward Everett Hale. Illustrated. In four parts. Paper, each part, 15 cents ; cloth, four parts bound in one, 60 cents.

Jordan's True Tales of Birds and Beasts. By David Starr Jordan. Illustrated by Mary H. Wellman. Cloth, 40 cents.

Fouqué's Undine. Introduction by Elizabeth Stuart Phelps Ward. Illustrations after Julius Höppner. Cloth, 30 cents.

Melville's Typee : Life in the South Seas. Introduction by W. P. Trent. Illustrated by H. W. Moore. Cloth, 45 cents.

THE HEATH READERS

A new series, that excels in its

1. Interesting and well graded lessons.
2. Masterpieces of English and American literature.
3. Beautiful and appropriate illustrations.
4. Clear and legible printing.
5. Durable and handsome binding.
6. Adaptation to the needs of modern schools.

THE HEATH READERS enable teachers, whether they have much or little knowledge of the art, to teach children to read intelligently and to read aloud intelligibly. They do this without waste of time or effort, and at the same time that the books aid pupils in acquiring skill in reading, they present material which is in itself worth reading.

The purpose of the HEATH READERS is, *first*, to enable beginners to master the mechanical difficulties of reading successfully and in the shortest time; *second*, to develop the imagination and cultivate a taste for the best literature; *third*, to appeal to those motives that lead to right conduct, industry, courage, patriotism, and loyalty to duty. The larger purpose is, briefly, to aid in developing an appreciation of that which is of most worth in life and literature.

The series contains seven books, as follows:

Primer, 128 pages, 25 cents.	Fourth Reader, 320 pages, 45 cents.
First Reader, 130 pages, 25 cents.	Fifth Reader, 352 pages, 50 cents.
Second Reader, 176 pages, 35 cents.	Sixth Reader, 352 pages, 50 cents.
Third Reader, 256 pages, 40 cents.	

Descriptive circulars sent free on request.

D. C. HEATH & CO., Publishers, Boston, New York, Chicago

www.ingramcontent.com/pod-product-compliance
Lightning Source LLC
Chambersburg PA
CBHW080148060326
40689CB00018B/3890